Holy Hills of the Ozarks

Lived Religions

Series Editors: David D. Hall and Robert A. Orsi

Holy Hills of the Ozarks

Religion and Tourism in Branson, Missouri

AARON K. KETCHELL

The Johns Hopkins University Press

Baltimore

© 2007 The Johns Hopkins University Press

All rights reserved. Published 2007
Printed in the United States of America on acid-free paper
2 4 6 8 9 7 5 3 1

The Johns Hopkins University Press
2715 North Charles Street
Baltimore, Maryland 21218-4363
www.press.jhu.edu

Library of Congress Cataloging-in-Publication Data

Ketchell, Aaron K., 1971–
Holy hills of the Ozarks : religion and tourism in Branson, Missouri /
Aaron K. Ketchell.
p. cm. — (Lived religions)
Includes bibliographical references and index.
ISBN-13: 978-0-8018-8660-7 (hardcover : alk. paper)
ISBN-10: 0-8018-8660-0 (hardcover : alk. paper)
1. Branson (Mo.)—Religious life and customs. 2. Recreation—Missouri—Branson.
3. Amusements—Missouri—Branson. 4. Amusements—Religious aspects—
Christianity. 5. Recreation—Religious aspects—Christianity. 6. Popular culture—
Religious aspects—Christianity. I. Title.
BR560.B76K48 2007
277.78'797—dc22   2006039423

A catalog record for this book is available from the British Library.

Contents

Acknowledgments

Most of this project was completed while I was a graduate student or faculty member at the University of Kansas, and many individuals affiliated with that institution are due thanks. Gratitude must first be extended to Pete Shortridge. His keen eye for detail, thorough editing skills, and perceptive comments transformed this subject matter into a work that I feel is clear, concise, and informed. Norm Yetman, Bob Antonio, Tim Miller, Sandi Zimdars-Swartz, and Ed Canda must also be recognized for their contributions to the dissertation from which this manuscript emerged. I have known most of these scholars for over a decade, and in addition to regarding them as skilled mentors, I am also thankful to count them as friends. Throughout this process, Brad Carter has been an invaluable colleague, comrade, and volunteer research assistant. From its inauguration, he has offered thoughts, critiques, and pertinent materials that course their way through all chapters.

A number of researchers and scholars working in and around the Ozarks have also been of tremendous assistance. Lynn Morrow, director of Local Records at the Missouri State Archives, has been ever willing to share his bounty of insights on the region and his wonderful collection of postcards, some of which appear in this book. Lynn has authored dozens of articles on the Ozarks, and his study of turn-of-the-century Branson tourism was an inspiration for my own initiative. Laura Jolley also generously assisted with the preparation of the book's illustrations. John Schmalzbauer at Missouri State University has provided multiple opportunities for me to present my work to audiences. These occasions allowed me not only to fine-tune thoughts during the latter stages of the project but also offered excellent venues for critique from individuals intimately familiar with Branson. John's ongoing interest in and support of my scholarship is deeply appreciated.

I was fortunate to receive funding from two sources for this study. Money provided by the State Historical Society of Missouri allowed for substantial fieldwork and archival research. A yearlong dissertation fellowship from the Louisville Institute offered the ability to focus solely on writing, and input from other Institute fellows and scholars proved indispensable. I thank both of these organizations for their assistance.

I have also received much support and encouragement from people associated with the Johns Hopkins University Press. I first met Henry Tom at a conference in 1998, when this project was in its infancy. Thankfully, he remained in contact and expressed his continuing enthusiasm for my scholarship as it grew and matured. I have also appreciated the opportunity to work with series editor Bob Orsi, whose studies of lived religion were truly inspirational while I was a graduate student. His comments on and critique of my manuscript helped to mold it into a work that I hope at least partially reflects the skillful and rigorous nature of his own scholarship. This book also profited from the superb editing of Grace Carino, who is to be commended for both this effort and her patience during a time when I was mired in difficult personal circumstances.

The roll of individuals in Branson who have offered their thoughts and time is too extensive to enumerate. However, hundreds of people have expressed an interest in this project and worked with busy schedules to meet with me and discuss their views on the topic. I hope their generosity is reflected in the ethnographic quality and detail found throughout. I would like to mention a few who offered substantial contributions in many forms. These include Howard Boyd, Richard Freihofer, Don Gabriel, Peter Herschend, Michael London, and Raeanne Presley. Nahum Tate, while not an Ozark resident, is also owed much gratitude for sharing family documents, genealogical materials, and personal stories about his ancestral links to the region. Finally, when researching in the field, basics like room and board can sometimes be difficult to arrange. I was often fortunate to be accommodated by Carol and Terry Smith, who offered their home and willingly listened to the travails of my research undertaking.

I have been a student for all but a few years of my life. Such utter immersion in learning would not have been possible without the constant support of my parents. Their unwavering confidence in my abilities has allowed me to cultivate a sense of inquiry that they initially instilled. My one great regret concerning this project is that my father passed away just months before its completion. He was an erudite man, and for many years, I looked forward to pridefully handing him a copy of the book and thanking him for making it possible. While working on a study that often involves miraculous things, two miracles did indeed come into my own life. Clara and Gus have encouraged this project in ways too numerous to list. Their captivating smiles, hearty laughs, simple words, and boundless wonder have truly been catalysts for this work. Finally, since the nascence of this study, Marcia Fisher has always unconditionally believed in my ability to complete a daunting enterprise and has taken every step along this long road with me. Without her strength, confidence, patience, insight, and love, I would never have made it to this point.

"The Moral Vineyards"

A city of less than 7,000 permanent residents, Branson, Missouri, annually attracts more than 7 million tourists, with vacationers swelling its population to 65,000 during peak season. Located in the southwestern corner of the state, it is often described as the "heart" of the Ozarks and has prospered for nearly a century as a result of a multifaceted fusion of recreation with religious sentiment. The tone was set early. In an 1862 letter, infantryman Robert Fyan called the region "one of the greatest countrys for Baptists that [he] ever saw—as they could be made 'elect' almost any place in this part of the moral vineyards." Fyan's remark, offered forty years before the city was platted, explicitly addressed the preponderance of rivers in southern Missouri that allowed for baptism by immersion. The meaning quickly became more general, however, and Branson developed into a site where travelers could embrace tourism-mediated piety in a setting ripe for the cultivation of moral fruits.[1]

Visitors to Branson today are enticed by many attractions: recreational lakes, rolling hills, and scenic vistas; an outdoor drama that reenacts Harold Bell Wright's place-defining novel *The Shepherd of the Hills;* a re-created nineteenth-century mining village–cum–theme park called Silver Dollar City; and variety show theaters that feature big-name talent such as Andy Williams and Glen Campbell. A popular variant of Christianity has underscored all these tourist draws and fortified every consumer culture success. The physical landscape has attracted sojourners since the 1880s, but it was not until the publication of Wright's novel in 1907 that Branson established itself as a true tourist mecca. The city is now, by some estimates, the second most popular "drive-to" destination in the country and ranks in the top twenty American overnight leisure spots. It is safe to say that many contemporary visitors have not read *The Shepherd of the Hills* and do not realize that it was written by a Christian minister. Nevertheless, Wright's work continues to function as a master narrative for Branson. The author's embrace of the inherent sanctity of the Ozarks, the necessity of manifesting belief in lived existence, and the conviction that popular culture can be a powerful evangelistic force are outlooks that have permeated local tourism and continue to provide it with a sense of religiously motivated vitality.

I arrived in Branson in September 2002 for an extended period of fieldwork. My first discussion was with Kathryn Buckstaff, the local beat writer for the *Springfield (MO) News-Leader.* At our breakfast, she shared a recent turn of events that could not have better resonated with my focus on religion and recreation. Buckstaff revealed that in the next day's paper she would break a story about televangelist Jim Bakker's arrival in Branson. As we spoke, he was building a set to host a talk show with his new wife, Lori. This program would feature Christian celebrities, musical guests, and Bakker's sermons. When Bakker was not on the air, backers hoped the venue could additionally be used for faith building and fellowship.

When this story appeared, some people in the area were leery of Bakker's presence and its effect on the local image. His checkered past is certainly well known. Founding Praise the Lord Ministries (PTL) in 1972, he amassed a $129 million fortune with his former wife, Tammy Faye, which included the 2,300-acre Heritage USA Christian theme park in Fort Mill, South Carolina. However, in 1987 he resigned from PTL after admitting to a 1980 affair with church secretary Jessica Hahn and a subsequent payment of "hush money." In that same year he was dismissed from the Springfield, Missouri–based Assemblies of God, with which he held credentials. In 1989, Bakker was convicted of a wire and mail fraud scheme involving the sale of more than 150,000 lifetime partnerships planned for Heritage USA which bilked followers out of $3.7 million. After being sentenced to forty-five years in prison and serving five, he emerged as an emblem of the corruption that many felt was inherent in 1980s televangelism.[2]

Amid negative reactions to Bakker's arrival, many area religious leaders, performers, and tourism administrators supported his ministry. Even people who had lost investment money when Heritage USA collapsed offered words of encouragement. Jess Gibson, pastor of Springfield's Cornerstone World Outreach Center, had purchased a lifetime partnership at the theme park. Despite losing $2,000, he stated that Bakker had been "restored spiritually" and should be given the opportunity to prove himself anew. Cecil Todd, founder of Branson-based Revival Fires Ministries, took this notion of renewal a step further by alluding to a gospel narrative. Asserting that "if there is somebody here that is a qualified judge of Jim Bakker then let them throw the first rock," Todd held that Branson could function as a "safe haven" for any Christian seeking restoration. Bakker also talked of praying with local stars such as Andy Williams, Tony Orlando, and the Osmonds on arrival, with these headliners embracing him like they were "old friends." Even the Branson/Lakes Area Chamber of Commerce, which could have been the most guarded because of a charge to represent the entire industry, added that his production company brings another element to an area that has a strong "Christian base." As stated by Ross Summers, director of the chamber, "He's good for Branson and he's good for his ministry."[3]

The Jim Bakker Show debuted at the Studio City Café on January 2, 2003—sixteen years to the day after Bakker had hosted his last television program. The enterprise was bankrolled by Branson businessman Jerry Crawford, who was born again during a PTL visit in 1986 and credits Bakker with saving his marriage. By June, the hour-long, five-day-a-week program was being carried across the country on thirty Christian television stations and two hundred cable channels and reached nearly one hundred countries via the Christian Television Network's "Angel" satellite. Moreover, Bakker has attracted renowned guests such as fellow television ministers Kenneth Copeland and Rex Humbard and nationally celebrated Christian entertainers like Dino Kartsonakis, Barbara Fairchild, and Doug Gabriel.[4]

Recently, Bakker has commenced other religio-tourism ventures. In January 2005, plans were announced for a Christian-themed residential community with the evangelist's new broadcast studio as its centerpiece. Again funded by Jerry Crawford, the community will be situated on a 590-acre site in Blue Eye, Missouri, which is roughly 20 miles south of Branson. It will occupy a locale that formerly hosted the Camelot theme park and will include thirty condominiums surrounding "Main Street," a climate-controlled atrium with shops and a food court, and Bakker's television facility. In addition to the TV program, Bakker will also offer seminars, workshops, Bible study, and "restoration." Reflecting on his renaissance in Branson, Bakker stated that he finally feels "back home" and hopes to stay "until death or rapture, whichever comes first."[5]

MAPPING BRANSON'S RELIGIOUS LANDSCAPE

With a long-standing interest in the merger of religion and tourism in the Ozarks, I thought the correspondence between Bakker's arrival in Branson and my own propitious. Undoubtedly, his advent validated many people's suspicions that Branson was a bastion of conservative Christian hucksterism. Arthur Frommer, the nation's foremost travel writer, has criticized the city's entertainment industry for professions of "fundamentalist, sectarian faith" and equated such proselytizing with a "physical assault." Merle Haggard, who had a short-lived stint in Branson during the early 1990s, stated after his departure, "If you're not a born-again Christian . . . they won't even loan you money to build a place. If you don't believe as they do, then you're just out." Although these commentators were remarking on the contemporary Branson scene, others have described the entirety of Ozark history as reliant on a brand of religiosity rooted in unwavering dogmatism. For instance, geographer Milton Rafferty identified "adherence to fundamentalistic religious belief" as a primary cultural trait of the Ozarks. Reiterating this assertion, *Kansas City (MO) Star* writer Charles Gusewelle characterized regional faith as "an uncompromising fundamental kind practiced with fire and brimstone fervor."[6]

Such rigid descriptions do a disservice to the tapestry of religious expressions found within the past one hundred years of Branson tourism. The industry was spawned from Social Gospel impulses. Harold Bell Wright was trained in the Christian Church (Disciples of Christ) tradition and drew thorough literary inspiration from that movement's most heralded novelist, Charles Sheldon. During his brief stint as a minister, Wright sought to combat ills and address issues that were on the Social Gospel agenda, including alcohol, the plight of labor, and prostitution. However, his primary contribution took the form of literary inspiration rather than socially oriented perspiration. Feeling that he could convey the movement's dictates to millions rather than hundreds through a "ministry in print," he sought, in the words of Erin A. Smith, to facilitate "provisional, personal faiths created by individuals in the course of their daily lives." Wright did pastor a church in Pittsburg, Kansas, when that town was an early twentieth-century locus for socialism. Yet he shared little with Christian socialists of the era who actively politicized their stances—for example, W. D. P. Bliss or George D. Herron. It is also difficult to ally him with Social Gospel moderates like Washington Gladden or Walter Rauschenbusch. Wright certainly appreciated these men's emphasis on the immanence of the divine. However, whereas Gladden served as president of the Ohio State University and prolifically published heady texts and Rauschenbusch was on faculty at Rochester Theological Seminary while he produced the somewhat esoteric manifestos of the movement, Wright was always reticent about his intellectual prowess and characterized his books as "plain food for plain people." Thus, he best represents what John P. Ferre has labeled the "conservative" wing of the Social Gospel, a faction that recognized societal problems but advocated few structural adaptations. This cohort instead relied on "individual moral enlightenment" for social and cultural change—a method Wright believed was best actualized through the writing of fictional texts that inspired original tourist visitation to the transformative Ozark hills.[7]

It is more difficult to link midcentury tourism innovators with a specific religious movement. The Lynch family, which made Marvel Cave into a popular local attraction, and Hugo and Mary Herschend, who opened Silver Dollar City atop this fissure in 1960, never professed a sectarian stance. Instead, these individuals embraced a Christian-informed yet nebulous approach to lived ethics, with their worldviews resembling stances being analyzed by contemporary sociologists such as Talcott Parsons and Will Herberg. For instance, Herberg posited a 1950s faith that was "common to Americans and genuinely operative in their lives," thereby describing the style of marketable Christianity prevalent in Branson during this period. Nancy Ammerman's paradigm of "Golden Rule Christianity" is also a useful heuristic for understanding these vantages. Although she employed this model to explain late twentieth-century American belief, its emphasis on applied Christian principles and use of scripture defined "more by choices and practices than by doctrine" (tenets that nicely bridge with Social Gospel impetuses) certainly informed these regional boosters. As Hugo Herschend's son, Peter, described, "If there ever was an embodiment of the Golden Rule, Hugo was it. . . . I never, ever knew that man to compromise his values." In addition, Peter's mother, Mary, best expressed this concern through her Christian-informed environmental stewardship, and the Lynch sisters hoped to facilitate experiences of sublimity through literally immersing tourists in a cavern replete with spiritual rhetoric. Such methods thus mesh with Ammerman's description of believers who "would like the world to be a bit better for their having inhabited it" and base their religious stances on "experience" rather than well-defined "belief."[8]

In the late twentieth century, especially after the city's boom in the early 1990s, Branson adopted a more specifically evangelical flavor that partially derived from the preponderance of Pentecostal and Southern Baptist influences in the region. Boosters rallied around the four key ingredients of evangelicalism identified by David Bebbington. This list includes "conversionism" (emphasis on a born-again or life-changing experience); "biblicism" (reliance on the Bible as ultimate religious authority); "activism" (concern for sharing the faith); and "crucicentrism" (a focus on Christ's sacrifice as the catalyst for salvation). However, rather than being communicated through churchly establishments, Branson has employed a time-tested evangelical strategy by broadcasting such theological concerns into the realm of culture. Local institutional manifestations of faith have certainly played a vital role in maintaining Branson's sanctified atmosphere, but the trenches of proselytism are today reserved for recreational venues that ardently fuse sacred and secular, thereby replicating strategies found throughout the tourism industry's hundred-year existence.[9]

As witnessed in the following chapters, Branson's tourism promoters and religious authorities have been vehement critics of sectarianism and facilitated religious experiences beyond both the bounds of orthodoxy and traditional locations for the pursuit of faith. Harold Bell Wright frequently disparaged "churchianity"—an approach that put more stock in creeds and church politics than in lived experiences of devotion. Claiming that such a vantage "makes a mockery of religion," he affirmed that individuals should instead focus on "the gospel of Christ as he preached it, not as the churchmen say it should be preached." This sentiment has pervaded all historical and contemporary tourist attractions and has thus functioned as an industry lynchpin. Throughout his corpus, Wright advocated for a style of Christianity that was intelligible to the common folk, thoroughly integrated into other value-creating arenas, and attentive to larger social concerns. In doing so, he offered a template for Branson's brand of pious leisure couched in "lived" or "popular" religiosity.[10]

The definitions of both lived and popular religion are somewhat imprecise, but their constructions rely heavily on the thoughts of Peter Williams, Charles Lippy, Robert Orsi, and Colleen McDannell. Williams identified popular religion as "extra-ecclesiastical," or outside the structures of an authoritative clergy and formal church walls. In his approach to such anti-institutional manifestations, Lippy has written that a majority of Americans possess "a sense of the supernatural so lively that it cannot be contained in creed and doctrine." In a 1997 essay, Robert Orsi demanded a reorganization of the language of the religious studies field which creates polarities between the sacred and the profane by disregarding the spiritual nature of lived existence. Finally, Colleen McDannell, in an examination of the materiality of Christian belief, challenged a historical duality between the divine and matter while reiterating calls for an emphasis on what people do rather than what they are urged dogmatically to think. Taken together, these vantages seem appropriate for an examination of Branson's religious tourism—a form of devotion expressed within theatrical and amusement-oriented venues which seeks to impart everyday experiences of leisure with sacred values.[11]

Moreover, Mark Hulsether has offered a four-part typology of popular religion. Scrutiny of each element reveals acute resonance with the Branson approach to faith. The first component entails practice by "ordinary people." Although this introduction began by discussing Jim Bakker's reemergence in Branson, the larger study places much greater emphasis on less heralded purveyors of religiosity (boosters, performers, and so on) and the everyday tourists who consume these vantages. Thus, when examining the city's contemporary history, I have hoped to abide by Christian Smith's caveat that one should not presume that "evangelical leaders speak as representatives of ordinary evangelicals." Hulsether also held that popular religion involves practices deemed "authentic" or "folk-oriented" in opposition to contemporary culture. Branson's history is indeed sated with examples of antimodernism informed by religious stances, and the larger region has often been put forth as one of America's chief resisters of modernization. A third aspect of this construct is a mass-mediated approach—a method that has obviously been central in Branson for decades. Finally, Hulsether posited elements of counterhegemonic cultural contestation by nonelites versus elites as elemental for understanding this mode of religious expression. From Harold Bell Wright's chastisements of ethereal theology and theologians to the anti-intellectual antics of modern-day hillbilly comics and the "down-home" morals they are said to represent, this populist aversion to social privilege has permeated the area's promotion of lived Christianity.[12]

Throughout this study, it will become apparent that popular Christianity mediated through the vehicle of recreation has undergone compound permutations in Branson. However, Harold Bell Wright's call for a nondenominational approach that integrates Christian principles into everyday existence still fuels the tourism industry. Today, both implicit and explicit expressions of religious ethics and precepts still find their way into all attractions. In addition, the sentiments of vacationers and local residents recall Wright's vision of the Ozarks as a locale inherently imbued with an ability to enhance spiritual prowess and moral wherewithal. By presenting this amorphous Christian outlook in a buoyant and consumable manner, Branson tourism has appealed to a range of audiences. When viewed in its totality, the city has therefore served as one of the nation's premier examples of popular religion for nearly a century.

THE VARIETIES OF AMERICAN RELIGIOUS TOURISM

Numerous scholars have crafted interpretive models that elucidate the relationship between religion and tourism. For instance, John B. Allcock has asserted that the process of vacationing in modern societies possesses certain "quasi-religious characteristics," including a quest for "authentic" experiences; implication in civil religious rituals that sacralize public ideals; and performance of an "implicit" mode of religiosity that corresponds with the privatized nature of vacationing. Consonant with these suggestions, the production of authentic experiences has been a primary goal for various Branson attractions. Sites such as the Shepherd of the Hills Homestead and Outdoor Theatre and Silver Dollar City seek to provide a glimpse of bucolic premodernity and so imply that the larger Branson context is one that resists modern accretions of urbanization, technology, and secularized philosophies. Similarly, for more than thirty years the city's theaters have provided amusements that put forth an Ozark ideological construct easily consumed within acts that often take the form of religious rituals.[13]

Furthermore, George Karlis, Sotiria Grafanaki, and Jihan Abbas demarcated three possible transcendental effects of the tourist experience: "leisure as a means of connecting with God" through facilitating spiritual growth; "leisure as a means of creating/finding meaning in life" through opportunities for self-discovery; and "leisure as a means of connecting with self/others" through providing a sense of belonging in an increasingly fragmented social existence. In line with these thoughts, tourists arriving in the area since the late nineteenth century have expected both an Arcadian landscape capable of facilitating harmony with the divine and a set of tourist offerings able to assist with self-enlightenment fostered amid a community of like-minded seekers.[14]

Theoretical models are useful when analyzing the history of Branson's tourism complex. Also of interest for this study, however, are the ways that this industry has exemplified more substantive stages and paradigms within the history of American religious leisure. Only in recent decades have scholars begun to investigate the interface between religion and recreation. Most accounts of American faith have commenced with portraits of stern and solemn Puritans who supposedly viewed amusement as anathema to the Calvinist mind-set and work ethic. By stationing New England Puritanism as a guiding narrative necessary for understanding U.S. religion writ large, this eliding of pleasure has left little room for religiously oriented frivolity.

Colonial historians such as Edmund Morgan, Bruce Daniels, and David Hall first began to shed new light on this aged New England supposition. Morgan's landmark work *The Puritan Family* (1966) suggested that these people liked "good food, good drink," and other modes of "innocent play." Building on this thesis, Daniels surmised that, although Puritans were undoubtedly serious about their religious stances, they found ample time for moderate pleasures of "cake and ale." Subject to theological proclamations that encouraged relaxation as a way to refresh body and soul, he utilized early eighteenth-century cleric Benjamin Coleman's concept of "sober mirth" to illustrate the importance of music, dance, courtship, sport, and other recreational activities. Finally, David Hall attended to a central problematic within Puritan history—the difference between what religious leaders said about pleasure and what practitioners actually did. His *Worlds of Wonder, Days of Judgment* (1989) enumerated many ways that popular religious sentiment refashioned formal theologies of godly transcendence to allow for supernatural presence within all everyday activities, including multifarious forms of leisure.[15]

In his work on the marketing of American religion, historian R. Laurence Moore demonstrated that faith has always been a salable commodity. Devotees and religious authorities, in fact, have often spearheaded consumer culture innovations such as stage performance, novel reading, and mass media advertising. Ultimately, Moore concluded that such "innocent pleasures need a justification." Thus, the goal of any pious product or consumer must be to rationalize how sacred sentiment is not cheapened through its implication in capitalist modes and to demonstrate how consumption can be validated by infusing commodities with devout tones. Although the salability of religion has been much criticized, especially within the arena of secularization theory, many scholars have come to accept this market-based approach as a viable guide for understanding religious development in the United States. From Dean Kelley to Laurence Iannaccone to Roger Finke and Rodney Stark, commentators in the past thirty years have employed supply-demand and cost-benefit notions to track the permutations of American faith.[16]

Regardless of one's stance on the commodification of religion or the use of economic models to analyze religious development, faith and consumer culture have been inextricably linked throughout U.S. history. A brief glance at the development of tourism in the United States also suggests that religious impulses have provided a foundation for that industry instead of standing in opposition to it. The banner tourist destinations of the early nineteenth century—Niagara Falls, Mammoth Cave, the White Mountains, and other natural attractions— were extolled partly because they offered a glimpse into the awesome character of godliness. Often referring to themselves as "pilgrims," individuals who participated in the American Grand Tour claimed to discover an ethereal presence amid the consciously crafted consumer culture that surrounded these locations. Reflecting this sentiment, Niagara Falls guidebook author J. W. Orr wrote in 1842, "Crowding emotions swell the bosom; thoughts that defy utterance, fill the mind. The power and presence of the Almighty seem fearfully manifest. You gaze, and tremble as you gaze!" Such sublimity sanctified leisure pursuits and granted otherworldly credence to the practices of vacationing and consumer fulfillment. Nineteenth-century Americans who inaugurated national tourism found justification for their leisure through veiling seemingly secular experiences of nature in a language of religiously grounded reverence and wonder.[17]

Nature idolatry wrapped in a Christian idiom is evident in a wide variety of

Branson attractions. Chapters 1 and 2 of this study demonstrate that *The Shepherd of the Hills* consecrates the Ozark populace and topography by marking the region as inherently righteous and equating its landscape with divinely constructed natural "temples." Chapter 3, in part, explores ways that Marvel Cave (the antecedent to Silver Dollar City) has welcomed for more than a century visitors who regularly observe a palatable godly presence within this subterranean world. Most topically, in Chapter 5 I augment Harold Bell Wright's pastoral descriptions with the voices of local pastors, entertainers, and tourists to consider the area's Christian placefulness. While examining the various ways that regional lakes, rivers, and hills have historically been draped in divine language, this chapter also notes connections between these vaguely transcendental conceptions and Branson's contemporary Christian-themed industry. In addition, it discusses the many things that threaten the city's sacred landscape, including legalized gambling, risqué entertainment, unemployment, crime, and environmental degradation—dilemmas that have all precipitated from the vacation industry and pose serious risks to a vaunted Ozark social and geographic terrain.

R. Laurence Moore has written that the rural camp meeting, which lies at the foundation of numerous types of religious leisure, "succeeded as an institution because it satisfied competing desires of piety and play." By enhancing opportunities for the cultivation of religiosity with occasions for socialization and recreation, nineteenth-century Methodists, Presbyterians, and other revivalists provided the first instances of communal leisure on the American frontier. Commenting on the theatrical and emotive nature of preachers and the pleasures available at such events, Walt Whitman referred to camp meetings in 1830 as "the most important of our amusements." Despite accounts that frequently remark on the chaos surrounding these occurrences, they possessed a rationalized nature that tempered recreation with a semblance of deferential order. The organized design of the grounds, the uniformity of public housing, and the establishment of moral premises to guide crowd behavior distinguished revivals from their secular counterparts in the world of mass leisure.[18]

By the mid-nineteenth century, camp-meeting grounds began to establish themselves as fixed tourist sites. With the birth of the Chautauqua movement in the 1870s, these locales offered lectures and lessons for Sunday school teachers in addition to concerts, plays, and games. Reflecting this turn, the Methodist-instituted Wesleyan Grove on Martha's Vineyard, Massachusetts, became the first permanent camp meeting in the Northeast in 1835. By 1869, there were more than two hundred cottages on the site, and many middle-class New Englanders came to the island well in advance of its religious festivities to swim, sunbathe, and commune with friends. Wesleyan Grove served as a "home away from home" for guests, a place where they could enjoy most household comforts in a bucolic setting. In addition, the locale was ideologically positioned as the antithesis of more aristocratic and profane tourist spots such as Newport, Rhode Island, thus ensuring that domestic values were furthered alongside familial attitudes. This augmentation of an ostensibly religious gathering with the machinations of morally guided tourism prompted historian Dona Brown to claim that Wesleyan Grove fused "the secular and the sacred, the profit-making and the pleasure-seeking."[19]

The most thorough study of an American religious resort is Troy Messenger's *Holy Leisure* (1999), a history of Ocean Grove, New Jersey. Ocean Grove was founded in 1869, and until 1979 it operated under a charter that allowed the Methodist-guided Camp Meeting Association to exercise municipal powers. According to Messenger, this group of "social architects" hoped that by "playing and praying together" vacationers would imbue all daily activities with the pursuit of holiness. Tourists filled their weeks with exercise, parades, pageants, and other frivolities to supplement religious services and sermons. By making no separation between sacred and profane, Ocean Grove was "dedicated to perfecting people in a perfect environment" while allowing guests to model the "ideal self" through experiences of tourism.[20]

The Branson area also has a long history of revivalism and has hosted camp meetings since before the Civil War. According to historian Robert Gilmore, these events involved fellowship, group singing, and emotional religious experience, but attendees most cherished the opportunity to be "entertained by a minister." As I detail in Chapter 1, fixed camp-meeting grounds that reflected Harold Bell Wright's Social Gospel emphasis were established near Branson by a group of Springfield, Missouri, Presbyterians shortly after the publication of *The Shepherd of the Hills*. In addition to welcoming Presbyterians, this White River Chautauqua Ground catered to Baptists, Disciples of Christ, the Woman's Christian Temperance Union, and other assemblies that relished a merger of pastoral scenery, outdoor recreation, religious programs, and prohibitions on alcohol consumption and card playing. A similar site was subsequently established nearby by the YMCA in 1910. In the mid-1920s, Kickapoo (later Kanakuk) Camp was founded on the banks of Branson's Lake Taneycomo with the intention of teaching children social and ethical graces. Currently, Kanakuk Kamps operates six facilities in southwestern Missouri focused on Christian athletics with an evangelical flavor. These facilities attract tens of thousands of youths per year who come for sports programs meant to inculcate "Christ-like attitudes" and promote experiences of spiritual rebirth.[21]

Since the late 1960s, Branson has supplemented its recreation offerings with an assortment of variety shows featuring country, gospel, and popular music alongside distinctively Ozark hillbilly comedy. As of 2005, more than one hundred such acts were performing at nearly fifty venues. In Chapter 4, I document the growth of this genre and its promotion of antimodern nostalgia, civil religious patriotism, and a distinct construction of "family values." These ethically laden premises, all subsumed under an often nebulous banner of evangelical Christianity, form the bedrock of every theater, and the degree to which these virtues are encouraged directly correlates with their success or failure. Furthermore, by offering wholesome entertainment in religious trappings, these theaters mimic the form and function of their camp-meeting antecedents and situate Branson as a city-sized "resort" that caters to a well-defined variant of popular Christianity.

In the twentieth century, the orientation of American religious tourism partially shifted from resorts serving a Christian clientele to more performance-oriented arenas that resembled the larger sphere of popular culture. Beginning in 1937 with the *Hill Cumorah Pageant* near Palmyra, New York, tourists began to frequent outdoor dramas that reenacted religious accounts. Hill Cumorah is unique because it is located at an important Mormon historical site and thus dramatizes stories from the Book of Mormon as well as the Bible. The *Black Hills Passion Play* in Spearfish, South Dakota, which commenced in 1939, was the first American production to enact the trial, death, and resurrection of Jesus. In the Ozark context, this narrative has been recounted since 1968 at *The Great Passion Play* in Eureka Springs, Arkansas. This event has become the most popular outdoor drama in the United States and has welcomed more than six million guests since its inception. Currently, eleven national outdoor religious dramas are in operation, ranging in location from Puyallup, Washington, to Disney, Oklahoma, to Cambridge, Ohio.[22]

Beginning in the mid-twentieth century, re-creations of biblical geography and material culture have become a major aspect of religious tourism. Eureka Springs' Sacred Arts Complex was a primary contributor to this movement. This site (which includes *The Great Passion Play* and the 67-foot Christ of the Ozarks statue) hosts a thirty-eight exhibit tram tour called the New Holy Land. It offers replicas of Moses's tabernacle in the wilderness, the setting of the Nativity, Golgotha, Jesus's tomb, and a host of other scriptural locales staffed by employees in period costume. Similarly, the Holy Land Experience opened in 2001 in Orlando, Florida. Billed as a "living, biblical history museum," the site re-creates the city of Jerusalem as detailed in Old and New Testament accounts. This premise permeates crafts, music, and even the food and beverages served at the park. Not only an educational and recreational locale, the Holy Land Experience also professes to be "a Bible-believing, Christ-centered ministry."[23]

Jim and Tammy Faye Bakker's Heritage USA is certainly the most renowned late twentieth-century addition to the arena of American religious tourism. In 1986 it attracted six million guests to a site described by one American studies scholar as hoping to "recycle old Methodist camp meetings into Six Flags Over Texas." Demonstrating that Pentecostal Christianity could effortlessly exist alongside seemingly secular amusements, the park surrounded a 2,500-seat church with a 500-room hotel, gigantic mall, water park, and nostalgic Main Street USA. Although it met its demise with the onset of Jim Bakker's scandal, this attraction once was the third most popular theme park in country behind Disney World and Disneyland.[24]

Numerous scholars have claimed that even the Disney theme parks contain elements that relate to religious tourism. Anthropologist Alexander Moore, for example, has written that "at a time when some proclaim that God is dead, North Americans may take comfort in the truth that Mickey Mouse reigns at the baroque capital of the Magic Kingdom and that Walt Disney is his prophet." By employing terms such as "pilgrimage," "rites," and "national shrine," commentators have sanctified Disney's promotion of a sanitized and nostalgic family-oriented past. Directly addressing Walt Disney's aspiration to undermine the carnivalesque elements of traditional amusement parks and alluding to the amorphously spiritual environment he sought to create, the Project on Disney avowed, "Disney World will surely never mount a springtime fertility rite, but its attraction taps a deep-seeded, perhaps unconscious, longing for the possibility of renewal." Thus, although some may question the inclusion of theme parks within a brief account of religious leisure, it cannot be denied that more Americans travel to Orlando and Anaheim than any other place in the country to engage in tourist experiences laden with the endorsement of a marked ideological vantage.[25]

If some vacationers make a "pilgrimage" to the Disney parks, one might rightfully assert that other sites with a similarly devout atmosphere deserve inclusion in a summary of religion and recreation. This list would perhaps take account of Graceland, the various national monuments in Washington, D.C., and even conventions for Star Trek enthusiasts. Such locales are important because the United States lacks traditional pilgrimage venues. Devotees do travel to heralded Marian apparition sites in Conyers, Georgia; Falmouth, Kentucky; or Belleville, Illinois, to be sure, yet the popularity of these places pales in comparison with that of their more illustrious counterparts at Lourdes, Fatima, or Medjugorje.

Additionally, they do not overtly fuse religion and consumer culture. American pilgrims are more likely to journey toward a set of sacred ideas with only a vague reference to the divine, and it is these popularly religious ventures that best exemplify this country's mode of pilgrimage.[26]

As I detail in Chapter 2, the Shepherd of the Hills Homestead and Outdoor Theatre was built on the site where Harold Bell Wright frequently sojourned in the region. Since the 1930s it has enshrined Wright's characters, enacted and sanctified Ozark pseudohistory, and staged a religiously laden production of Wright's novel. Within its drama, boosters have opted for pageantry that unequivocally performs Christian belief by way of traditional theater. Although not a bona fide Passion play, it includes numerous Christological themes, offers a well-defined portrait of core Ozark social and cultural values, and promotes *The Shepherd of the Hills* as a work that underlies all subsequent Christian attractions in Branson. In this manner, the play deserves recognition as a popular religious experience.

Similar to other religious theme parks, Silver Dollar City seeks to inculcate visitors with a sense of Christian ethics and values through the conveyance of pious dictates in popularly consumable form. This site currently draws more than two million guests per year to its presentation of late nineteenth-century Ozark culture. One may not instantly locate religious sentiments amid craft displays, performances of traditional Ozark music, and roller coasters. However, Silver Dollar City has an on-site church and a full-time pastor, its employee guidelines compel staff members to handle their work in a fashion that is consistent with Christianity, and sacred music subtly wafts through the grounds. Moreover, many religious organizations are associated with the park, thereby demonstrating its linkage with proselytizing impulses and its aspiration to "preach the gospel always, using words only whenever necessary."[27]

It may be mere coincidence that Walt Disney spent his boyhood years in the small Missouri town of Marceline. Still, he repeatedly acknowledged that this hamlet inspired the "Main Street, USA" entryways at both his parks. Like Disney's properties, Branson attractions mediate a set of essential "down-home" values that attract "pilgrims" to a set of sacred ideas. Also like Disney's locales, Branson has historically utilized an at least partially imaginary character—the hillbilly—to represent these principles. Chapter 6 traces the development of this icon from its early twentieth-century roots to the present and marks it as a prime example of a religious trickster figure. Like similar signifiers, this regional variant is framed in duality through its role as both a cultural creator and a continuing embodiment of behaviors and attitudes that threaten this creation. Yet despite this figure's function as taboo transgressor, local people and area attractions have persistently posited the hillbilly as a virtue-laden construct. Therefore, by examining this icon's many manifestations, one is privy to a paradigm that underscores all local religious entertainment offerings.[28]

It is overstatement to claim that Christianity has been the sole cause of Branson tourism. A comprehensive account of this industry would discuss infrastructural developments, political debates, legal battles, and a score of other topics. Still, an undeniably robust association has existed between religion and recreation throughout nearly one hundred years of local history. Richard Freihofer publishes the *Branson Church Getaway Planner*, a magazine distributed annually to tens of thousands of Christian congregations which alludes to this correspondence in almost every issue. He has written that Branson has a divine "plan and purpose at work"; that the city is a "celebration of faith toward God"; and that, if approached in the right manner, any vacation in the Ozarks "should be supernatural." Although Freihofer is certainly addressing an audience with a preconceived desire for the blending of faith and leisure, Branson's attractions have continuously suggested that the city and its amusements have an inextricable connection with the divine. In doing so, they have also made it apparent that the city's ever mutating body of leisure opportunities serves as a consummate example of the amalgamation of religion and tourism in the United States.[29]

MEMORIES AND METHODS

I am neither a Missourian nor an Ozarker. In fact, for thirteen years I lived in Lawrence, Kansas, a place that may express more anti-Missouri sentiments than anywhere in the world. In the predawn hours of August 21, 1863, William Quantrill and a band of proslavery advocates from Missouri descended on abolitionist Lawrence amid a larger conflict concerning whether Kansas would enter the Union as a slave or free state. More than a hundred male inhabitants were left dead or dying, and a large portion of the town lay in ashes when the raiders departed. Of course, this saga is told in different terms depending on the side of the state line from which one hails, with such a malleability of history nicely demonstrated in Ang Lee's *Ride with the Devil* and elsewhere. Compounding this acrimony is a historical and often quite rancorous basketball rivalry between the University of Kansas (where I did my graduate work) and the University of Missouri. Although such a Kansas-Missouri feud is often hyperbolized for the purposes of sport, its texture was revealed when I traveled to Columbia, Missouri, in 2002 to receive a research award from the State Historical Society. Arriving after the prizes had been given out because of a scheduling mix-up, I sat in the audience as a speaker commented in jest that perhaps a "Jayhawker" was afraid to cross over into hostile territory. Such remarks have indeed permeated my research when interviewees learned of my contentious university home.

On the other hand, I was born and raised about a mile from the Missouri border in Kansas City, Kansas, and have spent all but three years of my life within a four-hour drive of Branson. My paternal great-grandparents came from Miller County, which is on the periphery of the Ozarks. I also have relatives in Springfield and Nixa, Missouri—towns within a stone's throw of my topic. Finally, my father's side of the family has always professed a disputed genealogical link to Stanley Ketchell (sometimes spelled "Ketchel"), who was middleweight champion of the world from 1908 to 1910. While training for a fight in October 1910 on a farm in Conway, Missouri (roughly 75 miles north of Branson), he was shot and killed by Walter Dipley, who had caught Ketchell chatting with his girlfriend the night before. Although this account is of no consequence for my academic work, as a child it was ever intriguing to think of my most famous relative meeting a tragic and sordid demise in a region I frequently visited.

While I was growing up in Kansas City, my family would travel to the Ozarks three or four times a year. Tourists came to the region throughout the twentieth century for a multiplicity of reasons, and we were no different. Often we arrived to camp and canoe on one of many local rivers or stay in a cabin and boat and swim in area lakes. On occasion we sojourned in Branson and visited the city's banner attractions prior to its boom in the early 1990s—Silver Dollar City, *Shepherd of the Hills*–inspired sites, and hillbilly-based variety show theaters. In all honesty, we did not come for the merger of religion and recreation described in the following chapters. Throughout, I posit Branson as primarily a site for Protestant religious experience, and my family has for many generations been staunchly Catholic. Yet at the same time, my childhood memories are oriented around water sports, miniature golf, bumper cars, and roller coasters rather than often subtle fusions of piety and pleasure. Furthermore, these vacations ceased prior to the 1990s, when such amalgamations became more explicit. Despite familial links to the region, frequent visits as a child, and countless hours spent there while researching this book, I would never claim to be an Ozarker. A local resident stated in 1998, "You're only a stranger for five minutes, but you're a newcomer for fifty years." Thus, I have always fully admitted my "outsider looking in" status, and throughout nearly a decade of scholarly study, I have continued to be on tour.[30]

Two months before starting a graduate degree program in religious studies in 1994, I recruited a friend to accompany me on a camping trip to the Boston

Mountains in northern Arkansas. After a few days in the woods, we decided that a bit of sightseeing was in order. The previous year, my traveling mate and I had undertaken a 5,000-mile journey through the western states in search of wilderness and curious roadside attractions. During that trip I cultivated a taste for the touristic unusual, and I was soon to discover that the Ozarks offered more than its fair share of vacation-oriented exotica. This Ozark adventure led us to Eureka Springs, Arkansas, where we witnessed the nearly 70-foot Christ of the Ozarks statue and its accompanying sacred attractions. Leaving that city, we headed northward to Branson, Missouri, for the night. There had been no family vacations to the Ozarks for a number of years, and I was therefore not aware of Branson's enormous growth in the early 1990s. Although not a fan of Mel Tillis, Andy Williams, or Yakov Smirnov, I was fascinated by the thousands of individuals traversing the streets on a crisp fall night en route to one of perhaps forty variety shows emphasizing God, country, and family. Finally, on the return home we stopped at the Precious Moments Chapel in Carthage, Missouri, a site venerating the world's most popular collectible items and their much revered creator, Sam Butcher. A loose replica of the Sistine Chapel, Butcher's house of worship depicts various Bible scenes with scriptural characters replaced by his figurines, and it is said to allay existential anxieties through its comforting messages and aesthetics. When we returned to Lawrence, friends asked about the trip. Without hesitation I could say that the camping was good, but it was more difficult to describe or analyze our additional ramblings through the hills.

As my graduate work in religious studies began, I soon became intrigued with popular religiosity. My adviser, Sandra Zimdars-Swartz, had recently published *Encountering Mary* (1992), a study of modern Marian apparitions. Furthermore, Catholic popular religion struck home because of an upbringing in the faith, many years of parochial schooling, and a boyhood enchantment with the saint tradition. Immersing myself in this subfield, I came to realize that there was a body of academics seriously interested in considering paraliturgical devotions and willing to examine the concerns of the folk with earnestness and empathy. Harking back to my earlier Ozark experience, I recalled that in that region one could not find statues of Mary or paintings of Saint Sebastian skewered with arrows, yet its religious attractions were comparable mixtures of sacred and secular. In addition, they fused contemporary consumer culture with religiosity in a way that mimicked the descriptions of many Catholic extraecclesiastical practices. But in a fashion that confounded my understanding of the Reformation, they also seemed primarily Protestant in tone. Finding that these sites befuddled conceptions of the iconoclastic and world-denying nature of Calvinism, I became determined to grapple with a perceived scholarly lacuna—the apparent disregard for popular expressions of Protestantism and their seeming Ozark manifestations. Although the region possesses numerous lived religious spectacles, I quickly settled on Branson as my chief focus—the most visited and spectacular of this array.

Cursory investigations quickly revealed that little academic work had been done on Branson. Moreover, entering an American studies doctoral program with a background in religious studies, I hoped in my own small way to address a disciplinary critique from Mark Hulsether. As he wrote, "Religion, especially contemporary religion, is among the most understudied topics in American studies, compared to its weight in the larger culture." As witnessed in the following chapters, Branson's boom was amply covered by journalists from the coasts who mainly heaped words of ridicule on the types of entertainments offered and the people who consumed them. As an aspiring academic, I quickly noted that few topics remained uncommented on in the scholarly world. However, Branson was in the national spotlight, had been a sizable tourist draw since the opening decade of the twentieth century, and was perhaps America's foremost example of popular Christianity. Why, then, no rigorous and prudent examination of this cultural phenomenon?[31]

A partial answer to this question was supplied when I reexamined Colleen McDannell's thoughts on "kitsch" put forth in *Material Christianity* (1995). Her analysis of the ways that high culture–low culture distinctions pervade perceptions of popular religious wares and the class-oriented and gendered assumptions that accompany these divisions led me to believe that Branson was not an overlooked scholarly focus but rather one that might possibly be an affront to many scholars' ideologies and sensibilities. This thesis was reinforced during a recent phone interview for a position in a religious studies department. As I talked about interests in American evangelicalism and the relatively few academics who approach the topic without an accompanying theological and sociocultural commitment, the interviewer responded, "That's because most scholars don't like evangelicals." Although I have no data to verify or falsify this contention, its sentiment speaks mightily to sweeping assumptions that underscore an American "culture war" and the deficient study of conservative expressions of faith on university campuses nationwide.

I began serious fieldwork in Branson in 1998. During the fall of that year I sent letters of inquiry to every variety show theater and attraction in the area soliciting literature, tourist comments, and tickets. More than half of these venues responded with information, and perhaps a third offered passes to their shows or attractions. Because I was both taking and teaching classes at this juncture, acting on such invitations was limited to occasional weekends and four- or five-day jaunts during holiday, spring, or summer breaks. Since that time, I have visited notable and long-lived destinations like the Silver Dollar City theme park and the Shepherd of the Hills Homestead numerous times and perhaps seen half of the variety shows now featured. Accounts of these visits are strewn throughout the following chapters. In combination with words from boosters, performers, and tourists, they provide a peek into the style of entertainment offered and the generally unified religious, social, and cultural vantages that have been proffered in albeit varied ways during Branson's history.

I was able to spend most of the fall of 2002 in Branson interviewing tourism officials, owners of attractions, performers, local clergy, and residents. Nearly forty discussions varying in length from thirty minutes to two hours were recorded during this period. These accounts, coupled with materials gleaned from archives, newspaper stories, tourism magazines, and other historical sources that inform coverage of Branson in earlier periods, speak to the creation and maintenance of religiously motivated consumer culture. This production of a regional ideology, with its associated material expressions, has certainly not been without contest. Branson's past and present have often been described in terms of homogeneous beliefs and desires, but as John Urry has noted, because the space of a toured site is limited, "there has to be competition and conflict over its organization and control." Throughout the city's history, such discord has arisen around a variety of issues. Battles have frequently been waged over the degree to which it should modernize on numerous fronts (and thereby perhaps do damage to the selling of nostalgia); cater to constituents outside the aspiring middle-class audience that has always fueled its market; diversify its entertainments to include nonwhite or nonrural perspectives; and, most important, advertise its experiential commodities as explicitly Christian. Through this focus on the production of culture, I have thus acted on Jane Desmond's call for research that posits tourism industries as arenas where "notions of identity are sold, enacted, debated, and occasionally contested."[32]

Scholars of tourism and consumer culture can usually speak more precisely to the selling of experiences than the buying of them. It is certainly much easier to get at the motivations and aims of a tourist goods creator than at how such commodities are received and rendered meaningful by consumers. During my research, issues of reception indeed proved more difficult to gauge and tourist voices harder to procure. When investigating Branson outside the contemporary period, I was compelled to exercise a bit of ethnohistorical creativity. Some vaca-

tioner accounts were available in newspaper articles and regionally focused tourism periodicals. I was also able to acquire a number of letters and memoirs that
documented the experiences of visitors. Several of the most fruitful accounts
were gleaned from an incredibly underscrutinized primary source—the back of
postcards. With the aid of individuals who volunteered their collections, I pored
over hundreds of quips and brief narratives. Lynn Morrow, who is the director
of local records at the Missouri State Archives and has written an insightful book
on early tourism in the Branson area, was especially forthcoming and allowed
me access to a basement full of fruitful items. In my experience, such messages
fall into four categories, and unfortunately only one of these proved useful for
my purposes. Many are totally unrelated to vacationing and ask things like "How
is Aunt Martha doing?" Others simply identify the location on the front and add
"Where we went today." Some are indeed partially related to toured sites but
mostly comment on fishing or the weather. Finally, with enough combing I was
able to locate messages that offer interesting and provocative information. Reminiscences from this fourth category are interspersed throughout and, in conjunction with archival materials, exhibit the diverse ways that tourists throughout the
twentieth century have situated Branson and its attractions.

One might speculate that obtaining opinions from contemporary vacationers would be an easier endeavor, and with the aid of a dissertation fellowship
from the Louisville Institute during 2003–2004, I was able to seek these out in a
variety of manners. I have certainly had innumerable conversations with visitors
while waiting for a tram to arrive at Silver Dollar City, a craft demonstration to
commence at Shepherd of the Hills Homestead, or intermission to end at a variety show theater. I have also tried when possible to fraternize with tourists at
restaurants, motels, and other key locales within a vacation setting. Quotes and
impressions from these discussions occasionally make their way into this study,
but structural aspects of the Branson experience often impeded in-depth interviewing. Sojourners typically come to the area for only a brief stay. In 2004, the
average visit was less than four nights. Yet during these few days, most travelers
keep a frenzied schedule. For instance, 84 percent of all who currently arrive in
Branson see at least one variety show. However, venues normally offer three
productions a day (morning, matinee, and evening), and nearly all visitors see
multiple shows. In addition, local theme parks and historical re-creations can be
parlayed into full-day entertainment, and the majority of vacationers also hope
to engage in some type of water sport while in town. When one adds meals and
a bit of rest to this agenda, it becomes evident that there is little time left over to
engage in protracted dialogue with a curious researcher. Finally, Branson's main

thoroughfare has few sidewalks and thus offers little opportunity for even casual conversations among pedestrians as they rush from attraction to attraction. Instead, a flood of cars inching a long the Strip (86 percent of all vacationers arrive in personal vehicles) is the city's modus operandi. Even at places like Silver Dollar City and the Shepherd of the Hills Homestead, where people have adopted a more leisurely pace, one is confronted with a privatized "public sphere." These sites gather their own tourist data, but solicitation of any type by nonemployees is clearly discouraged.[33]

Often frustrated by an inability to engage tourists face to face for more than a fleeting moment, I resorted to following up through electronic means. Over the years, e-mail correspondence has offered an opportunity to gauge visitor opinions more fully and allow for more thoughtful and elaborate responses. Some of these correspondences have even been mediated through fan club Web sites and message boards. Coverage of Silver Dollar City in Chapter 3 is informed by multiple voices from guests who actively post to a site devoted to discussion of that theme park. In addition, similar Web pages facilitated the gathering of comments from individuals who frequent a number of popular variety show theaters and thus fit into Chapter 4's analysis of that phenomenon. I was also able to cull many useful voices from more broad-based sites that offer tourists the opportunity to review destinations worldwide. For instance, TripAdvisor.com is the largest global travel information and advice destination on the Web. It includes more than 4 million reviews and opinions, covers more than 200 thousand hotels and attractions, and receives input from 19 million unique monthly visitors. This site, and many smaller ones, contain appraisals of a multiplicity of Branson tourist locales and a wealth of untapped material that aided my exercise in virtual ethnography.

I was also privy to survey data from a number of sources. Silver Dollar City is the primary collector of such information in the area. The theme park not only amasses figures and brief qualitative accounts from its guests but also is the major compiler of demographics and data for the city at large. Early in my research I was offered some of this material. However, in 2003 the attraction came under new management. I was subsequently informed that its parent corporation had adopted a policy that forbade the sharing of different types of customer information with the press, competition, or educational pursuits. I have, however, been given access to smaller caches of tourist comments from a number of other venues that are integrated throughout.

While looking to fill a partial lacuna of tourist voices, I was told of a survey conducted in 2004. To celebrate Branson's more than one hundred distinct variety shows, a local agency held a contest in which tourists throughout the city wrote twenty-five or fewer words about why the city's attractions are "fun for everyone" (the marketing slogan for the celebration). These 3 × 5 inch cards were then deposited in drop boxes, and one hundred prizes were awarded through a random drawing. After being given permission to use these accounts as long as anonymity was preserved, I spent a weekend paging through 362 submissions from vacationers throughout the country, with various reviews and testimonies appended in chapters that follow. All the aforementioned sources, coupled with testimonies gathered from more traditional print materials, constitute my approach to issues of reception. Although the voices of cultural producers admittedly outnumber those of consumers, I feel that a sufficient representation of the latter group finds its way into the study and thereby demonstrates a long-standing and multifaceted discourse of religiously inspired tourism.

In May 2005 I was invited to give a public lecture about Silver Dollar City at Missouri State University in Springfield. This proved to be a unique experience because the respondent to my talk was Peter Herschend, co-owner of the theme park, crafter of its Christian-inspired entertainment, and, in most people's estimation, chief guardian of the entire region's morally driven industry. To promote the lecture, I agreed to be a guest on a morning radio program that airs on the region's most historic station, KWTO ("Keep Watching the Ozarks"). After a day of chatting with callers on the air, doing newspaper and TV interviews, and speaking to a hall of more than two hundred individuals (many of whom were local residents or Branson boosters), I walked away with one last dose of material to inform pending manuscript revisions. This experience, in fact, elucidates my overall approach to studying the area's tourism offerings. *Holy Hills* does not qualify as pure ethnography if that method is defined exclusively as talking with people and organizing and analyzing these reflections. However, one frequently finds issues of protracted fieldwork, participant observation, thick cultural description, and qualitative detail appended to this definition, and that more broad-based rendering is a better reflection of my research on the modern-day milieu. As with my 2005 presentation, I have interacted with people connected to Branson tourism in a variety of ways and sought information and insights from a wide range of historical and contemporary sources. Additionally, I have woven aspects of literary studies, cultural geography, social theory, and semiotics into a primary focus on religion and consumer culture. Ethnographic methods have been used to explore one period of Branson's history. However, to adequately represent the intricacies and vitality of the city's religion-recreation synthesis required the interdisciplinarity that suffuses this study.

BORN AGAIN IN BRANSON

At the close of *The Shepherd of the Hills,* the novel's protagonist claims to be "born again." Harold Bell Wright, like his hero, was also regenerated in the Ozarks. After spending time in the region, he went from penniless and sometimes suicidal to arguably America's most popular fiction writer. From this first instance of Branson-inspired re-creation, many others have followed suit. Important boosters discussed in this study such as Otto Rayburn, Peter Herschend, Bruce Trimble, and even Jim Bakker have found spiritual succor in the hills. In addition, tourists arriving to consume the experiential wares of these promoters have also used Branson and its attractions to renegotiate identities within differing historical contexts. Such negotiations have certainly included religious awakening, but the city has always thrived by conjoining spiritual renewal with a focus on subjective adaptations in other arenas of society and culture.

Harold Bell Wright valorized the supposedly premodern Ozarks at a time when the United States was undergoing rapid modernization. Commenting on the relationship between tourism and modernity, Dean MacCannell has written that vacationers engage in a serious quest for "real" experience facilitated by "a collective striving for a transcendence of the modern totality" that incorporates its fragments into a "unified experience." For many decades, Branson has not only touted its pioneer heritage but also functioned as a national hub for popularly mediated antimodernism. This sentiment has been expressed through an omnipresent pitting of upright rural life against often contemptuous urban existence; promotions of unwavering patriotism amid a larger culture supposedly unloosed from national pride; visions of unified nuclear families within a world struggling to preserve this elemental social unit; and endorsements of the foundational nature of Christian belief meant to combat perceived secularization.[34]

Thus, the city and its amusements have not only offered vacationers escape from troubling modern accretions but, through the political and cultural power of nostalgia, proffered strategies for enduring and even altering their lived existences. As geographer Yi-Fu Tuan has stated about the tourism process, "An argument in favor of travel is that it increases awareness, not of exotic places, but of home as a place." Moreover, an article in the *Economist* smugly discussed Branson as "utopia" and held that the city has always offered answers to "the fears and longings" of American life. This assessment is even more cogent when one considers that the city has prospered, and continues to prosper, by attracting sizable crowds from the senior tourism market, thereby playing on notions of an ethically sound and socially cohesive past juxtaposed against a somewhat degenerate present. Rather ironically, however, the selling of this sensibility has always been beholden to modern entertainment media, technologies, and economic modes. Furthermore, Branson's Christian-driven consumer culture has had to grapple with scriptural injunctions against the merging of God and mammon. Yet even these seemingly insurmountable paradoxes have been rationalized and gently assuaged by the industry and its audience.[35]

Central to Branson's reenvisioning of modernity are the semimythical stories that the city tells about itself. As Ivan Strenski has written, myth is never a singularity; instead "there is a thriving *industry,* manufacturing and marketing what is called 'myth.'" This study therefore addresses the creation of regional mythology and its pliability over time. Aside from this production vantage, it also broaches the many ways that tourists have utilized Branson's ontological fables and accompanying ideological constructs to conceivably refashion their nonvacation lives. In a poetic assessment of the city's allure, a recent vacationer from Illinois wrote, "Water, hills, shows & food / Nice people, Christians, good / Beautiful land, rocks & dales / Good stories, are they tales?" Although the author draws attention to a Branson artifice, this possible lack of historical candor is of little consequence. The touristic experience depends on the area's sanctified topography, the good nature of its residents, an atmosphere of like-minded belief, and the various ways that these attributes inform the reconstruction of identity outside the realm of leisure.[36]

Vital for such identity-oriented new birth has been the mediation of class status within the area's offerings. For a century the city has fielded visitors aspiring toward the middle class. This dynamic forges ahead into the modern day: in 2004 the average family income of visitors was roughly $52,000. Although many tourists have sought respite from the machinations of the modern class system, Branson's bucolic visions of a bygone era have always been supplemented by ostensibly incongruous displays of affluence—from the Lynch sisters serving supper on fine china after guests emerged muddied from descending into their primordial cave to the city's most popular contemporary variety show entertainer, Shoji Tabuchi, who advances nostalgic notions of rapidly vanishing "American values" while treating guests to bathrooms equipped with granite and onyx pedestal sinks and marble fireplaces. Still, attractions have at all times promised visitors that they could forge consistent notions of class identity and propriety (replete with accompanying ideas related to God, family, and nation) through following their examples and injunctions.[37]

As will be demonstrated, resistance to "modernity," the portrayal of an "authentic" past, and the promotion of waning "values" (all quite loaded terms throughout Branson's history) have not only facilitated a certain class consciousness but also greatly informed issues of citizenship, race, family life, and a variety of other social categories. Religion has too often been situated in isolation from these fields, but crucial for understanding the Branson experience is recognition of the city's keen ability to intertwine a brand of popular Christianity with related spheres of existence. Erik Cohen has posited a number of correlations between practices of play and the pursuit of ultimate meaning, including an "existential mode" in which travel allows for discovery of one's true self and life's rightful meaning. Although a casual glance sometimes does not reveal how seemingly hackneyed Branson attractions facilitate grandiose quests for ultimacy, the enigma of the Ozarks is its ability to straddle what Nicholas Entrikin has described as the "betweenness of place"—the modern relationship between unique experiences in a given location and the broader sociocultural implications of those geographically situated occurrences. Religious discourse in Branson, itself sitting astride a dichotomy of sacred and secular, has always orchestrated these nimble ambivalences, and comprehending its bedrock status then provides awareness of Christianity's linkages to presumably nonreligious domains.[38]

The foundational nature of religion in Branson and the Ozarks is keenly illustrated within a regional folktale. In this story, a farmer's daughter named Ruthie and her sweetheart flee from a spiteful and covetous father called "old Devil," who has forbidden the marriage of his child. As the couple attempts to halt his pursuit through the hills, the two engage in a mythological process of creation that speaks to Branson's tourism endeavor. Pulling bramble briars out of her pocket, Ruthie casts them on the road, and they magically grow to fill the valley with a thicket. However, the persistent father rides around the impediment. Throwing gravel on the trail, Ruthie next creates 50-foot-deep quicksand, but old Devil once again skirts the obstruction. Pouring a bottle of water on the route, the daughter creates the region's heralded rivers and lakes, but her father prevails by circumventing the flood. In a final moment of desperation, Ruthie takes a Bible out of her pocket and hurls it to the ground. At that moment "the little Bible took root and growed a mile a minute; the whole country was full of paper with holy words on it, and everybody knows the old Devil cain't stand Bibles. He couldn't get through and he couldn't go round, so finally he just gave up and went back home." Once the Devil is deterred by scripture, the couple lives happily ever after. So according to this saga, it is not the region's natural features that provide its underpinnings. Instead, the Ozarks is buttressed by biblically derived principles and ethics.[39]

In Psalm 15:1 (NRSV) the Lord is asked by David, "Who may dwell on your holy hill?" The verse immediately following this question states, "Those who walk blamelessly, and do what is right, and speak the truth from their heart." The chapter then continues with a series of more specific attributes labeled by some commentators as "The Marks of a True Worshipper." Amid this brief catalog of suggestions is a call for unwavering religious conviction, with readers being prompted to "stand by their oath even to their hurt." Access to Branson's holy hills has historically involved a similar steadfastness, and tourists and boosters alike have championed the ethical inventory put forth in this psalm. Moreover, like the aforementioned folktale, such blessed sentiments have indeed had a culturally generative capacity, and pious commodities continue to allay sacred and secular tensions through unified experiences of religion and recreation. Because of its many mitigatory roles the tourism industry has consequently offered visitors heterogeneous opportunities for worship, renewal, and rebirth.

Holy Hills of the Ozarks

CHAPTER ONE

"Temples of God's Own Building"

Harold Bell Wright and the Roots of Branson Tourism

In 1895, Harold Bell Wright was unemployed and living in Ohio. He suffered from serious respiratory problems and was plagued by an acute eye condition that had forced him to withdraw from college preparatory school. Contemplating suicide, he instead decided to construct a canoe and float to the White Oak district of the southwestern Missouri Ozarks to recuperate among extended family. Embarking down the Mahoning River and connecting with the Ohio, Wright traveled as far as Cincinnati before high water forced the abandonment of his boat. The remainder of his 1,000-mile journey was completed by train and horseback, with this would-be clergyman and author arriving at Springfield, Missouri, in early 1896.[1]

At the time, Wright was twenty-three years old, and few signs pointed to his pending career as a minister and best-selling novelist. Although he had attended a Disciples of Christ school and could count a number of Congregationalist preachers among his distant relatives, he frequently expressed misgivings about dogmatic theology and institutionalized faith. And while he had written a manuscript when at Hiram College, he was too ashamed of its quality to send it to a publisher. It was within the Ozarks hills, a setting he would exalt and extol throughout his career, that Wright realized his calling. Drawing on a decade of experiences in and around this region, he published *The Shepherd of the Hills* in 1907—a work that both catapulted him onto the literary scene and attracted the first substantial body of tourists to an Ozark locale heretofore unknown to most Americans.[2]

Although Wright was mostly forgotten or ignored by the middle of the twentieth century, he was extraordinarily popular in earlier decades. From 1903 to

1942 he conducted a self-labeled "ministry in print" by penning nineteen books, numerous play scripts, and many magazine articles. Six of his books appeared on best-seller lists from 1911 to 1923, with five selling half a million copies by 1934. According to Asa Dickinson, he was the third most read American writer from 1895 to 1926 and the first in popularity from 1909 to 1921. Moreover, in 1945 Frank Luther Mott developed a system to compare top-selling books, defining a book as a best seller if its sales equaled 1 percent of the U.S. population. Mott's system ranked Wright as the fifth most successful writer since 1665. According to these estimations, only he, James Fenimore Cooper, and Gene Stratton Porter had written five best sellers from the arrival of the Pilgrims through the first quarter of the twentieth century.[3]

Such dominance of the American fiction market was achieved by offering maudlin melodramas to white working- and middle-class readers. Constantly emphasizing the moral responsibility of those at the forefront of consumer culture, he plied fans with an embrace of rural sentimentality, wholesome family values, and simple moral lessons grounded in Christian precepts. This approach was berated by reviewers like Irvin Harlow Hart, who wrote, "No critic has ever damned Wright with even the faintest praise." Predictably, H. L. Mencken extended this vitriol to the author's readership, claiming that the texts appealed only to "naïve and half barbarous people." However, millions or ordinary Americans welcomed such antimodern nostalgia. As a woman who ran a small library in France during World War I recalled, "I soon came to know that ten out of a dozen of the boys who asked for a book would say first: 'Got anything by Harold Bell Wright?'" His status as the king of popular literature even became a begrudging litmus test for publishers. When confronted with a manuscript from a new author, they often asked, "Is he a writer or a Harold Bell Wrighter?" Although his fame began to wane in the 1920s, *The Shepherd of the Hills, The Calling of Dan Matthews, That Printer of Udell's,* and five other novels remain in print, and fifteen movies have been made from his body of work.[4]

The word *recreation* implies physical and mental refreshment through a process of creating oneself anew, and it was such an opportunity for remaking that initially drew Wright to the Missouri Ozarks in the late nineteenth century. Though the logistics of leisure often necessitate painstaking planning, exhausting travel, or an ability to cope with sometimes uncomfortable social and physical circumstances, tourism continues to offer the possibility of subjective reconstruction or maintenance. Codifying this prospect into his literature, Wright similarly placed before millions of readers the idea of restoration by means of escape from the stings of modernity. In this way he drew Branson's first literary tourists beginning around 1910. Furthermore, Wright sensed that the region's inhabitants and topography could facilitate spiritual, social, and cultural rebirth, and it was this occasion for replenishment that stimulated the development of the area's original religiously oriented tourist attractions.

Although suggesting a direct causal connection between Wright's Ozark-based novels and all facets of the historical and contemporary Branson tourism industry is a tenuous proposition, it does seem undeniable that these writings established a religious and ethical framework that inaugurated regional consumer culture—a moral scaffold that continues to bolster Branson's recreational offerings. Commenting in 1931 on such Wright-inspired tourism in the Missouri Ozarks, L. C. Milstead wrote, "The last twenty-five years have seen trade grow from a few hundred dollars into twelve millions annually." By valorizing both the physically and spiritually curative qualities of the Ozark hills, praising the simple yet virtuous character of their residents, and legitimating the promotion of Christian principles in a variety of forms and lived contexts, Wright expressed attitudes that are reiterated by tourism producers and consumers to this day. Glorifying the inherent holiness of Branson and its environs in *The Shepherd of the Hills,* the book's protagonist states, "There is not only food and medicine for one's body; there is also healing for the heart and strength for the soul in nature. One gets very close to God . . . in these temples of God's own building." Even though this city's modern vacation enterprise now extends far beyond sanctified topography and Christian-motivated attractions, many people would suggest that this facet still provides its core vigor. Thousands have contributed over the past decade to the persistence of such themes, but Wright continues to be memorialized as the individual who initiated this union of religion and recreation.[5]

THE OZARK EXPERIENCE AND THE MINISTRY OF
HAROLD BELL WRIGHT

Harold Bell Wright was born on May 4, 1872, in Rome, New York. Two days after the death of his mother, Anna, in 1881—an event marked by a biographer as the author's "first Gethsemane"—his alcoholic father, William, sent him to live with a local farmer. This relocation was the first of many during his adolescence, as he lodged with various family members, slept under bridges or in haystacks, and occasionally reunited with his father for brief periods in cheap boardinghouses. During his teenage years, Wright was left to his own devices and subsisted by hauling wood, driving a grocer's truck, laboring in a glass factory, and consenting to other odd jobs that he encountered during his travels. After fleeing his abusive parent and their squalid living quarters above a saloon in Findlay, Ohio, Wright rode rails upstate to Grafton, where he gained employment as a sign painter. In 1893, a ministerial student from local Hiram College held a tent-meeting revival, and Wright was asked to paint its advertising signs. His signage prompted him to attend a service and to join the evangelist's church, the Christian Church (Disciples of Christ). As he recounted, this event introduced him to the "simplicity of the idea that it was enough to be a Christian, and to be a Christian was to accept the teachings of Jesus as the guiding principle of one's life."[6]

Formed in 1832, the Christian Church (Disciples of Christ) called for an end to divisiveness among Protestant groups and sought to restore early Christian accord through a return to New Testament principles. Adherents to this tradition felt that scripture contained a pattern for all religious thought and behavior. Putting forth slogans such as "Where the Scriptures speak, we speak; and where the Scriptures are silent, we are silent" and "In essentials, faith; in non-essentials, liberty, and in all things, charity" (catchphrases Wright may have painted for the aforementioned revival), members pursued a "primitive" style of religion and took the Bible as their only existential guide. Spreading rapidly throughout the Midwest and South in the latter part of the nineteenth century, the movement protested the sectarian and creedal nature of extant Christianity and called for an ultracongregational polity that ceded all control of theological and structural matters to the local church. A sporadic attendee of Congregational churches since his youth, Wright professed that this older church was "all right for those who did not know life in the raw as [he] had experienced it." But its preachers, with their "immaterial and irrelevant theological discussions, seemed to be apart from life." Within the Disciples' fold, he would find instead a theological vantage that satiated his desire for a more action-oriented and less doctrinaire form of religiosity.[7]

Based on his revival experience, Wright quickly embraced the Disciples' theology and therefore found the themes that would eventually permeate his literature. With monetary assistance provided by a wealthy Grafton resident, he enrolled in Hiram's preparatory department in the fall of 1893. However, after two years of schooling, he was still uncertain about the preaching profession and continued to contemplate other avenues through which he could apply biblical social ethics. When his brief stint as a student ended, he returned to a life of physical labor, but he soon contracted tuberculosis and began to lose his eyesight. These maladies would prove to be the first of many throughout his life, with the search for physical well-being becoming a primary impetus for his original and consequent visits to the supposedly curative Ozark hills.[8]

It was Wright's feeble health that prompted an uncle to invite him to the Ozarks. Within pristine and undeveloped Stone and Taney counties (parcels of land now spanned by the Branson tourism industry), he pursued painting and drew general inspiration from a topography that he would hallow in six separate novels. During his first sojourn in 1896, Wright attended services at the one-room White Oak School near what would become Branson, Missouri, and was appalled by the itinerant preacher's lack of preaching skills and his misreading of scripture. When this same minister failed to show up for a Thanksgiving service, congregation members who were aware of Wright's truncated theological training asked him to conduct the meeting. Relating both his attempts to pastor in a mode that was comprehensible to untaught Ozarkers and their acceptance of his leadership in spite of his academic training, he quoted a congregant in his autobiography as stating, "He's got larnin', all right, but he sho' talks so's we-uns kin understand what he's a meanin'." Embraced by many rural churchgoers after this inaugural sermon, he frequently preached at schoolhouses and country churches before moving to Mount Vernon, Missouri, to minister to a small congregation.[9]

In the summer of 1897 Wright was invited by the Christian Church of Pierce City, Missouri, to preach on weekends and eventually served as its resident pastor until September 1898. Espousing a belief that "life was worth the effort only as one made whatever contribution lay within one's ability toward the more abundant living of all," and hoping to offer a "simple presentation of Jesus' teaching power," he was remembered by locals as a "very plain and somewhat unkempt person" who preached without pretense or undue theological argot. Resisting distinctive pastoral garb and abhorring being called "Reverend," he advanced an anti-institutional and anticreedal theology with a gentle reserve that appealed to Pierce City residents exasperated by the prevalence of late nineteenth-century "denominationalism."[10]

Near the end of his second year at Pierce City, Wright was invited to pastor a church in Pittsburg, Kansas, a booming coal-mining town in the southeastern corner of the state. At the turn of the twentieth century, Pittsburg was a locus of much ethnic diversity, with laborers from a dozen European countries seeking employment as deep-shaft miners. Partly as a consequence of this labor presence, the city was also a hotbed of populist and socialist political activity. In nearby Girard, J. A. Wayland had since 1895 published the nation's most important socialist newspaper, *Appeal to Reason,* with Eugene V. Debs serving as a contributing editor. Such a presence made southeastern Kansas a breeding ground for radical politics and revolutionary social thought. This turbulent milieu was also augmented by a remaining vestige of frontier culture—one that brought with it a considerable amount of violence, prostitution, drinking, and gambling. In Pittsburg, Wright found brothels a mere two blocks from his house of worship and counted twice as many saloons as churches. Yet despite these apparent impediments to piety, he described his five years in Pittsburg as "the most satisfactory" of his life. During this period he married, had two sons, furthered his reputation as a persuasive public speaker, and wrote his first novel, *That Printer of Udell's* (1903).[11]

It was in Pittsburg that Wright fully embraced Social Gospel advocate Washington Gladden's notion of "applied Christianity." In essence, the Social Gospel supported Christocentric philosophies premised on the conviction that Jesus's role as moral exemplar should overshadow his redemptive sacrifice and atonement for sins. Essential for such development was the positing of divine immanence and the call for greater involvement of the church within society. Thus, a remaking of the social order that accounted for dramatic social and cultural changes accompanying the rise of the city and the growth of industry was viewed as the only way to ensure the ceaseless advancement of the kingdom of God on earth. As individuals such as Theodore Munger, Walter Rauschenbusch, and Gladden persistently emphasized the progress of the Social Gospel made manifest in American civilization and the conjoining of the natural and supernatural into a unified whole, their themes deeply affected young Harold Bell Wright. His writing clearly promotes a mode of Christianity that emphasized putting faith into action within one's home, business, or community. Similarly, it often derided insular denominational wrangling over issues of finance, social standing, and leadership politics which impeded the church's necessary mission of service to the world.[12]

Although Wright embraced the practical directness of the Social Gospel, he at the same time shunned the academic rendering of the movement offered by its best-known advocates. In fact, he admitted that in "the company of a bookish person," he was "ill at ease." Direct attention to new liberal modes of biblical interpretation or explicit engagement with social-scientific thought is absent from his writings. Instead, Wright opted for the fiction genre and thereby added to the roughly one hundred Social Gospel novels published in the late nineteenth and early twentieth centuries which were aimed at bringing the movement's tenets to the masses. His disquiet with scholarly matters and high culture was parlayed into works that frequently rebuked the nonpragmatic intellectualism of spiritual elites and churchly establishments. In this manner, he melded his Social Gospel tendencies with an early nineteenth-century religious populism promulgated by evangelicals of the Second Great Awakening. Groups born out of this revivalistic climate, such as the Disciples of Christ, espoused a democratic variant of religiosity prefaced on razing distinctions between learned theologians and ordinary believers and calling attention to the play of the supernatural in everyday life. This lived and popular approach to Christianity would be invoked in his first novel and later serve as the foundation for Branson's unique brand of pious leisure.[13]

That Printer of Udell's, initially published as a serial in the liberal Protestant periodical the *Christian Century,* tells the story of an unemployed printer named Dick Falkner who attempts to escape poverty and an alcoholic father by traveling to a small Ozark town. Unable to find help among Boyd City's (read Pittsburg's) religious elite, he happens upon George Udell, a local unchurched publisher who demonstrates to Dick that a strong work ethic and unwavering moral principles can be solidly cultivated outside the confines of institutionalized faith. In opposition to the Jerusalem Church of Boyd City's prominent elders, a Young People's Society forms with the intention of putting Christian principles into practice. Aspiring to "talk less and do more," this group is led by renegade pastor James Cameron, who along with Udell epitomizes the merits of lived devotion. Presented as a series of sermons to his Pittsburg congregation, *That Printer of Udell's,* like Charles Sheldon's renowned Social Gospel tome *In His Steps* (1896), was meant to offer practical religious lessons. That Wright saw this impetus sorely lacking among his town's most pious individuals is evidenced when he has George Udell state, "Your church members are all right on the believe, trust, hope, pray, and preach, but they're not so much on the do. And I've noticed it's the 'do' that counts in this life."[14]

A modestly successful work, *That Printer of Udell's* was thinly veiled autobiography. By broaching the concerns of unemployment, alcoholism, crime, and class bias, Wright not only chastised Christian devotees in Pittsburg but also inaugurated a melding of personal narrative and spiritually oriented fiction which would guide his entire body of writing. Further, this work is replete with moral uplift, as the protagonist relinquishes drinking and drifting, adopts a virulent work ethic, marries an affluent Christian girl, and is finally elected to the U.S. House of Representatives. Such inspirational conclusions, which can be found in all the author's texts, led critics to label his works sentimental and chide them as having "the rosy, empty features of banality." With 1,000 copies initially printed and 450,000 eventually sold, *That Printer of Udell's* in no way rivals the popularity of Wright's later texts. However, its promotion of a style of Christianity that was intelligible to the common folk, thoroughly integrated into other value-creating arenas, and attentive to larger social concerns would recur in every subsequent offering.[15]

Shortly after publishing his first book, Wright accepted a pastorate at the Forest Avenue Christian Church in Kansas City, Missouri, where he preached from 1903 to 1905. Cautioned by doctors that a persistent cough might grow worse in the mining environs of Pittsburg, he took a brief recuperative vacation in the Ozarks before heading north to his new congregation. During two trying years in Kansas City, he once again sought to combat a wealth of saloons, brothels, and gambling houses through an applied Christian approach and grew increasingly discontented with his fellow ministers' inattentiveness to these social matters. Chastising their self-centeredness and lack of popular focus, he wrote in his church's newsletter, "When is a preacher not a preacher? When he cannot forget that he is." Feeling throughout his career that he was "a thorn in the flesh of the body ministerial" and frequently criticized by his cohorts for failing to embrace the air of distinctiveness that is supposed to accompany the profession, Wright decided in 1905 to work on a second novel. He ventured alone to the Ozarks in the summer of that year and boarded with John and Anna Ross.[16]

Wright first met the Rosses while pastoring in Pittsburg. The family had settled in Springfield in 1879 and moved to a homestead in Stone County in 1895. Farming a 160-acre parcel with their son Charles, they took advantage of plentiful game, tillable soil, and abundant water to fashion a prosperous life atop a hilltop now called Inspiration Point. Wright's initial visit to their cabin was prompted by the frequently flooded White River. On the way to join his father and younger brother for a hunting and trapping expedition in Arkansas, he was unable to ford the waterway. Seeking sanctuary with John and Anna, Wright passed time by investigating the idyllic mountains and their residents. As John Ross wrote, "It was on this trip that . . . the scenery charmed him. The peaceful quiet of the hills held his interest. It was the beauties that he saw on this trip that he afterward proclaimed to the world in print." During his second visit to the homestead in 1901, Wright and his family camped near the Rosses' home as he explored the region, painted, and worked on *That Printer of Udell's*. He called on the family again during the summer of 1902 while in the area for a fishing trip. In July 1903, he revisited with a horse-drawn wagon packed with a tent, furniture, and other household items. Erecting his shelter in the midst of a recently harvested cornfield, he spent three months absorbing the local landscape and culture. He arrived once again during the summer of 1904, and in 1905, after resigning from his church in Kansas City, he returned permanently to begin his masterwork, *The Shepherd of the Hills*.[17]

Not yet ready to end his formal work as a Christian minister, Wright accepted a call to become pastor of the First Christian Church in Lebanon, Missouri, in September 1905. There, for fourteen months he continued to emphasize the merits of a lived Christian approach to theology. In October 1906, he offered a variation of Charles Sheldon's question "What would Jesus do?" by proffering a sermon entitled "What Does Jesus Say about It?" More important, it was in Lebanon that Wright completed most of the manuscript for *The Shepherd of the Hills*.[18]

THE THEOLOGICAL, THE SOCIAL, AND
THE SHEPHERD OF THE HILLS

Published in 1907, *The Shepherd of the Hills* emerged within an American culture that was witnessing the ascendancy of urban lifestyles, the rise of industrialization, and the dawn of new forms of subjectivity dependent on the consumption of mass-produced commodities. At the time of Wright's first visit to the Rosses' homestead, 60 percent of Americans lived either on farms or in towns of fewer than twenty-five hundred people. However, by 1920 more than half of the population lived in cities. The decade in which *The Shepherd of the Hills* was published also included one of the most sizable waves of immigration in U.S. history. By 1910, one out of every seven Americans was foreign-born. Urbanization and new economic modes also facilitated labor unrest and unionization, with thousands of working-class men arrested during the opening years of the century. Yet despite these upheavals of modernity, Wright's text claimed that it was still possible to produce and maintain the sanctity of the family, the vitality of Christian-based ethics, the integrity of the individual, and the overall value system of an older rural American society.[19]

Set in the late nineteenth century near what would become the city of Branson, *The Shepherd of the Hills* tells the story of Daniel Howitt, a learned and cultured Chicago minister who comes to the mountains "staggering under a burden of disappointment and grief" that is product of years spent in degenerate urban confines. Keeping his background a secret, he is befriended by Grant Matthews Sr. (Old Matt), a farmer and miller whose only daughter died giving birth to an enigmatic son named Pete. Hired as a shepherd by Matthews, Howitt mentors the entire community, giving special attention to Grant's son, Young Matt, and his love interest, Sammy Lane. Most significant, the Shepherd plays an instrumental role in safeguarding the Ozarkers against physical, ethical, and spiritual dangers. Throughout the novel, residents are tormented by Wash Gibbs and his band of vigilantes (a group Wright modeled on the Bald Knobbers, who terrorized Taney County during the 1880s). While Howitt attempts to protect the mountain folk from this obvious threat, he must also counter the more subtle coercions of temptation and materialism. During the story, Sammy is faced with choosing a mate. At the outset she is engaged to Ollie Stewart, a former Ozarker who has left the hills for the corporate world. Young Matt also seeks Sammy's love, and as the "giant" of the hills he epitomizes the virility and raw power of rural naturalism. At stake for the author, of course, is more than the hand of his unspoiled heroine. The competing sweethearts serve as a representation of the clash between city and country, with meritorious and productive physical labor squaring off against spurious mental work and the quest for monetary gain. Ultimately, Ollie is portrayed as meek and physically feeble, unable to protect himself when bullied by mountain misfits, and feminized by a modern consumerist impulse that decays authentic manhood—traits that the book claims easily precipitate when loosed from the confines of the bucolic Ozarks.

Wright used such dichotomous characterizations and moral conundrums to valorize the inherently ethical fortitude of rural inhabitants, a sentiment with much currency at the time of the novel's publication. The turn of the twentieth century marked the beginning of the Country Life Movement in the United States, an initiative that mirrored Progressivist programs simultaneously popular within urban America. Country Life, essentially a "rural version of the Social Gospel," sought to reclaim a lost sense of community among farming peoples and to valorize an agrarian myth of once unproblematic and entirely cohesive social arrangements. The chief impetus for the movement was the National Commission on Country Life, created by President Theodore Roosevelt in 1908. The group was led by urban Progressives with training in both theology and rural sociology. Individuals such as Liberty Hyde Bailey, Kenyon L. Butterfield, and Warren Wilson blurred traditional lines between church and society by prompting country churches to become community centers and sponsors of cultural activities. They also implored rural pastors to relegate soul saving to social betterment. Finally, in a related initiative spearheaded primarily by members of the United Presbyterian Church in the USA, the Methodist Episcopal Church, and the Moravian Brethren Church, religious leaders stressed the need for federated community houses of worship grounded in nondenominational cooperation. All these ideas clearly echoed Wright's personal agenda and his Disciples of Christ training.[20]

Although Wright never claimed a formal affiliation with the Country Life Movement, its glorification of the yeoman farmer lifestyle, promotion of a rural simplicity that translated into uncomplicated rectitude, and claim that agricultural life would always be superior to urban existence all found expression within *The Shepherd of the Hills.* Liberty Hyde Bailey's sentiment that "the land is holy" and Warren Wilson's injunction to "make country life a religion" are mirrored in the opening page of Wright's text. Here, a character referred to as "Preachin' Bill" exclaims, "When God looked upon th' work of his hands an' called hit good, he war sure a lookin' at this here Ozark country." Though Wright, with his seeming detestation of modern accretions, may not have condoned the Country Life Movement's sponsorship of contemporary scientific techniques to further commercialize and mechanize agriculture, he assuredly welcomed the movement's attempt to reemphasize American agrarian righteousness. This premise, which traces its roots to Jeffersonian idealism, would hold currency until approximately 1920, with such outlooks informing all of Wright's Ozark-based novels.[21]

Seeking to uphold the values of rural decency and spiritual prowess by citing the quest for materialism as their antithesis, Wright uses the characters of Ollie Stewart and Wash Gibbs to illustrate two different but equally injurious brands of acquisitiveness. Ollie's once solid ethics had been quickly decayed by his urban lifestyle, replete with its accoutrements of "faultless linen, well gloved hands and shining patent leathers." Similar to C. Wright Mills's "morally defenseless" white-collar workers who could look only to mass culture for ethical guidance, he had discovered urbane nobility but lost "the aristocracy of heart and spirit."[22]

Wright's fears of an overly feminized modern culture also found support within religious initiatives of the early twentieth century. For instance, the Men and Religion Forward Movement of 1911–1912, the first evangelistic campaign to target a specific gender, stressed a masculine spirituality allied with church leadership, social service, and domestic responsibility. Purveyors of religious art such as Bruce Barton, meanwhile, attempted to divest representations of Jesus of feminine attributes and emphasize Christ's manliness. Finally, men like John R. Mott, general secretary of the International Committee of the YMCA from 1915 to 1928, sought to cultivate "Muscular Christianity" and thereby assuage the ill effects of feminized faith. As cultural historian Erin A. Smith noted, Wright was implicated in this attempt to masculinize American religion. Although his works contain many traditional elements of the nineteenth-century sentimental novel, he separated himself from authors such as Harriet Beecher Stowe or Susan Warner by "eschewing domesticity and the world of women." Most of his texts draw on the western genre and through a variety of archetypal frontier themes offer

protagonists who have resisted the decay of authentic manhood and virile spirituality which results from modern life. Such trappings of civilization are thoroughly evident within Ollie Stewart. On his transition to city life, "cheap culture"
not only facilitates the demise of manly aesthetics but also converts once solid
religious principles into nothing but "foam and froth."[23]

Alternately, Wash Gibbs's quest for material gain is accompanied by a vio-
lent streak unfathomable to the dandyish Ollie. Killing, robbing, and constantly
putting Sammy into physical and mental peril, he is willing to thwart the law
to satiate his desires. Only Young Matt can resist the temptations of the time,
and it is therefore obvious throughout that he will triumph at the book's end.
Wright resists characterizing this hero as driven by animality, a depiction regularly assigned to "hillbillies" or mountain folk throughout the twentieth century.
Instead, Young Matt is the consummate virtuous Ozarker who avoids leveling
undue force on either Wash or Ollie. Throughout the novel he heeds the Shepherd's advice that "it is always God's blessing . . . when a man masters the worst
of himself."[24]

Even the gentle and moderate Old Matt must fend off the temptation for re-
venge to maintain his status as an intrinsically righteous hill man. On the arrival
of the Shepherd, Grant is still tormented about the death of his only daughter, who had been abandoned by a lover prior to the childbirth that precipitated
her demise. Old Matt constantly battles feelings of hatred toward this wayward
man who deserted her at the urging of his conceited father. Seemingly willing to sacrifice his spiritual good standing for retribution, he tells the Shepherd,
"Many's the time I have prayed all night that God would let me meet him again
just once, or that proud father of his'n. I'd be glad to go to Hell if I could only
meet them first." When at the end of the text it is revealed that Howitt himself is that fulsome father who had urged his son not to further a relationship
with such an uncultured mountain girl, the Shepherd fears that justice will soon
be brought to bear. However, like all of Wright's rural ethical exemplars, Old
Matt controls his rage, forgives the perpetrator, and acknowledges the divine
providence that guides all Ozark happenings when he states, "It's sure God's
way."[25]

Like Wright himself, Howitt comes to the Ozarks in search of physical and
spiritual rejuvenation and an escape from the tribulations of materialistic city
life. Although he finds individuals such as Ollie and Wash in the hills, the merits
of Young Matt, Old Matt, Sammy, and others far outweigh the ethical shortcomings of the handful of immoral inhabitants. Concurrent with the sentiments of
the author, Howitt's Christianity is linked more to a sense of nature-driven spiri-

tuality and concern for social well-being than to any particular creed or theological vantage. For example, it was a comparison of his experiences in the Ozarks with those of Christ in the wilderness which prompted the Shepherd to associate the hills with "temples of God's own building." Similarly, Harold Bell Wright's son has described his father's spirituality in a manner somewhat analogous to that of the nineteenth-century transcendentalist movement: "He came to a little different concept of God, not so much as a personal entity you can talk to and pray to, but as a great overall power. . . . He believed that the all pervading, all powerful, all the laws of physics, all the laws of nature, everything in the whole cosmos, represented God to him." At the novel's end, the Shepherd claims to be "born again," a sentiment that not only reflects the spiritual refreshment enjoyed by this character but also mirrors Wright's own sense of rebirth within the hills. As will be documented in subsequent chapters, this amalgamation of leisure with spirituality and its accompanying product of soulful renewal would function as a model for many tourists throughout the next century. [26]

Although thoroughly embracing the Social Gospel movement, Wright and his shepherd alter ego were hesitant to view communal and religious betterment as solely a result of a philanthropy of affluence. In the early decades of the twentieth century, tomes such as Simon Patten's *The New Basis of Civilization* (1907) extolled the beneficial social functions of capitalism and urged Americans to view their checkbooks as objects "as spiritual and poetic as the grime and bloodstain of ministering hands." Furthermore, consumers were increasingly being told that "real" naturalness required the subordination of nature to technology rather than a valorization of a bygone way of life and its antiquated economic arrangements. However, Wright resisted both of these intellectual currents and instead, according to John P. Ferre, situated morality as "embedded in nature," where it could be "discerned by those who look earnestly." In *The Shepherd of the Hills,* only those who cultivate a melding of grace and works are able to overcome the threats of modernity that swirl around this pastoral Ozark community, with characters embracing capitalist acquirement marked as dissolute pariahs who have unquestioningly accepted wayward "progress." [27]

A union of ethical action and steadfast faith, which reflects the plea for an amalgamation of liberal and conservative approaches to salvation put forth by the Christian Church (Disciples of Christ), is made manifest by the characters Old Matt, Young Matt, and Sammy. Throughout, they stay the course of their moral quest by recognizing the ethical merits of country life and its concomitant simple yet fruitful value structure. Never does a reader find these individuals attending a formal church service or engaging in any type of prescribed ritual.

Instead, their spiritual strength and moral vigor are cultivated in natural temples. In 1931 Wright wrote, "I have come to feel God in the most commonplace acts of everyday life. In the familiar and common objects of my daily experience, I recognize the divine." It is this popular or lived religious sentiment that the Shepherd both learns for himself during his Ozark pilgrimage and demonstrates to the people he mentors.[28]

In *The Calling of Dan Matthews,* Wright's 1909 sequel to *The Shepherd of the Hills,* his condemnation of nonpragmatic "churchianity" and promotion of an applied Christian approach are further articulated. Set in the midwestern city of Corinth, this work describes a town filled with churches and dogmatic pronouncements but lacking in the Christian charity so essential to the author's conception of religion. Dan Matthews, son of Young Matt and Sammy Lane from *The Shepherd of the Hills,* assumes his first pastorate within this environment, and a struggle ensues between his socially active intentions and the dogmatic and financially preoccupied stances of Strong Memorial Church's two prominent elders. Early in the narrative Dan meets a young nurse named Hope Farwell, who professes to be a devout Christian and demonstrates knowledge of things biblical. Nevertheless, she also rejects church establishments in favor of putting faith into action by means of her vocation. Dan steadily embraces her anti-institutional piety and loathing for the town's religious elite. Functioning as a mouthpiece for Wright's vision, she states during her first encounter with the novel's protagonist, "To the churches, Christianity has become a question of fidelity to a church and creed and not to the spirit of Christ. . . . Man serves God only by serving men. There can be no ministry but the ministry of man to man."[29]

Befriending perceived "undesirables" such as Charity Conner, the daughter of a murderer, and emphasizing accomplishment over intellectual suppositions to the chagrin of Strong Memorial elders, Dan realizes that he must leave Corinth. Like the biblical Corinthians addressed by Paul, Wright's townspeople suffer from a variety of theological and practical problems. Paul's correspondence was prompted by the increasing division of his targeted church community into factions. Urging this community to combat social divisiveness, he marked love and service to other Christians as imperative and chastised those who prioritized esoteric knowledge over a concern for this-worldly betterment. By invoking a church constituted of "many members, yet one body" who "suffer together" and "rejoice together," Paul recommended a service-oriented religiosity grounded in Christian humility which is remarkably similar to Wright's conception of proper faith. When the New Testament author advised the Corinthians, "If you think that you are wise in this age, you should become fools so that you may become wise," he was offering a directive that could just as easily find expression in *The Calling of Dan Matthews* and throughout Wright's literature.[30]

In large part it is the novel's urban setting that dictates its dilemmas and outcomes. Dan was "born with the passion for service in his very blood and reared amid the simple surroundings of his mountain home . . . where every soul was held a neighbor." In this context each individual was "judged upon his own life and living" and not by the stolid dictates of creeds or confessions. Seeing that the members of his flock are incapable of exhibiting the uncomplicated communal virtues inculcated under the tutelage of the Ozark shepherd, he becomes ever cognizant of their preoccupation with "useless speculation." Much of this banter is again the result of a feminized church replete with women's committees that waste time "discussing the most trivial matters with the most ponderous gravity." As a result, Dan abandons the hypocrisy and inaction of the supposed devout, returns to the hills to supervise mining on his family's property, and makes the causes of local labor his chief priority.[31]

By fleeing the corrupt city and returning to this ethical sanctuary, Dan becomes reacquainted with Hope and truly realizes the verities of lived religiosity. As he professes in the closing pages of the text, "The ministry of the farm, and mine, and factory, and shop . . . wherever men toil with strength of body and mind for that which makes for the best life of their kind—that ministry is sacred and holy." Dan's choice of a ministerial vocation is well intentioned, but he quickly grows to realize that an assumed willingness among the devout to take principled action was naive. Thus, Wright once again expresses his conviction that the most viable avenues for Christian belief and practice lie outside the parameters of the institutional church and that it is in these popular forums that the real work of faith is done. In taking such a stance, he effectively outraged pastors throughout the United States. *The Calling of Dan Matthews* was even rebutted by evangelical novelist Alexander Corkley one year after its publication. In *The Victory of Allen Rutledge: A Tale of the Middle West,* a young pastor in another midwestern town confronts moral challenges similar to those faced by Wright's hero. But in Corkey's book the preacher refuses to renounce his denominational establishment and instead reforms the church and remains in the ministry.[32]

An expansive vision of "ministry" is Wright's chief legacy within the century-long religio-touristic Branson environment. In *The Calling of Dan Matthews,* service to the common hill folk is the mark of true Christianity. Similarly, the author himself soon realized that he could better fulfill his vision of religious charity and practiced ethics outside the confines of a preaching career. Reflecting on this transformation in his autobiography, he stated, "All of who in any capacity serve are God's ministers. . . . The pen of the writer . . . is the sacred furnishing of the temple of life which is the temple of the living God. . . . Certainly I have looked upon my writing as a ministry."[33]

In 1906, Wright abruptly left the Ozark region to seek a milder climate in California and eventually retired from formal preaching in 1907 because of declining health. Although he seldom returned to the area during the last three decades of his life, his Ozark-based novels inspired scores of devotees to visit Branson as tourists. Moreover, they also prompted numerous individuals to adopt religious vocations or convert to Christian lifestyles. For instance, Guy Howard, known as the "Walkin' Preacher of the Ozarks," was born in Iowa in 1892. Initially a farmer and teacher, he began his evangelistic work in 1933 after his first wife made a deathbed request that he leave agricultural life and preach. At the time of this tragedy, Howard recounted:

> I lost myself in reading. . . . A school patron loaned me copies of two of Harold Bell Wright's books, *The Shepherd of the Hills* and *The Recreation of Brian Kent.* . . . The very word Ozark became to me a symbol of haven—a symbol of peace and quiet. I determined that some day I too would seek out this country which had become the refuge of another weary man. And I felt that in this land so far away in feature and situation I too might experience recreation.[34]

Seeking the solace of the hills so valorized by Wright, Howard moved to Hickory County, Missouri, to become a schoolteacher. Soon thereafter he decided to spend ten years walking from one community to another preaching the good news. Though raised in a Methodist family, he adopted the nondenominational approach of the itinerant minister, willingly sermonizing to any and all during 4,000-mile yearly treks in which he conducted an average of 280 meetings throughout northern Arkansas and southern Missouri.[35]

Like the author who inaugurated his illustrious preaching career and countless Branson pastors over the past century, Howard undertook a ministry prefaced on both spiritual uplift and this-worldly betterment. His best-selling autobiography, *Walkin' Preacher of the Ozarks* (1944), is replete with stories that detail creative ways he used his meager salary to supply food and clothing, as well as religious education, to the hill people. His services combined frenzied praying, testifying, tears, laughter, dance, and tongue speaking with discussions of Christian service that could affect others "in works as well as in words." Though he traveled throughout the region, he made Branson his home for a number of years in the 1950s and there wrote two books. Perhaps no one has had more firsthand experience with the entirety of the Ozarks than Howard. After a decade of surveying the land and traversing tens of thousands of miles on foot, it was the "Shepherd of the Hills Country" that he dubbed his "promised land." Like Harold Bell Wright, Howard indeed found solace and restoration in the "spiritual nectar brewed in the out-of-doors." As told in all his written works, *The Shepherd of the Hills* was the motivation for both his personal religiosity and that which he instilled in thousands of Ozarkers.[36]

Although Howard achieved much renown within the Ozark region and became known nationally on the publication of his autobiography, the most illustrious individual who was spiritually inspired by Wright's Ozark literature was former U.S. president Ronald Reagan. At ten or eleven years of age, Reagan borrowed *That Printer of Udell's* from the Dixon, Illinois, Public Library. He read it from cover to cover and became impressed by the traveling printer Dick Falkner. As Reagan wrote in a 1984 letter to Wright's daughter-in-law, "After reading it and thinking about it for a few days, I went to my mother and told her I wanted to declare my faith and be baptized. We attended the Christian Church in Dixon, and I was baptized several days after finishing the book." As will be discussed in Chapter 4, the modern Branson tourism industry finds its roots in Reagan-era America. Although claiming that Reagan's administration is directly connected to this consumer culture emergence is an unfounded assumption, his 1984 claim that Wright set him on a path that he "tried to follow even unto this day" certainly speaks to the politico-social impetus of the contemporary tourism industry and its connection with Branson's early twentieth-century roots.[37]

In language similar to Reagan's unadorned political rhetoric, in 1917, Wright credited his pastoral and literary successes to an egalitarian approach and characterized both undertakings as "plain food for plain people." The Book Supply Company, Wright's publisher from 1903 to 1920, offered no original texts except for his books. The remainder of its catalog consisted primarily of Bibles, Sunday school curricula, and other popular religious literature. The correspondence between Wright's texts and more explicitly pious materials was recognized by his second publisher, Appleton, which claimed that "people to whom all other books but the Bible are idle and profane read Harold Bell Wright." In 1910, Sears, Roebuck, and Company began advertising and selling his books through its catalog, a technique that would soon provide him with the epithet the "Dickens of the Rural Route." The presence of his works within country homes soon became so pervasive that it prompted literary scholar Grant Overton to write, "It was the interesting inevitability of the visitor to humble homes in out of the way American places to encounter, on the parlour table, a Bible, a gift edition of Longfellow's poems, *The Wreck of the Titanic* . . . and a copy of *The Shepherd of the Hills.*"[38]

Though reaching his prime as a best-selling novelist with *The Winning of Barbara Worth* (1911), *The Eyes of the World* (1914), and *When a Man's a Man* (1916)—books written while he was residing in California and Arizona which reiterated earlier critiques of urban vice and unmeritorious capitalism and promoted the natural integrity of rural communities—Wright is still primarily remembered for his place-defining Ozark novels. The author infrequently visited the region once established out West, and he died in 1944. However, in a 1935 letter to distant relative Marian Wright Powers of Carthage, Missouri, he stated that he "would like to make a pilgrimage back to the Ozarks," thus continuing to imbue the area with the spiritualized aura present in his first novels. Even though Wright's poor health and business obligations prohibited regular return visits, the region just west of Branson, Missouri, would adopt the sobriquet "Shepherd of the Hills Country" shortly after the publication of his place-defining novel—a moniker that has compelled visitors to revisit his Ozark legacy on a daily basis for now nearly a century.[39]

CHAUTAUQUAS, CAMPS, AND THE INSTITUTIONALIZATION OF RELIGIOUS LEISURE

Even prior to the publication of *The Shepherd of the Hills,* the area around Branson, Missouri, was viewed by outsiders as a consecrated Arcadia. The region's first tourist attractions were game parks meant to draw hunters and fishermen to the untouched Ozark terrain. In 1891, a group of St. Louis businessmen purchased 5,000 acres in south central Taney County for the St. Louis Game Park. Stocking the land with deer, elk, wild goat, bear, pheasant, turkey, and quail, the park opened in 1896 and attracted dignitaries such as frequent visitor William Jennings Bryan and affluent sportsmen from across the country. Following this lead, another group of St. Louis residents established the Maine Hunting and Fishing Club in 1905 by moving the Maine Building of the 1904 World's Fair to a bluff overlooking the White River and purchasing 207 acres of land south of Hollister in Taney County. These ventures, frequently touted in the leading sportsmen's magazines of the day, would quickly become catalysts for journeys by city dwellers to the "exotic" Ozarks in search of the antithesis of their modern urban existence.[40]

The abundance of the land was a primary draw for early tourists in the Branson area, but it was the region's waterways that were the most heralded aspect of this Ozark topography. While lake sports currently are a chief enticement for tourists, float fishing inaugurated this relationship between water and consumer culture. Vacationers began to frequent the rivers of southwestern Missouri in the 1890s, and by 1904 enough were coming to Stone and Taney counties to warrant the establishment of the area's first commercial float-fishing company in Galena. Individuals arrived primarily for the "Famous Galena to Branson Float," a 125-mile trip that began at the confluence of the James and White rivers and terminated at Branson. This week-long adventure (and other shorter variants) not only offered abundant bass and other game but also immersed visitors in "the Ozone of the Ozarks," a pastoral and spiritual aura that could cure "the ails and ills of man."[41]

The Shepherd of the Hills may have lamented ever encroaching modernity and a pending loss of agrarian simplicity, but it also suggested to readers that there was a place where the perceived troubles of industrialization or urbanization could be allayed—a locale populated by folks who, according to the text, "pause in the hurried rush to listen to the call of life" and who serve as examples of "what God meant men and women to be" away from "the shame and ugliness of the world." Utilizing an Ozark vacation to assuage such pressures, a St. Louis businessman floated on the James River in 1908 for an escape from the "awfully hard" business climate of his day. As he wrote, "I have had so much work at home that I simply don't get any time to get away." Despite this lack of leisure, he was still offered brief reprieve within an environment deemed immune from the tribulations of capitalism. While the hills and rivers around Branson could offer fleeting solace and time for contemplation to vacationing urbanites, the place could also function as a means for finding sanctuary from or briefly disregarding the stings of technological progress, social differentiations, moral relativism, or even global conflict. As a Branson vacationer wrote on a 1918 postcard, "We don't get war news all the time and are forgetting everything about it."[42]

At a general assembly of Springfield, Missouri, Presbyterians in 1908, eighty prominent elders hoping to partake of the region's pastoral accoutrements agreed that their district needed a site where conferences, conventions, and group meetings could be held. Pastors of the First and Second Presbyterian churches were instructed to make a 300-mile trip through the Ozarks to investigate potential locations, and they ultimately purchased 160 acres near Hollister in 1909. In 1913, the articles of incorporation for this site, named Presbyterian Hill, identified that the locale would serve as a "suitable place for religious educational assemblies and conventions"; host activities aimed at "the development of Christian character"; and provide "a place for the rest, recreation and entertainment of its members and their guests." Situated atop a bluff that overlooked Branson and the White River, Presbyterian Hill was reached by climbing 330 concrete steps—bringing one nearly 300 feet above the river. Visitors were offered a commanding view of Branson and the increasingly famous Shepherd of the Hills Country. Dewey Bald, Sammy's Lookout, and Old Matt's Cabin were all visible with the aid of a telescope. John and Anna Ross then helped to make this initial association with the novel more concrete by donating their old dinner bell to the new center and presenting lectures there about their connections to the book. Operated under Presbyterian ownership until the mid-1940s, this complex became sanctified terrain not only because of its sectarian affiliation but also because of the surrounding landscape. Peering down at the valley below from atop Presbyterian Hill's summit, a traveler in the 1920s commented, "Man may have made the Hudson, but only God could have made the White River."[43]

Initially, programs at Presbyterian Hill ran only three weeks. However, by the 1920s the site hosted a variety of annual encampments, lecture programs, and conferences. Attendees lodged in floored tents, rentable privately owned cottages, or even the somewhat lavish Grandview Hotel. Because accommodations were equipped with an abundance of water, lighting, bathing facilities with showers, and even a rudimentary sewer system, visitors could enjoy outdoor recreation and *Shepherd of the Hills*–based attractions without forsaking the comforts of home. A 1928 program for the midsummer gathering at Presbyterian Hill highlighted this notion of rusticity augmented by modern convenience in its information on Branson: "Here in our little city nestled in the beautiful surrounding hills on Lake Taneycomo you will find all the comforts and accommodations of a large city combined with all the scenic beauties and recreation that appeals to the tourist in this most romantic and scenic spot in the Ozarks." Moreover, a similar resort, Shepherd of the Hills Estates, boasted that although vacationers would not hear "a single city noise," the site was "easily reached by the completed system of modern highways" and "not too great a distance from home and office." In this way, these original tourist destinations nimbly negotiate a divide between the premodern and modern worlds through assurances that guests could consume the bucolic wonders of the Ozarks yet still enjoy "necessary" innovations of the industrial age. Such a union of seeming contradictions also indirectly reflected the amalgamative theological vantage present in Wright's literature, which according to Erin A. Smith promised readers that they could "be both citizens of a modern, disenchanted world and Christians inhabiting a profoundly sacred space."[44]

Presbyterians from the five-state area that included Arkansas, Kansas, Missouri, Oklahoma, and Texas had access to the assembly grounds, but Presbyterian Hill also drew national meetings and guests from across the country. Making

Pulpit Rock and Grandview Hotel, Presbyterian Hill, circa 1930. Courtesy of the Lynn Morrow Postcard Collection, Jefferson City, Missouri

its accommodations available to other denominations and religiously affiliated groups, the site hosted gatherings of the Southwest Missouri Baptists, the Disciples of Christ, the Woman's Christian Temperance Union, and the Masons by 1915. Attesting to an ecumenical spirit, a promotional brochure proclaimed, "While the Assembly bears the name Presbyterian it would be hard to be sectarian in the presence of the eternal hills bathed in splendor. Here Jew and Gentile, Catholic and Protestant, persons of all faith and persons of no faith, meet and mingle on the broad terms of a common humanity." Boosters asserted furthermore that the site was "Evangelical" and "Evangelistic" rather than "denominational" and thereby echoed Harold Bell Wright's implicit understanding of the relationship between spirituality and the Ozarks. Branson and its surroundings were thereby vested with the ability to proselytize across faith traditions and even to reach those lacking religious inclination. The hills and hollers offered a means of encountering the transcendent in a fashion grounded in orderly experiences of nature, pious recreational enjoyments, and escape from the tumult of modern urban life. For those seeking "rest, refreshment, and recuperation" in a place "away from the dust and dirt of cities," Stone and Taney counties were increasingly portrayed as ideal.[45]

Augmenting the ability of Presbyterian Hill's natural beauty to bestow spiritual prowess, the grounds also engaged in the promotion of religiously based morality and social conduct. Supporters claimed that the site was consecrated for the purposes of providing "physical, intellectual and spiritual improvement" and sought to shield vacationers from a gamut of vices. By prohibiting card playing and alcohol, Presbyterian Hill joined the early twentieth-century temperance movement in trying to preserve a vestige of morality amid rapid American urbanization. Drawing inspiration from the rural camp-meeting tradition, proprietors offered seemingly secular leisure opportunities such as fishing, boating, and dignified dancing within a sanctified social climate.[46]

Beginning in 1912 and continuing throughout the 1920s, Presbyterian Hill hosted a late summer Chautauqua. Established by prominent members of the Methodist Episcopal Church in 1873, the national Chautauqua Association sought to create a space within Protestant America that dissolved distinctions between religious and worldly activity. With an educational rather than revivalist intent, the organization was nondenominational and sought to offer high culture to working- and middle-class individuals through schooling in the arts and public affairs, with all offerings gently clothed in indistinct Protestant theology. Cofounder and eventual Methodist bishop John H. Vincent wrote in 1886 that such leisure opportunities allowed "the cable of divine motion" to stretch "through seven days, touching with its sanctifying power every hour of every day." If it was effectively instated, there should then be "no break between Sabbaths."[47]

The Chautauqua movement achieved its zenith about 1915, with more than ten thousand communities hosting events in that year. Like them, Presbyterian Hill offered celebrations of Christian ethics, patriotism, and family, with an observer portraying its program as "mother, home, and heaven lectures." Sold to the Missouri Baptist Assembly in 1946 and renamed Baptist Hill, the grounds were employed by the Southern Baptist Convention for similar summer meetings until the late 1950s. By seeking to realize John Vincent's call to "turn all secular nature into an altar for the glory of God," Presbyterian/Baptist Hill stood as

Tabernacle at Presbyterian Hill, circa 1920. Courtesy of the Lynn Morrow Postcard Collection, Jefferson City, Missouri

the first institution in the area to blend recreation with explicit Christian themes. By doing so it inaugurated the intricate conjoining of sacred and secular that now characterizes many of Branson's most visited attractions.[48]

In 1910, a second institution joined the Branson area tourist mix when the YMCA established a campground on a 60-acre site below the bluff of Presbyterian Hill. Named the Hollister YMCA Interstate Recreation Camp and Summer School, and also known as Camp Ozark, this locale sought to further the overall aims of the association by offering a wholesome environment through which individuals could combat the vices of urban America; embrace Protestant virtues of thrift, temperance, and industriousness; and build healthy minds, spirits, and bodies.[49]

Unlike its male-oriented urban counterparts, Camp Ozark was billed as "An Ideal Vacation Resort for the Entire Family." Begun with only one small cabin, the facility boasted by 1919 a registration center, a handicraft area, a small library, a 283-seat gymnasium, numerous lodging options, and landscaped drives and walking paths. Like Presbyterian Hill, the YMCA opened its camp to people outside its association and hosted Boy Scouts, physical education clubs, and private vacationers. By the early 1930s, a wide variety of religiously unaffiliated camps had joined Presbyterian Hill and Camp Ozark in the promotion of the Branson area's Arcadian landscape and links to an idealized history of resident righteousness. Places such as Kohler's Health Resort, Camp Ideal, and Camp Perfecto beckoned tourists to enjoy, in the words of the White River Booster League (a marketing organization for the Shepherd of the Hills Country incorporated in 1919), a "land of scenic splendor, romance, health, contentment, happiness, sunny days, cool nights, and all else that makes this truly the vacation Paradise of the Ozarks." In 1930, attracted by such pastoral promises, an average of 150 cars per day streamed into Branson during the summer months, and vacationers could choose from 550 cabins and cottages found at area resorts. Attesting to the difficulties of choosing one idyllic spot over another, a traveler wrote during this period, "It would be hard to decide which camp is prettiest. It [the White River] is the most beautiful river I ever saw."[50]

Enhancing this milieu of religiously motivated vacation options were Kickapoo Camp (at the mouth of Bee Creek on Lake Taneycomo downstream from Branson) and Kuggaho Camp (across the lake from its sister site). Built in the mid-1920s, these destinations were intended exclusively for young adults, with Kickapoo serving girls and Kuggaho boys. The camps were begun by Dallas schoolteacher C. L. Ford with the intention of helping city children learn ethical and social graces in a pristine setting, and this vision came to fruition under the leadership of Bill Lantz. Described by his friends as "the best 24 hour a day, 7 day a week Christian we ever met," Lantz took over the sites in 1929 and renamed the boys' location Kanakuk Kamp after a Kickapoo leader and prophet. As director, he prefaced the camps on two primary religious doctrines entitled "I'm Third" and "Four Square Life." The former principle urged attendees to adopt a mind-set that proclaimed, "God First . . . Others Second . . . I'm Third." Drawing on Luke 2:52, the latter augmented this sentiment of service and selflessness by advocating a life course intent on increasing one's wisdom, stature, favor with God, and assistance to humankind—injunctions that today continue to function as Kanakuk's guiding philosophy.[51]

Filtering lake sports and other athletic recreations through the lens of Christian values, Ford laid the groundwork for an enterprise that would be most fully developed by Spike White, who came to Kanakuk as a junior counselor in 1931 and assumed ownership of the venture in 1954. Nearly fifty years after the White family began to direct the camps, they still offer an "Exciting Adventure in Christian Athletics." In doing so, Kanakuk continues to emphasize the concern on which it was founded and which was central to Harold Bell Wright, who in 1934 identified the "real social enemies of the day" as people who "make vice fascinating" and attire miscreants "in heroic guise for the worship of young children too young to detect the lie."[52]

Throughout the hundred-year history of the Branson tourism industry, boosters and sojourners have persistently struck a sometimes uneasy bargain with modernity. This situation was even more complicated for Wright himself. He realized, for example, that a sizable portion of his readership was of the middle class and that this contingent was in search of a resolution that somehow united nostalgia and progress. Therefore, despite the abhorrence of city living found in *The Shepherd of the Hills,* Sammy Lane is remade by the Shepherd into a genteel and well-mannered lady by the book's end. Moreover, despite the constant berating of the railroad as a symbol of the machine menace that threatens rural life in *The Calling of Dan Matthews,* Dan embraces industry by the work's conclusion (though he does hope to employ wealth for the good of mountain folk). Caught in this betwixt and between position, Wright increasingly turned to divine sanction of progress to appease people who themselves needed an endorsement of their increasingly progressive lifestyles. As Edward Ifkovic has noted, "By attributing the new industrial America to God, there is nothing to fear. A highly industrialized nation is, indeed, God's country. . . . The turn-of-the-century romancer created a new America—the industrial pastoral."[53]

Ironically, tourism was one of Wright's most loathed modern practices. In *The Re-Creation of Brian Kent* (1919), Brian's urbane and egotistical estranged wife is reunited briefly with her husband while on tour in the hills. However, her avaricious sophistication is brought to an end when she drowns in a raging river, her wickedness checked by the adjudicating waters of the Ozarks. In his last regionally based novel, *Ma Cinderella* (1932), the author portrays wealthy city dwellers vacationing near Branson as pretentious snobs who select the area as their destination only because of the opportunity to throw wild parties and ridicule mountaineers. Finally, in the closing pages of *The Shepherd of the Hills* the author issues a caveat concerning the fate of his much beloved mecca which squarely situates tourism as a symptom of modern ills. As stated by the Shepherd, "Before many years a railroad will find its way yonder. Then many will come, and the beautiful hills that have been my strength and peace will become the haunt of careless idlers and a place of revelry."[54]

Although Harold Bell Wright clothed Branson, its surroundings, and its residents in a spiritualized aura and connected this portion of the Ozarks with religious sentiments that still drive its tourism market, his literature also initiated a process of discovery whereby outsiders and modern infrastructures overran the hills. In addition, though Wright frequently censured consumer culture and the ethical dilemmas it produced, *The Shepherd of the Hills* prompted the birth of a still vital vacation market. Commenting on this explosion of spending in the region, L. C. Milstead noted in 1931, "More money changes hands in an hour than in a year a quarter of a century ago." Milstead, like most literary critics, recognized Wright's "shortcomings as a man of letters"; nevertheless, he admitted that the author should be "crowned king of press-agents" as a result of such economic growth. As will be seen in Chapter 2, even as most local residents welcomed consumer culture and actively incorporated themselves into this development by becoming the folks envisioned by tourists' imaginations, others invariably begrudged Wright and his role in unmasking their Arcadia. As told by Chris Meadows, who for many years played the role of Old Matt in local theatrical productions of *The Shepherd of the Hills*, "The story . . . did the one thing the mountain people hated the most. . . . It gave the outside world a view into their lives and their way of living. They resented this invasion of their property and their lives. These were sacred to them."[55]

Employing familiar Ozark terminology to express his contempt for people who unduly complicate straightforward Christian principles, Harold Bell Wright wrote that "plain and understandable truths" were increasingly convoluted by "weird, fantastic theological moonshine." Since the publication of *The Shepherd of the Hills*, Branson's tourism industry has advanced such a practical and lived religiosity that posits God in daily experience. It has also drawn vitality from tourist attractions that lionize the "sacred" lifestyles of regional inhabitants and the inspired topography in which they live. By offering camps prefaced on an interdenominational approach, early boosters crafted a market that resisted religious offense and accommodated vacationers seeking refuge from the perceived immoralities and mounting godlessness of modernity. In decades to come, this brand of popular religion would continue to motivate millions of Branson visitors. Though the status of Wright's literature waned during the less sentimental and optimistic depression years, bucolic and spiritual themes persisted in attracting people seeking the solace of sanctified terrain and the succor of the imaginary premodern.[56]

CHAPTER TWO

"Hills of Truth and Love"

Authenticity and the Sacred in
Shepherd of the Hills Country

Dow Tate was born in 1884 in Cotter, Arkansas, a town 75 miles southeast of what would become Branson, Missouri. As a boy he grew to be familiar with Ozark religion because his father, Van Buren, was a Baptist preacher who traversed the state line between Arkansas and Missouri serving disparate congregations. In 1913 while living in Waco, Texas, Dow embarked on a 600-mile journey by train and horseback to visit sites made famous by *The Shepherd of the Hills*. Like another tourist who ventured to the region in 1915 and wrote back to family in Maine that travel over the past few weeks had been "both humorous and terrible," Tate assuredly encountered many adversities while on his literary pilgrimage. However, thousands of Harold Bell Wright devotees committed themselves to such circumstances and poured into Shepherd of the Hills Country shortly after the publication of the text, hoping to glimpse its bucolic lifestyle and meet its righteous heroes.[1]

On July 29, 1913, Dow wrote a letter to his sister, Sammy. In it he described recent visits to places memorialized in Wright's novel such as Mutton Hollow (the site of the Ross homestead) and Dewey Bald (a mound featured prominently throughout the text)—"holy ground" sanctified by a writer "touched like the prophets of old by the hand of God." A day earlier, Tate had sat on the spot where Wright penned portions of the novel, and like his fellow sojourners he drew inspiration from the "magic value" of the hills and a lingering presence of the man who first expressed its wonders. As he wrote, "Here the Ozark flower-laden air supplied the breath that in the beginning helped to make man a living soul. The bubbling mountain springs filled his thirsting veins with the nectar of the gods. . . . The fountains of power and life were supplied with wholesome viands from the hillside gardens that smile here and there like so many patches in the human heart, cleared away for fruitful deeds."[2]

Dow Tate was an aspiring poet and songwriter, and few visitors have so eloquently praised Shepherd of the Hills Country. In addition, his absolute devotion to the region's masterwork was codified when he named his daughter Sammy Lane after the heroine of the text. However, millions have ventured to Branson, Missouri, over the past century to similarly implicate themselves in Wright's saga, draw spiritual inspiration from its still persistent legacy, and encounter, according to the letter's portrayal, "a natural health and a heavenly rest unknown in the Sanitoriums of science and unguessed in the marts of men." In his closing, Tate beckoned individuals to the region and, while intoning Wright's prophetic status throughout, offered what has proved to be an accurate personal divination in light of Branson's paramount status within the American tourism industry. Marking the area as one where vacationers could authentically experience a variety of eternal values and virtues, he wrote, "The world must turn for their supreme delight to the suncrowned hills of truth and love where the light lingers even when the sun goes down."[3]

FACT, FICTION, AND THE CONSUMPTION OF LITERARY HERITAGE

In 1976, Dean MacCannell offered a groundbreaking analysis of the tourist mind-set by introducing the concept of authenticity to sociological studies on the subject—a heuristic device that keenly elucidates Dow Tate's experience in the Ozarks. In *The Tourist,* he claimed that alienated moderns suffer from a schism between self and a sense of bona fide reality. Tourists are thus individuals in search of the pristine, the primitive, and the natural—entities unavailable within the confines of a highly individualized, technologically driven, and consumption-oriented milieu. The past thirty years have witnessed seemingly endless commentary on notions of authenticity and heritage within modernity, many of which have censured MacCannell's thesis. However, his suggestions were certainly innovative in light of earlier observations from social critics such as Daniel Boorstin, who easily dismissed the tourist experience as a frivolous reflection on the superficiality of contemporary mass culture. Ultimately, MacCannell's assessment, one that has been characterized by anthropologist John Taylor as a "central orienting principle" of tourism studies for the past twenty years, inaugurated a new era of structuralist analysis. According to this approach, ultimate values are formed and negotiated within leisure contexts replete with sojourners pursuing authentic cultural experiences, thereby disparaging "false conscious-ness" as the only way to situate a vacationer's subjectivity.[4]

Lionel Trilling held that in the modern period "authenticity" references "the peculiar nature of our fallen condition, our anxiety over the credibility of ex-istence and of individual existence." Thus, Western peoples are increasingly engaged in a search for something "exceptional in its actuality." Furthermore, within his typology of tourist experiences, social anthropologist Erik Cohen de-scribed the quest for authenticity as "essentially analogous to a religious quest, i.e. a quest for a Center or transcendent Reality." Through such an encounter, the tourist "discovers his real self and meaning in his life" while behaving as "the prototypical pilgrim." Functioning as a substitute for serious ritual in a secular, modern world, this style of tourism seeks to regain a sense of groundedness and to reaffirm the presence of foundational principles and values within a larger society deemed morally suspect and lacking a relationship with otherworldly inspiration.[5]

Certainly MacCannell's template does not hold for all types of contempo-rary tourism. Banner destinations of the late twentieth and early twenty-first centuries such as Disneyland or Disney World, while offering a sanitized vision of Main Street America, engage more fully in a deconstruction of the concept of authenticity by blurring boundaries between the copy and the original or between signifier and signified. According to postmodern theorists such as Um-berto Eco or Jean Baudrillard, these sites are prefaced on the fantastical or the imaginary and, functioning as "simulacrum," rely on identification with "hy-perreality" rather than claiming to represent some verifiable event, period, or personage. Even MacCannell himself was skeptical of one's ability to experience genuine authenticity while on vacation, concluding that what most people come across is in fact "staged" and that visitors to these sites are in effect victimized by a ruse of legitimacy perpetrated by tourism boosters bent on inspiring feelings of genuineness rather than actual knowledge of some "objective" reality.[6]

Although much heralded theorists such as John Urry have marked the search for authenticity as "too simple a foundation for explaining contemporary tour-ism," the historical and current Branson industries have relied heavily on a con-structed and idealized past. According to Eric Hobsbawm and Terence Ranger, traditions are created in relation to the needs of the present and are therefore subject to social processes and relationships of power. Within such a rendering, there is not and never has been an authentic object available for consumption or reflection. Rather, authenticity is a projection of tourists' own beliefs, expecta-tions, stereotypes, and consciousness onto toured things and peoples. Tourist attractions are thus perceived not as originals in and of themselves but as symbols of one's desires and concerns pertaining to present situations and circumstances. As will be seen, Branson tourism has been involved in the construction of authenticity and heritage for nearly a century, with vacationers looking to its assembled vision of "pastness" to allay apprehensions about the present and, by way of that industry's dependence on soteriological religious themes, the world to come.[7]

By 1908, Harold Bell Wright enthusiasts began arriving in Branson via the Missouri Pacific Railroad eager to meet bona fide characters from the text and partake of their simple and upright lifestyle. As a writer for the *St. Louis Post-Dispatch* remembered, "Nobody expected to see Scarlet O'Hara in Georgia, of course, but tourists in the Ozarks did hope to see Old Matt and Young Matt, Uncle Ike, Sammy Lane, and other characters in *The Shepherd of the Hills*." The primary locus for this pilgrimage was the Rosses' residence, as John and Anna quickly melded into literary creations in the minds of tourists seeking the authentic individuals on which the characters were based. Demonstrating such desire, Sammy Lane Tate and her brother, Ewing, were photographed during this early period with the Rosses. However, on the back of the image, the children's mother labeled the couple "Uncle Matt and Aunt Mollie." In 1906, the Rosses fled years of drought conditions by moving from their hilltop farm to nearby Garber. There they opened a general store and post office adjacent to the newly completed railroad. With their farmstead sitting empty, souvenir hunters who rode the train to Branson began hiking across the hills and dismantling the cabin in order to take their own small piece of the novel home with them. After a series of renters occupied the cabin and fed meals to hungry tourists, M. R. Driver, a physical education instructor at Fairmont College in Wichita, Kansas, purchased the land in 1911 and made the homestead into an inn for curious travelers. In 1913, nearly seven hundred vacationers dined at the site. Converting the property into an inn, however, was not enough to prevent further looting by leisure enthusiasts, as the Rosses' gristmill was stripped of all its siding and most of its equipment during that same year.[8]

Tourist pilgrimages focused on acquiring a slice of the "real" *Shepherd of the Hills* were not limited to the purchase or theft of material relics. Travelers also pined to experientially consume the hypothetically genuine subjects of the novel. As Branson historian Kathleen Van Buskirk has written, "Visitors hoping to meet Wright's characters had little trouble getting directions. For the rest of their lives, J. K. and Anna Ross at Garber, and Uncle Ike at Notch were essentially 'on stage.' Almost any nearby pretty girl was likely to be pointed out as Sammy Lane."[9]

Ewing and Sammy Lane Tate with "Uncle Matt and Aunt Mollie," Branson, Missouri, 1919.
Courtesy of Nahum Tate, Missouri City, Texas

A whirlwind of myths concerning the identity of "actual" characters began to
arise, thereby creating an image of Branson and the surrounding area as a site of
"true" and ongoing rural culture within a historical climate witnessing the sharp-
est divide between city and country in America's history. In the decades following the work's publication, local residents unabashedly claimed to be prototypes
of the story's characters or put forth their kinfolk as such. In a correspondence
that addressed the validity of these assertions, Wright would only acknowledge
that Levi Morrill, the postmaster at Notch, Missouri, was indeed "Uncle Ike"
from the novel. Hoping to clarify his intentions, the author wrote to Hollister,
Missouri, resident W. Gibbons Lacy on September 1, 1932:

> I am very glad for this opportunity to settle some of the many conflicting legends
> as to the characters. . . . "Uncle Ike," the old postmaster in the story, is the only
> character which could be definitely placed as an actual portrait of a living person.
> "Old Matt" and "Aunt Molly" were near portraits—I mean that Mr. and Mrs. Ross
> inspired these characters but . . . I idealized and created characters which their
> lives suggested, rather than actually personified. "The Shepherd," "Sammy Lane,"
> "Wash Gibbs," "Jim Lane," "Ollie Stewart," "Young Matt," and all the others were

creations of my imagination and never so far as I know existed as living human beings. Not one of these characters is even near a portrait.[10]

Such admonitions, however, had little effect on eager tourists looking to become corporeally a part of this Arcadia and on willing locals offering a fleeting premonition of the consumer culture mecca that is modern-day Branson.

In a 1936 missive, a distant relative informed Wright that he was "almost worshipped" in "Shepherd of the Hills Country." Additionally, she reported that each local could "'cash in' on his connection with the book" and that many were "living off the publicity" Wright had given them. Branson natives did almost immediately seek to profit from their ambiguous fiction-turned-assumed-fact relationship with the book. A 1922 tourist brochure held, "Residents of the city take pride in pointing out to strangers the places of special interest to those acquainted with that popular and tragic romance." It also guaranteed potential vacationers that they would encounter "unshakable evidence" of the characters' verisimilitude. Intoning a fusion of spirituality and private enterprise which still pervades Branson, an author for the *Midwest Motorist* stated, "By the time of World War I, even the natives began to believe that the ground might really be sacred, not to mention profitable."[11]

By the early 1920s, people engaged in pilgrimages of literary authenticity could partake of a tour that included myriad sites mentioned in *The Shepherd of the Hills*. For instance, a 1930 article from *The Decatur (GA) Review* described a 1,260-mile motor trip made by a group of residents which included visits to Old Matt's Cabin, Uncle Ike's Post Office, the cave where Little Pete's father sought refuge, and the cemetery where Sammy Lane was buried. Apropos for this period, the travelers sought to separate regional truth from literary invention. Even within a brief, one-column article, the author noted that the group met Sammy Lane's husband but that he "is not the 'Young Matt' of the story, who now lives in California." Although failing to come across this genuine protagonist, they did manage to purchase postcards embossed with "the same seal used by 'Uncle Ike' in his lifetime." Such explorations came not only with the promise of walking where "real life" personages walked and meeting those still alive but also with a guaranteed flesh-and-blood encounter with Ozarkers who modeled the humility, rectitude, and purity represented by Wright's main characters.[12]

When the Powersite Dam impounded the White River to create Branson's Lake Taneycomo in 1913, businesses established on the waterfront to capitalize on anglers and floaters also sought to identify with the region's newfound literary fame. Shortly following the creation of the lake, Hobart McQuarter and

Shepherd of the Hills boat on Lake Taneycomo, circa 1930. Postcard from the author's collection

Charles Givauden founded the Sammy Lane Boat Line. This business boasted vessels named the *Sammy Lane,* the *Jim Lane,* and the pride of the line, *The Shepherd of the Hills,* each carrying mail, freight, and passengers between Branson and nearby cities while providing special dancing tours. To accommodate masses of vacationers seeking to enjoy rustic nature and literary realism, a variety of resorts soon lined the banks of Taneycomo. The oldest of these, the Sammy Lane, was opened at the end of Main Street in downtown Branson in 1924 and after eight decades continues to operate.[13]

As this process unfolded, the Ross family and other people linked to characters in the original story also made several attempts to "set the record straight" through their own reminiscences. A primary impetus for the Rosses' decision to abandon their homestead and move to Garber was the annoyance of having groups of tourists arrive unannounced for visits to a *Shepherd of the Hills* locus, or as John asserted, the "plague" of "picture takers." Around 1910, he wrote a little booklet entitled *Old Matt's View of It* in the hope of answering "numerous persons who by letter or in person" sought to interview him and his wife. Seeing himself as victimized by "the great multitudes of book worms," the author offered a comprehensive autobiography detailing his family's genealogical roots, travels, settlement in the Ozarks, and encounters with Harold Bell Wright. While verifying his and his wife's identities as "Old Matt" and "Aunt Molly" and authenticating the existence of an actual Sammy Lane, Young Matt, and Shepherd,

Ross also claimed that the characters Wash Gibbs, Ollie, and Pete "belong to the author." Attempting to answer the question on the mind of any visitor, he stated, "Many have asked us is this a true story. Our answer is, Yes, in the sense that it was intended for, as the locations and landmarks are being almost daily traced out, not only by the curious and sentimental, but by professional people of all callings." Here Ross seems to be saying that the codification of literary tourist sites by enthusiastic patrons validates their legitimacy. He implies that shows of faith in authenticity by people frequenting this burgeoning consumer enterprise are all that is required to blur already fuzzy lines between verity and fabrication. Clothing this entire endeavor in spiritualized language, the author concluded that tourists have discovered a "haven" and that in this way "the prophecy of Harold Bell Wright has been fulfilled."[14]

In 1948, O. R. Morrill, the son of local postmaster Levi Morrill ("Uncle Ike," the only character from the *Shepherd of the Hills* who Wright claimed was based on an actual person), published an account of his father's experiences in the Ozarks. In this book, Morrill also sought to unravel truths and myths concerning Wright's novel. After telling of Levi Morrill's early years in Maine, his apprenticeship under Horace Greeley at the *New York Tribune,* and his establishment of numerous newspapers, the narrative focuses on his opening of a post office in Stone County in 1893. Characterizing this Ozarks region as a "Utopian land" and implicating his uncle in Wright's nature idolatry and antimaterialism, Morrill wrote that the cultured and educated Levi "found contentment in these hills and wouldn't swap places with any city man, for all his earning power." Reiterating a now familiar theme, the author also recounted his uncle's displeasure with the onset of "modern facilities and conventions" in the area, accretions that would crowd out "the simple life" and natural beauty that are a "tonic to the soul." Until Levi's death in 1926, he had been perhaps the most sought after "living souvenir" on *The Shepherd of the Hills* tourism circuit. Welcoming visitors at his post office at Notch, he was at the time of his passing the nation's oldest postmaster. Even after his death, vacationers continued to flock to the site, with one man claiming in 1948 that "thousands of tourists come yearly" to see the tiny building that had by the late 1940s become a "primitive shrine" for consumers of literary heritage.[15]

Amid this flurry of hyperbolic stories and claims of authenticity, it was difficult, if not impossible, for tourists and residents to discern the facts behind the fiction. Such conflation of veracity and sham is not necessarily a bad thing, of course, and the mix has always been essential to Branson heritage brokers. As tourism scholar Barbara Kirshenblatt-Gimblett has written, "Live displays . . .

create the illusion that the activities one watches are being done rather than represented, a practice that creates the illusion of . . . realness. The impression is one of unmediated encounter . . . for people become signs of themselves." A classic confrontation from 1918 illustrates this issue. That year Harold Bell Wright returned to the region with moviemakers who were considering an adaptation of *The Shepherd of the Hills.* As Wright was standing on the veranda of a hotel in Branson, a man sitting nearby commented, "I reckon you have read that book, *The Shepherd of the Hills.*" Wright responded, "Yes, I have read the story." The gentleman then pointed out, "Do you see that girl? That is Sammy Lane." After Wright asserted that considerable time had passed since the work's publication and that Sammy would seemingly be much older, the man responded, "I live here and I reckon I know," and he proceeded to provide much more information about the story and its "true" characterizations. Taking a break from his diatribe, he asked Wright, "Who are you anyway?" To which the author responded, "Nobody, mister, I'm just the feller who wrote that story."[16]

Thus, in a climate of consumer culture increasingly driven by its link to a certifiable past of righteousness and sincerity, it may have been only the "the feller who wrote that story" who could hope to verify the host of allegations mounting in his absence. As the enticement of spiritual regeneration drew more and more tourists to the area, virtually all locals were willing to accentuate this process by rooting themselves in a predominantly legendary past. Of these purveyors of image, Pearl Spurlock was clearly the most important in the early years.

Beginning in 1923, Spurlock became the region's first tour guide and conducted nearly one hundred sightseeing expeditions a year throughout Stone and Taney counties in her Buick taxi. Moving to Branson from Bethany, Missouri, in 1917, she and her husband operated the city's only garage. In a region lacking any semblance of developed roads, her automobile scaled rocky trails while she lectured to people who had traveled from as far away as Australia, Denmark, China, Japan, Turkey, and Sudan. In 1936, Spurlock collected her various tales and talks in *Over the Old Ozark Trails in the Shepherd of the Hills Country,* in which brief comments concerning regional flora and fauna are interspersed with local folklore and humor. Biographical details about Harold Bell Wright mix with "true to life" accounts of his novel's characters and their history in the area. Throughout, the author reiterates the uniqueness of the place and the feelings of reverence one gets "alone with God in a land of his special favor."[17]

Two of Spurlock's stories offer special insights into the way she melded tourists' quests for antimodern and literarily authentic consumer culture with religious sentiment and sanctified topography. In the first account, she tells of an old woman who had lived in Branson all her life but decided she needed a change of climate and moved to California. There she quickly became ill, and a doctor wired her family back in Missouri to drive west. Arriving as the mother lay on her deathbed, her son was told that no cure existed and that his parent's end was in sight. However, claiming he had a sure remedy, he "jerked one of his tires off of his old Ford car, took the inner tube in the house, stuck the valve stem down his maw's mouth and let this Ozark air into her lungs. She immediately came to and was able to come to Branson in the Ford." In another story, Spurlock tells of a tourist who came to Branson and dreamed he had died and gone to heaven. Peeking through the Pearly Gates, he commented to Saint Peter on the beauty of the afterlife but wondered why so many people were "chained to the golden streets." Saint Peter responded, "Well, all those people are from Taney County, and if we didn't keep them chained they would all go back!"[18]

Although such amusing anecdotes are meant to match the jovial mood of sightseers, they simultaneously resonate with deeper associations between place and spirituality. This profound appeal has become the touchstone for leisure activity throughout twentieth-century Branson history. In a demonstration of thematic continuity within the city's vacation industry, contemporary boosters, theater owners, and performers often restate Spurlock's hallowed sentiments, with the conception of Branson as an enchanted land demonstrating dogged perseverance.

ENSHRINING AND ENACTING THE OZARKS' SACRED TEXT

After John and Anna Ross sold M. R. Driver the cabin literally sanctified by Harold Bell Wright, this site initially attracted hundreds of travelers each year. The building began to fall into disrepair in the early 1920s, however. Were it not for the efforts of Elizabeth (Lizzie) McDaniel, the daughter of a wealthy Springfield banking family, the neglected homestead might have never become the attraction that it now remains. Described as a "true believer" in *Shepherd of the Hills* lore, McDaniel liquidated her business holdings and purchased the property in 1926. Prior to this acquisition she had become fascinated by the book and took numerous 50-mile trips on horseback from her home to examine its setting. Finding that land overrun by livestock and squatters, she bought the cabin and re-collected its belongings. Her intention throughout a ten-year process of refurbishment and repair was, according to a *Springfield News & Leader* reporter, to open Old Matt's Cabin as a "shrine and museum.[19]

Lizzie McDaniel, born on August 31, 1871, and raised in affluent southeastern

Springfield, was active in that city's turn-of-the-century social scene. However, she uprooted in 1926 to reside in the Ross cabin and devote the remainder of her life to preserving its semifictional history. After inhabiting the site for a decade and allowing the occasional visitor to tour, she opened it fully to the public in 1936. McDaniel was a longtime board member of the Young Women's Christian Association and one of the leaders in the construction of Springfield's YWCA. One can imagine that, like her YMCA predecessors in the region, she felt that a revamped Shepherd of the Hills Country would serve as a similar wholesome influence on people jaded by the glitz of Jazz Age America.

Before the cabin's reopening, McDaniel implemented numerous changes that would make it better conform to tourists' visions of a romanticized frontier homestead. By building a screened dining room on the structure's north side, converting a barn into comfortable sleeping quarters, and transferring many furnishings from her home in Springfield, she offered initial guests a whitewashed attraction devoid of any suggestions of the many trials and tribulations of pioneer existence. Instead, her cabin presented late nineteenth-century Ozark history in a manner that catered to early twentieth-century bourgeois culture—clean, orderly, and lacking in the violence and social tumult that often afflicted post–Civil War Stone and Taney counties. Through this reconstruction of Reconstruction, McDaniel, according to Branson historian Lori Robbins, created a place that has "long served as the definitive emblem of the Ozarks region."[20]

In a recent exploration of literary places, tourism, and heritage, geographer David Herbert wrote, "There is fascination about places associated with writers that has often prompted readers to become pilgrims." Not in search of absolutely verifiable historical evidence, and perhaps only partly interested in historical reality, such sojourners instead seek to experience a new truth based on the tangible remains of the past. By presenting the Ross homestead to tourists, Lizzie McDaniel facilitated such a process of subjective and objective re-creation. During the 1930s, she provided guests with comforts of home at "Miss Lizzie's Tearoom" and built a new residence for herself on the north slope of a nearby bald—a structure that now serves as the Shepherd of the Hills Homestead's ticket office. Lavishly decorated, the abode boasted a vaulted ceiling with beams constructed of local oak and mantels of solid mahogany adorned with marble. These luxuries offered tourists in depression-era America an escape from social and economic upheaval by eliding such problems through reminders of Arcadian simplicity and promises of emergent modern decadence—a technique that made Branson one of the few vacation destinations in America that did not suffer from declining tourist numbers during the 1930s. Though in sharp contrast with the humble ac-

HAROLD BELL WRIGHT

AND OLD MATT'S CABIN, SHEPHERD OF THE HILLS COUNTRY, NEAR BRANSON, MISSOURI, ON HIGHWAY NO. 80

Old Matt's Cabin, circa 1940. Postcard from the author's collection

commodations and surroundings described in Wright's novel, McDaniel's modifications satisfied early visitors who sought an experience of the rural past that still bore witness to the technological innovations and cultural appurtenances of the day. As a Los Angeles–area tourist staying in the ostensibly rustic environs of Branson wrote to her family, "everything modern just like home."[21]

McDaniel's opening of the cabin to tourists in 1936 prompted other *Shepherd of the Hills* sites to launch shortly thereafter. A formal attraction labeled Uncle Ike's Post Office and Homestead commenced that same year. Although the famous postmaster had been dead for a decade, the locale still promised visitors an immaterial encounter with "the intimate friend of Harold Bell Wright." In 1937, the Diesroth family unveiled a replica of the Jim Lane Homestead, which advertised that the cabin was memorialized within a text whose readership was trumped only by "The Holy Bible." By the mid-1950s, tourists could also visit the Wash Gibbs Free Museum and Ghost Town. Not a testament to the lawlessness epitomized by Gibbs in Wright's novel, this museum instead served as a repository for antique guns, saddles, wagons, and other curios from the Ozarks' past. Regional booster G. H. Pipes characterized site owner "Chick" Allen as "one of the very few authentic native hillbillies who are today operating a public business" while assuring vacationers that the attraction was "free of bandits, and as peaceful and pleasant as a box-supper at a country schoolhouse." Through such advertising, tourist aspirations for genuine hill life were again offset by promises of charming creature comforts. Individuals traversing Highway 148 from Reeds Springs to Branson during this era could also enjoy Little Pete's Zoological Park and the Old Shepherd's Book Shop, which aptly distinguished itself in a 1964 advertisement as "quaint and antique." Thus, the ever mounting attractions of Shepherd of the Hills Country all resorted to a now familiar constellation of marketing devices. In addition to trumpeting their locales as filled with bona fide nostalgia, the sites promised encounters with a sanctified material culture thoroughly linked to the region's sacred text.[22]

While living in Springfield, Lizzie McDaniel orchestrated a series of sunset vesper services at St. Paul Methodist Church and coordinated a number of YWCA-sponsored sunrise Easter pageants. Stationing a rock pulpit halfway up a cliff and releasing a flock of doves at the play's close, she often expressed interest in Christian-themed outdoor drama. At the beginning of 1936, the cornfield where Wright camped while working on portions of *The Shepherd of the Hills* was christened "Inspiration Point." Leased by McDaniel for fifty years to the State of Missouri for one dollar a year, the site became a historical park. From this vista, the proprietor perpetuated her love for religious theatrics by hosting an Easter sunrise pageant that year on April 12.[23]

On a hastily prepared stage, thirty Branson adults and eighty-seven children dressed in monochrome costumes (black on one side and white on the other) re-enacted the Passion as Karl Klein read a script that was projected via loudspeaker and broadcast by Springfield radio station KWTO (Keep Watching the Ozarks) on specially installed telephone lines. As recounted by local historian Kathleen Van Buskirk:

> The players moved silently through the pageant as Klein's solemn voice read the ancient words. Then, as the players rearranged themselves for the final events of the first Easter morning, the sun's rays broke over the ridge tops and caught, on the hill to the north across a steep, rocky creek, the bright form of a giant cross. For more than an hour, 87 children had waited in the pre-dawn gloom, the dark side of their costumes turned toward Inspiration Point. Their cue came at sunrise, and all turned at once so the white half of their costumes would gleam in the Easter dawn.[24]

In retrospect, this public Easter celebration, the first among many in Branson's history, was an important event for the city's religio-touristic undertaking. Roads recently constructed by the Works Progress Administration now supplanted the rocky trails that earlier tourists had to use to access Shepherd of the Hills Coun-

"Taint no wonder 'tall
God rested when He
made these here hills-
He jest naturally had
t' quit, fer He done
His beatenest an' war
plumb gi'n out"

Preachin Bill

View from Inspiration Point, 1942. Courtesy of the Lynn Morrow Postcard Collection, Jefferson City, Missouri

try. These modern designs allowed approximately two thousand visitors to attend the play while thousands more tuned in to the radio broadcast. Structural and media-oriented developments thereby opened the area to a much larger market. Furthermore, although the region had been wrapped in spiritual tones since the beginning of the twentieth century, this first celebration of Christianity's major holiday on the hallowed grounds of the Ross estate made explicit the link between religion and leisure in and around Branson.

In addition to reopening the farm to tourists and reinforcing its Christian associations, McDaniel staged the area's first theatrical production of the novel—a tradition that continues into the modern day. In 1926 she produced a two-act play for several hundred patrons, using the Ross cabin as the main stage. Dramatized productions of the novel began shortly after its publication, with the first Missouri enactment occurring in St. Louis on August 18, 1912. Performances took place frequently throughout the 1920s as troupes toured the country for Chautauqua and similar meetings. In the first few decades of the century, the most influential organization to produce *The Shepherd of the Hills* was the Federal Theatre Project, organized during the depression to offer free entertainment to the economically struggling populace and to provide employment for out-of-work actors. Though McDaniel's rendition was an infrequent event at the homestead, it did "set the stage" for regularly scheduled performances beginning in 1960.[25]

Film versions of *The Shepherd of the Hills* also amplified the book's popularity. In 1919 the Harold Bell Wright Story-Picture Corporation released a silent adaptation scripted, directed, and produced by the author. Emphasizing the utopian notions solidified over the previous decade and accentuating the ways that modern consumers sought to valorize the premodern values of their Ozark "other," a brochure described the movie as "a delightful story of the Ozarks portraying the lives of these hardy mountaineers who are as clean cut and unaffected by the veneer of civilization as the rock bound hills in which they live." A second silent was offered by First National Pictures in 1927, but the most popular (and most locally controversial) version was Paramount Picture's 1941 release starring John Wayne as Young Matt. This adaptation, Wayne's first Technicolor film, debuted with much fanfare in Springfield on July 4. When it opened in Branson atop Inspiration Point, however, residents derided liberties taken with both characterizations and plot. For instance, Paramount presented Aunt Mollie not as Wright's tender and affectionate matriarch but rather as an ill-tempered moonshiner who spearheads her family's illegal ventures. Old Matt, Wright's steadfast and virtuous patriarch, was put forth as a "blind drunk fool" with a "fire spittin' tongue." And Young Matt and his literary antithesis, Wash Gibbs, were depicted as half brothers.[26]

The Shepherd of the film, though still shown as a regional savior, brings physical and psychic relief to the Ozarkers by means of his economic endowments rather than the inculcation of a new ideological vantage. Throughout, hill people are portrayed as rubes who cannot comprehend the workings of a market economy and who stand awestruck as the protagonist writes checks for cash. Contrary to Wright's disdain for modern materialism, Paramount's Shepherd brings salvation through the purchase of a controversial and supposedly haunted piece of land and heals blind Granny Becky, not through some type of reliance on faith but by sponsoring her trip to a city doctor.

Perhaps the most upsetting aspect of the Paramount movie for Branson residents was the retitling of the novel's location to "Moanin' Meadow," which was described by Sammy Lane as "a land of seed ticks and chinch bugs and whoopin' cough." Plagued by "haints" and hexes, Shepherd of the Hills Country is populated by inhabitants wrought with ghostly superstitions and dependent on magical schemes to ward off malevolent spirits. Gone is Wright's infusion of godliness into the Ozark hills. His "temples of God's own building" are instead marked as homes for horrifying apparitions and ill fortune. As a product of this resident evil, locals bear stains of immorality. Aunt Molly is described as "full of the devil's sin," and Young Matt is said to engage in all types of "devilment." Resonating with Ozarkers discontent over the ways that the movie divested the novel of its sacred intentions and underscoring the manner in which the protagonist's religiously grounded ethics are replaced with salvation through economic wherewithal, a *New York Times* reviewer wrote, "The Shepherd of the Hills is a lachrymose bore. His holiness is synthetic; he sells his homilies cheap."[27]

At the film's end, the Shepherd demonstrates that the Moanin' Meadow ghost is a hoax, teaches residents the merits of temperance, and transforms Young Matt into a redeemed character who feels as though he has been "borned all over again." Despite many reviews that praised the movie's legitimate characterizations, including a *Variety* critic who felt that it captured "the authenticity of the Ozark characters and country," Wright's consecration of the hills and his conviction that its residents were naturally imbued with blessedness are noticeably lacking. Unlike its religiously saturated literary inspiration, Paramount's interpretation makes reference to the divine only on three occasions. The Shepherd does bring communal deliverance by the film's end, but this occurs only by means of Aunt Mollie's death—the eradication of an inequitable presence that has cast a pall on the vice-ridden Matthews family for many years.[28]

When the film opened at the Owen Hillbilly Theater in downtown Branson on July 11, 1941, a banner hung from the entrance reading, "We Don't Like It, But Here It Is." Protesters representing the fictitious "Hillbilly Local No. 0001" carried placards that chastised the studio for its unfair treatment of the novel's original characters.[29] A *Newsweek* review from July 21 reacted to these demonstrations as follows:

> Some descendants of the Ozarks clan are willing to admit that no Ozarker could embody half the virtues, intelligence, and energy that Wright gave them in the novel. The majority, however, have come to believe that they themselves, their neighbors, and kinfolk, are actually prototypes of the novelist's characters. So, when Hollywood has the temerity to veer from the romanticized original and present a more realistic picture, the Ozarks don't take kindly to the idea.[30]

In response to this review, local resident Townsend Godsey replied, "Few Ozarkians would be so braggy as to think their living kinfolks could embody the virtue, wisdom, and strength that Wright gave the hillfolk of the novel. But their ancestors might have been such folk. That's what makes them legendary." As this retort suggests, even if mid-twentieth-century Branson residents could partially recognize their own moral shortcomings, they were not prepared to ascribe these same vices to a previous generation already ensconced in myths of spiritual prowess and ethical aptitude. Furthermore, by perpetuating an ongoing process of making these ancestors "legendary," locals protected family heritage and preserved virtuous sentiments vital to the success of regional consumer culture.[31]

When Lizzie McDaniel died in February 1946, her property and buildings were purchased by the Civic League of Branson. Later that year, all but Inspiration Point and Old Matt's Cabin were sold to Dr. Bruce Trimble and his wife, Mary. Prior to this acquisition, Dr. Trimble received a Ph.D. from Cornell, wrote a two-volume biography of Supreme Court chief justice Morrison Waite, and was chair of the political science department at the University of Kansas City. In addition, he and Mary were the owners, editors, and publishers of the *Jackson County Times*. Like Harold Bell Wright, Trimble came to the Ozarks seeking health and solace. He was feeling well worn after twelve years of teaching and endless political feuds in Kansas City, and the peaceful Ozark countryside beckoned. Though the Civic League was unwilling to sell the cabin, it entered into an agreement whereby the Trimbles could take over its operation, conduct tours, and sell souvenirs. Besides continuing to present Old Matt's Cabin as a museum of Ozark history, the Trimbles converted a portion of Lizzie McDaniel's extravagant home into the Shepherd of the Hills Memorial Lodge. Furthering its earlier owner's decadence, this second museum housed an eclectic mix of accoutrements that included Greek sculptures, relics from the ruins of Pompeii, fifteenth-century throne chairs, and a sizable collection of curios fashioned by local artist Rose O'Neill.[32]

Best known as the creator of the Kewpie doll, O'Neill was born June 25, 1874, and demonstrated a talent for drawing from a young age; Omaha, Nebraska, newspapers commissioned works from her while she was still in her early teens. In 1893 she moved to New York to draw for *Harper's Weekly, Life, Collier's,* and *Puck*. At one time she was the highest-paid female illustrator in the country. Supplementing her career with writing and sculpture, she amassed great wealth in her early twenties, and it was with this fortune that she constructed a home in the Ozarks.[33]

In 1893, while the artist was in New York, her family homesteaded a small tract of land on Bear Creek, just a few miles north of modern-day Branson. Here family members built two log cabins and tried their hand at farming. One year later, Rose first visited the place that would become her lifelong sanctuary. Immediately loving the region, she made plans for a fourteen-room mansion later named "Bonniebrook." Afflicted by marital problems throughout her life, Rose sought solace there after divorces in 1901 and 1908. In 1909, while she was napping in a treetop studio at the homestead, her famous Kewpies—plump, puerile, angelic children—revealed themselves to her in a dream. In this vision, a Kewpie was "perched in her hand like a bird," and she recognized that the dolls were "bursting with kindness," a result of having hearts "as rounded as their tummies."

Kewpie drawings accompanied by verses that highlighted their propensity to perform good deeds first appeared in *Woman's Home Companion* and *Good Housekeeping* in late 1909, and bisque dolls were manufactured in Germany beginning in 1912. In 1925 O'Neill created a second impish character, Scootles, an infant dubbed "the Baby Tourist." Though she also owned an apartment in Greenwich Village, a castle in Connecticut, and a villa on the Isle of Capri, O'Neill branded her Ozark home, where "the brook gurgles its song of peace," as "better than any place on earth."[34]

By the time of O'Neill's death in 1944, the popularity of her Kewpies had waned, and her fortune had been exhausted. However, her creations were given a prominent place in the collection at the Shepherd of the Hills Memorial Lodge. At a site that was already subtly blending Wright's saga with more explicitly religious themes and events, the innocent and beatific Kewpies meshed nicely with other displays of "traditional" values and sanctified regional heritage. Attesting to the principled intentions of this doll collection, a visitor wrote, "On my next visit to the Museum, I intend to rob my piggy bank and enshrine one [Kewpie] in every room as a morale builder."[35]

By the late 1940s, through the efforts of Lizzie McDaniel and the Trimbles, the Shepherd of the Hills Farm had become a testament to the righteous heritage of the Ozarks and a site for the intermingling of tourism with Christian themes. To further this connection and to emphasize already implicit links between Wright's characters and biblical persons and events, in 1948 the Branson Chamber of Commerce commissioned a series of murals. These images were to accompany festivities surrounding the city's first Adoration Parade and lighting of its Nativity scene. This parade, even now held every year on the first Sunday in December, was begun in 1949 by artist Steve Miller (the creator of the Shepherd of the Hills murals) and businessman Joe Todd. Floats sponsored by churches and civic organizations still accompany high school marching bands that proceed through downtown, with the festivities culminating in the illumination of a massive crèche atop Mount Branson. Though arising from modest beginnings, the pageant currently draws approximately forty thousand people a year who come to celebrate "Keeping Christ in Christmas." By directly allying *The Shepherd of the Hills* with a Christmas festival, Branson boosters continued to blur the lines between sacred and profane and to staunchly suggest that the novel could be situated among other great narratives of Christianity.[36]

Even a decade after Paramount's rendition of Wright's novel, Branson residents were still smarting over its perceived liberties and injustices. As a partial attempt to "set the record straight," Dr. Howard Long, a former Crane, Mis-

Adoration scene atop Mt. Branson, circa 1950. Courtesy of the Lynn Morrow Postcard Collection, Jefferson City, Missouri

souri, newspaper publisher, suggested to the Southern Illinois University Players that they use Branson as the site for their summer theater and produce a version of Wright's novel. Seeking to write a script that used language drawn directly from the text, Charlotte McLeod fashioned a dramatic adaptation that first ran in Branson in 1955. Performed at the Shepherd of the Hills Theatre, a venue located near Lake Taneycomo and built through the combined efforts and funds of the Branson Chamber of Commerce and local business owners, the play was offered six times each season, with approximately two hundred people attending each show. Primarily featuring collegiate actors, the production also included locals such as Pete Herschend, who would later bring the Silver Dollar City theme park to prominence in the region. To supplement McCloud's quest for greater authenticity, "Walkin' Preacher" Guy Howard and folklorist Vance Randolph served as coaches to teach actors "genuine" regional dialect.[37]

In 1957, Central Missouri State College (now Central Missouri State University) assumed occupancy of the theater and staged *The Shepherd of the Hills* until 1960. Scriptwriter Ruth Kline diverged somewhat from McCloud's realism to offer an interpretation that presented Wright's characters as hyperbolic emblems of virtue. In addition, the play's perceived links to Branson personages was further advanced when fourteen locals (including the grandson of "Uncle Ike," Alfred R. Morrill) were cast for the 1957 season. Nearby School of the Ozarks, located in Point Lookout, Missouri, was the next to offer performances at the theater. That institution staged its rendition of the novel until 1962 before moving to a venue adjacent to the campus. It was in 1959, however, that the most heralded and long-lived version of the book began when the Old Mill Theatre opened at the Shepherd of the Hills Farm.[38]

By the late 1940s, *The Shepherd of the Hills* had fallen out of print. Fearing that tourists would not have access to the book that justified the Farm's existence, the Trimbles persuaded Grossett and Dunlap to publish a new edition in 1951. With this publication in hand, visitors swarmed to the family's attraction in the mid-1950s. Old Matt's Cabin was still the location's primary draw. In those years, tourists purchased more than half a million souvenirs annually that bore some replica of the edifice as reminders of a uncomplicated era quickly vanishing in the face of post–World War II industrial prosperity. To augment the Farm's offerings and further memorialize Wright's characters, Roberta Stoneman Baker was commissioned to sculpt a number of their likenesses on a hill above Old Matt's Cabin. By 1955, 7-foot-tall images of the Shepherd, Pete, and Aunt Molly adorned the spot, and tourists were asked to provide tithes so that the entire cast of players could be assembled. Visitors could also ascend Dewey Bald to Sammy's Lookout and there reflect both on the heroine's goodness and the majesty of the hill country that lay below. According to Bruce Trimble, vacationers now were privy to "the gentle spirit of the good Shepherd of the Hills," a benign specter that seemed "to hover like the morning mists over the silent crags, bringing a wonderful sense of peace and contentment to all."[39]

Trimble died in March 1957 and left the operation of Shepherd of the Hills Farm to his wife. Aided by her son, Mark, she continued to add structures and attractions. Meanwhile, Mark decided that a more true-to-life version of *The Shepherd of the Hills* could be fashioned by using adult actors rather than college students. He cleared the north side of the property and remodeled it so that theater patrons could sit on the hillside and look out on a newly constructed version of a village street, the Ross family's old mill, and the Shepherd's cabin. Local entrepreneur and craftsman Shad Heller and Coffeyville, Kansas, play director Jim Collie were hired to cast the production and write its script. Though the pair derived approximately 85 percent of the dialogue from the novel, they (like their predecessors) opted to condense the storyline for dramatic effect. On August 6, 1959, the Old Mill Theatre debuted with 385 folding lawn chairs as well as bales of hay for seating. During its first full season in 1960 the performance drew more than three thousand guests from Memorial Day to Labor Day.[40]

At the production's onset, Mark Trimble played the role of "The Stranger," a character who introduces the story. Recounting this experience and encapsulating the primary intent of the Farm's theatrical rendition, he stated, "I was the link between the present and the past." Feeling that he was reenacting "the most significant historical event" in the community, Trimble facilitated his performance's quest for authenticity by situating it amid rolling hills and shaded arbors, leading audience members in a square dance at intermission, setting a cabin afire during the play's climax, and trotting out an array of livestock throughout the drama. By doing so, he and his cohorts sought to bring heritage to life while valorizing a terrain already sanctified by thousands of tourist pilgrims. This strategy proved effective, as the theater attracted thirty-six thousand patrons in 1963.[41]

In a 1964 publication entitled *A Day at the Shepherd of the Hills Farm*, tourist Alma Jones Laugeson described her visit to Trimble's attraction as "like being suspended between heaven and earth." Emphasizing that the site lacked "garish signposts or color," she said that the buildings seemed "conjured out of the hills." In her mind, she was allowed to "revert to childhood," "return to an age when people lived graciously," and partake of a place where "past and present knew no boundaries." She concluded her stay by attending the nightly drama, with "God's great out-of-doors" as the stage. Reflecting on the encounter as a whole, she sought adjectives to describe her experience but surmised that its ineffable quality rendered all words "too trite" for this "near-to-heaven spot." Thus, in a brief, twenty-one-page booklet Laugeson invoked the gamut of spiritual themes promoted by Branson boosters and incorporated to this day within the offerings at the Shepherd of the Hills site. Using pious language devoid of reference to institutionalized religious practices or dogmas, she nevertheless consecrated Ozark topography, history, and populace. By intoning such themes, she offered the faithful a site where they could seek spiritual experiences vested with popular, albeit nontraditional, religious accoutrements of pilgrimage-oriented devotion, liturgical drama, and everlasting scripture.[42]

Laugeson concluded her book with the "The Legend of the Dogwood." Familiar to Ozark visitors throughout the past century, the dogwood tree's springtime blossoms continue to draw scores of tourists. Laugeson's poem, however, goes further than just extolling the plant's beauty by making explicit connections between this emblem of the Ozark hills and Christ's Passion:

The Dogwood once grew tall and strong
So the legend goes;
Until it formed the Cross on which
The savior died, and rose.

As Jesus hung there on the tree,
He sensed its great distress,
At having had its branches used,
For such cruel purposes.
In gentle pity Jesus vowed
Henceforth the dogwood tree,
Should grow too small to make a cross
And bend and twisted be.
And now the blossoms form a cross,
A nail print in each petal;
Each flower depicts a crown of thorns
Which on His brow did settle.
Thus, the Dogwood stands today
Protected in its loss;
A symbol of His agony,
And death upon the Cross.[43]

Somewhat ambivalent in tone, the poem offers a lucid example of the way that vacationers might fuse religion and leisure in this region. Each year the dogwood puts on its flowers during the Lenten season, a period marked by both repentance and anticipation. Though recreation has never been fully prohibited within Christian theology, such opportunities have frequently been accompanied by a caveat that mandates spiritual sanction for pleasure. In Laugeson's rendering, the most heralded of Ozark trees signifies this uneasy melding of ostensibly dichotomous categories. The dogwood exists for the sensory enjoyment of nature lovers, but its constitution is also wrought with symbols of Christ's suffering, death, and resurrection. Through its representational qualities, the tree thus imbues the terrain with an unequivocal reminder of divine presence and reminds people inspired by Ozark topography of the doctrinal foundations of this oft consecrated land.

Beginning in 1963, tourists visiting the Shepherd of the Hills Farm in search of Christian premises found them far more overt than the dogwood. In January of that year, the Lake Area Parish of the Presbyterian Church was created to "discover new ways to minister to the many guests and tourists" coming to the Branson region. Though under the auspices of a specific denomination, the parish displayed an interdenominational intent by hosting Methodists, Assemblies of God adherents, and other Christians. By conducting summer worship services aboard the *Branson Belle* (an excursion boat that cruised on a local lake), sponsoring Saturday campfire meetings at nearby state parks, offering boat-in veneration at a waterside chapel, and sponsoring a summer a cappella choir for students working in the resort area, the organization brought religion in multifarious forms to vacationers. At the Shepherd of the Hills Farm, the faithful were invited to "Worship in the Outdoors" by attending Sunday services held at the site's amphitheater. Through choosing this locale and stressing that church would be held at the "principal setting of Harold Bell Wright's famous novel," the Lake Area Parish thus obscured lines between the deliverance offered at morning worship and that to be found through attendance of the nightly drama. This association's integration of unambiguous Christian devotion into extant regional attractions has become a hallmark of the contemporary Branson tourism industry. As will be seen, modern-day visitors find theaters used as churches, churches used as theaters, houses of worship given prominence within local theme parks, and a number of other unique syntheses of piety and amusement.[44]

The outdoor drama and other attractions at the Shepherd of the Hills Farm grew and prospered throughout the 1960s and 1970s by continuing, in the words of a press release from that period, to "spread the gospel of the Ozark Mountains in enviable proportions." Attendance at the production during the 1966 season was double that of the previous year, the theater employed seventy actors, and the Farm at large attracted more than 500,000 visitors. In an article about the site written during the social and cultural tumult of the late 1960s, Gene Gideon still put forth time-tested promises of nostalgia when he noted: "The only modern aspect is the Jeep-drawn conveyance used to haul visitors on tours each day." In 1971 the seating area was expanded to accommodate 1,500 guests, and the cast grew to almost a hundred. The viewing section was again enlarged in 1971, and that year's turnout numbered 162,000. In 1978, the Old Mill Theatre increased its seating capacity to 2,800 and counted 249,000 attendees. At that juncture the production was well known nationally and ranked as the most popular outdoor drama in the country. However, with the onset of the energy crisis and a recession in 1979, attendance dropped by 40,000. Mary Trimble died in 1982, and amid declining interest in the Farm and its play, the attraction was purchased by Gary Snadon in 1985.[45]

Although Mark Trimble received numerous offers from investors, many of those people wanted to install children's rides and other nonthemed amusements at the Farm. Trimble preferred to sell to Gary Snadon because the latter man did not intend to add elements that "conflicted with the philosophy of the Shepherd of the Hills." Snadon, a real estate developer and entrepreneur, came to Branson in the 1960s and familiarized himself with the Farm by portraying

Wash Gibbs during the 1966–1968 theater seasons. Soon after taking over the property, he renamed it "The Shepherd of the Hills Homestead and Outdoor Theatre" and expressed interest in keeping the play and its surroundings faithful to Wright's novel. When the state's lease on Inspiration Point expired, he began developing that site and adding other attractions—a number of which furthered the location's ties to Christianity.[46]

In 1989, Snadon opened Inspiration Tower—a 230-foot-tall, 3-million-pound observation platform built on Inspiration Point. Since it offered a 360-degree panorama from its summit, visitors now could embrace even better the scenery so beloved and glorified by Harold Bell Wright. That same year the Homestead purchased a trim Lutheran church building in Morgan, Missouri, that had fallen on hard times. Featuring a boxed-entry bell tower, the structure dated from 1901, but its congregation had waned. Snadon saw similarities between this house of worship and ones pastored by Harold Bell Wright during his ministry in the Ozarks. He therefore purchased the building, moved it intact to Taney County, and restored failing walls, floor, and roof with new materials. These changes prompted writer Kathleen Van Buskirk to label it a "born-again church." Currently it rests at the base of Inspiration Tower and is open to visitors, many of whom use it as a site for relaxation and mediation. A gospel group frequently performs in the sanctuary, and the church has also become a popular wedding venue.[47]

Beginning in the late 1980s, the Branson tourism industry sought to extend its season by implementing "Ozark Mountain Christmas." Many of the city's major attractions, restaurants, and motels collectively decided to stay open beyond a traditional early fall closing date in the hope of attracting winter vacationers. The Shepherd of the Hills Homestead contributed to the inaugural effort by merging its celebrated narrative with gospel accounts. Braving November-December weather, eight thousand people attended eleven performances of *The Newborn King*—a sixty-five-minute play in which Wright's Shepherd conveys the story of the birth of Christ to his grandson. The outdoor theater transformed its sets into scenes from the Holy Land and incorporated donkeys, sheep, and camels into the production, thereby accentuating the quest for genuineness and furthering its ties to other Christian pilgrimage sites. And by employing the advertising slogan "From the folks who brought you the first story of the Ozarks . . . we proudly present the first story of Christmas," the site solidified its standing as the historical and ideological antecedent of all Branson tourism. Although production of the play ceased in the late 1990s, the Homestead is still visited at Christmastime. Tourists can partake of a drive-through Trail of Lights, marvel at Inspiration Tower adorned with nearly twenty thousand colored bulbs and Santa

Morgan Community Church, Shepherd of the Hills Homestead, 2002. Photo by the author

on a sleigh, display reverence at various Nativity scenes throughout the attraction, and hear hymns and carols at its church—a conglomeration of sacred and secular reminders of the season which epitomizes the site's nearly century-long approach to holy leisure.[48]

Despite this ongoing process of remaking the Homestead, its outdoor drama is still the primary draw. To cater to changing audience composition, the script is continuously revised. Keith Thurman, who recently asserted, "Harold Bell Wright made Branson what it is today," first acted in the play in 1967 and has directed the production since 1982. Responsible for many contemporary modifications, he supplied more mystical overtones to the ending in 1986. Instead of the primary characters exiting the stage in tears after the death of Little Pete, the new conclusion depicted the ghosts of Maggie (the Matthews' deceased daughter) and Howard (Maggie's lost lover) emerging from nowhere with the aid of black lights and fog machines and then disappearing into darkness. Additionally, Thurman struck the occasional "hell" or "damn" uttered by Wash Gibbs from the script, opting for a profanity-free presentation to satisfy conservative church groups who had written letters of disapproval and felt that even seemingly benign expletives conflicted with the production's pious intent.[49]

A promotion of explicitly Christian themes was evident during my September 2002 visit to the production. Throughout the play, actors engaged in a much more forthright discussion of divine providence than what was even put forth in the original book. Wright's story is undeniably wrought with spiritual tones, but in this contemporary production, Howard (the son of the Shepherd) is painted as an Ozark Christ figure. He, not Young Matt (as in the text), saves Ollie Stewart from a threatening cougar and fires some shots that scare off the Bald Knobbers as they prepare to hang the Matthews' son (an episode of deliverance not found in Wright's original). Howard also is described by Little Pete as being a spirit that looks over everyone as "God is looking over us." He offers gold (to supplement immaterial manna) to villagers which allows them to subsist through a drought. And he is the centerpiece of a Pietà-like scene that concludes the performance, in which all cast members gather to mourn his dying body. The play's final lines were spoken by an unseen narrator who eulogized Howard and his long-deceased lover as follows: "Is the end of life really the end or is it just the beginning?" Accentuating the Christological themes written into this character and the ways that this modern-day rendition partially displaces messianic hopes vested by Wright on the fathering Shepherd by granting them to his misunderstood, persecuted, yet numinous son, a number of people in the crowd responded to the narrator's existential query with "Amen."

Amid the boom of musical theaters in Branson during the 1990s, the Homestead's production suffered declining attendance. Often its 2,000-seat auditorium drew only between 700 and 800 patrons per night, with some weekday shows attracting only 100. To try to overcome these losses, the play's logo (a portrait of the Shepherd in an oval) was altered in 1991. As Doug Sullivan, operations manager at the Homestead, recounted, "The Shepherd's [original] face, bearded, smiling, resembles Jesus. People who have no preconceived notion as to what *The Shepherd of the Hills* is about think it is some kind of hillbilly passion play." This conflation of Wright's narrative with that of Christ is not limited to individuals unfamiliar with the production's content. A tourist from suburban St. Louis, recalling a recent visit to the site, stated, "I'm not particularly religious (and usually turned off by such things) but the outdoor Passion Play at the Shepherd of the Ozarks [*sic*] still lives in my memory as quite a spectacle." Because of this confusion, proprietors removed the Shepherd's visage from the emblem. But in the face of resistance from tour group operators, local ticket-booking agents, and fans who received the new brochures and thought the production was changing (i.e., becoming more secular), the original logo was restored in 1996.[50]

It is apparent that a key strategy for combating increased tourism competition is to emphasize Christian tones more blatantly while extrapolating themes and theologies not present in the original text. Storylines have been remade to better accommodate socially and culturally conservative Christians. Altered characterizations consciously or unconsciously intertwine the performance with events and beliefs from the Passion narrative. The production's logo is complicit in the merging of the Shepherd and the divine. To solidify this intent, in the late 1990s the Homestead added "Christian Family Weekend" to its special events calendar. Promotional materials publicize this happening as a "perfect setting for Christian communities to learn and share their faith" by experiencing an attraction and a message that can be "taken home to share at Sunday school, VBS [Vacation Bible School], and church activities." The weekend blends performances by Christian music groups and hymn singing at the on-site church with backstage tours and VIP status at nightly performances, and marketers promise all participants "fellowship, fun, and inspiration."[51]

Yet despite these deliberate presentations of Christianity, a more indefinite brand of religious experience continues to be described by patrons of the Shepherd of the Hills Homestead and Theatre. For instance, in June 2006 the popular vacation review Web site Tripadvisor.com contained eleven appraisals of the site. Included in this lot were now familiar, partially accurate testimonies concerning the authenticity of the place ("'The Shepherd of the Hills' is performed on the very site of the author's home"); praise for an attraction that makes travelers feel as if they are experiencing archetypal small-town America ("It has a way of making you feel like you're not even a visitor. Everyone is helpful, courteous, and friendly"); and admiration of semicontrived regional history ever resistant to deleterious progress ("This place gives you a view into the past and shows what life should really be about, even in today's modern age"). Although many of the appraisals pointed to the production's romance or action as highlights, most also made mention of the play's message, which a visitor from Dallas asserted "is one that we all need to be reminded of." Providing specificity and contour to the vaunted meaning of the production, an Asheville, North Carolina, guest wrote:

Prior to our trip to Branson, we read the book, "Shepherd of the Hills." While the outdoor drama highlighted the essence of the story, the emotionally packed drama had us attentive to the threads of love and honesty flowing through the entire program. The story helped us to reminisce our historical past, giving credibility to the valor and social stability of our family ancestral designs for a nation under God. Thanks for the superb entertainment and the sense of togetherness that was represented at the theater. There was a real sense of cohesiveness demonstrated by the entire cast even though Mr. Gibbs tried his best to corrupt his neighbors. But Mr. Lane was a good example of overcoming the complexities that divide our world into schisms of disbeliefs and fractured wounds—thanks to the sincerity and trustworthiness of his daughter, Sammy. May the Lord bless you—as "dad" would say!

In this brief assessment, the tourist draws attention to many aspects of the show that have inspired visitation over the past fifty years. Witnessing a story panned by critics as simplistic and mawkish, she instead was reminded of the loss of community in America and offered a momentary salve for the ills of splintered society. While the play prompted her to consider the advances of secularization, it also harked back to a mythical past when all were united in Christian belief. Finally, by drawing on the words of the novel's protagonist, "Dad" Howitt, the missive linked the region's metanarrative to the divine and highlighted an age-old belief that blessings are available to people who venture into the Ozarks.[52]

Though the contemporary Homestead attraction is seemingly a far cry from Lizzie McDaniel's initial transformation of the Rosses' property, tourism at the site has demonstrated an ever mutating yet ever present relationship with Christianity. Beginning with a 1936 Easter pageant, the Shepherd of the Hills Farm/Homestead has enhanced Wright's already spiritually laden novel with a variety of pious adornments. Over the past eight decades, these devotional extras have in many ways superseded the original narrative to provide visitors with an experience of lived Christianity only tenuously underscored by a now seldom-read novel. Currently, as the Homestead competes with a set of Branson attractions that multiplies exponentially on a yearly basis, it is apparent that both subtle and evident presentations of Christian themes and values may be the only way to retain its status as an icon of Ozark tourism.

At first glance, the amusements historically offered at the Shepherd of the Hills Farm/Homestead appear merely to be part of a larger valorization of a mythical Ozark past that has underscored and continues to provide foundation for the region's tourism industry. Although this frontier legacy is undeniably a primary impetus and calling card for Branson leisure, close examination of this locale reveals that, for more than a century, Christian sentiment also has been woven into a fabric of nostalgia, premodern longing, and whitewashed rusticity. Out of this amalgamation has been crafted what cultural theorist Pierre Bourdieu labels a "habitus," or a "system of dispositions" that constitutes a symbolic universe and helps individuals cope with unforeseen and ever changing situations. Specifically, *Shepherd of the Hills*–based attractions have embraced Bourdieu's "popular ethos." This notion denies separation between art and life and presents artistic production in a manner that is emotional and pragmatically oriented (as opposed to a "pure aesthetic," which embraces art for art's sake and calls for distanced contemplation). Such an ethos is said to have appeal for middle-class audiences, Branson's primary historical cohort. As witnessed, the Shepherd of the Hills Farm/Homestead has always offered visions of rustic escape from the tribulations of urban, working-class America while at the same time dangling displays of high culture in front of individuals pining for elevated economic status. By linking a popular artistic philosophy to a popular religious style that similarly fuses applied Christian principles with poignant staging, the site has aided in the crafting of middle-class identity since the birth of that socioeconomic group in the early twentieth century.[53]

The Shepherd of the Hills instigated tourism in Branson, and the novel continues to be memorialized in a variety of ways. For instance, an expressway named after the book creates the northern border of the city. Homes can be purchased from Shepherd of the Hills Realtors. Visitors in need of a motel can overnight at Old Matt's Guest House. And the faithful can attend services at the Shepherd of the Hills Episcopal Church or the Shepherd of the Hills Lutheran Church— houses of worship that testify to the ongoing link between Wright's narrative and Branson's religiously motivated vacation industry. Few contemporary visitors read the novel, yet an exhaustive knowledge of its plot has never been a precondition for immersion in the region's mystique. Theatrical enactments do offer a vacationer direct engagement with the book. However, the true legacy of Wright's lore surpasses this semiliteral rendering. His saga may no longer be in the forefront of a vacationer's consciousness on arrival in the Ozarks, but notions of sanctified topography, virtuous local residents, and authentic experiences of social and spiritual regeneration still beckon many to Shepherd of the Hills Country.

CHAPTER THREE

"I Would Much Rather See a Sermon Than Hear One"

Faith at Silver Dollar City

Since its inception in 1960, the Silver Dollar City theme park in Branson, Missouri, has offered patrons a sometimes anachronistic fusion of the Missouri frontier, preindustrial craftsmanship, and simple faith. In a 2003 interview, Peter Herschend, co-owner and vice chairman of the Herschend Family Entertainment Corporation (Silver Dollar City's parent body), discussed the ways his attraction seeks to inculcate visitors with a sense of Christian ethics and values. Vocalizing the experiential nature of his park's piety, he declared, "I would much rather see a sermon than hear one." This statement keenly speaks to the visual and pragmatic character of a site that currently draws more than two million guests per year to its presentation of late nineteenth-century Ozark culture, purportedly timeless "family values," and unique rendering of religiosity. Silver Dollar City has continuously appended thrill rides and artisan demonstrations, but even such seemingly secular updates are designed to satisfy the values of their producers and consumers and thus subtly support more overt exhibitions of Christianity.[1]

Not all contemporary visitors to Silver Dollar City arrive expecting to be blatantly inculcated with Christian principles. In 2005, a $43.65 single-day adult admission offered access to many ostensibly worldly offerings. There were five yearly festivals ranging from World-Fest in the spring to Old Time Christmas in the winter; twenty attractions and rides, including some of the nation's best roller coasters; sixty specialty shops and hundreds of craftspeople; forty musical shows per day; and a host of dining opportunities. However, according to Peter Herschend, these attractions were built on a supernatural foundation—one that is encountered on different levels by different patrons. As he stated, "Sometimes people will never know why they feel good about this place. There are people who are Christians who spot it rather readily in the feeling of the park—you do not hear swearing, or the Lord's name taken in vain. People who are not Christian say this place has a special feeling. People often write back and say this is where they met the Lord." An investigation into the popular brand of Christianity offered at the site requires an unearthing of the various ways that this imprecise sense of faith is conveyed through the theme park medium. As tourist S. T. Lambert commented by paraphrasing an interpretation of enigmatic parables offered in Matthew 13:16 (New Revised Standard Version [NRSV]), Silver Dollar City's devotional aspects are available to all who have "eyes to see and ears to hear."[2]

Silver Dollar City was built atop Marvel Cave, a site that for nearly one hundred years welcomed visitors who regularly observed an indefinite yet palatable godly presence within a subterranean world. When the theme park was constructed above the fissure, its founders envisioned an attraction that approached guests with the Golden Rule ("In everything do to others as you would have them do to you" [Matthew 7:12, NRSV]) as a guide and honored divine creation through the stewardship of nature. Employee guidelines since the 1980s have codified these initial dictates by compelling staff members to handle their work in a fashion that is consistent with Christian values. Missionary sentiments, while present, have intentionally been merged with the site's thematic attempts to create a seamless presentation of religion and recreation. Sometimes one must even look to more explicitly sectarian organizations and initiatives associated with Silver Dollar City to realize how thoroughly it has been linked with proselytizing impulses.

Ever growing attendance and revenues indicate that this melding of faith and frivolity has been a successful strategy. The Herschend family took ownership of Marvel Cave in 1950 by investing $7,000. That summer they welcomed 8,000 guests for tours. By 1959, 65,000 vacationers visited the site, generating $200,000 in revenues. The company opened Silver Dollar City one year later and, with only a dozen employees, served 125,000 visitors. By 1966, nearly 500,000 people visited the park, and it brought in $3 million in revenues. In 1967, several episodes of *The Beverly Hillbillies* (whose characters purportedly hailed from Silver Dollar City) were filmed on site. This produced the park's greatest one-year increase in visitation and inspired a national interest. By the early 1970s, more than 1 million guests visited. By 1977, "the City" welcomed 1.5 million patrons and employed more than 1,000 individuals. In the early 1990s, revenue totals approached $40 million, and by the end of that decade attendance surpassed the 2-million tourist mark with approximately 2,500 full-time and seasonal staff working on site.[3]

Silver Dollar City's success allowed its proprietors to add additional locales to their tourism holdings. As of 2005, the Herschend Family Entertainment Corporation owned and operated Celebration City in Branson (a theme park that nostalgically remembers various "golden eras" of twentieth-century American history), Dollywood in Pigeon Forge, Tennessee, a southern-themed attraction within Stone Mountain State Park in Georgia, a showboat on Table Rock Lake, an additional Ozark cave, various water parks, and a shopping center. Although Silver Dollar City is the best illustration of the company's relationship with popular Christianity, each site has tried to integrate Christian values into leisure activities. All these attractions generated well over $100 million in revenues in the year 2005, and they collectively earned brothers Peter and Jack Herschend a spot in the Theme Park Industry Hall of Fame in 2004. Most important for this study, Silver Dollar City has been Branson's most popular tourist attraction for the past forty years. Through its leadership's focus on preserving a local religious ethos, it has impacted the social, cultural, and economic climate of the city and the region in a wide variety of ways. Finally, despite the tendency of some commentators to view religion as a sociocultural sphere mired in stoic demeanors and languid creeds, the history of Christianity in the United States demonstrates an overriding concern for lively enactments of devotion meant to inspire and entertain. In light of the various attractions, marketing approaches, and ideological vantages discussed below, Silver Dollar City has fully involved itself in this historical merger of faith and frivolity while functioning as a premier twentieth-century standard for the integration of a nebulous variant of evangelicalism into consumer culture.[4]

SUBTERRANEAN SPIRITUALITY

The foundation of Silver Dollar City arose hundreds of millions of years ago and grew out of the region's unique geology. The area surrounding Branson, Missouri, can be categorized as a karst landscape, one in which the underlying limestone has been partially dissolved by groundwater. Throughout time, rain moving in cracks and crevices has caused large amounts of rock to soften and created nearly seven thousand Ozark caverns. In *Sacred Places,* a work that explores the relationship between nineteenth-century American tourism and religious sentiment, historian John Sears described how natural attractions such as Mammoth Cave in Kentucky possessed the ability to inspire a sense of sublimity. In his assessment, vacationers considered the site to be a type of "axis mundi " (or meeting point between heaven, earth, and hell) and so bestowed on it a variety of ritualistic meanings. A 1992 promotional video for Silver Dollar City described the origins of its cave and park in a fashion that resonated with ideas of sublime transcendence: "The story begins with the Creator. It was he who fashioned a land of calm that would attract those of adventure, retain people of enterprise, and spawn fruits of vision." Though associations between Branson area caves and the divine would remain indistinct for the first half of the twentieth century, Silver Dollar City is underscored both figuratively and literally by a fissure entrenched in numinous rhetoric since its discovery.[5]

The formation now known as Marvel Cave was originally dubbed Devil's Den by Osage Indians who inhabited the Ozarks prior to the Louisiana Purchase and demarcated both the physical and mystical dangers of the site with V-shaped notches cut in nearby trees. Frequently compared to Mammoth Cave by early explorers and visitors, Marvel's Cathedral Room is the largest cave entrance in the United States, and its passages and chambers have never been challenged as the grandest of Ozark natural wonders. Still, the first arrivals to Missouri caves came in search of mineral deposits rather than spiritual insights. In 1869, a St. Louis speculator bought the property from railroad interests hoping to discover lead. Finding no minerals, Henry T. Blow did mistakenly believe that much of the cavern was lined with marble and thus retitled his property "Marble Cave." Blow's interest in the cave quickly waned, and he abandoned his undertaking within the year. Evidence suggests that the cavern then remained undisturbed for thirteen years, except for occasional visits by vigilantes who purportedly used its opening as a repository for murdered bodies. Knowing this and that the cave was populated by thousands of bats, locals avoided the grotto because, in the words of longtime guide Ronald L. Martin, they were convinced that "the Almighty had not intended man to enter."[6]

In the 1870s Marble Cave changed ownership a number of times, and in 1884 it was acquired by T. Hodge Jones of Lamar, Missouri. Jones and members of his fraternal organization, the Lamar City Guards, formed a mining company in the hope of extracting bat guano—a natural fertilizer and important ingredient in gun powder—which then sold for $700 per ton and could be found 25 feet deep in many portions of the cave. In 1884, the Marble Cave Manufacturing and Mining Company developed a small town at the mouth of its holding, and investors hoped to further their profits by capitalizing on a late nineteenth-century boom in tourist spas and health resorts through exploiting the "healing waters" available at their site.[7]

In the first published piece to detail the cave's formations, stockholder Captain J. B. Emery described its surroundings in 1885 as "a bracing, invigorating atmo-

Cathedral Room, Marvel Cave, circa 1950. Postcard from the author's collection

sphere" of "springs of pure water, and medicinal springs, chalybeate, sulphur, etc." Water cure, or hydropathy, was popular at the time, and people throughout the United States sought healing baths and springs as treatments for a wide range of ailments. Moreover, individuals such as Phineas P. Quimby, a celebrated mid-nineteenth-century mental healer, promoted the eradication of physical ailments through the cultivation of healthy attitudes rather than topical remedies. A great influence on those who championed ideas of faith-oriented treatments such as Mary Baker Eddy (founder of Christian Science) and Julius A. Dresser (a leader in the New Thought movement), Quimby joined promoters of homeopathy in acknowledging the power of suggestion and the workings of nature as viable means for encouraging wellness.[8]

The best-known healing waters in the nineteenth-century Ozarks were at Eureka Springs, Arkansas, a town one hour south of Branson. When incorporated in 1879, Eureka Springs had a population of only four hundred clustered around more than sixty local springs. After a series of accounts claimed that consumption of the city's water could cure ailments as diverse as hay fever, insomnia, and paralysis, however, the population grew to an estimated fifteen thousand residents by April 1880. Shortly thereafter, Eureka Springs' water was bottled and shipped nationally, and investors constructed the elegant, Gothic-styled Crescent Hotel to house a massive influx of visitors. Closer to Branson, Panacea Springs in Cassville, Missouri, and Eau de Vie and Reno Springs in Christian County also flourished briefly as summer resorts in the 1880s by promising natural treatments for rheumatism, kidney disease, dyspepsia, and bowel troubles.[9]

The Marble Cave Manufacturing and Mining Company intended to draw on these regional success stories for its own resort community. Initial plans called for a housing development and a number of parks, but by the mid-1880s the only businesses were an ordinary general store, a one-room school (predominantly used to train aspiring cave guides), a blacksmith shop, and a sawmill. With its dream gone, the company dissolved itself in 1889 and sold the property to Arthur J. Lynch, a businessman from Jackson County, Missouri. A month later, Arthur sold Marble Cave to his brother, William Henry Lynch. Lynch, a Canadian miner, dairyman, and amateur archaeologist, bought the property primarily as a place to hunt for prehistoric animal bones. After five years of futile searching, he, along with daughters Miriam (an opera singer) and Genevieve (a nurse and poet), decided to develop the site as an Ozark attraction.[10]

The Lynch family allowed tourist access to the cave via wooden ladders that descended 200 feet into the Cathedral Room (a huge chamber 200 feet high, 400 feet long, and 225 feet wide). Though the attraction possessed many breathtaking qualities, transportation was problematic at the turn of the century. For instance, in a recollection by Miles H. Scott, the author described a harrowing 50-mile journey from Marrionville, Missouri, to the cave which took his party over some of the "roughest hilly roads" in the state. His 1922 visit was undertaken with twenty others who traveled to the Branson area in the flat bed of a Model T truck. Along the way, multiple stops were made to refill the radiator, patch tires, and push the vehicle up steep hills. On arrival, the group was outfitted with coveralls, equipped with candles, and led down a steep slope on "rickety ladders and wooden steps." Despite the dampness, mud, narrow passages, and "long strenuous climb" to the surface, Scott concluded his narrative by invoking the "awe and admiration" felt by the tourists amid "the beauties of the magnificent works of nature beheld." Considering the travails necessary to both arrive at and tour the cave, it is not surprising that the Lynches were lucky to welcome ten or twenty visitors a day during the summer months.[11]

Over time, Henry Lynch took steps to make the cave more accessible and urbane. In the 1920s, he and nine-year-old Lester Vining blazed a winding trail with a gas-powered saw which would eventually become the Branson Strip. Lynch was also a primary lobbyist for the rail line that reached Branson in 1906. At the cave itself, he replaced wooden ladders with scaffolding, constructed gracious cabins, built an auditorium inside the Cathedral Room (said to be able to seat ten thousand spectators), and equipped this subterranean theater with a grand piano so Miriam could showcase her operatic talents for guests. Through such an incongruous merger of leisure opportunities, boosters drew on a time-tested regional tactic by attempting to imbue a vacation in the wilderness with the sophistication of Victorian culture, thereby offering an image of a rustic past nevertheless replete with modern comforts. After traversing rocky hills, dressing in coveralls, and plunging 200 feet on treacherous steps, guests could then relax in temperature-controlled surroundings and partake of arias from a classically trained singer.[12]

By the 1920s, the Lynches' cave had become a heralded Branson-area tourist draw. Visitors increasingly proclaimed the other-worldly qualities (both terrifying and astonishing) of the site, which had aptly changed its name to "Marvel Cave" in 1913. An account from that period detailed vacationers' concerns over "hobgoblin perils" that gripped "the soul with a dread that precludes passage into the unventured beyond." Another guest recalled that her tour in 1920 produced "the kind of feeling that one might experience upon a visit to another planet." Scientists joined tourists in extolling the cave's ability to produce a sense of "mysterium tremendum." In 1893, representatives from Missouri's World's Fair Commission and researchers from the state geological survey declared the cave a "new wonder of the world." G. Kingsley Noble, a curator at the American Museum of Natural History, recorded his experiences in an article for *Scientific American* magazine. Though primarily interested in the cavern's blind salamander, Noble was "spellbound" by the "inky blackness and perpetual coldness" he found. Visitors thus departed with emotional imprints, not at all dissimilar from those available at more traditional grottoes, cathedrals, and sacred spaces.[13]

Little evidence suggests that the scholastic and scientifically minded Lynch ever envisioned his holding as a location where tourists could encounter the divine or the sublime. When he died in 1927, however, the property came under the ownership of his daughters, and the mood changed. These women began to employ their training in the arts and humanities to vest the cavern with spirituality and sentiment. For the next twenty-two years, the "Misses Lynch" worked to cloak their attraction in transcendent language that allied the cave with other piously grounded Ozark destinations.[14]

Miriam and Genevieve Lynch were good friends with both Lizzie McDaniel and Rose O'Neill and shared those women's desire to merge the refined and luxurious elements of early twentieth-century America with the pastoral quaintness of the "frozen-in-time" Ozark hills. In an account offered by visitors from Chicago, Genevieve is described as a stylish proprietor clad in "tight fitting jodhpurs, a tight little woolen bodice, and a colorful scarf bound round her head." Miriam, in contrast, is deemed "as picturesque as a character doll." During this visit, the guest was not only awed by the cave but also amazed by the property's hundreds of flowers and the Lynch sisters' knowledge of botany. After only a few short paragraphs devoted to cavern exploration, this missive instead focuses on the owners' impeccable decorum, a meal of chicken and asparagus served on rare English china after the exploration of the cave, and a cache of items from Rose O'Neill displayed with reverence and "devotion" in a large glass case. This report suggests that Miriam and Genevieve sought not only to valorize Marvel Cave's attributes but to also showcase a variant of progressive culture for people aspiring toward middle-class status. By augmenting their attraction with a tea room, an antique shop, and a spacious lodge, the sisters celebrated and sanctified a vision of overly sentimental modernity within a locale supposedly immune to modern change.[15]

Harold Bell Wright also often toured Marble Cave while sojourning at the Rosses' homestead. By 1904, the proprietors had even named his favorite grotto the "Harold Bell Wright Passage." Because of his frequent visits, local lore began to hold that the cave was the model for the one mentioned in *The Shepherd of the Hills*—a hideaway for Maggie's illegitimate son (Little Pete) and the refuge of the Shepherd's outcast son (Howard). In fact, early twentieth-century tourists stopped at a chamber known as "Mad Howard's Room" and were told that a small cabin built into the side of the cavern (actually meant as a retreat for the Lynch sisters to escape the public) was the character's Ozark home. By the 1930s, the cave's ties to the book had been cemented as promotional brochures subcaptioned it "The Famous Shepherd of the Hills Cave" and advertised cabins at the Marvel Cave Lodge named after Wright's characters. The site's operators thus joined all attractions and personages of early Branson tourism history in implicating themselves in the production of regional folklore (or "fakelore") to entrench their cavern within a master narrative that sanctified Ozark people and places.[16]

In a tourist pamphlet from the 1930s, Miriam and Genevieve Lynch wrote that visitors to their cave would encounter a "veritable doorway to adventure, recapture youth, and in the almost endless welter of common things behold a star-like vision of sublimity." Here, familiar Branson area promises of untamed nature, recaptured virility, escape from urban drudgery, and encounter with spiritual forces all merged around this subterranean attraction. When tourists guided by the sisters dipped tin cups into a natural spring christened the "Fountain of Youth," they may have reckoned the experience as merely fanciful participation in a time-tested legend of American exploration. However, Marvel Cave's advertising and reminiscences by visitors suggest that interpreting the cave through a religiously based lens was possible and often probable for guests. Though no explicitly Christian themes found their way into early promotional materials, the Misses Lynch certainly couched their attraction in general pious language and symbolism that pointed to a godly presence. For example, in a poem that memorialized the cave's Cathedral Room, Genevieve wrote: "Here, something lingers, subtle, fine, / Irradiations, veiled, devine [sic]; / God's temple and the age's tomb." Such poetics thus seem to promise psychical and spiritual wellness to those with "eyes to see and ears to hear."[17]

When Chicago-area residents Hugo and Mary Herschend first visited Marvel Cave in 1946, it was drawing roughly four thousand visitors a year. They, like many urbanites, had come to the Ozarks to fish, hunt for wildflowers, and vacation at Mac and Annabelle McMaster's Rockaway Resort. The Herschends returned to Branson for four consecutive springs and were introduced to a wide variety of local attractions by their hosts. During one trip, they met Miriam and Genevieve Lynch and toured Marvel Cave. Now both in their seventies, the sisters were looking to sell the property. The Herschends and McMasters entered into a partnership, brokered a ninety-nine-year lease for the cavern, and became its proprietors in April 1950. Because tour revenues were initially unable to support the Herschends and their two sons (Peter and Jack), Hugo kept his job with the Evanston, Illinois, vacuum manufacturer Electrolux and left operation of the property to Mary and the boys. Although they doubled previous totals by hosting eight thousand visitors during their first summer, no one could have predicted the amazing future of the enterprise.[18]

The McMaster-Herschend partnership lasted only two years before the latter family assumed sole management. During the winter of 1950–1951, the Herschends replaced wooden stairs and walkways with concrete and installed electric lights. However, they were not content with a solely underground focus. Tourists often asked for something to do while waiting to visit the cave, and so

Hugo negotiated with Marlin Perkins, a Carthage, Missouri, native, to install a small zoo in the early 1950s. When this proved successful, Hugo dreamed further. According to Peter Herschend, his father believed that "visitors coming to the cave would like to see men and women of the hills . . . doing their own thing." Not content merely with gimmicks such as underground square dances and séances, the family decided to purchase 640 acres around the site to showcase local culture. Silver Dollar City developed on this land (originally named "Marvel Cave Park") and an additional 1,600 acres.[19]

Hugo Herschend died of a heart attack on November 14, 1955. But prior to his death, he laid the groundwork for an attraction that would come to define regional mythmaking and heritage marketing. Under his management, cave guides developed tall tales about the cavern and the surrounding country's local history. Devoted not only to the manufacture of legend, Hugo also envisioned an area-wide valorization of Ozark craftsmanship through cottage industries that showcased the arts of the blacksmith, basket weaver, or potter. While researching his plot of land, he encountered the short-lived history of the guano company's Marble City (or as he preferred to call it, "Marmaros," Greek for "marble"). The former existence of this actual nineteenth-century village on the grounds inspired him further. Though Hugo failed to see his plans realized, Silver Dollar City—described by one St. Louis Post-Dispatch writer as "a mixture of fantasy, history, and just plain 'hillbilly fun'"—would be the fruition of his aspirations.[20]

THEME PARK THEOLOGY

Silver Dollar City opened on May 1, 1960. A frontier-style blacksmith shop, general store, ice cream parlor, doll shop, inn, and two reconstructed, late nineteenth-century log buildings made up the village. One of these last structures was the Wilderness Church, a house of worship that continues to serve as an emblem of spirituality within the park. Guests were treated to local music performed by the Mabe brothers (who would later open Branson's first music show) and entertained by staged "feuds" between the stereotypical Hatfields and Mc-Coys. Later that year the park would append its first rides—a tilt house called Slantin' Sam's Old Miner's Shack and a stagecoach-mule ride. The overall aim of the park was declared in a press release: "The Ozark Village is not a museum or a ghost town, but a living, working village."[21]

Though early promotional materials adamantly proclaimed the park's authenticity and boasted that "everything about the City remains just as it was nearly a century ago in the Ozarks," promoters consciously elided problematic histori-

Silver Dollar City, circa 1960. Postcard from the author's collection

cal happenings. For instance, although the site did recognize and portray the existence of Alf Bolin, the region's most notorious post–Civil War bushwacker, it benignly restricted (and continues to restrict) his murderous ways to a jovial attempted train robbery as patrons circumambulate the grounds. Reflecting on this reworking of the past, park historian Crystal Payton wrote, "Frontier bad behavior was recycled into good entertainment. History, bloody and painful the first time around, is enacted as playful amusement." Thus, although Silver Dollar City owners, directors, and administrators have, since the attraction's inception, stressed its accurate portrayal of history and its ability to educate patrons about the Ozarks' past, the locale has continually offered only a sanitized and refined variant of earlier days which coincides with its equally genteel vision of proper ethics.[22]

Throughout its history, everyone involved with Silver Dollar City's management has resolutely stated that the site is a theme park, not an amusement park. Though the difference is seemingly small, this distinction is important for understanding the ways that the locale integrates promotion of Christian ethics and values with craft presentations, variety acts, and thrill rides. The creator of the theme park genre, Walt Disney, spent his boyhood in the northwestern Missouri town of Marceline, which subsequently served as a model for his quaint enactments of heartland America. Like Branson boosters who have followed his lead, Disney hoped to offer a leisure space quite unlike the existing models of Coney Island or Riverside in Chicago—attractions he characterized as "dirty, phony places, run by tough-looking people." When Disneyland opened in 1955, its proprietor perceived American society as troubled by failing families, a lost sense of community, and a mounting disregard for moral principles, courtesy, and decorum. Thus, at Disneyland (and later Disney World), guests were offered a nostalgic portrait of what once was (or, to be more accurate, an imagined past grounded in the staging of sociocultural cohesion which lacked the messy elements of postindustrial America). A stroll down each park's Main Street USA was to be a reembrace of a fabled public square prior to civil rights battles, ethnic divisiveness, or the muddling of conventional gender roles. For a hefty fee, patrons are still offered psychical reassurance that there is one spot where things are uncomplicated and "traditional"—a strategy described by E. L. Doctorow as the production of "abbreviated shorthand culture."[23]

Commentators on the Disney experience have continuously described the parks' presentations of stereotypes, archetypes, and historical pastiche in religious language, thereby more firmly indicating the sites' desired ideological functions. Terms such as "pilgrimage," "national shrine," "Disney rites," "New Eden," and "secular mecca" find their way into descriptions and critiques. Though elements of sacred space, ritual, and clergy can be teased out of an analysis of Disney's properties, his "imagineers" have chosen to interpret their version of core values as shaped, sanitized, and sanctified recollections of the past rather than using any overt reference to divinity. Silver Dollar City undoubtedly drew inspiration from this model on its opening in 1960, but it went beyond Disney by augmenting its brand of utopia with the workings of popular Christianity.[24]

No accounts of Silver Dollar City's development indicate that Hugo and Mary Herschend were strong advocates of institutional religion, but Peter Herschend remembers his stepfather's business practices as "an embodiment of the Golden Rule." Additionally, Mary had an abiding concern for conservation motivated by a belief that she was protecting divine design. The park's official history claims that this "almost obsessive reverence for the things of God's creation" manifested itself sometimes antagonistically through the firing of people who harmed trees, but it was more often gently evidenced by her protection of the locale's abundance of wildlife and natural features.[25]

When Silver Dollar City opened, the Wilderness Church was its one unambiguous religious space. The church was an abandoned log sanctuary designed to seat approximately eighty. It was found by Mary Herschend near a local creek in 1959, dismantled, and brought piece by piece to the park. The site chosen for

reassembly was occupied by a massive sycamore. Ever reluctant to fell such speci-
mens, Mary acquiesced when the tree's trunk was hewn into a pulpit. Shortly
thereafter, she insisted that a huge picture window be installed so that worshipers
could draw inspiration from the site's scenic vista. To reinforce this relationship
between geographic place and transcendence, a placard quoting the King James
Version of Psalm 121:1 ("I will lift up mine eyes unto the hills from whence cometh my help") was stationed prominently above the outlook.[26]

Touted as a site for spiritual refreshment amid the frequent disarray of the
vacation experience, the Wilderness Church has, since the early 1980s, been conducting services for employees and guests with the aid of an on-staff parson.
Sunday ceremonies are offered to staff prior to the park's opening, and visitors
are invited to the church for both formal worship and hymn singing. In keeping
with the interdenominational thread that courses its way through the park's presentation of Christianity, these events are billed as free of creed. Nevertheless, despite such nonsectarian attempts, it is easy to characterize the brand of religiosity
offered at the site as Reformation-derived and often Manichaean. Referencing a
classic Protestant contempt for the prioritizing of church tradition over the injunctions of scripture, former Wilderness Church pastor Bob Burton stated, "If I
have a theme, it is that the message has to get out to Christians that we have tended
to put religion over relationship with Christ. . . . We're all ministers of the Word."
As a former Catholic priest turned member of a nondenominational fellowship,
Burton was a good fit for Silver Dollar City's brand of evangelicalism.[27]

Currently, the Wilderness Church offers three Sunday morning services, including an 8:30 a.m. event for staff. When this practice began, administrator Don
Richardson claimed that the theme park was the only one in the nation that
provides worship services, weekly Bible study, and an on-staff minister for its
employees. Research indicates that this is still the case and thus demonstrates
Silver Dollar City's distinctive focus and unique place within the wider industry.
Once the park opens, it offers two other morning rites for visitors. Both services
are usually full. Additionally, hymn singing occurs five times daily. The singing
is often led by employees who have left the ranks of institutional evangelism for
the more popular variant offered at the park. For instance, Linda and Bob Frie-
del are retired missionaries who work on the grounds and frequently spearhead
the hymns. Their efforts regularly inspire sizable crowds who had not ostensibly
come to the site for devotion, with upwards of one hundred people gathering at
the church for song. Wedding vow renewals are also available in the afternoons,
and more than two hundred couples annually have their nuptials performed in
the sanctuary.[28]

I will lift up mine eyes unto the hills from whence cometh my help

Picture window, Wilderness Church, circa 1970. Postcard from the author's collection

As the site is within the confines of a theme park, it must tailor its religion to conform to tourist expectations of the frontier past. According to Bob Deeds, who had a thirty-four-year career as a Methodist minister before becoming pastor of the Wilderness Church in 1986, this message is extraordinarily straightforward: "We just preach Jesus Christ and the love of God. And once in a while we tell them there's a Hell." Fielding vacationers from across the Christian spectrum, the locale must serve a double function by putting forth a brand of spiritual succor that has appeal to millions of vacationing devotees and showcasing the religious intentions of the park at large. Such authenticity is evidenced by the lack of bulletins distributed to congregants, a simple presentation of both theology and liturgy, and a populist ceding of song choice to attendees. Though not presenting the attraction as one with an explicitly religious theme, Silver Dollar City's proprietors still feel that their holding must demonstrate Christian epistemology. As Pastor Deeds asserted in a 2003 interview, "If you really want to know the truth, this church is the basis for this park."[29]

Mary Herschend underwent surgery for cancer in 1963. Though she continued to be active in the park's management until her death in 1983, administrative decisions gradually were ceded to her sons, with Peter fronting public relations and Jack overseeing day-to-day operations. Throughout these early years, the

Exterior, Wilderness Church, circa 1970. Courtesy of the Lynn Morrow Postcard Collection, Jefferson City, Missouri

attraction continued to grow. In 1963 it became Missouri's foremost tourist destination. In the late 1960s and early 1970s it added other craft displays such as glassblowing, metalsmithing, candle making, and a print shop. Regionally themed rides like Jim Owens Float Trip (named in honor of a longtime promoter of Ozark rivers and multiterm mayor of Branson) and Fire in the Hole (a ride that invokes the tumultuous post–Civil War period in the region) were also added to the site. By the mid-1970s the park was one of the nation's most popular tourist attractions and garnered more repeat business than any other similar locale. Throughout the 1980s and 1990s, Silver Dollar City became more hi-tech: state-of-the-art roller coasters joined its offerings alongside craft displays and musical acts.[30]

This period also saw the birth of many yearly festivals on site, such as a summer event for children, a Christmas celebration, and a global folk culture fair. Yet despite this growth and embrace of contemporary technologies, Mary Herschend was ever cognizant of offering predominantly urban midwesterners a glimpse of fabled premodernity. As she told a reporter during the park's expansion, "My job is to keep the modern from creeping in." Peter and Jack Herschend followed their mother's lead. For them, avoiding the modern meant not only a supposed allegiance to late nineteenth-century artisanship and material culture but also a thorough yet muted integration of Christian morality into the park's attractions and tone. Although raised by parents who looked to religious precepts for business guidance, the sons were not exposed to institutional faith in their youth. As self-described "baby Christians" in 1960, they sat down on a log bench behind the Wilderness Church for a "board meeting" that solidified Silver Dollar City's future direction. Peter recalled that during that session they decided "to look [the] Lord in the eye" in terms of their business and subsequently coined the phrase "Making decisions with Christ in the room." Peter Herschend married in 1966. In 1969 he and wife, Jo Dee, were "baptized in the Holy Spirit" while at a meeting in Springfield held by renowned Episcopal renewal leader Dennis Bennett; began to attend Shepherd of the Hills Episcopal Church in Branson; and, in Herschend's words, "went from 'sorta' to 'saved.'"[31]

Peter Herschend's religious journey reflects a critique of theological liberalism within mainline American Protestantism which has been under way since the early twentieth century. This opposition was inaugurated by seminarians engaged in an ongoing fundamentalist-versus-modernist battle over issues such as evolution and biblical higher criticism, and it continues to simmer by way of a contentious "culture war." American Protestant "renewal movements" began in the early 1960s as efforts within individual denominations to combat perceived threats of women's leadership, homosexuality, ecumenism, and theological diversity. The Episcopal renewal movement has roots in John Stott's Evangelical Fellowship in the Anglican Communion, which established an American branch in 1961. Since that time, liberal congregants and clergy within the Episcopal Church have faced opposition from a wide variety of right-leaning organizations, including Charles Fulton's Episcopal Renewal Ministries (an association that formerly had Peter Herschend as its vice president) and Pat Robertson's Regent University (with Peter Herschend serving on its board in the early 1990s). Ultimately, renewal movements have prospered because of their ability to integrate conservative religious stances into other sociocultural spheres and, by focusing on charismatic religious experience, to enliven allegedly wearisome faith practices. These tactics have certainly been utilized by Herschend when molding Silver Dollar City's "public face" and organizational directives over the past forty years.[32]

In the late 1990s Peter and JoDee Herschend abandoned spirit-filled Episcopalianism to join the Pentecostal group the Assemblies of God, whose world headquarters is only 40 miles from Branson in Springfield, Missouri. This change reveals an ambivalent yet palatable interplay between institutional and popular religiosity. According to Father Richard Kellogg, current rector of Branson's Shepherd of the Hills Episcopal Church:

They left here not because of any difficulties with this parish but because of the liberal attitudes of the entire Episcopal Church—the national church. But I would say they tend to be toward charismatic and probably a very conservative attitude. Part of what went on is that their charismatic tendency was almost divisive. This congregation, as far as Episcopalians go, is little more conservative than I anticipated. It's kind of a subtle conservative.

Concomitantly, the promotion of a subtle yet transformative experience of Christianity is indeed the modus operandi at Silver Dollar City. According to Peter Herschend, "A friend once told me, 'Preach the gospel always, using words only whenever necessary.' We go out of our way not to be preachy, but if people leave here feeling good or a little closer to God, then I feel like maybe we've done our jobs."[33]

The Pentecostal tradition has often been posited as an adversary of modernity because of its roots in the Holiness tradition and expressed disdain for immodest culture, social intemperance, and vice-ridden secular entertainments. However, numerous prominent adherents have undertaken a melding of religious message with popular and mass culture. Aimee Semple McPherson, founder of the International Church of the Foursquare Gospel and a revivalist, started the nation's first Christian radio station in Los Angeles in the 1920s. Drawing inspiration from McPherson, fundamentalist Charles E. Fuller created the California-based *The Old-Fashioned Revival Hour,* which was carried on 575 stations and reached 20 million homes in the mid-1940s. In 1953, Pentecostal minister Rex Hubbard bought time on a local television station in Akron, Ohio, and set the standard for later manifestations of televangelism, including a faith healing ministry inaugurated by Oral Roberts in 1954. In 1961, Pat Robertson, an ordained Southern Baptist minister who yet espouses Pentecostal theology, began airing programs over his Christian Broadcasting Network (CBN) and eventually launched the first privately owned communications satellite in the world. CBN featured the popular *700 Club,* which was originally cohosted by Robertson and then unknown Jim Bakker. Bakker left the network in the early 1970s to host the equally popular *PTL Club;* fellow Assemblies of God minister Jimmy Swaggert commenced his own show in 1973; and Paul Crouch founded the Trinity Broadcasting Network that same year. Scholar of Pentecostalism Grant Wacker has accounted for the success of the movement by detailing its ability to blend a "primitivist" focus on returning to a purer and more spiritual past with a "pragmatic" impulse that encourages the use of modern methods to facilitate the spread of religious messages. In light of Silver Dollar City's emphasis on a semimythical history and its creative methods for evangelism, Wacker's explanation seems an apt paradigm for understanding the park's connections to a larger Pentecostal history.[34]

Pentecostals have also been active in the realm of religious theme parks. Most notable among this group are Jim and Tammy Faye Bakker, whose 2,300-acre Heritage USA in Fort Mill, South Carolina, ascended to the nation's third most popular park (trailing only the two Disneys) in the mid-1980s. In 1986 it attracted 6 million visitors, who came to enjoy a 500-room hotel, 2,500-seat church, 5-acre water park, gable-fronted "Main Street USA," and enclosed mall. During its tenure, evangelical and charismatic Protestantism was blatantly evidenced as lifeguards occasionally shut down their pools to perform baptisms and secular variety acts transformed themselves into Passion plays at Eastertide. Such moves led a writer for *Time* to characterize the overall experience as "the triumph of born-again nice." Interestingly, in 2002 Bakker chose Branson as the place to re-vitalize his ministry after serving a prison sentence. In January 2003 he began broadcasting a daily television show from the Studio City Café on the Branson Strip, and he has recently acquired a 590-acre parcel of land just outside town for a Christian-themed residential community.[35]

As Bakker's experience demonstrated, Christian-based leisure can be volatile and perilous when stripped of its perceived ethical underpinnings. However, in-dustry experts also agree that Calvinistic and transparently proselytizing recre-ational offerings do not result in profits. As Tim O'Brien, an editor with *Amusement Business,* stated, "No one wants to go on vacation and be preached to. Just imagine the kind of rides you'd see. I think a 'Fires of Hell Funhouse' would be a bit too much to take on vacation." Silver Dollar City boosters seem to have gen-tly negotiated all these examples and caveats to offer a product that is perceived as sincere yet unassuming. As Peter Herschend has explained: "The phraseology my brother and I have long time used is, 'What would we do if Jesus were in the room?' It's the guiding principles, the moral values that make a difference in the business." Adding biblical precedent to this notion of Christly emulation, he has also asserted that Matthew 25:35 (NRSV; "For I was hungry and you gave me food, I was thirsty and you gave me something to drink, I was a stranger and you welcomed me") offers a template for the park's approach to customer ser-vice.[36]

The religious path of Jack Herschend, though institutionally dissimilar to that of his brother, has exhibited a comparable focus on methods of popularly medi-ated evangelism and religious instruction. Jack and his wife, Sherry, drew on the consecrated nature of their attraction when they married in the Cathedral Room of Marvel Cave. For more than thirty years they have been active congregants at

Branson's First Presbyterian Church. In 2002, their longtime service to the congregation was recognized when they were awarded the Sunday School Teachers
of the Year Award by Gospel Light Publishers, a distributor of children's curricula
and resources. Throughout this period, the couple has emphasized the motto
"Being a Christian is fun," a maxim that is certainly at the root of Silver Dollar
City's approach. This delicate mix of prudent proselytism and entertainment
within the theme park context was recently framed by Jack through the analogy
of a spiritual feast: "Witnessing is like seasoning a meal. Too much spoils the
meal. We don't want to cross the line from what is tasteful and appropriate."[37]

Sherry Herschend has also been involved with a more explicitly religious
theme park venture. Nazareth Village in Israel, which opened in April 2000, is a
re-creation of the first-century town where Jesus grew up, replete with authentic
crafts and guides in period costumes. Existing as a site where the life and teachings of Jesus can be conveyed in a manner true to biblical text, Nazareth Village is
also designed to bring people to Christ through multisensory exhibits of his ministry that are exciting and engaging. Throughout the past twenty years, Sherry
has led more than twenty tours of the Holy Land. She is on the Board of Trustees
of the Miracle of Nazareth International Foundation and donated $1 million for
the building of the attraction. Sherry feels that the site not only offers a glimpse
of ancient Hebrew history but can also help to facilitate Middle Eastern peace
by stressing Christly emulation. As she stated, "Regardless of their cultures, they
[Jews and Muslims] all know that Jesus was the great peacemaker."[38]

In the late 1980s, Silver Dollar City Inc. (now Herschend Family Entertainment Corporation) codified its approach to religiously inspired tourism by crafting a mission statement that compelled employees to provide experiences "all in
a manner consistent with Christian values and ethics." According to Jack Herschend, the company recruits and trains its thousands of employees, religious or
nonreligious, "based on Christian values." Each is thereby expected to provide a
"Christian witness" to the park's guests without "wearing faith on our sleeves."
Evidence suggests that this obligation is welcomed by employees. Many staff
members have been with the enterprise for multiple decades, and 70 percent of
all promotions come from within.[39]

Verbalizing this mandate to missionize and allying Silver Dollar City's Christian underpinnings with the historical period it seeks to represent, current employee Orville Conrad stated:

> Christianity is integral to the Ozarks way of life in the late 1800s and cannot be sep-
> arated from the theme. Many of us are really offended by non-Christian attitudes

and behaviors of a few of our guests but the only Christian way to deal with these is to provide an appropriate example for them with gentle suggestions of what might be more appropriate without making any accusations. We can show the evidence of gods love in non offensive ways just as the early settlers of this area did.

Alicia Bolin, a singer at one of Silver Dollar City's many shows, added that the park "supports God in a lot of things" and claimed that a majority of the site's guests visit because it is a Christian-based attraction. As she wrote, "I know this because I sing at SDC and over half my audience comes up to me and the rest of the cast after the show and tells us how much they love the fact that there is a dress code, and that they play Christian music through the entire park all the time."[40]

To further substantiate the ways that employees are compelled to provide Christian witness, Peter and Jack Herschend frequently have told stories about longtime street cleaner Luke Standlee. Jack recalled one instance when he was watching Standlee in action as he talked to a disabled and distraught girl visiting the park with her parents. As the child cried, Luke's attention and effort to cheer her up became more resolute. After the family departed, Jack inquired about the circumstances. In his rendering, "Luke aw shucked, then said, 'Whenever I see youngsters who have had a hard road, I try to get them to smile. Then I ask them to do things that would make their mom and dad happy and to please the Lord.'" Luke had apparently been utilizing this approach daily for many years and sealing each promise from a child with a shiny silver dollar. Marking Standlee as an exemplar of Matthew 25:35, Peter Herschend held that this is only one instance of a pervasive method used by Silver Dollar City "citizens": "It's simply living out what we as Christians are called to do. Our people know what it is to share love."[41]

Additionally, an endorsement of Christianity has not been limited to on-site employees. Although the Herschend brothers are often listed as "co-owners" and are unquestionably responsible for the site's spiritual impetus, Peter currently serves as vice chairman of the board of directors and Jack as chairman emeritus for the Herschend Family Entertainment Corporation. Since 1972 the still private company has been run with the assistance of a board that is given formal say on strategic decisions and sizable capital expenditures, and the company now has more than thirty owners with varying stakes in the enterprise (though the Herschend family retains the majority share). Individuals active within the realm of evangelical Protestantism have been part of this leadership structure from its instigation. For instance, Sam Moore, head of Bible publisher Thomas Nelson Inc., was an original board member. In the late 1980s, the company received frequent consultation from Harry Hargrave, the chief operations officer for PTL

Network, who claimed that his first job priority was to "glorify God." On his retirement in 1998 as president and chief executive officer of the corporation, Cary
Summers claimed that the Lord led him to service at the park. Finally, in 2003 Joel
Manby was named CEO. Among Manby's many credentials was the founding of
Family Wise, a nonprofit Christian ministry focused on offering to corporations,
public schools, and churches tools that can facilitate the rediscovery of wholesome family time, trust in God, and behaviors guided by the Golden Rule.[42]

Although Silver Dollar City's millions of guests are not fully aware of the
ways that the Herschends ideologically position and justify their property, it is
easy to identify these techniques. Though the park has featured a saloon since
1973, visitors are not able to imbibe Ozark moonshine (or any alcoholic beverage
for that matter). In fact, the on-site "saloon" has roots in an embrace of physical
restraint rather than drunken revelry. According to Jack Herschend, a park tavern
was planned because one was included within the site's original mining town.
However, not wanting to promote inebriation, he linked the tavern to Carrie
Nation, the ax-wielding leader of the nineteenth-century temperance crusade,
who was born in nearby Eureka Springs, Arkansas. To showcase this regional
connection, Silver Dollar City's saloon show once started in a typical can-can
girl fashion only to be interrupted by a Nation impersonator who broke whiskey
bottles, called sinners to the stage, and closed down the business five times daily.
A century after Nation's campaign, temperance is still a calling card for the park.
As stated by Ron Farris, a trucker who delivers supplies to the site and frequently
visits as a guest, "It's an incredible place. . . . I can bring my family and never have
to worry about drunks because there aren't any." Other aspects of the attraction
further equate it with Christian-based social and cultural decorum: visitors can
enjoy bloodless bouts between law enforcement and outlaws, re-created nineteenth-century miners with sparkling hygiene and profanity-free dispositions,
and stand-up comedians who resist the risqué jokes that exemplify their trade.
In this manner, aspirations of wholesomeness fuse with a recent stockholder
statement of objectives that mandated a "Christ-centered company" to produce
a variant of "family fun" firmly entrenched in popular religiosity.[43]

While an amorphous translation of decency finds its way into all entertainment venues at the park and easily meshes with the upright brands of country, bluegrass, and "hillbilly" tunes continuously featured, a guest can also easily
locate traditional gospel performances. Many of the gospel entertainers often
claim that they appreciate the unique prospect of evangelizing to unchurched
park visitors. As Tim Martin, lead singer for the a cappella group First Day,
stated, "We welcome opportunities such as Silver Dollar City to be able to sing

about our Lord to those who may not have a relationship with Christ. It is our hope that others will be moved to seek God and his word." Furthermore, each day (except Sunday) concludes with a showcase of religious music at the site's amphitheater. As a capstone to the week, a program currently entitled "Gospel Jubilation" is offered after the park's close. Gary McSpadden, who holds credentials as a former Southern Baptist minister, member of the Oak Ridge Boys and the Gaither Trio, and inductee into Gospel Music Hall of Fame, has frequently hosted this Sabbath-day event. In addition, McSpadden also operates a ministry out of Branson that hopes to bring gospel music and biblical truths to Europe and Latin America. Silver Dollar City has also made devotional melodies ubiquitous throughout its acreage. As one strolls the winding paths, such songs are always heard though speakers shaped as rocks. These devices, which demonstrate the site's commitment to fusing religion with the greater theme park experience, perfectly embody the dictum to preach while not being "preachy."[44]

During a typical summer season (which amounts to half of overall visitation), four-fifths of all Silver Dollar City's guests arrive with children. In light of this core constituency, the site is permeated with nondistinct "family values" rhetoric that reflects its similarly imprecise religious product. Appropriately, the performing of Christian precepts is therefore not exclusively aimed at adults. In 2002, animated Veggie Tales characters joined the park's annual National Kids' Festival. The creation of Phil Vischer and Mike Nawrocki, Veggie Tales cartoons feature fun-loving vegetables that entertain children with Bible stories and help their parents teach Christian values. A remarkable business venture in its own right, the Veggie Tales enterprise began in 1993 and has never been supported by a cable TV network or syndicated show. Nonetheless, it is currently the most popular children's video series in the world, with more than twenty-five million copies sold. Prior to their arrival, Peter Herschend labeled the pious plants a "glove fit" for his property. Considering that Veggie Tales has prospered by presenting easygoing moral lessons in inventive ways, it is not surprising that Vischer declared, "Most parents want their kids to be more forgiving, more kind, more compassionate. It's the same thing Silver Dollar City's been doing for 40 years." Attesting to ways that Veggie Tales conjoined with the restrained religiosity of all the locale's offerings, tourist Shelby Sears stated, "It's not a direct message. They [her children] don't even get it that they're getting preached at."[45]

The theme park's celebration of Christmas also brings to light its unique negotiation of sacred and secular sentiments. The holiday is commemorated with a living Nativity presentation, an Angel Garden that provides the story of cherubs throughout the Bible, and ornate crèches from all over the world. The venue also offers a five-story Christmas tree decorated with two hundred thousand lights and a "Wonderland" where children can make their requests to Santa. Seemingly profane Christmas displays such as these can be viewed while aboard the park's steam train, where riders often sing nonreligious seasonal melodies en route. However, at the climax of this journey through signifiers of the secular holiday, the train rumbles to a stop in the woods. There a woodsman standing near images of the manger scene tells the story of Christ's birth, wraps all the sights encountered into an overarching Christian narrative, and, in the locale's typically understated fashion, lets guests know that Jesus is the "reason for the season."[46]

The Herschend Family Entertainment Corporation often reiterates that its goal is not proselytism. As Peter Herschend maintained in 2000, "This is not Billy Graham. We're not trying to convert anyone." Still, although the park may not station preachers on its street corners, it is undeniable that the attraction and associations sponsored by its parent company engage in evangelism by broadcasting their variant of Christian values to larger society, with the site's proprietors claiming that many people have "met the Lord" during their visits. Herschend intoned this approach when he was part of Billy Graham's Heart of America Crusade held at Arrowhead Stadium in Kansas City, Missouri, in 2004. Prefacing his address, he stated, "What I will speak about is ultimately how living with Jesus has directed my life and how important He has been to my life and our business." Considering Silver Dollar City's amorphous spiritual approach, a Herschend-Graham revival pairing makes much sense. Scholar of American evangelicalism Mark Noll has accounted for Graham's remarkable success by highlighting his ability to "reduce friction" among Christian groups and trade "angularity for access." Utilizing a "particularly inoffensive way of reminding people that they are sinners in need of grace," Graham has opted for a focus on "mere Christianity" that greatly resembles Herschend's own business strategies.[47]

As a central part of this religio-tourism mission, each spring the company sponsors "Young Christians' Weekend," an event that draws up to sixteen thousand teens for a combination of entertainment and dating, self-image, and sexuality seminars. Christian artist-ministers perform for youths, and despite attempted missionary restraint, Peter Herschend claimed that many attendees have "accepted Jesus" as a result of their stay. At the 2001 event, for instance, teens attended a sermon by Ryan Dobson, son of Focus on the Family founder James Dobson, who told them that they are loved by God despite their flaws. Minutes later, the Christian boy band Plus One took the stage to the delight of hundreds of junior high girls. The park also used this occasion to unveil the $18 million looping roller coaster, Wildfire. Beyond braving the ride, attendees gathered on Sunday morning for a rousing service at the Wilderness Church. After this weekend of faith and fun, the park received calls from a bevy of youth leaders and estimated that nine hundred young people made a commitment to Christ as a result of these activities.[48]

Furthermore, all Herschend Family Entertainment Corporation holdings are required to give a percentage of their yearly profits to Christian ministries, and Jack and Peter Herschend have been active as board members with a variety of these groups for more than a decade. Organizations supported by Silver Dollar City donations include Habitat for Humanity, Lives Under Construction Boys Ranch (an association that offers alternative programs and homes for troubled boys), the Young Life/Discipleship Focus Program (a discipleship training and Bible study initiative for youth group members), and Ozarks Food Harvest (a mission intended to alleviate hunger in southwestern Missouri and northern Arkansas). Supplementing these endeavors is the Silver Dollar City Foundation, formed in 1996 to serve as a grant-giving umbrella entity for Branson-wide community programs. By offering funds that assist needy Ozarkers in paying their utility bills, "adopting" impoverished families at Christmastime, and providing conflict management classes to schools and community organizations, the foundation utilizes, according to President John Baltes, a "grass roots approach to growing a community centered in Christian values" and hopes to ultimately lead "people into a personal relationship with Jesus Christ."[49]

In addition to his business enterprises, Peter Herschend has engaged in a variety of political pursuits that inform the tenor of Silver Dollar City and signal his importance outside the Branson area. A lifelong Republican, Herschend avowed, "I am a conservative, both philosophically and politically." This claim was solidified in 1992 when President George Bush chose Silver Dollar City as the place to emphasize his "family values" message and celebrate his nomination to a second term of office—an event that attracted ten thousand people in the August heat to a brief rally. Also notable is Herschend's long-term relationship with John Ashcroft. Ashcroft was raised in Springfield and practiced law in that city before beginning his political career; is a fellow member of the Assemblies of God and comes from a family of ministers; and was both senator from and governor of Missouri before serving as the U.S. attorney general from 2001 to 2005. This religious and political like-mindedness led Herschend to contribute tens of thousands of dollars to Ashcroft's campaigns of the early 1990s—generosity that was rewarded by an appointment to the Missouri State Board of Education in 1991. He still sits on this board, and in 2005 he assumed the office of president for the second time.[50]

The Herschend-Ashcroft relationship has not been without controversy. In 1992, Branson was burdened with traffic congestion as thirty thousand cars a day jammed its Strip during peak season. At a press conference that year where he was introduced by Herschend, then governor Ashcroft declared an "economic emergency" in order to build additional roads. A $140 million, 18-mile bypass was quickly approved, and it soon came to light that the new highway would benefit several of the governor's key political contributors, most of all Herschend. Skirting the city's overcrowded primary road, U.S. Highway 465 (dubbed "Pete's Pike" by disgruntled local residents) would offer people traveling to Branson from the north a direct route to Silver Dollar City. In addition, it was to cross three stretches of Herschend-owned property, including one parcel sold to the state for $2.2 million in 1993. Amid the planning and construction of the bypass, campaign contributions from Herschend, his family, and business continued to pour into Ashcroft's coffers, with $33,000 donated between 1994 and 2001.[51]

Although this saga indicates a symbiotic, and perhaps suspect, economic arrangement, the men's religious affinities clearly influenced the deal. Aside from their shared affiliation with the Assemblies of God, they are mutually acquainted with important figures of the Christian Right such as Pat Robertson and James Dobson. Famous for his integration of conservative Christian principles into public stances, Ashcroft has sought to "invite God's presence into whatever [he is] doing." Like-minded evangelicals, including Herschend, showed support for this union in the 2000 election cycle, when Ashcroft received more political money from religious groups and clergy than any other candidate for the U.S. Senate. By holding voluntary daily prayers with his staff and anointing himself prior to being sworn into political offices (a ritual meant, as he stated, to "replicate the ancient kings of Israel"), he therefore reproduced the blurring of a line between sacred and secular promoted by Silver Dollar City. And, through his renowned Christian-guided conservatism, he has advanced a variety of social policies fundamental to Herschend's own agenda, with an opposition to gaming central to this overlap.[52]

Herschend has vigilantly campaigned against gambling in the Ozarks for more than a decade. The possibility of gaming in the area has caused consternation among many residents since it was first proposed by a New Jersey–based company and the Eastern Shawnee tribe in 1994. Throughout a decade of battles over this issue, Silver Dollar City has indeed led Branson's charge against what Herschend has termed the "cancer of gambling." On several occasions, the company has paid employees to conduct studies of its effect on local economies and to assist people combating its influences with fund-raising and resource gathering. In an attempt to defeat 1998's Amendment 9 to the Missouri constitution, which legalized gaming in artificial moats, it donated more than $25,000 to a lobbying group. Illustrating the union of tourism boosters and clergy around this and other social matters, Howard Boyd, pastor of Branson Hills Assembly of God Church and opponent of local gambling, praised Silver Dollar City's efforts when he stated, "I probably will not know until I get to heaven just how much the Herschends have influenced this community."[53]

The most sizable challenge by gambling advocates arose in 2004 when Rockaway Beach, a tiny town 12 miles from Branson, proposed the construction of a casino that promoters claimed would bring year-round jobs to its depressed economy. In a now familiar refrain, Peter Herschend voiced his opposition by claiming that the enterprise would damage the "image" of Branson—one that relied on "wholesome, family-oriented, good entertainment." To counter roughly $12 million spent by the pro-gaming coalition, the Herschend family and its corporation bankrolled the "Show Me You Care" campaign. Finance reports showed that Peter Herschend contributed $125,000, his brother and sister-in-law added another $125,000, and the Herschend Family Entertainment Corporation donated $970,000. These three gifts amounted to nearly 90 percent of the campaign's overall budget. On August 3, 2004, Missouri voters defeated a constitutional amendment that would have made Rockaway Beach's plans legal. While money and grassroots political effort certainly aided the antigambling cause, Peter Herschend also suggested that divine intervention led to victory: "The Lord's on our side. I have such a tremendous prayer group working. I have consciously sought out prayer groups around the nation to be in prayer about this."[54]

Because Silver Dollar City relies on Billy Graham's innocuous mode of evangelism rather than John Ashcroft's more brazen attempts to integrate Christianity into the public sphere, no contemporary visitor would find evidence of the Herschends' opposition to gambling or to any other hot-button political initiative that is part of the larger evangelical "family values" agenda. While placards do not adorn the grounds in protest of abortion or homosexuality or in support of school prayer, a religiously derived focus on families is thoroughly commented on by guests and other observers. Although the American "culture war" is thought by most to be a product of the 1980s, it has a century-long history in the Branson area. Throughout the past one hundred years, regional attractions have promised an escape from the ills of modernity by means of retreat to a changeless and pristine environ. Many technological transformations and other progressive innovations arrived on Ozark soil during this period, but boosters (including those at Silver Dollar City) continued to tout the area as an escape from ethically bereft aspects of the country at large. Here was a place where people could leave their car doors unlocked without fear of theft; where children could safely play without constant parental supervision; where vulgarity was an infrequent occurrence rather than a way of life; and where the seeming chaos of contemporary existence was calmed by a core group of amusements focused on God, country, and the traditional nuclear family. Reflecting such promises, the three-million-member American Family Association (AFA), whose mission statement claims that the entertainment industry "has played a major role in the decline of those values on which our country was founded and which keep a society and its families strong and healthy," offered a review of Silver Dollar City on its Web site in 2003. In it, the AFA praised the park's emphasis on putting "God first" in all its endeavors and highlighted the understated yet effective ways that "Christian values are expressed in the thousands of small details that go into running a family attraction."[55]

In contemporary exit surveys, Silver Dollar City patrons similarly extol the site's "safe, family atmosphere," "friendly" employees, "clean" and "orderly" environment, and overall "Christian values." Often these attributes are juxtaposed against comments about competitors within the tourism market said to have a less welcoming, mannerly, and pious disposition. As one tourist wrote within a recent online review of the park:

> During our June trip my mother lost track of my 4-year-old son. The staff not only kept him entertained, they sent someone out to find my mother. Later in the day she decided to buy the kids some ice cream, not thinking she left her billfold sitting on the counter. When we returned to the cabin she had rented we called the park, they had her billfold. I would like to add that there was nothing missing, not even a dollar, do you think that would happen anywhere else? . . . I went to Six Flags St. Louis recently and was really grossed out by the conditions of the park. Since they added the water park all you see is half naked women, running around half drunk, and trash all over the park. I may never go back there.

Thus, the nonthemed, urban, lascivious, and unrestrained competitor paled in comparison with its diametric Ozark opposite. Another Internet review perhaps summarized Silver Dollar City's aura most succinctly by labeling the site "clean (in all ways)."[56]

Each of the aforementioned "family values" elements is integral to the vision of appropriate religiosity represented by the park and subtly preached to its guests. As Peter Herschend explained: "The greatest ministry that we have is the operation of the company properties. The greatest witness we have to who Jesus

was and is, is how we operate day in and day out." Although not every guest may
ally characteristics of decorum, integrity, and modesty with imitation of Jesus,
the link was apparent to a tourist from North Carolina, who wrote:

> At so many amusement parks the attendants are all young people who could care
> less about their job and they let it show. SDC has mostly older people as attendants
> and they were so friendly. They also had some young people working for them,
> and they too were very nice and friendly. Also you didn't see immodestly dressed
> people like you do at some parks, where you have to pray your children don't see
> their lack of clothes. The entertainment was wholesome, we loved Chapter 6 [a
> Christian a cappella ensemble], and the Veggie Tales show was so fun for the kids.
> We are Christians and this was a fabulous wholesome place to take my children.

Through such an account, one therefore becomes even more aware of the ways
that the park's unwritten (yet thoroughly scripted) "sermons" are enacted within
the everyday workings of the site and interpreted by patrons through a religious
lens.[57]

In the minds of many visitors, Silver Dollar City has served as the antithesis
of other American recreational locales. Moreover, the consciously crafted culture of the place, solidified within the park's motto "Creating Memories Worth
Repeating," has often resisted the cultural inclinations of America at large. The
site's attendance surged in the late 1960s not only because of its national exposure through episodes of *The Beverly Hillbillies*. As administrator Brad Thomas
explained, "With Vietnam and other uprisings . . . a lot of people were purposely looking for ordinary people and simple themes that they could relate to.
. . . Places like Silver Dollar City offered families a chance to escape from those
turbulent times and get back in touch with their roots." In the latter part of the
twentieth century and the beginning of the twenty-first, Silver Dollar City has
employed its brand of antimodernism to combat a perceived severing of morals from daily life, the ever increasing degeneracy of popular culture, and the
decline of wholesome leisure opportunities for families. In this manner, it may
ostensibly represent the turn-of-the-century Ozarks, but on a larger level, it has
always sought to enact an alternative culture for people able to see and hear its
message.[58]

Marvel Cave has consistently had a spiritual dimension. Under the propri-
etorship of the Lynch sisters, the stress was on divinity. Contemporarily, nearly
half a million people still take the cave tour while visiting Silver Dollar City,
and its mystical nature remains palpable to many. As a recent guest from Illinois
wrote, "It is amazing the treasures that our earth holds that God has created that

are just waiting for us to discover." Since the Herschend family bought the site, the cavern's mystique has become part of a thorough, aboveground embrace of amusement-oriented Christian evangelism. A thread of piety indeed winds its way through park employees, guests, and attractions alike. The site has always framed itself as a simple place populated by plain folk who provide glimpses of a trouble-free age. However, its experiential brand of remembering, imagining, and worshiping has spoken to the complexities of culture for many decades and offered tourists unique reaffirmations of the place of Christianity within American life.[59]

CHAPTER FOUR

Jesus Is "the Greatest Star"

The Variety Show and Contemporary Branson Tourism

In 1999, Wes Neal, of Branson's Champions of Excellence Ministries, pro-
duced the *Branson Stars Booklet*—a forty-page tract of Christian testimony. Its
contributors included area entertainers such as Roy Clark, Tony Orlando, and
Trinity Broadcasting Network mainstay Dino Kartsonakis, plus local resident
and nationally known marriage counselor Gary Smalley and business leaders Jack
Herschend (co-owner of Silver Dollar City) and Joe White (owner of Kanakuk
Kamps). Meant to be distributed to every tourist as part of the "Reach Out From
Branson" project, it highlighted the impact of faith on the lives of these performers and dignitaries and described various religious revelations received and spiri-
tual transformations undergone while in town.

In addition to testimonies from the stars, Neal's pamphlet included a thumb-
nail sketch of Jesus's life and a mock "reporter's interview" with the Messiah
that outlined major evangelical Protestant themes (the ascendancy of faith over
works, Christ's role as the exclusive mediator between humanity and God, and
the importance of rebirth through accepting Jesus as one's savior). Following
this biography and question-and-answer session, readers were asked to offer a
"prayer of commitment," to realize the contemporary relevance of Christianity,
and to fill out a decision card attached to the back cover which indicated their
newfound devotional steadfastness. Engaging in a bit of spiritual mathematics,
the author claimed that 6,855,000 people visited Branson in 1998, and he assumed
that 10 percent were already Christians (an incredibly modest hypothesis considering the religious identities of the American people and the religious nature
of regional tourism). Neal hoped that his booklet would inspire an additional
10 percent of visitors and that 30 percent of that total number, on departing the

Ozarks with renewed or new faith, would introduce people in their home communities to Christ. If this course of action proved cogent, nearly 1.8 million individuals would be affected by the ministry's handout.

Although there is no way to confirm the statistical efficacy of this initiative, it does speak to an overarching thread that integrates the diversity of offerings found within Branson's variety show theaters. The primary impetus of Neal's "free souvenir" was to give tourists the opportunity to literally "meet Jesus Christ 'face to face'" and to suggest that they could wage a war against Satan's work by consuming Branson's ideological vantages and then sharing them abroad. People who attend one of the region's theatrical performances will not encounter an explicit missionary presentation, but they will find religiously tinged country music, a plethora of gospel numbers, spiritual and nostalgic renderings of an antimodern past, deference to civil religiosity, and "family values" rhetoric derived from theological perspectives. Despite extolling the merits of virtue-laden entertainers and encouraging experiential consumption of their popular religious wares, the *Branson Stars Booklet* concluded with a reminder that the Christian underpinnings of the tourist market must never be overlooked. By suggesting in its final pages that Jesus is "the greatest star" in Branson, it forthrightly iterated what all local acts imply—Christ is the fabric of the music and the message.[1]

In 2004, more than seven million vacationers went to Branson and spent nearly $1.5 billion. That year, the city hosted forty-seven variety show theaters with more seats than New York City's Broadway district and more than a hundred different live productions. Prior to 1991, it was primarily a summer destination for midwesterners. However, the contemporary market greets families, seniors, and other sojourners from March through December who seek entertainment that valorizes distinct visions of God, family, and country. Beginning with acts tendered by local families in the late 1960s and 1970s, continuing with the arrival of more recognizable talent such as Roy Clark and Boxcar Willie in the 1980s, and culminating with the advent of entertainment icons like Andy Williams and Wayne Newton in the 1990s, such acts have been the primary catalyst for Branson's emergence as an international phenomenon. The country standards, wistful pop tunes, and patriotic harmonies proffered by these performers seem to be secular at first inspection. However, a closer look at the shows and the principles that inform their headliners reveals the perpetuation of a popular religious undercurrent that has coursed its way through Branson tourism from the beginning.[2]

A BRIEF CHRONOLOGY OF BRANSON AREA
MUSICAL ENTERTAINMENT

Radio station KWTO (Keep Watching the Ozarks) began operation in Spring-field, Missouri, in 1933. Founder Ralph Foster, who was responsible for the live 1936 Easter broadcast from Shepherd of the Hills Farm in Branson, envisioned KWTO as a vehicle for local entertainers who would transmit traditional Ozark music. As the originator of mass-mediated family entertainment in the region, Foster sought musical performers who could don pseudonyms such as "Aunt Martha" Haworth or "Uncle" Carl Haden and thereby draw on kinship networks vital to Ozark community life in the early twentieth century. KWTO prompted its audience to forge a conception of entertainers as proverbial relatives able to enter households via the airwaves. Moreover, according to historian Edgar D. McKinney, when Ozarkers tuned in to hear time-honored regional music on commercial radio, they "opened their homes to the philosophy of the market economy" and readily purchased medicines, detergents, and other advertised wares. Thus, by uniting traditional song with consumer culture, the station forged a formula of family-based amusement that still defines Branson.[3]

Although KWTO's offerings were dominated by fiddling and Ozark ballads, they also included gospel. The first gospel group to appear on the station was the Goodwill Family, a quartet that consisted of Clyde "Slim" Wilson, his sister, her son, and fundamentalist minister Guy Smith (who later became famous as the composer of Roy Acuff's hit "The Great Speckled Bird"). Other groups ad-opted the approach of Albert E. Brumley—the most popular of all white gospel composers and a longtime Ozark resident. Creator of more than eight hundred songs, Brumley had a style that emphasized visions of a caring, personal savior and a pastoral heaven which were well received by poor, rural southerners dur-ing the depression years. His trademark arrangement, and one that epitomizes such themes, was "I'll Fly Away"—the most recorded gospel song in history. Drawing on Brumley's work, KWTO performers such as the Matthews Broth-ers (four evangelist siblings) entertained and inspired listeners during the mid-1940s.[4]

Seeking to expand his undertaking after World War II, Ralph Foster teamed with Springfield businessman Si Siman to create RadiOzark Enterprises. This ini-tiative sold recorded programming to stations outside the Ozarks and achieved its first success with "Sermons in Song"—a program of popular gospel music sponsored by the Springfield-based Assemblies of God and purchased by more than two hundred stations nationwide. With their radio programs attracting talent from Nashville such as Tennessee Ernie Ford, the pair decided to produce a network TV program in 1954 and lured Red Foley away from his job as master of ceremonies at the Grand Ole Opry to host it. Known as *The Ozark Jubilee* and aired on Springfield's KYTV, the show blended elements from vaudeville and variety show radio to offer wholesome family programming that accentuated Ozark values of self-sufficiency, working-class pride, patriotism, and religiosity. Described by commentator Dickinson Terry as a production "with a strong leaning toward songs with a spiritual note," *The Ozark Jubilee* found a wide following among Ozarkers and non-Ozarkers alike. Benign and innocent in presentation, the program also offered a unified social and political stance that appealed to a cross section of post–World War II Americans seeking common, mass-mediated culture.[5]

In the late 1950s, five members of the Mabe Family, which had originally showcased its musical talents at church dinners in Christian and Taney counties, began performing on KWTO as the Blansit Trio (under the sponsorship of Blansit Auction Company). The children of Southern Baptist preacher Donald Mabe, Bill, Jim, Lyle, Bob, and Margie played live music three mornings a week beginning in 1957. Another local group, the Presley Family, also drew on the success of Foster's enterprises. Springfield-area natives Lloyd and Bessie May Presley, and children Gary and Deanna, originally performed on KWTO as part of the Ozark Playboys. Capitalizing on the popularity of regional caverns, they also became the featured act at a Stone County cave in 1963.[6]

KWTO ceased live performances in 1959 in favor of an all-recorded music format. That year, the Mabe children began performing twice a week at the fifty-seat Branson City Hall Community Building. Beginning in 1960, they secured jobs with Branson's newest tourist attractions when they were asked to play the intermission square dance at the Shepherd of the Hills drama and to display their talents for guests awaiting the cave tour at Silver Dollar City. Now firmly situated in Branson's burgeoning tourism industry, the Mabes acquired their own position within the region's process of historical remaking by adopting the title the Baldknobbers. A far cry from the late nineteenth-century vigilantes who were their namesake, the group presented popular country music and Ozark hillbilly humor. In response to a growing audience in the early 1960s, the Baldknobbers relocated to the 200-seat Sammy Lane Pavilion on Lake Taneycomo and then to an old skating rink that accommodated 500 patrons.[7]

Meanwhile, the Presley Family continued to perform at Herman Mead's Underground Theatre (now Talking Rocks Cavern) throughout the 1960s. In 1967 the Presleys purchased a 10-acre site on Missouri Highway 76 in Branson. Titled the Ozark Mountain Jubilee, this 363-seat venue, strategically located between downtown Branson, Silver Dollar City, and the Shepherd of the Hills Farm, was the first on the city's now famous Strip. In 1968, the Mabes purchased a 14-acre plot across the highway from the Presleys and built an 865-seat theater to house the Baldknobbers Hillbilly Jamboree. Both locations remained open from late April through October. Although the city drew nearly one million tourists in 1970, performers all held additional jobs during this early period because Branson largely grew silent at nightfall. Over the past thirty years, however, the theaters have been remodeled and expanded on a number of occasions, and each now seats approximately two thousand people. And although many recent performers have deviated from the combination of country music and Ozark comedy which still epitomizes the Baldknobbers Jamboree and the Presleys' Country Jubilee, these two acts are recognized as the bedrock of Branson musical entertainment.[8]

A late 1960s brochure for the Baldknobbers Hillbilly Jamboree advertised the show as "Good Clean Family Entertainment," a credo that still can be applied to all Branson performances. The basic elements of this construct (to be discussed more fully below) include country and gospel tunes, nostalgic and patriotic melodies, and a patent vision of the virtuous nuclear family. While the Mabes and Presleys have in recent years added nonfamily session players, electric instruments, sequined costumes, and sanitized rock-and-roll classics, these accretions have not detracted from the promotion of a well-defined, Christian-informed creed.[9]

Additional groups soon ventured into the Branson area. Joplin, Missouri's Foggy River Boys organized in 1967, with all members coming from a background of quartet gospel music. Lead singer and Christian Church (Disciples of Christ) minister Bob Hubbard was a founding member of the Jordanaires— an act from Springfield that became one of the most famous of all Nashville groups by recording spirituals for Decca and Capitol Records and backing legendary figures such as Chet Atkins and Elvis Presley. First opening a theater in nearby Kimberling City in 1971 and performing both gospel and country songs, the group relocated to Branson in 1974 and remained in town until 1993. Hailing from southeastern Missouri, Darrell and Rosie Plummer and children Melody and Randy opened a theater on the Strip in 1973. Although the Plummer Family Country Music Show emphasized secular songs over sacred numbers, Randy Plummer has stressed notions of divine providence that brought his family to the area. Feeling that "the Lord plopped them down in a perfect location for their theater," he stated in a 2001 interview: "I really believe it's a Godsend for the tourist, because no other place has the kind of music, variety, and Christian atmosphere that Branson has." The Plummers' attraction was sold in 1990. However, Randy continues to perform at various locales and to sanctify the region through recorded songs such as "An Ozark Prayer"—a track from his 2000 album which beseeches listeners to "thank the Lord" for Branson and the Ozarks. Finally, in 1977, Bob Mabe, one of the founders of the Baldknobbers, left that show to build the Bob-O-Links Country Hoe Down. Beginning a trend in guest appearances by nationally known entertainers, Mabe opened his 1,800-seat venue with a performance by Ronnie Milsap. Until 1980, Branson hosted only these five shows.[10]

In 1980, Paramount Pictures' *Urban Cowboy* spurred a western fashion vogue that prompted many nightclubs throughout the nation to replace their disco balls with mechanical bulls and led patrons to trade polyester attire for leather and denim. By showcasing the talents of John Travolta and communicating a clichéd version of roadhouse culture to urbanites in search of alternatives to a 1970s nightclub ethos, *Urban Cowboy* initiated a nationwide embrace of stylized country music that contributed to a swelling of Branson's entertainment ranks. With the arrival of Chisai Childs in 1981, the Branson industry assumed this more ostentatious style, which contrasted sharply with the down-home fashion of its founding families. Childs was creator of the Grapevine Opry in Grapevine, Texas—a venue that in the late 1970s hosted the second largest country-and-western stage show in the world. When she opened the Starlite Theatre on Highway 76, it facilitated the merger of religion and recreation in the Ozarks by presenting the first Christmas and Easter specials. Additionally, she introduced several new performative elements to the area such as contemporary dance numbers and elaborate sequined costumes. As stated by Jean Trent, wife of *Hee Haw* star Buck Trent and Branson theater manager, "She kind of fancied up the town. . . . Before, it was the overalls and that type of stuff. She's kind of responsible for bringing all the glitter in."[11]

Since Childs's creation of "Branson chic" in the early 1980s, all shows have followed suit. Consonant with the mixing of rustic vacationing and Victorian opulence put forth by earlier tourism leaders, contemporary Branson entertainment has been labeled "a mixture of the Grand Ole Opry and Caesars Palace," or as described by a twenty-three-year-old tourist from Arkansas, "a G-rated, country version of Las Vegas." By melding the Ozarks with its seeming Nevada antithesis, the city has adopted a truly postmodern aesthetic—a disjointed artistic mode that is evident when one peruses the dizzying array of neon and flashing lights along its Strip. However, this fusion has not disturbed the Branson's marketed values, which continue to stress decidedly anti-Vegas wholesomeness. According to local costume designer Jan Rousseaux, "I think you can make the girls cute and even sexy without being seductive. We are the home of the clean-cut, grass-root, American style."[12]

Although Chisai Childs brought a new fashion to the Branson scene, it was the arrival of Roy Clark that first garnered national attention. Clark was a showman who won national music competitions as a teenager and played Las Vegas in the early 1960s. His career took off when he became cohost of *Hee Haw* in 1969. Though one may not easily identify a theological intent in this lighthearted and hackneyed program, Clark has testified that "behind all the foolishness" that he did there was "nothing but Jesus." Well worn from ceaseless recording and concert giving during the 1970s, he opened Roy Clark's Celebrity Theater in 1983 for "a chance to have a normal lifestyle." The year before Clark's arrival, Branson's Strip hosted thirteen venues perpetuating earlier Ozark themes. This emphasis was soon to be drastically altered, however, for as former communications director at the Branson/Lakes Area Chamber of Commerce, Dawn Erikson, has asserted, "I generally measure the growth of Branson as an entertainment mecca from the arrival of Roy Clark." Because Clark committed to only one hundred shows a year and maintained his residence in Tulsa, Oklahoma, big-name performers such as Conway Twitty and Mel Tillis began singing at the theater in his stead. Some of his substitutes then decided to open their own venues in Branson, with Boxcar Willie debuting in 1987 and Mickey Gilley and Tillis in 1990. Clark's theater existed for only five years, but on its closing in 1988, Branson was on the verge of an entertainment explosion.[13]

In the late 1980s, Branson witnessed the arrival of numerous bigger-name stars who either established their own venues or did guest appearances. In 1989, twenty-two theaters and twenty-four shows lined Highway 76. That year, an estimated 3.8 million individuals vacationed in Branson, and an average of 21,740 vehicles traversed the Strip during summer months. Of these visitors, two-thirds saw at least one music show, nearly one-third saw three or more productions, and for the full year, all locales combined took in $32.9 million for tickets, concessions, and merchandise. Though these were impressive numbers for a town with a population of then less than four thousand, 1991 would prove to be the year that saw the creation of a tourism phenomenon.[14]

In March 1991, Mel Tillis announced plans to build a 2,100-seat venue off the Strip on U.S. Highway 65. In April of that year, plans were made for a $30 million theme park centered on Johnny and June Carter Cash to be called "Cash Country." Deviating from the city's country theme but remaining within the time-tested realm of nostalgic entertainment, Andy Williams began publicizing plans for his Moon River Theatre in August. In mid-September, Willie Nelson agreed to assume Tillis's former location and retitle it the Willie Nelson Ozark Theater. And as the year closed, Merle Haggard revealed that he would perform seventy dates at Nelson's venue beginning in 1992. In light of this flurry of proclamations, *Time* ran a feature article on Branson's theaters and christened the town "Country Music's New Mecca." Moreover, *60 Minutes* aired a thirteen-minute special about Branson in which correspondent Morley Safer called it "the live music capital of the universe" and Mel Tillis boasted that his enterprise brought in "$6 million in six months." As a result of this upsurge of notable talent and national press, the number of overnight visitors to Branson increased 116 percent from April 1991 to April 1992.[15]

All observers of Branson's tourism history mark 1991–1994 as the city's "boom years." During that period, the number of lodging rooms and restaurant seats both increased by nearly 10,000, the number of indoor theater seats swelled from 22,788 to 50,065, and construction values skyrocketed from roughly $20 million to nearly $140 million. In 1994, 5.8 million guests came to the area for its now overwhelming entertainment offerings and were welcomed by a host of new stars that included Tony Orlando, the Osmonds, Kenny Rogers, and Wayne Newton. With the town featured on *The Today Show, The Larry King Show, Entertainment Tonight,* and numerous other national programs; ranked as the number one destination point by the American Bus Association in 1993; and quickly becoming known as the premier place for senior travel in the United States, it appeared as though Branson was primed for unlimited growth.[16]

Although Branson theater owners and boosters have often expressed reservations about the sustainability of the region's tourism success, the city has remained a banner destination for seniors, veterans, and families over the past decade. For instance, the number of yearly overnight visitors remained near seven million from 1996 through 2005. Throughout this ten-year period, the area has maintained its primary tourist cohorts—it was ranked as the number one destination by *Senior Group Traveler Magazine* in 1995; as the number one motorcoach destination by the American Bus Association from 1995 to 2001 (and the number one motorcoach destination of the decade in 2002); and as the top family-friendly tourist town by *FamilyFun Magazine* in 1999. In the face of legitimate concerns about the pitfalls of unchecked development in the early 1990s, a declining number of visitors from the World War II generation, and disinterest by baby boomers in Branson's offerings, this city of then still only 6,050 permanent residents remained the number two "drive-to" destination (trailing only Orlando, Florida) and the sixteenth most popular overnight leisure vacation spot in the United States in 2003.[17]

Although many factors have contributed to the monumental growth of area tourism, any deeper understanding of this success requires a return to the industry's long-established ideological structure. Variety show entertainment in Branson was built on and continues to thrive by means of innocent country and gospel music, the promotion of antimodern nostalgia, civil religious patriotism, and a distinct construction of domestic appropriateness expressed through the rhetoric of "family values." These ethically laden premises, all subsumed under the often nebulous banner of Christianity, form the bedrock of every tourism venue, and the degree to which they are encouraged directly correlates with the success or failure of attractions.

Michael Ediger, a frequent Branson tourist and now a resident, affirmed this multifaceted appeal. Describing the city's allure, he cited "friendly and helpful stars" who are "just everyday people like us 'common folk'"; entertainment that offers "something for everyone"; an atmosphere that is "proud of our country's veterans"; a "crime-free and safe" environment; and, rounding out this list, an ever present promotion of "family and religious values." It would be in error to claim that the contemporary Branson undertaking has proffered an entirely homogeneous body of vacation options or that the mere inclusion of these themes amounts to assured economic vitality. However, there exists a quite recognizable Ozark entertainment genre founded on a very identifiable set of moral principles and spiritual dictates. As many performers have discovered, if one is not willing to "Bransonize" his or her act, it will most likely be short lived.[18]

COUNTRY, SOUTHERN GOSPEL, AND POP CULTURE EVANGELISM

What is today known as country music finds many of its roots in southern folk songs of the early nineteenth-century camp meetings and revivals. Predicated on notions of universal salvation for people willing to seek it diligently, the frontier evangelist's message was conveyed by familiar melodies easily recognizable to the uneducated, rural masses who gathered at revival grounds. As historian Bill C. Malone has claimed, it was these "simple, singable" tunes characterized by "choruses, refrains, and repetitive phrases" which have always been the "obvious characteristics of country music." Within his discussion of the history of American camp meetings, Dickson Bruce Jr. has argued that revival songs serve as repositories of "plain folk" theology. Offering an alternative to the closed-system polity and stoic hymnody of early nineteenth-century mainline Protestantism, such harmonies laid the foundations for an emotive, antidogmatic religiosity that still characterizes much of evangelical Christianity. When heaven became the object of desire, revival sounds highlighted a pious pragmatism and mastery of paradisiacal destiny that mimicked promotions of self-guided religious experience—a sentiment that lies at the root of all popular religion. According to Bruce, "The other world which camp-meeting religion propounded was the other world the plain-folk needed."[19]

As revivalism spread to urban areas in the latter part of the nineteenth century, its melodic repertoire became more firmly allied with popular music of the day. Such revivals coincided with the nostalgic nature of Victorian religiosity, with the Christian savior characterized as a loving shepherd who tended his flock rather than the austere and removed deity of eighteenth-century Puritanism. The musical rhetoric of entrance into heaven became enveloped in optimistic tones that accented individual volition rather than the helplessness of predestination. Evangelist Dwight L. Moody was the great systematizer of the urban revival. According to religious historian Peter Williams, Moody's theology "could be reduced to the proposition that salvation was available for the asking. . . . Judgment was largely gone, and mercy was everything. Sentimentality—the appeal to the heart . . . had been raised to an ultimate principle."[20]

This later wave of revivalism spawned the southern gospel tradition—the style of religious music most performed in Branson. The genre arose at the turn of the twentieth century as part of a larger theological and cultural discourse regarding the value of modern change. Offering solace to conservative white Christians who felt alienated by the rapid pace of urbanization and technological ascendancy, it posited family and home as the bases for morality and country life as the bastion of religious virtue. For example, standards such as "This World Is Not My Home" forthrightly expressed displeasure with a purportedly inhospitable world of ceaseless transformation and found solace only in a heaven that resembled the idealized rural domestic sphere. Furthermore, with the dawn of commercial country music, many performers perpetuated the relationship between earlier southern gospel themes and popular piety. Stephen Smith and Jimmie Rogers, for example, have written that the genre is characterized by a lack of faith in institutions—whether political, social, or religious. As Don Williams sang in his 1980 hit "I Believe in You," country music fans "don't believe that heaven waits only for those who congregate." Or as the son of a Southern Baptist minister, Tom T. Hall, declared in his 1972 song "Me and Jesus," "Me and Jesus got our own thing going / We don't need anybody to tell us what it's all about." Thus, even the most truncated examination of country music reveals its steadfast connection with a brand of individual theological autonomy that offers a revivalistic, musically motivated, and informal mode of worship.[21]

In 1981, Branson's Highway 76 was given the new promotional moniker "76 Country Music Boulevard." Although this name highlighted the brand of music that was bringing the town to national prominence, the choice also solidified Branson's standing as a place that melded recreation and popular religious sentiment. As a locale that turned theaters into sanctuaries for the propagation of Christian faith and values, it was put forth as unique among leisure destinations. This fusion is exemplified by the Braschler Quartet, one of Branson's longest-lived acts, which came to town in 1985. On arrival in Branson, Cliff Braschler, the patriarch of the quartet, had been a Church of God pastor for twenty-eight years, and lead singer Johnny Walters had co-pastored with him since the early 1980s. Planning to perform for only one year, the members of the quartet realized that the entertainment market would allow them (albeit nontraditionally) to advance their religious calling, and they have remained in Branson ever since. As Cliff Braschler avowed, "I've never felt any withdrawal from the ministry because I feel like I've been a minister ever since I've been here." Just as members of the group have always treated their performance as a sacred vocation, their fans have frequently embraced a similar juxtaposition. As Braschler detailed in a recent interview: "When we first started we had business men and women in town who would make their reservations for the same night every week because they worked on Sunday and they counted it as their worship for the week. We didn't get up and read the Bible and pound the pulpit but we've always tried to maintain a level of discipline in the group that would reflect what we say we are." Thus, like the popular religiosity from which country music draws inspiration, this show has always offered the opportunity for Christian worship outside formal church parameters. And like the camp meetings that first inspired the genre, it continues to do so within a context of regimented leisure.[22]

Like all Branson acts, the Braschler Family Music Show integrates some nonreligious numbers into its set. This fusion of sacred and secular prompted one critic to write, "The show is not 'religious' or preachy . . . but the spiritual influence is obvious." During a 2002 performance I attended, the program featured songs such as "The Tennessee Waltz" and "Blue Moon of Kentucky" and was occasionally punctuated by appearances of hillbilly comic Homer Lee. However, gospel music was its defining feature. The crowd seemed most captivated by "Have a Little Talk with Jesus," "Please Let Me Sing in the Choir," and a rousing rendition of "The Battle Hymn of the Republic" that served as the finale. The

The Braschler Music Show advertisement, 2003. From the author's collection

group's ministerial background and its long-standing, all-gospel performance on Thursdays provide further accentuation to the plethora of gospel songs. Patrons who do not fully appreciate the Braschler Quartet's emphasis on religious recreation might be further inspired by a poem by Carol Wimmer, entitled "When I Say I Am a Christian," which hangs prominently at the theater's entrance. Proclaiming "When I say . . . 'I am a Christian' / I am not trying to be strong. / I am

professing that I am weak / and pray for strength to carry on," this verse emphasizes age-old evangelical themes that are presented more lightheartedly by the
theater's performers. As confirmed by members of Topeka, Kansas's Eastside
Baptist Church who visited the theater in 2003, such premises are not overlooked
by guests. Asked how they liked the show, congregants simply responded in uni-
son, "Amen."[23]

Although the Braschlers' show has been in Branson for nearly twenty years,
other predominantly gospel acts have been less successful. The Collins Family
offered an all-religious music set that lasted only four years in the 1980s, and
the Blackwood Singers presented a gospel show that drew only modest crowds
throughout the 1990s. In 1992, the 2,000-seat Celebration Theater opened featuring contemporary gospel artist Bill Gaither—publisher of more than 500 hym-
nal standards and host of the *Gaither Gospel Hour* (a program with more than 75
million viewers worldwide). In light of Branson entertainment's penchant for
religious music, one would think that Gaither would have met with an excep-
tionally warm reception. However, this venue closed its doors after less than two
months. Although the city's style of leisure harks back to Christian liturgical
elements and often intends to inspire as much as entertain, its tourism history
has demonstrated that patrons want their mix of religion and ostensibly secular
entertainment finely mingled—a desire that may account for the failure of many
explicitly gospel acts. Thus, to find the true stories of accomplishment one must
look to those performers such as Barbara Fairchild who have put forth a more
well-rounded package of value-laden amusement that, while holding Christianity paramount, opts to evangelize in a more unassuming fashion.[24]

Fairchild is best known for her child-themed hits of the early 1970s, including "The Teddy Bear Song." Raised in rural Arkansas, she got her start singing
with two aunts in a gospel trio. A series of sugary sweet odes to the innocence
of youth then made her a two-time Grammy nominee and secured a number of
appearances on *The Tonight Show* and *Hee Haw*. By the late 1980s she had found
God with the help of born-again country star Ricky Skaggs and established a new
career in country-gospel. Fairchild began doing guest appearances in Branson
during the late 1980s. In 1991, a number of people told her that God was crafting
a distinctive mission for her in the Ozarks. As she recounted, "They said, 'God
wants to do something special in this area and He wants you to be part of it.'
. . . I said, 'I belong to the Lord and he can do whatever He wants to with me.'"
Fairchild performed at Mel Tillis's theater in 1992 and then at the venues of Glen
Campbell, Charlie Pride, and others. In addition to offering shows that mix gospel numbers with older pop hits, she and husband Roy operate Barbara Fairchild

Ministries and travel the United States singing and preaching at churches, fairs, and theaters. Their ministry blends evangelical Christianity with a patriotic, pro-life agenda that also advocates prayer in public schools, and the ministry's aims find their way into her Branson performances. Unapologetically explaining her station within the local tourism industry, she stated, "If they come see me they are going to get to hear about Him." And in a fashion that reflects the mind-set of many performers who couch their future in Branson in terms of godly providence, she maintained that predicting the play of divine will on her career is folly: "I don't know what the future holds, but I know who holds the future."[25]

Branson commentator Bruce Cook has written that "there isn't a show in town that doesn't include a few gospel numbers." He also could have added that most shows contain elements of Christian testimony. Singer Doug Gabriel could not get a job with any theater when he first came to the Ozarks. However, after he learned to "relax in God," auditions became available, and he began to "know the reality of Psalm 37:4" ("Take delight in the Lord, and he will give you the desires of your heart" [NRSV]). On stage, Gabriel is never hesitant to praise God for his Branson show and invites audience members to exude similar tribute.[26] Moreover, his father, Don, who is past president of the National Travel Agent Alliance and in 2005 founded BransonFunTrip (a team of travel specialists "dedicated to helping others experience the blessings of Branson"), has even more boldly proclaimed the evangelistic intentions of the city's entertainment industry:

> I believe God has raised up this community at this point of history for a ministry or a mission. . . . Maybe there is a couple praying for friends that need to know the Lord. They could bring them to Branson and take them to a number of shows. It would make wonderful opportunities to talk about the things of God in a very unthreatening way. In Branson they would have an opportunity to know Jesus. Many will not hear it in church but they will hear it in Branson up and down 76 Country Blvd. They'll hear it in song. They'll see it in deeds.[27]

Thus, for many a visit to one of Branson's musical venues involves much more than just enjoying variety acts heavily laced with pious song. The medium and the message are intricately bound together there and intend not only to reinforce the values and beliefs of people who are already Christians but also to recruit the nonbelievers by offering the possibility of conversion mediated by experiences of leisure. Warren Harmon, a member of Parkview Baptist Church in Decatur, Alabama, intoned this approach after bringing a group to Branson in 2004: "I'll recommend that our pastor talk to other pastors and ministers. . . . I'd tell them what a great atmosphere it would be and what a great evangelism effort it would be. With us, I've got people on my bus that are not churched, they just wanted to go on our trip to Branson. . . . So we're reaching out. It's like a mission effort."[28]

Well-known country-gospel stars such as the Gatlin Brothers have actualized Don Gabriel's call for Christian-infused Branson entertainment and recognized the curative effects of participation in this industry. As Larry Gatlin stated about the group's life prior to arrival in 1991, "We were emotionally and physically bankrupt." But once established in town, their theater proved to be a "miracle of God" that brought about sweeping personal change. Other marquee acts, however, have either failed to buy into the "Branson style" or offered performances in defiance of this template—actions that have led to their swift departure.[29]

In his discussion of Branson popular culture, anthropologist Damien Francaviglia suggested that a process of "local editing" administered by boosters and patrons safeguards the brand of entertainment and etiquette that must be followed by all performers. Citing a de facto ban placed on John Denver because he used profanity while on stage, the author intimated that this "family values" orientation is stringently enforced by a palpable yet uncodified set of rules that comply with conservative Christian dictates. For instance, many might have predicted the poor reception received by Merle Haggard when he became a Branson regular in 1992. A teenage runaway, frequenter of reform schools, and convicted felon who spent two and a half years in prison in the late 1950s, Haggard has built his career on an outlaw image. Although never known for gospel music, he was embraced by conservative political circles after he released his antihippy anthem "Okie from Muskogee" in 1969 and developed a relationship with Richard Nixon. These traditionalist credentials, however, were not enough to win him permanent support in Branson. Haggard lasted less than two years in town primarily because he refused to comply with the promotion of evangelical sentiment. As he alleged a few years after his departure: "Branson and me just don't mix. If you're not a born-again Christian, ready to stand up and tell them that, they won't even loan you money to build a place. If you don't believe as they do, then you're just out."[30]

Other Haggardesque performers have met with a similar fate in Branson. Willie Nelson, who originated country's "outlaw movement" in the 1970s as a means of recording outside the rules of the Nashville establishment, came to Branson in 1992 with IRS troubles and a history of illegal substance use. Although he was a good friend of local mainstay Mel Tillis, Nelson's stint at the Ozarks Theater lasted less than a year. By failing to augment his musicianship with glitzy stylings and sentimental tunes, and denying patrons the chance to symbolically absorb him into their own family because he performed infrequent dates, Nelson refused to "Bransonize" and thus had an aborted run in town.[31]

Johnny Cash, country music's legendary "Man in Black," came to Branson with a known affinity for prison culture and addictive drugs. However, by the late 1960s he had overcome his drug problems, made a public commitment to Christ, and even written a novel about the apostle Paul entitled *Man in White*—actions that would seem to have guaranteed him an audience in Branson. Ground was broken for his Cash Country amusement complex in October 1991. With the development 85 percent complete, primary investor David Green filed for Chapter 11 bankruptcy—a move that resulted in Cash receiving a $1.6 million settlement in 1993 for use of his name and shows contracted but not performed. From that point until his ultimate departure in November 1994, he occasionally sang at Wayne Newton's theater but was able (on average) to fill that venue only to 10 percent capacity. When he left Branson, Cash was coming off an incredibly successful year—one that saw the release of his critically acclaimed "American Recordings," an album that garnered him sellout crowds at Carnegie Hall and the Montreux Jazz Festival. Yet in spite of (and perhaps because of) this embrace by younger, more fashionable adults and those who had not trafficked in the country-and-western genre, he never was well received in Branson. Discussing his stay and implying that the Ozark audience was not a core body of admirers, he claimed, "I don't think I'm doing myself or my fans a favor by being here."[32]

Mel Tillis, a performer never associated with these renegade elements, sparked Branson's leap to nationwide prominence when he opened a theater in 1990. A composer of more than a thousand songs who first debuted on *Ozark Jubilee*, Tillis was on the road for thirty years before settling in Branson—a place he has described as a "miracle." His repertoire of traditional country and southern gospel made him a fan favorite prior to the conversion of his theater into an Assemblies of God church in 2002. Although this change is seemingly an odd transition, Tillis had for many years featured a morning show at his venue entitled "Smoke on the Mountain"—a musical story set in the 1930s which takes place at Mt. Pleasant Baptist Church in Mt. Pleasant, North Carolina, and one that showcased familiar hymns such as "Power in the Blood" and "Church in the Wildwood." Unlike Haggard, Nelson, and Cash, he readily embraced the religious climate and homey feel of Branson entertainment. As he stated about his decision to drop anchor in town, "You can go to church every Sunday and put your underwear in the same drawer every night." As Branson's entertainment history has demonstrated, the mere offering of country tunes laced with sacred numbers is not an assured recipe for success. An exhaustive embrace of hearth and pulpit must accompany these genres if one is to achieve longevity.[33]

In Don Cusic's history of gospel music, frequent Branson guest performer Barbara Mandrell offered an assessment of the relationship between the country sound and an evangelistic outlook which can be applied to all the city's performances: "Introducing a gospel song into a secular show has a larger strategy. . . . When I sing the gospel songs, they see something in my eyes that lets them know I mean what I'm singing about. . . . I've had kids who have gone back to church, that have gotten over family problems. Do you think they would have tuned into me had I been on a 'gospel' music show?" Over the past decade, numerous commentators have claimed that Branson has supplanted Nashville as the country music capital of the world. Although Nashville was built on a mix of country and gospel, that city has always been better known for its recording studios than its live music venues. As suggested by Mandrell's statement, Branson can be viewed as distinct from Nashville because it offers not only a style of musical entertainment that combines sacred and secular but also myriad "theater-churches" that facilitate the distribution of a Christian message through anti-institutional liturgies, celebrity clergy, and pop culture evangelism.[34]

NOSTALGIA AND THE SELLING OF SANCTUARY

Since the publication of *The Shepherd of the Hills,* tourists have traveled to the Ozarks in search of values deemed vanishing within the bewilderments of modernity. Vacationers have reaffirmed "lost" moral elements at sites such as the Shepherd of the Hills Homestead, Silver Dollar City, and the multitude of variety show theaters that continue to invoke home, rurality, and Christianity. National commentators on the Branson scene often have negatively appraised this embrace of nostalgia. For instance, in 1993, a writer for the *Village Voice* opined that area performers "cater to the phobia-driven inner life of the audience" through their presentations of "family, God, and country." A journalist for the *St. Petersburg (FL) Times* wrote in 1994 that people come to Branson because "they have found a place that looks, sounds, and acts like the America of their dreams, the one that they sense is eroding from the coasts inward." A writer for *Gentlemen's Quarterly* claimed that the town is a haven for Americans "feeling forsaken by the machinery of popular culture" who want to counterbalance the excesses of a contemporary milieu with entertainment that is "extremely anti-extreme." And finally, tour guide author Arthur Frommer wrote that Branson theaters are "a type of make believe, of denial, a fervent wish—if nothing else—a respite from the truths we otherwise face each day on our streets and on TV." Although meant as scathing commentaries, these urbane critiques are not totally accepted by most Branson visitors. Conservative syndicated columnist Cal Thomas has argued, "Some might laugh at Branson, but the town stands as a rebuke to much of the rest of the nation. . . . 'Sophisticates' who deride such things as unrealistic and not reflective of the times in which we live must give an account of the 'reality' they have imposed on the country. . . . This is a town that slime forgot."[35]

As Thomas's comments suggest, Branson's promotion of nostalgia entails a touristic retreat from modern or postmodern constructs of morality to a supposed sanctuary of wholesomeness devoid of the "slime" of gambling, alcohol, blue humor, lascivious presentations of the body, or secular philosophies. This citywide paradigm and its material manifestations led *TV Guide* columnist and *New York Times* book reviewer Joe Queenan to label Branson a "cultural penal colony" and a "Hades-by-the-Ozarks" that is "as close to Hell" as anything that he has ever seen. Alternately, Jay Scribner, who pastored Branson's First Baptist Church for twenty-five years and was the foremost ethical "policeman" of tourism offerings, addressed the uprightness of that industry when he stated, "My favorite phrase about Branson, and I've said it for years, is, 'Branson, Missouri is America the way it ought to be.' I'm convinced that if every community in America was like Branson, the United States of America would be like Branson, a wonderful place to be." Both comments clearly revolve around the infusion of religious sentiment into the city's leisure opportunities and the perceived sociocultural repercussions of this mixture. Both obviously also demonstrate a liberal/conservative tension within American culture related to the merits of historical remembrance and reenactment. As with all presentations of wistfulness, the Ozark industry has chosen to accentuate a created past while bedeviling a created present. By examining both, one deemed decent but waning and the other decadent but waxing, one becomes aware of the moral anxieties supposedly rebuffed by Branson entertainment.[36]

Within a tourism industry predicated on the accentuation of bifurcations, the divide between city and country originally emphasized by local marketers even prior to the arrival of Harold Bell Wright still fuels Branson's version of nostalgia. In 1987, Lecil Travis Martin (a.k.a. Boxcar Willie) became the first nationally acclaimed star to own his own theater in Branson. Known for an embrace of train songs and the hobo lifestyle, Boxcar achieved great success prior to his death in 1999 and opened a motel and museum next to his popular venue. Although he grew up in a three-room tool shed adjacent to the railroad tracks

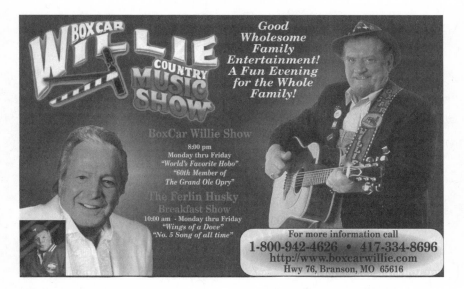

Boxcar Willie Country Music Show advertisement, 1999. From the author's collection

in Sterratt, Texas, his definition of poverty speaks to the various ways that rural experiences are given an air of ethical purity and urban lifestyles are in part demonized within Ozark tourism.

In a 1989 interview, Boxcar Willie recounted a visit to New York City with his wife, Lloene. Initially overwhelmed by the traffic from the airport into the heart of Manhattan, the couple later found the city's human composition no better than its swarm of automobiles. As he recounted, "When we got out, I bet we stepped over a hundred drunks. There was some gang on a street corner. . . . Lloene was wearing her diamond rings, and I told her to turn those rocks around and we hightailed it." Although many might not posit a distinction between the homeless who so repulsed the singing star and his own stage identity, he described this differentiation as unwavering: "Let me tell you, there's a big difference between hoboes and bums. Those folks I saw on the sidewalks of New York are bums. Hoboes were just transient workers. . . . Bums make me mad, there's so many of them strangling up this country. There are plenty of jobs out there if people just want to work, but they'd rather be on welfare."[37] Thus, while the itinerant, rural, and good-natured railroad traveler is wrapped in rhetoric of freedom and virtue, his ominous city-dwelling counterpart is depicted as inherently malevolent and content to be on the government dole—sentiments that speak to geographic, ideological, and political divides highlighted within Branson tourism. Reiterating this dichotomy and the ineffable and increasingly rare character of the locale, one tourist commented, "Word's can't really describe it. . . . [There are] not many places like that, that are left to go see." As the town's self-proclaimed "unofficial morality cop," Boxcar Willie presented a brand of nostalgia that made even the vagabonds of rural America into exemplars of a principled life. Eight decades after Harold Bell Wright's place-defining novel, he continued to conceive of Branson as an uncompromising site for the valorization of rustic righteousness and to "thank the good Lord" for his success.[38]

Despite such pastoral attitudes, visitors to Branson for the past hundred years have wanted their bucolic vacation experience accompanied by the contemporary comforts of home. As an Oklahoma tourist asserted, "It's an old fashioned, yet modern place." Addressing this amalgamation, a writer for the *Economist* claimed that the contemporary Ozark vacationer is seeking "the American ideal of *urbs* in *rus,* city glamour in mountain quiet," or "something very close to ideal and eternal life." Variously branded "Mayberry meets Las Vegas" or "Las Vegas without the sin," Branson continues to extol country life. But amid aesthetic flamboyance, it also seeks to offer a vision of shackled urbanity—an image of metropolis perhaps as contradictory as the city's most recent chamber of commerce slogan that proclaims Branson as the perfect combination of "neon and nature."[39]

The primary purveyors of such nostalgia within contemporary Branson entertainment are the bevy of aging pop stars who have arrived over the past fifteen years. Andy Williams initiated this turn when he opened his 2,000-seat Moon River Theatre in 1992. Built into the side of a limestone formation, designed by Frank Lloyd Wright devotee Warren Bates, and eclectically decorated with modern sculptures by Willem de Kooning and Henry Moore, this $11 million project is a far cry from the tobacco barns that dominated the Strip prior to the 1990s. The design of Williams's venue, however, was consciously meant as a diversion from traditional Branson architecture, just as his presentation of popular rather than country music was meant to depart from previous entertainment offerings. As his manager, Tennyson Flowers, explained, "The idea, you see, was to take these natural cliffs and have an urban building rising out of it. Using the natural thing, this is the concept—that we're combining the urban with country."[40]

Although Williams's theater acquiesced to a partial rural aesthetic, his sometimes coarse demeanor—gleaned from many years on the Las Vegas nightclub circuit—almost spelled his theatrical demise even prior to his arrival. In January 1992, he stated in the *Nashville Tennessean* that he was surprised at the success of many local acts and that he had deliberated deeply before deciding on his move:

"I had never heard of Branson—I wasn't interested in having some theater in f-cking Branson. . . . I think that the acts in Branson have been having a joy ride because there are all those people over there, and the shows, a lot of them, are just crap." Entertainers and tourists alike interpreted these comments as a rebuke of Branson's folksy and wholesome offerings, and comedian and musician Jim Stafford defended the "authentic" nature of area entertainment when he asserted, "People pick on country music all the time. Of course, you're not going to walk into a Branson theater and see 'Equus.' But you're going to see good family entertainment. The players are good, the singers are good. It's real people playing real music." To make amends and to display his allegiance to local mindsets and ethical vantages, Williams's opening-night performance was a benefit for the conservative College of the Ozarks' Camp Lookout (a Christian summer camp for needy Taney County children). Raising $40,000 and winning front-page coverage in the *Springfield News-Leader,* the event resituated a performer deemed out of the Ozark fold within the local entertainment prototype, thereby demonstrating Williams's ability to "Bransonize."[41]

Currently, tickets to the Moon River Theatre are among the most sought after in town because Williams has mostly consented to the Branson archetype and infuses his act with requisite religious and patriotic numbers. Although he still does not do country songs because he "does not want to intrude on what's established here," trademark pieces such as "Moon River" and "September Song" similarly evoke a more innocent age and may even spawn propitious visions that quiet the tumult of modern life. As a Japanese fan hoping to visit the Ozarks avowed, "Branson is something special place. I feel I may be able to find my dreamland. . . . Andy's warm voice makes me a woman with a gentle heart." Despite his complicity with local standards, Williams's approach to entertainment is still sometimes tinged with controversy. For instance, in 2003, he even briefly bucked the city's unwritten rule of theater temperance by offering beer and wine to his guests—a move that produced much consternation among visiting church groups. Notwithstanding such glitches, he has become Branson's most successful vendor of nostalgia and opened the door for many performers outside the country or gospel scene.[42]

One pop showman who tried to follow in Williams's footsteps was Wayne Newton. In May 1993, he launched a 3,000-seat theater in Branson. Though known for his Las Vegas panache, Newton was raised in Roanoke, Virginia, and toured with the Grand Ole Opry road show at the age of ten—facts that at least provided a bit of country currency on his arrival. However, his abbreviated stay in Branson had less to do with style and more to do with what might be termed personal substance. Like Williams, Newton put on a benefit when he first came to town, a show that raised several thousand dollars for the College of the Ozarks. Despite this gesture, however, the presence of curse words and other "racy" elements in his show led the college to refuse his money. More problems quickly followed. At the close of his first season, in which his leased theater filled to only 50 percent capacity, its owners put it up for sale. One month later, Newton sued the company for $5 million, claiming that the show was mismanaged and his reputation tarnished. In April 1994, the singer was officially fired and left Branson to tend to a pending personal bankruptcy case in Nevada.[43]

Beginning in 1995, Newton returned to Branson for occasional performances. In 1998, he teamed with Tony Orlando for an act at the Talk of the T.O.W.N. (an acronym for Tony Orlando Wayne Newton) Theatre. Following that season, this collaboration went sour, and the duo split. Subsequently, Orlando sued Newton for $15 million, contending that his partner violated terms of their agreement. Newton countersued for $20 million, claiming that Orlando had disseminated false statements while perhaps hoping to win over Ozark vacationers by stating that he would keep his former partner "in [his] prayers." Newton is known for his incredibly loyal and sometimes maniacal admirers. Echoing the sentiments of many, enthusiast Sue Baker claimed, "The thing that keeps me coming back is the man, the way he relates to you. It's like spending an evening with a relative and an old friend." Creating a sense of familiarity has always been vital to the success of Branson entertainment. Because Newton's controversies denied his ardent fans this ability to situate him within a psychic domestic sphere, he fulfilled the premonitions of many who doubted that he could comply with the "just folks" attitude on which Ozark entertainment was built. Though he could croon nostalgic numbers such as "Danke Scheon," he could not avoid being labeled "too Vegas" for Branson. In October 1999, Newton signed a ten-year contract with that Nevada city's Stardust Casino and thus returned to a place where ethical circumstances are lesser determinants for success. Applauding this departure and citing Newton's poor fit in the region, vacationer Peg Adams stated, "He's not Branson. We went home for the winter and he did too. But he never came back."[44]

Both Andy Williams's and Wayne Newton's productions have always included the mandatory gospel numbers that characterize all Branson shows, but neither explicitly emphasized Christian themes. However, other pop icons have mimicked the area's long-established fusion of religion and leisure nearly perfectly. Alan, Jay, and Merrill Osmond (siblings of Donny and Marie) opened the Osmond Family Theatre in 1992, and it remained in operation for a decade. These brothers and more than thirty other family members were brought to Branson by Andy Williams, who had launched their career on his television show in the 1960s. Reliving their adolescent successes of the 1970s, the performers offered tunes that reflected their decades-long promotion of clean-cut values. In 1994, they described the impulse that prompted their move from Utah to the Ozarks: "Branson is an oasis. America is going down the toilet." Claiming that God's work is in the process of being systematically undone by secularized politics and liberal media, Merrill Osmond cited the evangelistic capabilities of Branson entertainment in the face of a less than virtuous nation when he asserted, "The problem is, we don't have enough role models that have the basics figured out that can preach to the masses the correct way."[45]

Since its debut, the Osmond Brothers Show, which now performs limited engagements in Branson, has been filled with all the patented elements of reminiscence. Including in their show musical styles ranging from barbershop quartet, to big band, to country hoedown, to pop, these poster boys of a more innocuous era are conceivably the prime example of marketed nostalgia. As tour guide authors Kate Klise and Crystal Payton have written, "If Branson didn't exist, the Osmonds would've had to invent it." Seemingly out of context, the brothers frequently end their act with religious melodies such as "'Till We Meet at Jesus' Feet" backed by giant watercolor portraits of Christ beamed on the stage. The Osmonds were the first of an ever growing contingent of Mormon performers in Branson which now includes the Hughes, Dutton, and Lowe families. All of them take advantage of a well-known Latter-day Saints missionary impulse coupled with a theological vantage that posits things spiritual as refined essences of the material world. Moreover, because the Book of Mormon describes the United States as "a land which is choice above all other lands," the church's promotion of American exceptionalism nicely meshes with similar Ozark fusions of God and nation. The ability to theatrically enact these religious perspectives within a tourism climate that prizes extended families, heralds procreative inclinations, and values temperance has thus made Branson a site ripe for Mormon-operated entertainment.[46]

Jimmy Osmond, who operates the American Jukebox Theater, is also frequently a guest star at Branson's many special Christmas productions. Over the past decade, Christmastime tourism has become incredibly popular, making the city one of America's most renowned holiday destinations and exemplifying its Christian-themed nostalgia. Since 1949, the city's Adoration Parade has kicked off the season on the first Sunday of December with purposely noncommercial floats and the lighting of a 40-foot-high Nativity scene. Lauding this approach while attending a 2003 event that drew twenty-five thousand onlookers, Rex Jensen stated, "It's the way things ought to be. It tends to put the real purpose of Christmas into perspective." Although the aim of "Ozark Mountain Christmas" seems to be the castigation of the materiality of the modern holiday, it reaps huge profits from an avowedly nonconsumptive fete. As religious historian Leigh Eric Schmidt has observed, the twentieth century was wrought with Christian protests against a mounting "consumer gospel" that seemed to overtake heartfelt and meaningful memorializing of Christ's birth. Branson boosters, fully aware of this tension and seeking to assure their visitors that they stress the devotional aspects of the season, chose an unambiguously Christian moniker for their citywide celebration.[47]

This negotiation of seasonal title was described by Claudia Vecchio, former vice president for communications at the Branson/Lakes Area Chamber of Commerce and Convention and Visitor's Bureau, in a September 2002 interview:

> The interesting juggling act is as Branson grows, the goal is to attract more visitors. Calling ourselves a Christian destination does limit us. For some people here that's a very good limitation and they prefer that that be our target market. . . . We're Ozark Mountain Christmas not Ozark Mountain Holiday Season. There's absolutely no escaping and nobody really wants to, the Christian overtones of Branson.[48]

Central to clarifying an appropriate holiday designation is the conscious subsuming of the secular to the sacred within variety show Christmas pageants. For example, Tony Orlando has offered his "Santa & Me" for more than a decade. The crescendo of the production is a moment in which Santa hands a Nativity scene to the performer. According to Orlando, in doing so the figure who symbolizes the worldly aspects of the holiday becomes "a soldier of Christ." The singer, who is well known for thoroughly melding Branson's triptych of God, family, and country, admits that such sentiments might not be welcomed in other parts of the nation, but they are guaranteed a warm reception in a "a place that stands for all that makes America great."[49]

The popular Christmas show offered by Trinity Broadcasting Network (TBN) mainstays Dino and Cheryl Kartsonakis is a prime illustration of wistful Christmas renderings that assure tourists that the "real" reason for the season is not forgotten in Branson. Dino, a flamboyant pianist sometimes labeled the "Liberace of the gospel set," claims that the turning point in his career came when he played a solo show at an Assemblies of God convention in Springfield, Missouri. He recorded his first of forty albums in 1963, received a Grammy nomination

Dino's Christmas Extravaganza brochure, 2000. From the author's collection

for his "Chariots of Fire," and spent many years traveling with the healing and miracle ministry of Kathryn Kuhlman. As the host of a weekly TBN program entitled *The Dino Show,* Kartsonakis has for many years been the foremost Ozark booster among Pentecostal and charismatic Christians.[50]

Dino first performed his Christmas show in 1991 at the Mel Tillis Theater. Although this act has relocated from venue to venue in Branson, it continues to draw large crowds. At a 2002 performance I attended alongside more than a thousand other patrons, Kartsonakis and his wife prefaced their holiday spectacular by reminding attendees that they were there to "celebrate the Birthday of Jesus," to observe "the true meaning of Christmas," and to witness a presentation "based on the word of God." The entire first act was filled with similar homage, as sequined singers offered rousing versions of sacred Christmas music and Dino accompanied in an emblazoned tuxedo. Somewhat surprisingly, the second act opened with an appearance by Santa and the performance of large-scale secular numbers. These arrangements extolled the virtues of gift giving and merriment in a setting of nuclear families apparently unaffected by the anxieties of the contemporary holiday. Although deference to modern (although nostalgically presented) Christmas seemed to diverge from the production's earlier focus on sanctity, the show's finale more than reaffirmed the basic message. After a solemn rendition of "Silent Night," peculiar cherubim appeared on stage, a Nativity scene was lowered from above, and Dino and Cheryl dropped to their knees in prayer. Following a few moments of divine entreaty, Dino displayed three balls skewered onto a metal rod: one gold (representing God), one black (representing evil), and one blue (representing humanity). Dino claimed that, like the aligned balls, human beings are separated from God by sin. He then dramatically removed the black sphere with a crucifix, declaring that Jesus can similarly eliminate such moral tarnishes from our lives. He also noted that, even with the evil ball gone, humanity is still estranged from the supernatural. Many in the crowd vocally concurred and departed from what had been a predominantly jovial celebration with a somber reminder of their own iniquity.

For more than a decade, Kartsonakis has offered nostalgically motivated entertainment and promoted the Ozarks as a place where leisure is accompanied by divine sanction. As he has stated:

This town was founded on Christianity. . . . Churches throughout the US are becoming more aware of what's happening in Branson. They're wanting to come here not only for the entertainment, but to feel the presence of God. When they come to Branson they feel protected because the town is covered with the blessings of God. I am an entertainer, and I love to entertain, but I'm first a Christian. When people come to any of our shows, yes, they will see the glitz and the glamour of the costumes, the dancers, the lavish sets, all the entertainment part, but just before I do my finale I take five minutes and present the gospel of Jesus Christ. We have thousands of people coming to our shows, but not one of them can ever say they never heard the gospel.[51]

Within this quotation, one can locate many complexities that accompany the mixture of longing and religiosity in Branson. According to Kartsonakis, the city can function as a location for popular religious missionary work not only because of "the presence of God" but also because vacationers can emerge from their recreational experiences "nourished and refreshed." Affirming this sentiment, a fan from Georgia asserted after attending a show, "What a blessing I received. . . . The joy of the Lord spills out all over you. Thanks for blessing me and thanks for lifting Jesus high." Moreover, claims of miraculous healing have even arisen from the Kartsonakises' Branson productions. Cheryl recounted about their 2002 Easter Show, "A gentleman up in the nose-bleed section of The Grand Palace received a healing on his knees. He had been a carpet layer and his knees were damaged. He had a hard time walking. It's just awesome to see what God does for people."[52]

Certainly not all Branson shows that engage in remembrances and re-creations of the past have Dino Kartsonakis's overt Christian tones. However, lack of explicit religiosity does not preclude a forthright codification of appropriate ideals. In recent years, for example, Branson has witnessed a number of productions that take various decades of American history as their subject. In one such production, "Lost in the Fifties," a series of poodle skirts, greasers, and doo-wop hits may at first seem devoid of any overarching value structure. A review by the *Branson Church Getaway Planner,* a periodical distributed at the rate of eighty thousand copies a year to church groups throughout the country, suggested otherwise:

Mike Meece [the show's producer and director who also functioned in a similar capacity for the gospel-based musicals *The Promise* and *Two from Galilee*] finds a different and unique way to communicate eternal truths. He captures an era, then uses great music, festive dancing, and even comedy to once again probe every nook and cranny of our hearts. But something else happens. If we look for it, we will note a deft and subtle hand at work, once again underscoring those precious core values that bring blessings to our lives, and as history has proven, have brought blessings to our nation.[53]

Thus, at least in this reviewer's opinion, "eternal truths" must not necessarily possess a divine referent. Within the Branson milieu, they can even be located at the most understated and glib of locales.

Ron Layher, the owner of the Starlite Theatre (where "Lost in the Fifties" is staged), approaches this endeavor from a decidedly business-oriented perspective but has phrased its popularity in terms of marketing re-created values. Claiming that the show is "selling a memory," Layher candidly expressed the workings of nostalgia in a fashion that could apply to most Branson productions: "The truth of the matter is the fifties music, if you just look at the music itself, wasn't that good. We remember it as that good because we want to. It was pretty thin. . . . But we sell the time. We do the old music done like they want to hear it today and they think that's the way it was." Further commenting on "Lost in the Seventies," a similar jaunt down memory lane that opened during the 2003 season, Layher added, "Now the seventies was totally different. The seventies is a time that people don't necessarily have positive memories about the era. But the music was wonderful. . . . When we produce the seventies we will emphasize the music and not the era." Layher's collective observations express what all other Branson entertainment implies—that tourists are not looking for documentary renderings of historical turmoil or even accurate presentations of musical genre or style. Instead, they want gentle reminders and placid memories, all enveloped in a staging of "eternal truths" that evade the stings and arrows of the past rather than trying to heal them.[54]

In a 2002 interview with Dan Lennon, director of marketing at Branson's Welk Theatre and Resort and performer in that venue's swing music morning show, he discussed an act entitled "Century of American Music," which was staged the previous year. Describing this production, which featured hit songs from the 1960s, he portrayed that decade as "serious and dark" and held that "the cultural shifts that happened at that time have mixed feelings for the senior audience." As this age group is the Welk Theatre's primary draw, an era of strife and protest was represented by the music of Burt Bacharach and other "non-threatening" crooners. Defending this interpretation and claiming that one of the hallmarks of the Branson industry is its lack of "cynicism," Lennon asserted, "We're not obliged to put on a definitive history of the music. We're obliged to put on an entertainment product that pleases a lot of people."[55]

Although essayist Jerry Rodnitzky claimed that he "inadvertently found Harding's 1920s in Branson" during his visit, it seems clear that the millions of annual tourists to Branson do not come in search of accurate portrayals of the 1950s, 1960s, 1970s, or any other time period. However, they often do arrive believing that the place offers opportunities to glimpse at and perhaps internalize systems of morality and religious dictates from a very distant past. This, of course, is the myth first described by Harold Bell Wright and still glorified within the contemporary tourism market. Describing this dynamic, a vacationer from Arkansas stated in the late 1990s, "I feel at peace, harmonious, tranquil. In the middle of the busiest place I feel comfortable. . . . The Ozarks offer a simple way for most people. Look to the history of the Ozarks, the people who settled, and what they are about." Thus, it is not a specific sociocultural context that is desired but rather a set of virtues or truths that continue to be associated with this regional past and which are given the promise of return through vacationary implication. Reflecting on time spent away from town, Dan Lennon claimed, "Branson feels like it's far away from the world." By fostering this sense of otherworldliness, the city becomes a sanctuary for pilgrims fleeing the present and a site for nostalgic reminiscence about a time that never was.[56]

GOD AND COUNTRY

In an influential 1966 essay, sociologist Robert Bellah introduced the concept of "civil religion." Citing the possibility of ideological consensus forged around notions of religious nationalism rather than official Christianity, he dated the emergence of such functionalist spirituality to the dawn of the nation. As he wrote, "What we have then, from the earliest years of the republic is a collection of beliefs, symbols, and rituals, with respect to sacred things and institutionalized in a collectivity," attitudes thus capable of creating a nationally bound "church." Despite intoning the ability of America's foundational political documents and religiously motivated archetypes (Exodus, Chosen People, Promised Land, and so on) to bind individuals within an ever differentiating society, Bellah's essay is primarily a lamentation. In the face of mounting conflict in Vietnam, he expressed trepidation about nationalism left untempered by the ethical motifs of conventional religion. Addressing a demise of shared values in The Broken Covenant (1975), he pleaded for a "common set of moral understandings necessary for both cultural legitimation and a standard of critique for society." With "concerns over virtue" trumped by the "success ideal," a reinvention of overarching symbolic structures able to bind disparate individuals was now described as lost within the "nightmare" of modernity.[57]

Since publication of The Broken Covenant, few sociologists have commented on civil religiosity. However, in the wake of the terrorist attacks of September 11, 2001, expressions of religious nationalism reemerged in a variety of contexts.

Although intensified patriotism and a stronger alliance between nation and godly mission are viewed by many Americans as recent phenomena, civil religiosity is not a new subject in Branson. As Richard Freihofer, publisher of the *Branson Church Getaway Planner,* stated in an interview a little over one year after September 11, 2001:

> We get criticized by Arthur Frommer or whoever for jamming religion down people's throats or being really schlocky with waiving the flag in everybody's face. It's in fashion now because of the events of September 11th. . . . So suddenly we're waking up to who we are. We represent something, and the flag represents something. Maybe Branson isn't so corny after all. That's part of what Branson is and this is what people can't orchestrate. We're speaking to something in people's hearts.[58]

Further substantiating links between devotion to country and devotion to God within Branson tourism, Raeanne Presley (of the Presleys' Country Jubilee) acknowledged, "Almost all of us tend to have some type of a gospel segment that's very godly. . . . It's also very patriotic. [We did this] long before September 11th, when this seemed more popular and the thing to do."[59]

In fact, following the tragedies of 2001, a debate raged in Branson concerning the sectarian nature of the town's civil religious presentations. The Chamber of Commerce and Convention and Visitor's Bureau decided to respond to the events by means of a series of public service announcements broadcast on area television stations. Then vice president of communications, Claudia Vecchio, sent out an invitation to local entertainers soliciting their participation and encouraging them to make their message "faith-based" rather than "Christian-based" (as she felt that these stations would not air a message connected with a specific religious tradition). In her words, "By the end of the week I was the Antichrist. . . . Paul Harvey without calling said that the Chamber of Commerce was not letting its entertainers talk about faith in their commercial messages. . . . Very definitely this is a Christian-based community." Thus, unlike Bellah's notion of civil religion—one that suggested an ecumenical understanding of nation as object of veneration—Branson's version of the concept has always imagined the United States as safeguarded by a distinct formulation of the Christian deity. This message is fortified by the rousing patriotic finales and mandatory tributes to veterans found at each and every theatrical venue. In embracing this mode of civil religion, the city has become a model for American identity rather than the aberration criticized by a bevy of journalists. This transformation was highlighted by local entertainer Bucky Heard: "After September 11, the way people looked at Branson changed. People used to make fun of us—that we dropped the flag at every show, that we were hokey. To me, the rest of America could take a lesson from Branson."[60]

Branson hosted its first Veterans Day parade in 1934 and has continued the tradition ever since. It was 1993, however, that marked the beginning of a more forthright association between the city and civic worship. That year, Tony Orlando was the grand marshal of the Veterans Day parade and afterward emceed the "First Annual Yellow Ribbon Salute to Veterans." This tribute marked the earliest conscious targeting of veterans as a niche market. In 2000, more than one-third of Branson's seven million visitors were veterans and their family members. A 1999 economic impact study revealed that this demographic spent more than $109 million in November alone. Currently, the city sponsors the nation's largest Veterans Day celebration—a week-long festival titled "Veteran's Homecoming." The commemoration annually attracts approximately 150,000 former soldiers and their relatives, and its events are frequently punctuated with reference to John 15:13 ("No one has greater love than this, than to lay down one's life for one's friends" [NRSV]).[61]

Spearheading the patriotic veneration is the Branson Veterans Task Force—a nonprofit organization founded in 1997 which advances the motto "Honoring America's Veterans Every Day." Intent on making Branson a "mecca of veterandom," the group sponsors the city's yearly celebration, which currently includes more than sixty special events for former soldiers and garners participation from the Osmonds, the Gatlin Brothers, the Oak Ridge Boys, and many other Branson regulars. Because of these efforts and the ever present nationalistic sentiment at local theaters, Branson was given a "Stewards of Freedom Award" in 2000 by the National Flag Foundation for being the most patriotic city in America.[62]

Patriotic feelings are further enshrined at Branson's Veterans Memorial Museum, a venue that sits enveloped by flags on the town's Strip. The museum contains 18,000 square feet of exhibits and artifacts, along with personal pictures and emotional stories shared by families that lost loved ones in major battles. Composed of five sections, the museum covers World War I, World War II, Korea, Vietnam, and Desert Storm. Branson's first "Veteran's Homecoming" focused on World War II, and afterward some people felt that the city favored this age cohort (a group that was at the forefront of a senior tourism explosion of the early 1990s). As a result, since 1995 greater emphasis has been placed on veterans of more recent wars.

At the museum, a placard for the Vietnam War claims that the truth about this conflict "remains elusive," that what most people know about it was "generated by fragmentary and incomplete reporting," and that, however the war is judged, "the Vietnam veteran got a raw deal." Fred Smith, who fought in Southeast Asia, visited Branson in 2001. Attesting to the ways that the city intentionally caters to soldiers of "unpopular" wars, Smith stated, "One of the best parts of Branson was that every show we went to always recognized veterans. They had them stand up to pay honor to them. . . . There are a lot of veterans, especially from Vietnam, who haven't been appreciated. No one's ever said thank you." The purpose of all veteran-oriented events is to offer visitors a sense of respite that mimics the town's more general orientation toward nostalgia. By giving museum space to more recent and less valorized wars or singling out individuals who fought in these conflicts, the events are moved from the world of active debate into the realm of history—a bastion that within the tourism industry is not open to interpretation.[63]

In a room at the museum dedicated to captured artifacts from Nazi Germany and imperial Japan, a disclaimer reads, "Their display should in no way be taken as an endorsement of the beliefs or ideologies of our enemies. Far from it; the Veterans Memorial Museum has no sympathy for the beliefs of America's enemies." Further described as "tangible symbols of our triumph over evil," such objects (and the civil religiosity they represent) are implicated in the staunch production of dualisms that pervade Branson entertainment. Patriotism, like Christianity, is a put forth as a given for visitors. In a Manichaean world of absolute right and unconditional wrong—one that draws thick lines of ethical separation between religious and nonreligious, country and city, and old-fashioned and modern—debating the merits of military conflict (like arguing the intrinsic worth of other heralded categories of meaning) is not encouraged.

As mentioned, Branson's civil religiosity finds a home not only at veteran-focused events but also at each and every entertainment venue. Mike Radford, a motivational speaker, author, and performer billed as "America's Ambassador of Patriotism," stages the long-running "Remember When" show. Although this is primarily a patriotic set, Radford has described its dawn in a manner that is replete with signifiers of both nation and the divine:

> The "Remember When Show" was born on a lonely stretch of Wisconsin highway when an "angel" appeared to me in 1993. The evening sun was beginning to set, and I watched in awe as great American bald eagles soared high above the valley. Suddenly I noticed a van in the slow lane ahead of me. I could see the words painted on the spare tire cover, "The Men and Women Who Died for Our Country Must Never Be Forgotten!" An elderly man sat behind the wheel. As I pulled alongside, I smiled and gave him a "thumbs-up." He rolled down the window, pointed upward,

then covered his heart and pointed to me. I knew then I had to create a show that would honor his generation, the generation that literally saved the world. "Is this what you want me to do, Lord?" I prayed. "Is this my destiny?" God answered me by flooding my heart with indescribable joy. And the "Remember When" show was born![64]

Moreover, echoing the sentiments of most, if not all, Branson entertainers and brusquely pronouncing his religious nationalism in now familiar dichotomous terms, he stated, "You're either a believer in this nation and its tenets of God, family, and country, or you're not. I was taught there's only right and wrong. There's no gray area."[65]

Comedian Yakov Smirnoff first began performing in Branson in 1993 and opened his own theater in 1997. Through basing his act on a personal journey from Communist to American nationalist, he presents himself as a living example of Mike Radford's contention: "We [Branson entertainers] don't 'promote' patriotism—We are patriotism." In 1977, Smirnoff and his family immigrated to the United States from the Soviet Union with little money and no knowledge of English. In 1993, while performing his comedy act at a Farm Aid concert, he was told about Branson by Willie Nelson and decided to try his hand in that market. Smirnoff's success in town has been predicated on the debasing of a Communist government that had collapsed well before his arrival. Merging a barrage of patriotic hymns with clean humor that often belittles his former home country, Smirnoff exalts the United States. In addition, within a rousing finale he dances with the Statue of Liberty, explodes fireworks, and describes working in Branson as living the American dream. Immediately before coming to town he referred to his new location as "the land of opportunity" and has since stated that "God guides us to the place where we can really do the most service." Thus, in this rendering Branson becomes the hub of patriotic inculcation and the prime national example of a place where the opportunities and blessings of citizenship can come to fruition. Confirming the efficacy of these methods, a New York tourist stated," He is more american than alot of americans I know. Thank god for having him in the U.S.A."[66]

In 2004, a production entitled "Celebrate America" opened at Branson's Mansion America theater. No area spectacle better demonstrates how the promotion of patriotism becomes wrapped in other key industry themes. "Celebrate America" was the brainchild of Gene Bicknell. Bicknell was born into a mining family, eventually rose to prominence in the business world (he owns five hundred Pizza Huts), and has showcased his theatrical talents in dozens of film, television,

Yakov Smirnoff advertisement, 1998. From the author's collection

and stage roles. Set in the midwestern town of Promise, the show begins with a heart-to-heart discussion between a grandpa (Bicknell) and a granddaughter who is grieving over her father going off to war. Recounting the greatness of the nation from colonial times to the present, the production takes onlookers on a whirlwind singing and dancing tour through various archetypal periods and events within U.S. history (the founding fathers, the opening of the West, the construction of railroads, the 1904 St. Louis World's Fair, World War II, and so on). As one might expect based on prior discussions of nostalgia, every epoch and episode is offered in a manner that resists tumultuous circumstances, cultural strife, and other inconvenient historical details that might convolute a clear vision of American exceptionalism. Moreover, prominent in the mythical town square and nearly every scene of this nationalistic melodrama is the Church of Promise. The centrality of that sanctuary and Christianity at large is made evident within the finale when performers present a rousing rendition of "The Battle Hymn of the Republic." By way of this hasty tour through the nation's "past," "Celebrate America" thus hopes to demonstrate a generational continuity of excellence and achievement underscored by divine mandate. Although this show is the city's most forthright staging of such themes, all venues replicate its intentions. Reflecting this pervasiveness and its intended affect on future generations, a seventy-two-year-old Arizona tourist wrote, "The shows we saw are uplifting, patriotic and clean! Think of the world we are creating for our grandchildren!"[67]

On September 11, 2002, the "American Highrise" mural was unveiled on an exterior wall of the Grand Palace theater in Branson and serves as a mammoth reminder of the city's civil religiosity. This painting, a quarter of an acre in size, offers a view of downtown New York set upon an American flag background and bordered by the sayings "One Nation Under God" and "We the People, United We Stand." The image was created by Richard Daniel Clark, an Australian native who now resides in Branson. In 1989, it was chosen by George Bush as his presidential inaugural artwork. Since then, it has been displayed at the National Archives and the Statue of Liberty, on board most U.S. aircraft carriers, and at roughly 250 military bases around the world. In addition, it has been accepted as a gift by more than seventy world leaders, including the Reverend Billy Graham and Pope John Paul II (making it the first piece of art featuring the Stars and Stripes to be admitted into the Vatican Archives). According to a Web site that discusses the painting's history, such worldwide dissemination will soon make "American Highrise" "the most personally viewed piece of art in modern times" and, by association, situates Branson as a vital site for the propagation of its premises.[68]

The emergence of the Christian Right as a viable political force in 1980s is well documented and thus prompts one to consider the connections between the rise of this movement and the development of Branson as a tourist region catering to a similar brand of religious nationalism. As mentioned in Chapter 1, Ronald Reagan's conversion to Christianity was facilitated by Harold Bell Wright's vision of applied faith. During Reagan's first term in office, Jerry Falwell's Moral Majority exerted considerable influence over his administration. Introducing the notion of "family values" into common parlance (terminology employed by every booster of the Branson industry), evangelicals such as Falwell, Pat Robertson,

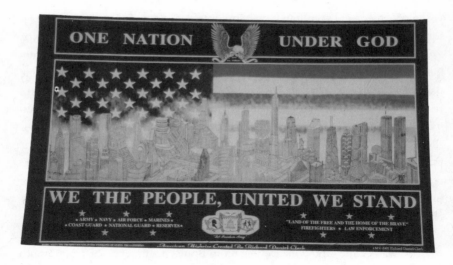

"American Highrise" mural, 2001. Photo by the author

and Tim LaHaye fiercely lobbied throughout the 1980s to revitalize America's ethical underpinnings. Meanwhile, the ever mounting number of theaters in Branson echoed such sentiments, albeit within a more muted recreational context. The city's emergence as a national destination in the 1980s coincided with other expressions of evangelical popular culture (e.g., Christian music, literature, and film). Reflecting on the growth of this subculture in a manner that keenly resonates with Ozark entertainment, Erling Jorstad commented that once insular evangelicals began during the Reagan era to emphasize more greatly how "God works in all activities of their everyday lives" and therefore created popular culture geared toward expressing that faith.[69]

Throughout Branson's rise to national prominence in the 1990s, numerous conservative Christian political leaders recognized the correspondence between the city's principles and their policy initiatives. Realizing the importance of evangelicals for his campaign and locating Branson as that constituency's leisure hub, President George Bush in 1992 chose Silver Dollar City as the place to emphasize his "family values" message and celebrate his nomination to a second term of office. In 1996, Ralph Reed, executive director of the Christian Coalition, spoke to a crowd of more than a thousand people at a local theater, where he attacked the evils of gambling, homosexuality, the liberal media, and "environmental wackos." Similarly, former presidential candidate and televangelist Pat Robertson addressed a large assembly of tourists in 1998. During his speech, he chided "political correctness" that discouraged talking about God in public arenas, reiterated his stance that the United States was founded by Christians, and suggested that Branson was crucial for the promotion of such sentiments because it was "the heartland of America." Finally, John Ashcroft, whose political involvement in the area was outlined in Chapter 3, blurred the lines between politics and show business when he, Senate majority leader Trent Lott, and a number of other conservative congressmen sang for a throng of onlookers at a local theater in 1997.[70]

According to American studies scholar Robert Schmuhl, "Branson is a metaphor for red state America. . . . The town represents what many conservative people in the Midwest see as America, the America they want, the America they hold in their heads from yesterday. Maybe it is part mythical—but it's the America they want to cling to." Central to this utopian and fabled construct is an unabashed melding of God and country. This union underscores a belief by the tourism industry and vacationers alike that the vitality of the nation depends on regular beseeching of divine sanction and a perpetual acknowledgment of America's providential status. With such civil religiosity gaining traction in the 1980s and fully emerging amid post–September 11 rhetoric of American exceptionalism, Branson has become the national point of emanation for spiritually tinged patriotism.[71]

CONSTRUCTING "FAMILY"

In a 1994 article in Gentlemen's Quarterly, Jeanne Marie Laskas wrote that, in Branson, "family values are talked about as objects. It is never said where these things are available or how you get them. Everybody just seems to know." Since the second decade of the twentieth century, Branson boosters have employed "family" rhetoric to attract visitors. Any contemporary marketer would assuredly reiterate this idiom by claiming that the city's entertainment possesses a wholesomeness that makes it accessible and acceptable to grandparents, grandchildren, and everyone in between. Moreover, tourist comments almost invariably cite this dynamic as a primary draw and ally it with other place-defining themes. As a visitor from Oklahoma asserted, "Branson is a place that honors God, family, and the things that hold America together." The city's definition of family is more than just benign presentations of ostensibly unobjectionable material, however. Deconstruction of its variety show entertainment industry reveals numerous ways that domestic identities are intertwined with and fortified by distinct, Christian-informed ideologies.[72]

Nationally known relationship counselor, author, and conference speaker

Gary Smalley resides in Branson. There, he heads the Smalley Relationship Center—his organizational center that focuses on allaying divorce rates, fostering accord between husbands and wives, and promoting a specific vision of child rearing. Todays Family is the nonprofit, Christian-based arm of this undertaking. Since Smalley's arrival in Branson, his organization has interfaced with the tourism industry in a number of ways. For instance, in 2000 he initiated a radio talk show broadcast from Silver Dollar City's Wilderness Chapel—a program lauded by the park's administrators as able to entertain and lead people to a relationship with Christ. Examination of Smalley's initiatives reveals a number of essential principles that course through Branson's presentation of "proper" family dynamics.[73]

Smalley's counseling-cum-ministry is predicated on scriptural precedents. He claims that God created us to need relationships by quoting Genesis 2:18 ("Then the Lord God said, 'It is not good that the man should be alone; I will give him a helper as his partner'" [NRSV]). Understanding that men and women are programmed by the divine in naturally different manners, he frequently includes in his advice the idea that men are emotionally guarded, sometimes inattentive to the needs of their mates, and often negligent in the realm of child care. Alternately, he portrays women as overly sensitive, prone to being nagging marital partners, and exceedingly neurotic about their parental duties. Although he admits that claims such as "Women Are from the Classroom; Men Are from the Playground" are "generalities," these dictates lie at the root of his counseling approach—one that seeks not to overturn such divine imprints but to assist couples in better understanding and managing an innate, preordained dichotomy.[74]

In *God's Daughters* (1997), an ethnographic study of the evangelical Women's Aglow Fellowship, scholar of religion R. Marie Griffith detailed the many healings and transformations brought on marital relationships through wifely submission. Although Smalley's suggestions evade the rhetoric of obedience, he has harked back to Griffith's thesis by recommending "gentle persistence" to wives—an approach that avoids direct confrontation in favor of the more tender discourse "inherent" in female personalities. Such counsel, coupled with his reliance on scripture, understanding of gender as a naturalized identity category, expressed definition of marriage as a union between a man and a woman, and admonitions concerning premarital sex, has bestowed him with much credence among American evangelicals. His honors include endorsements from Jerry Falwell, Pat Robertson's Christian Broadcasting Network, and the Trinity Broadcasting Network.[75]

Although Smalley has sold more than 5 million books and spoken to more than 2 million people at conferences during his thirty-year career, James Dobson, founder of Focus on the Family and syndicated radio and newspaper commentator, is assuredly the leading spokesman for conservative, Christian, family values. Like Todays Family, Dobson's organization situates church, family, and government as three basic institutions ordained by God and thereby seeks to combat the contemporary pervasiveness of "humanistic notions." Focus on the Family is based in Colorado Springs, Colorado, rather than Branson, but on a number of occasions Dobson has invoked the importance of an Ozark brand of family values. As he stated during a national radio broadcast, "Branson is the alternative Christians have been looking for." Thus, to understand the idealized family unit put forth by the town's multitude of entertainment venues, one must assess not only what the industry says family is but also what it claims it is not.[76]

Christian approaches to child rearing and family systems are also codified at Branson's Kanakuk Kamps. Founded in 1926, Kanakuk is the largest Christian athletic camp in the United States. Composed of eight different sites (seven in the Ozarks and one in Colorado), it welcomes seventeen thousand children every summer from elementary through high school age for "Excitement, Adventure, and Christian Athletics." Kanakuk campers can participate in a gamut of recreational offerings—from team sports, to mountaineering, to water slides. Although children primarily come for these activities, Ward Wiebe, the director of the junior high camp, has stated that "the pie plate that holds the pie is the biblical foundation or the whole Christian message." Kanakuk is officially a non-denominational enterprise, but its religious impetus is evidenced by owner Joe White's frequent appearances on Focus on the Family programs. To further its religious mission, committed Christian counselors offer a morning Bible reading that is supposed to underscore the remainder of the day's frivolity. Classes open and close with a prayer, and scriptural study supplements athletic offerings.[77]

Within all its activities, Kanakuk accentuates family situations and problems that echo those addressed within Branson's entertainment industry. Reminders of the evils of drugs, alcohol, and premarital sex pervade its endeavors. Children are counseled on issues of separation, divorce, and lack of parental involvement. Through a leisure vehicle, campers are introduced to the religious underpinnings of these tribulations, with their dynamics situated within a good-versus-evil dualism assuaged through the redemptive sacrifice of Christ—theological vantages that imitate the larger regional epistemology. As Ward Wiebe declared:

> We can introduce kids to the morality of the truth of what happens on the cross and I think that opens up their eyes to how life is meant to be lived. . . . The thief

comes to kill, steal, and destroy. Jesus came so that you could have life and have it more abundantly. . . . The Bible teaches that if you confess with your mouth "Jesus is Lord" and believe in your heart that God raised him from the dead you'll be saved. I think what we try to do is put in front of each kid, "According to the message of the cross, why did Jesus Christ have to die on the cross? What was accomplished there? And what does it mean?"[78]

Most broadly construed, Kanakuk's religious perspective revolves around the promotion of an "I Am Third" lifestyle—an ontology that emphasizes putting God first, others second, and oneself third. Such an ethic again imitates the self-sacrificial notions of family that are invoked within local entertainment. Like the myriad theaters adjacent to Kanakuk's Branson camp, recreation is posited as a ready medium for evangelism. During a child's stay, he or she can indicate a public profession to Christ by ringing a centrally located bell, and hundreds of such experiences occur over the course of a summer. As Wiebe has asserted, these rebirths entail more than an intellectual reunderstanding: "It's more than just saying I have religion. It's more than saying that I know there was a man named Jesus Christ. It's confessing with your mouth that Jesus is Lord and believing in your heart that God did raise him from the dead. Then you'll be saved." Thus, an active, embodied experience of Christian awakening is at the root of Kanakuk's endeavor—a mode of religiosity that reproduces the evangelical theology buttressing Ozark religion and recreation.[79]

In a 1992 essay on rural gender identity, anthropologist H. Jane Parker held that, in the Ozarks, "the social/symbolic representation of gender is a public sign system that dialectically reflects and produces a local epistemology, a system of ideas, of and about gender." Although she did not broach representations of maleness or femaleness within regional tourism, Parker did document various ways that cultural forms assist in the construction and negotiation of those categories. Furthermore, oral accounts from her subjects frequently posited Christian scripture as the basis for such understandings. As one interviewee (Laverne) attested, "I just feel like that a man should be the head of the house and head of the government. That's what the Bible teaches." Rhonda, from Rock County, Arkansas, furthered this claim when she stated, "Men excel at being out-going and dynamic, they exert their personality more. Being subjective is what I think the Lord created us for . . . to be the helpmate." Within Branson's entertainment, this perception of gender is corroborated, as such identities are put forth not as shifting matrices of meaning but rather as time-honored and God-ordained essences. Parker additionally claimed that storytelling is a primary vehicle for the conveyance of gender "models." Each and every Branson musical venue tells these stories through on-stage performance, thereby proffering a leisure-oriented channel for such indoctrination. Though the majority of Branson's headline performers are men, their spouses almost always play a significant role in the production. They sing and dance with their mates, work the theaters' gift shops selling homemade wares and glossy photos of their nuclear families, and, of supreme importance, are presented as matrons imparted with the most vital of domestic duties—the raising of sometimes stunningly large celebrity families.[80]

In the Branson entertainment industry, sizable families function as status symbols. Much is made of the fact that the Osmonds and Lennons now have thirty-plus members living in the area. The Presleys' Country Jubilee and the Baldknobbers Hillbilly Jamboree (the progenitors of family-based, family-operated amusement in the Ozarks) tender a parade of related stars, with grandparents and grandchildren at times sharing the stage. Space does not allow for an all-inclusive exposition of the various intermingling of entertainment and extended family in Branson, but suffice it to say that procreation is given paramount importance and that this reproductive impulse is subtly put forth as a godly mandate. In addition, the unbridled acquisition of offspring in Branson is not solely limited to biological breeding. Some musical families have augmented their ranks through the channels of KidSave International, a Christian nonprofit group founded in 1999 which helps children from orphanages in Russia and central Asia find homes in the United States. In 2002, the Dutton family (of the Dutton Family Theater) added five members to its ranks through this program—two siblings from Russia and four from Kazakhstan. Following suit, the Hughes family (of the Hughes Brothers Celebrity Theatre), whose matriarch hopes that "the Spirit comes across" in the way it represents family within its show, also adopted four children. Considering the religiously motivated importance placed on extended kinship networks in Branson and the fact that the Dutton and Hughes families are committed Mormons, their participation in the program seems fitting.[81]

Although leisure opportunities in Branson implicitly address female bodies and female sexuality through their procreative and child-raising emphases, corporeal display has no place within the industry. On-stage costuming is intentionally modest, and when the bounds of "appropriate" dress are overstepped, tourists frequently vocalize their discontent. The Legends Family Theatre is a venue that showcases celebrity impersonators imitating the likes of Elvis Presley, Judy Garland, Marilyn Monroe, and Little Richard. All in this list are connected with bodily expression to varying degrees—the gyrating king of rock and roll, the gay culture icon, the busty starlet, and the sexually ambivalent pianist. Surprisingly, these look-alikes have not been cause for consternation, perhaps because impersonators merely copy and are therefore exempt from critiques that question personal artistic creation. Female singers and dancers who accompany them on stage have been deemed too "Vegas" (read provocative) for Branson at times, however. A frequent vacationer in the region objected to a visit in the late 1990s as follows:

> We wanted to see the Blues Brothers and Elvis mostly. We didn't see Elvis at all and the Blues Brothers didn't perform long. What we mostly saw were showgirls in sexy costumes flaunting their bodies in our faces!! All consisted of low-cut, midriff bare tops, and high-cut or short short bottoms. I will never go back there and I have told everyone I know not to go unless they want to hear and see a bunch of naked women and husbands and boyfriends drooling and acting stupid. This show should be driven out of town or cleaned up.[82]

Such a comment demonstrates once again that many tourists envision Branson as the ideological opposite of Las Vegas. Although local performers have donned glitzy, sequined attire since the early 1980s, this garb is meant to present female bodies in a manner that reflects the "tasteful" flamboyance of "country chic" rather than lust-arousing scantiness found on America's other famous Strip.

This being said, not all female performers in Branson have limited their onstage persona to that of mother or caregiver. From 1993 to 2001, singer Jennifer Wilson portrayed a self-styled, late twentieth-century Betty Grable. (She even sold photos of herself striking Grable's back-turned, hand-on-hip pose so widely disseminated during World War II.) However, according to *Springfield News-Leader* journalist Mark Marymount, this appeal was tempered by a tourist vantage that viewed her as a "sexy granddaughter" rather than as a harlot. Another means by which the performer dispelled criticism of her ostensibly provocative numbers was "having a lot of Jesus around me." Throughout her stay in town, she was never reticent about the evangelistic intentions of her act: "Of course I witness on stage and give brief testimony. I'm proud to say I'm a born-again Christian. When I moved to Branson, it was just like coming home." Through these measures, Wilson enveloped what was assuredly the sexiest Branson act within the safety of domestically oriented Christian rhetoric and "comforted" guests by putting herself forth as a titillating relative rather than a true competitor for the affections of male guests.[83]

Since 1994, the leggy and scantily clad Rockettes have been performing a "Christmas Spectacular" in Branson. One might think that this presentation of Broadway-style glamour would not resonate well with Ozark tourists, but the show has always produced large, contented crowds. Unlike Jennifer Wilson, the Rockettes' sexuality is elided not through situating them as extended family members but by making overt references to the dancers' industriousness. Audiences are reminded that the performers devote eight hours a day to rehearsal, that they are versed in multiple forms of dance, and that they pay the utmost attention to even the smallest detail. This appeal to a Protestant work ethic is bolstered by the religious Christmas themes central to their show. The Rockettes climax their presentation with a living Nativity scene, and alongside references to the merits of hard work, this spiritual sentiment functions as an effective anodyne for what might be construed by some as a New York infusion of bodily inappropriateness into the local tourism scene.[84]

In 1999, Branson hosted the Miss USA Pageant. Boosters hoped that the event would increase national exposure and attract a younger tourist audience, but in its wake, numerous objections concerning the production's bawdiness surfaced. Local journalist Lauren Squires wrote, for example, "As wholesome and family-oriented as Branson claims its appeal to be, it is a shame that it chose such a sex-doused show to gain exposure. . . . Branson's 'heartland values' reputation is a bit tarnished." Many more Ozark aficionados reacted to the exploits of the Miss USA emcee, *Young and the Restless* star Shemar Moore, feeling he had engaged in overly sexual banter with contestants and proffered a too "racy rendition" of the song "Pussycat." Immediately following the event, retired newspaperman Ben Kinel drafted a petition stating that Moore "presented the Branson values, which we all cherish, in a very unfavorable light." After his text was circulated at churches and other civic organizations, within ten days more than a thousand residents and tourists signed it. Although the pageant had included a worship service coordinated by Branson pastors and business leaders and attended by most contestants, this infusion of Christianity was not enough to salvage the production. As Kinel proclaimed, such presentations might be suitable for Las Vegas or New York, "But when you're in the Ozarks, do as the Ozark people do, and tone it a little more to our fitting." Of paramount importance for such a fit is the promotion of a value structure that cherishes the procreative impulse, sanctions male authority, locates femaleness within the realm of child bearing and nurture, and stamps these dictates with a divine imprimatur that bestows them with a sense of naturalness rather than social construction.[85]

Since big-name stars began performing in Branson, boosters have made much of the fact that many of these famous people have decided to reside in this tiny southwestern Missouri city. Tourists thus arrive with the expectation that they might bump into Tony Orlando at Wal-Mart or see Andy Williams raking leaves in his front yard. As Mel Tillis quipped, "You go to Nashville, you see the stars' homes. You come to Branson, you see the stars." Though such happenings are, in fact, rare, even the possibility of their occurrence furthers Branson's status as "America's Hometown." By means of these marketing claims and the constant reminders that sojourners can be symbolically incorporated into already sizable celebrity families through their mere attendance of performances, the town functions as a second (and in many ways more desirable) domestic dwelling for visitors. According to one tourist, "it's like going home, where you don't meet a stranger." Through affirmation of all the "family values" discussed above, entertainment venues indeed offer images of unproblematic household units fortified by biblically grounded morality, and through participation in and consumption of these vantages, tourists thus acquire an arsenal of beliefs to be enacted outside the vacation context. Acknowledging this ability to apply Branson's sociocultural template to other arenas of lived existence, a St. Louis visitor stated, "Have dessert first! Visit Branson before you see the world."[86]

When Christianity finds a home within and buttresses country-and-western arrangements, nostalgic renderings of an antimodern past, rousing tributes to veterans and national government, or visions of domestic tranquility, it then is given the popular religious constitution necessary to thrive in Branson. Like any other tourist, the Christian one wants to be entertained. Ozark theaters may contain loosely knit liturgical elements such as sacred music or homiletics, but they are still primarily leisure venues. Jesus is certainly "the greatest star" within all shows, but like the camp meetings and other historical arenas for religious tourism from which Branson theaters draw inspiration, they must clothe this overarching premise in a recreational form that allows visitors to apprehend the infusion of Christian theology and ethics into all lived realms.

CHAPTER FIVE

"Near Heaven"

The Dynamics of Sacred Space in Branson

In *The Shepherd of the Hills,* Harold Bell Wright described an inextricable link between Ozarkers and their environment. Living amid "temples of God's own building," the hill folk possessed intimate knowledge of "how big God is" and spiritually profited from this divine presence expressed through "the language of the mountain, and tree, and sky, and flower, and brook." In a moment of spiritual upheaval toward the end of the work, the Shepherd entreated God to allow him to stay in this bastion of solace and righteousness. Confessing the error of his former urbane ways, he concluded with the plea: "Oh, drive me not from this haven into the world again!"[1]

Initiating a rural-urban dichotomy and lacing this dualism with a religious rhetoric that has since suffused countless descriptions of the Branson area, Wright's Shepherd heaped an array of criticisms on city life—an existence that produced "pale, sickly, colorless" inhabitants. In this "mad, cruel world that raged beyond the hills," individuals mired in superficiality were not able to discover "the deeper things in life." Although the Ozarks had been able to evade the perils of sophistication, modern threats were on the horizon. As the Shepherd presaged, "Before many years a railroad will find its way yonder." With the advent of mass transportation, many types of development would be offered an opportunity to invade this sacred landscape.[2]

Mass tourism is a modern invention, and, in an ironic twist, Wright's laudatory comments directly facilitated the emergence of that practice in the Ozarks. Although well-known Ozark pundit Charles Gusewelle has asserted that the region "as a place and a landscape and a social culture has very little to do with touristic things," this has certainly been a minority opinion over the past century. Sojourners and the development associated with their arrival have affected place and space at every turn. While some people have bemoaned this influence, many more have maintained that a sense of spiritual uplift can be salvaged from the practice by codifying vacationing within a language of potential transcendence.[3]

In the closing pages of *The Shepherd of the Hills,* the protagonist suggested a similar ambivalence to growth. Although the railroad certainly could make his "beautiful hills" into "the haunt of careless idlers," this loss was not a foregone conclusion. The Shepherd felt that spiritual "hard work" might be able to preserve the inherent virtue and sanctity of the Ozarks. If such vigilance was not upheld, however, and the region was divested of its sacred aura, this passing would be cataclysmic. As he proclaimed, "When the outside world comes, men will turn the page, and you may lose the place."[4]

In the almost one hundred years since the publication of Wright's work, analyses of Ozark sacred space have often similarly melded pious praise of the landscape with admonitions against the material and spiritual hazards that threaten its sanctity. Voiced by local tourism boosters, national commentators, area clergy, residents, and vacationers alike, the problems are seen as combinations of environmental degradation, sightseer-inspired commercialism, "outsider" ideologies, and urban vice. This list is frequently summarized under the label "modern," leaving the ever present mystery of how people with a vested interest in Branson and its surrounding region can simultaneously rebuke modernity and yet embrace many of that epoch's characteristics.

Similarly, contemporary geographic theorizations usefully pose understandings of place and space as contested categories of meaning. In a recent essay about methodological approaches to sacred landscapes, David Chidester merged perspectives that grant space a sense of independent agency with vantages that alternately see its meaning as the product of disputed power relations. Within this template, the former stance (the "poetics" of sacred space) marks consecrated sites as sui generis centers of meaning and significance, while the latter outlook (the "politics" of sacred space) understands such locations as "nodal points" in social and political networks of power. Adding nuance to the political vantage and censuring perspectives that posit sacredness as a "given" revealed through topography, Chidester and Edward Linenthal have held that place is not a fixed position in space but rather a "point of departure for an endless multiplication of meaning."[5]

Contemporary nongeographers investigating sacred space have also adopted paradigms that emphasize the production of meaning. For instance, religion scholar Jonathan Z. Smith illustrated the process of sanctification necessary to imbue a place with spiritualized overtones. According to Smith, a site is vested with these qualities only after a long process of cultural labor that involves issues of memory, design, and authority. Thus, many scholars examining the situatedness of the holy have moved away from earlier, myth- and symbol-inspired notions of peaceful centers and cosmic points of harmony to scrutinize the myriad ways that these sentiments are formed, negotiated, and reformed by human imaginations, cultural discourses, and social developments.[6]

For a century, Branson's tourism industry has utilized religious rhetoric to imbue landscape with a sense of inviolability grounded in utopian imaginings of the human-topography relationship. However, this construct has also met with a variety of problems that have threatened the seamless perceptions of place vital for the success of Ozark consumer culture. The region has often been viewed as set apart from the tribulations of worldly existence. Tourism promoters have championed this uniqueness as a site for divine contact and entreaty, with such godly acquaintance circumscribed within historical re-creations, theatrical production, variety show theaters, and the like. Branson's inimitable melding of premodern, modern, and postmodern; its use of consumer culture to codify and express theologico-geographic sentiments; and its struggle to maintain this sense of sanctity in the face of environmental, social, and cultural challenges make the city an ideal case study—one that stretches the limits of landscape poetics and necessitates examination through the lens of politicized space.

As illustrated throughout this chapter, a contested understanding of regional placefulness can be found in a multitude of written and verbal expressions. Poet R. A. Birdsong perhaps best encapsulated this sentiment within a 1950 ode entitled "Near Heaven." Published in *Rayburn's Ozark Guide,* the most widely circulated Ozark tourist magazine of the first half of the twentieth century, the poem begins with standard idealizations of the area's mountains, forests, and waters. Nevertheless, in the next verse Birdsong offered broadly construed words of anxiety that resonate with many analogous venerations: "As time goes on and on, / Will it always be the same? / Or will these beauties be destroyed, / Never to be seen again?" By not specifying the shape of these prospective destructions, the author left a substantive blank that has since been filled in with numerous concerns. Seeming to sense this pending change, he nonetheless clung to a utopian outlook as the poem closed: "I hope as time goes by / That the mountains meet the blue, / And when you want to be near Heaven, / This will be near Heaven to you." Here the poet takes the relative proximity of the sacred as his concluding subject. It has been the maintenance of this closeness, amid issues that threaten to put distance between place and the divine, which has permeated Branson's history.[7]

CONSENSUS, CONFLICT, AND THE CREATION OF OZARK SACRED SPACE

The founder of an American-based human geography tradition, Carl Sauer, is well known for advocating cultural particularism and adopting an antimodern stance that viewed the decline of rural society as a result of the homogenizing tendencies of urbanization and industrialization. Sauer's proclivity for the "premodern" began when he published *The Geography of the Ozark Highland of Missouri* (1920). This dissertation project was spawned from the lack of knowledge about this sizable region and the author's personal experiences (a familiarity that led him to label the work a "study in home geography"). Sauer was born in the east-central Missouri town of Warrenton and received a degree from its Central Wesleyan College. He thus possessed "vivid associations" with regional topography and sometimes offered them in terms that echoed the rhetoric of Wright and the cadre of early tourism boosters in Branson. Harking back to "the scenes of early years" that remained "forever green" in his memory, he wrote:

> The old white church, astride its rocky point, overtopped by cedars that grow on the warm rock ledges, forever looks forth upon the fairest valley. The lower slopes are abloom with red clover, or golden with wheat. Wide fields of blue-green corn border the shaded stream, where the bass lurk in transparent pools. In the distance forests of oak mantle the hillsides, up which, past spacious farmhouses, the country roads wind. The people who move upon the scene of this account are homefolks one and all. Some have succeeded better than others, some give greater promise than others, but they are all well worth knowing.[8]

Although the body of this book is empirical and predominantly resists romanticized tones, these introductory words reveal that even a scholar concerned with establishing disciplinary principles found it difficult to avoid painting the Ozarks in godly, pastoral, and morally upright terms.

In a 1922 essay, Sauer elaborated on the economic circumstances of the Ozark highland and offered an early example of the ways that one might examine both idealized imaginings of a place and material considerations that contest such Arcadian views. Eliding a vision of Ozark inhabitants as slothful, he laid primary blame for their poverty on an "inferior environment" that was not amenable to agriculture. Ancillary culpability was placed on immigration to larger cities by the region's young, a process that introduced them to "new standards and modes of life." Finally, some fault was attributed to a lack of common effort to improve economic wherewithal—a product of the Ozarks frontier heritage of individualism. This last critique, however, did not signal Sauer's belittling of the hill people's virtuous composition. He claimed that, in spite of their travails, acquisitive impulses were not strong motivators and that his subjects did not "live in want." In fact, much of the impression of poverty was a result of the "simplicity of the habits of the people" and their inclination toward "even distribution of wealth." Ozarkers may have known little about profit making through economic collaboration, but they were described as fully knowledgeable of "the relief of a neighbor in trouble." According to this description, residents (especially those living in what Sauer referred to as the "central region," a swath of the larger territory which included Branson) were "primitive" (read admirably bucolic) by choice.[9]

A year before the publication of *The Geography of the Ozark Highland of Missouri*, Will Ferrell expressed comparable notions of godly terrestrial intention and a distinctive regional blessedness in a verse entitled "The Ozarks":

> God clothed the Rockies with eternal snows,
> The Alleghenies with the juniper and the rose.
> When all was done some odds and ends remained,
> The choicest of them all—He retained.
> He painted and adorned each precious scrap
> And flung the whole into Missouri's lap.
> There shall they lie. There shall they bless mankind.
> The greatest spot of all the Earth designed.

In this "Land of the kindly Shepherd of the Hills," the author found much evidence of "Dame Nature's kiss." Although many of the Ozarks' wonders had now come to light and were readily available for aesthetic and spiritual consumption, Ferrell also proclaimed the as yet unseen possibilities of the place, or the "rare films of rapture yet unfurled"—words possessing an even more triumphant sense of potential and attitudes that echo prophetic millennial understandings found throughout the history of Branson tourism.[10]

In the arena of imaginings about place, tourism boosters were not to be outdone by scholars and poets. For instance, in a 1922 brochure for Branson's Sammy Lane Boat Line, the writer exclaimed that "no pen or brush could do justice" to nature's handiwork in the Ozarks. Although visual replication of such wonders by human hands was deemed impossible, the topography could leave a spiritual imprint on sojourners. The hills themselves (without the aid of human interpretation) could "communicate to your inner self a message that you will never forget" and impart a satisfaction that "will carry you back to this land of a million smiles for years to come." Commenting on such an affect, a visiting fisherman during this period wrote, "It is almost like floating into another land to glide into the mysterious blue and purple haze that makes the Ozark hills seem like some great painting rather than a thing of reality." Similarly, a 1926 brochure produced by the Lake Taneycomo Chamber of Commerce publicized the possibilities of the region in a manner that simultaneously emphasized a familiar construct of "authentic" rural America. As a site that prompted visitors to recall "forgotten days when man walked close to nature" and "unhurried days when people had time to really live," the place could introduce a bona fide reality to guests only familiar with the "artificiality of our modern life." By trafficking in the simple things, Branson's landscape would thus facilitate the reemergence of numerous waning virtues and traditions.[11]

Like Carl Sauer, early tourism boosters tended to conflate serene Ozark topography with a consequent serenity among the region's inhabitants. The friendliness and good nature of Ozarkers have always been a calling card for the area, and some commentators have attributed these characteristics to the correspondingly genteel attributes of the surrounding landscape. For instance, a 1924 brochure produced by the Kansas City Southern Railway noted that the mountains of southwestern Missouri

> have all of the true characteristics of true mountains but are devoid of those stern, bleak and desolate prospects that may move the beholder to feelings of wonder and awe, but scarcely can be said to inspire sensations of pleasurable enjoyment. . . . The scenery of the Ozarks is of a friendly sort that invites intimacy and direct contact. It is the kind of scenery that welcomes you right into its family circle and envelopes you in a cordial embrace. It is Nature wearing a serene and genial smile, rather than a gloomy and forbidding scowl.[12]

Thus, unlike the daunting Rockies, Missouri's peaks possessed a more kindly allure that could provide a sense of comfortable admiration. Reflecting the much heralded hospitality of the people who lived amid them, the Ozark hills thus greeted visitors as family members.

According to poets and promoters, a blessed terrain made the Ozarks a de facto garden of spiritual and social delights for vacationers. But in two articles from *Missouri Magazine* (the official publication of the Missouri State Chamber of Commerce) published in 1928 and 1930, the region was also hallowed for its agricultural possibilities. Author Harry A. Miller marked the place as a "land of strawberries and sunshine" and assured potential investors that even a plethora of rocks could be turned into "values as permanent as themselves." This essay also guaranteed easy access to Branson and its surroundings while pledging that such infrastructural progress would not detract from one's ability to "absorb inspiration" or "rest in the environs of perfect relaxation and peace." Although declaring that the state's highway program must continue to develop, Miller forthrightly asserted that an easy balance could be struck between a desire for retreat from modernity and an embrace of epochal elements that eased the difficulties of rural existence. Ultimately, if one came to the Ozarks for work rather than play, even labor would be inherently profitable within such an extraordinary atmosphere.[13]

Further translating a sacred landscape into one of economic profit, realtors regularly bestowed Branson with a sense of divine sanction. In the late 1940s, a brochure for the New York City–based E. A. Strout Realty Agency, the largest farm-selling organization in the world at that time, described the city as a locale "Where Nature Smiles and Opportunity Beckons." Here one could develop his or her "respect for nature's handiwork" and here "God's farmers prosper." Thus, in Stout's view, the Ozark region was a sacred space that could operate inside the cycle of economic exchange rather than being set completely apart from it. This interpretation, of course, was the norm in the Branson area.[14]

Spiritualized notions of Ozark placefulness were also consumed through recorded music. One example exists as early as 1893, when Henry DeMoss's "My Happy Little Home in Arkansas" praised the area's streams and woods. In Fred Rose's 1923 "Ozark Blues," he sang, "I was in heaven but I didn't know it, / When I left Missouri way." Patsy Montana's "Where the Ozarks Kiss the Sky" declared that the region was a place "where the angels rested." And numerous musicians forged a connection between the Ozarks rural nature/isolation from modern civilization and inherent virtue. This vantage was most thoroughly found in Jimmy Long and Gene Autry's "By the Ozark Trail," where the "busy city" was juxtaposed with a "quaint old mountain home." Creating what W. K. McNeil has labeled the "concept of Ozarks as Eden," these artists broadcast utopian notions of landscape to a national audience and added to an already sizable body of similar boosterism.[15]

As is evident, notions of sacred space were bolstered by language declaring an unspoiled natural setting and the climate's effect on visitors, current inhabitants, and potential residents. However, at the same time that this idiom was being proffered, a sequence of events was unfolding which geographer Milton Rafferty has labeled "the most tragic in the history of mankind's relationship with the Ozark environment." For nineteenth-century Ozarkers, trees were both an encumbrance and a bountiful resource. To establish farmsteads and grazing land, forests were chopped down and incinerated. When construction began on the Missouri Pacific's White River Line in Branson in 1904, vast tracts of oak and pine became available to outside commercial interests. In this newly platted city, most residents found employment with the Bagnell Timber Company, the largest manufacturer of railroad ties in the United States. Although this particular venture was short lived, Branson remained a log-shipping hub for several decades. Tie hacking employed many citizens, but the timber industry also began to destroy the natural surroundings that were needed to sustain a tourist trade.[16]

By the mid-1930s, much of the area's vaunted plant and wildlife populations had been destroyed. The felling of stands of trees produced exposed soil and led to massive erosion down the hillsides and into stream valleys. Oak sprouts grew up, choking out annual grasses. This led to an increase in fires set to control this woody growth—a method long used by Scots-Irish settlers in the region. The climax of this tradition occurred on Easter Sunday 1941 (known as "the day the Ozarks burned down"), when 40-mile-an-hour winds facilitated the destruction of more than two-thirds of the area's woodlands. Although burnings eliminated brush, in the words of one farmer it also rendered the soil "so worthless that the only way you could grow a crop would be to tie two rocks together around a seed." According to Rafferty, these customs and consequences greatly reduced the amount of usable land and thereby resulted in lowered income, poorer health, and reduced education standards—effects that gave rise to popular conceptions of the place as ridden with "poverty and hard times."[17]

Many Ozarkers throughout history have decried the influence of outsiders on their landscape. When in the 1930s the Civilian Conservation Corps sought to cease annual burnings, some locals saw its efforts as a threat to a regional way of life and intentionally set "grudge fires." However, the U.S. Forest Service and other external interlopers were in fact largely responsible for saving the Ozarks from catastrophic destruction in the early twentieth century. Seeking to make Taney County into a middle-class tourist area, for example, urban businessmen from eastern Missouri formed the St. Louis Game Park in 1891. This private reserve was located on the west side of the White River and, when opened in 1896, included 5,000 acres of creeks, caves, and forests stocked with native and non-native species. Garnering national attention, the park attracted many famous visitors, including frequent guest William Jennings Bryan. Replete with an eighteen-room hunting lodge overlooking the White River, which was used by sportsmen to float downstream to the preserve, the site was christened a "hunter's paradise." Until its sale in 1917, the St. Louis Game Park was at the forefront of the Ozark conservationist movement—a lobby constituted of tourists and tourism boosters and the first of many efforts by outside interests to protect a landscape ostensibly disregarded by the people who called the area home.[18]

Non-Ozarkers once again modified the region's topography with the authorization of Powersite Dam in 1911, the largest hydroelectric structure in the country on its completion in 1913. Erected near Forsyth to manufacture energy for Springfield and Joplin, Missouri, the edifice also created the 2,000-acre Lake Taneycomo. Powersite was built by the Ambussen Hydraulic Construction Company with moneys supplied by the Ozark Power and Water Company, a group of private investors. In addition to concerns over lost farmland and the taming of the White River, locals also vehemently objected to the licensing of a private company to profit from a public waterway. However, the project employed more than a thousand workers (many of whom earned a livable wage for the first time in their lives) and added $2 million to the local economy during construction. Thus, the endeavor serves as another early example of regional ambivalence concerning foreign modifications to topography. Standing only 70 feet tall and producing only 52 miles of shoreline, the dam would seem incredibly diminutive in years to come when other more gargantuan structures generated even greater contests over the use and transformation of landscape in the Branson area.[19]

Although some homes in Taney County received electricity as a result of Powersite Dam, the most extraordinary effect was on local tourism. Just as visitors began arriving at sites made famous by *The Shepherd of the Hills,* they were confronted with the added bonus of fishing and a gamut of other water-related activities. In addition, the dam's completion created two new local tourist havens. Hollister, due south of Branson across the lake, was platted by landscape architect William J. Johnson and was meant to resemble an Old English village. Rockaway Beach, upstream and northeast of Branson, was founded by Willard and Anna Merriam of Kansas City, Kansas, and named after the famous New York vacation spot. All three cities subsequently exploded with resorts and tourist-oriented businesses. Commenting on this development, a writer for *Technical World* stated in 1913:

The thrill of a new day is felt everywhere. New hotels have been going up all summer. Fishing and hunting clubs are going up all along the lake. . . . Already the people of the Ozarks are adapting themselves to the new conditions, which promise not only to attract thousands of sightseers, summer visitors, and permanent

Lake Taneycomo, circa 1950. Postcard from the author's collection

residents, but also to develop industries undreamed of in this hitherto sequestered region of romance and mystery.[20]

Although journalists of the time saw Powersite as a technological innovation that would revolutionize the entire Ozark region, twentieth-century history demonstrates that tourism administrators had other ideas. Their objective was to situate Taneycomo and ensuing recreational lakes as part of the region's premodern heritage rather than as emblems of waxing modernity. As boats with names such as the *Sammy Lane* and *The Shepherd of the Hills* began embarking from Taneycomo's shores, boosters built rustic cottages alongside its waters and wrapped the whole development into a burgeoning process of historical re-creation.

For many, Lake Taneycomo served as an example of the ways that human beings could modify the Ozark landscape to further the region's natural beauty. To combat the abuses of deforestation, wildlife depletion, and the polluting of the area's rivers, a coalition of predominantly urban sportsmen and conservationists met on September 10, 1935, in Columbia and formed the Restoration and Conservation Federation of Missouri. The group empowered publisher E. Sydney Stephens and a nonpartisan committee to lobby for a commission charged with restoring Missouri's wildlife and forests. This meeting marked the origins of the Missouri Department of Conservation—a body that would become the model for similar state departments nationwide and would be influential in fighting environmentally damaging practices in and around Branson.[21]

When an amendment to create the Department of Conservation came to a statewide vote in 1936, only 54 percent of the residents of Stone and Taney counties supported it. In contrast, the strongest backing came from metropolitan counties such as Jackson (77 percent) and St. Louis (83 percent). Ozark residents undoubtedly viewed the enterprise with trepidation because of its strong urban espousal, but when the department was formally created in 1937, Branson inhabitants were not without representation.[22]

Missouri native and soon-to-be Branson resident Townsend Godsey was appointed director of information and education for the Department of Conservation in 1938. Born in Maryville, Godsey moved to Branson in 1939. While with the department, he made a number of original contributions to its mission. These included the drafting of a conservation curriculum for children instituted at rural schools throughout the state, the filming of *Back to Missouri* (a film shown in more than four hundred small-town theaters in the late 1930s which helped to defeat politicians opposed to conservation efforts), and the creation of *Missouri Conservationist* (the department's monthly magazine). He continued throughout his life to draw attention to environmental concerns in the Ozarks, particularly through publication of *Ozark Mountain Folk*—a collection of 140 photographs taken prior to 1950 which documented the natural environs and folk life of the region. As Branson began its monumental growth in the mid-1980s, Godsey expressed concerns that had permeated his tenure as a conservationist and Ozark booster. Amid the dawn of theaters, new highways, and scores of tourists, he stated in 1990, "The development pressure is too great, and people have let short-term economic gain override any concern for long-term damage to the environment. . . . Whenever you change the quality of the environment, you're going to change the quality of life."[23]

Branson's unique status within the region and the need to balance preservation issues with an ever growing tourist culture have produced anxiety for the Department of Conservation throughout its history. Aldo Leopold, the philosophical guru of wildlife conservation in the United States, lent his counsel when the department was being created. Addressing what he perceived as that organization's primary motive, he stated, "Conservation, at bottom, rests on the conviction that there are things in the world more important than dollar signs and ciphers. Many of these other things attach to the land, and to the life that is on it and in it." In Branson, however, a gentle merger of conservation and "dollar signs" has often been the most effective remedy for environmental ruin. For instance, in 1929 M. B. Skaggs, Ozarker by birth and owner of the Safeway Grocery chain, purchased the former St. Louis Game Park property. Skaggs repaired the dilapidated hunting lodge, bought additional land that increased the site to 9,000 acres, and forged a management agreement with the Department of Conservation which created the Drury Refuge. Skaggs began restoring the natural surroundings in 1939 by restocking deer herds and turkey populations. In this way, and unlike other ventures that pitted commercialism against conservation, his endeavor melded seemingly oppositional currents into a unitary effort. In doing so, he also provided an example that was emulated, though not always realized, throughout the twentieth-century Ozarks.[24]

The delicate conjoining of landscape-related preservation and modern progress took many forms in the midcentury Ozarks. In April 1943, *National Geographic* ran a feature article on the region. Written in the midst of World War II, this piece highlighted soldier training at Fort Leonard Wood, the mining of zinc used for cartridge shells, and cattle ranching to feed hungry troops. Additionally, it underscored industrial endeavors like the mass production of poultry in northern Arkansas. Then, in a manner similar to that of regional boosters and conservationists, the magazine balanced this progressive portrait with visions of simplicity by including narratives of fishing on area rivers, hunting razorback hogs, attending one-room schoolhouses, and visiting sites made famous by Harold Bell Wright's literature.

Although the *Geographic* offered a more modernized view of the Ozarks than many previous commentators, it advanced a belief that the place was imbued with a special religiosity. While no explicit discussion of regional faith was offered, the spread included photographs of a hill preacher conducting a Pentecostal revival, students at the School of the Ozarks singing hymns, a pie supper at a local church, and a baptism in the White River. A lack of overt mention of religion may have resulted from the article's focus on industry, but it also may suggest that Ozark spirituality was assumed as a given for national readers who believed that hill people were primitive yet moral. In the sole mention of the divine, the second sentence of the piece stated, "They say God lifted these hills so near to heaven that children may reach up and tickle the angels' feet!" In this way, readers were reminded of what they perhaps already knew—that the different industries and amusements discussed in the article were fortified by a sense of divine presence.[25]

Despite environmental problems and the birth of industry, post–World War II boosters forged ahead with their exaltations of pristine landscape. More theologically minded writers, however, sometimes warned of threats to this status from

America's ever increasing secularization. In 1952, a reporter for the *Bull Shoals Gazette* in Forsyth, Missouri (the Taney County seat), described colorful displays of fall foliage that were directed by the "Master Painter." But then, in a move that invoked ideas of human unworthiness in the face of wondrous spectacle (a mind-set that still has currency in the contemporary Branson tourism market), the author went on to enumerate the dangers of insufficient "brotherly love and good-will" and the "weak" constitution of people who experience such "glories." Asking "why all the blessings He bestowed on us when we are so unworthy?" the article linked notions of sacred space to an explicit religious vantage—one that suggested to readers that they could still profit from Branson's heavenly topography in spite of their inherent sinfulness and an unscrupulous contemporary milieu.[26]

Although the constitution of Branson's sacred space at midcentury was contested by way of its ongoing struggles with material and spiritual hazards, imaginings on the topic continued to offer poetic paradigms of consensus and harmony. For example, a 1954 promotional brochure suggested ways that the divine and humanity worked together to fashion the nation's consummate "family vacationland." For author Charles C. Williford, the "Oracle of the Ozarks," the White River lakes area functioned as a "refuge from the stress and strain" of urban life and represented a sanctuary where one may "regain an undistracted mind." Promoting the gamut of outdoor recreational activities and appealing to tourist aspirations for escape from "existing world chaos," Williford also touted an Ozark ability to acquiesce to the modern. Mimicking the strategy of promoters throughout the twentieth century, he described the place as a perfect mixture of the simple yet rugged days of old and the "convenience and comfort" of the modern world. By smoothing out the rough edges of progress, the brochure thus attempted to deflect mounting concerns about the growing numbers of Ozark tourists and their effect on the landscape.[27]

Williford's article was printed in the same year that Congress authorized the building of Table Rock Dam. Since the early twentieth century, engineers had sought ways to control flooding on the White River. Table Rock Dam was the fourth structure built to this end by the U.S. Army Corps of Engineers. Plans initially were devised in 1928, but the initiative did not move forward during the depression or war years. Begun in 1954 and completed in 1958, the dam impounded a reservoir that covered more than 43,000 acres of land and created nearly 1,000 miles of shoreline.

Like Powersite Dam, Table Rock generated hydroelectric power for area inhabitants while simultaneously augmenting the range of outdoor recreational

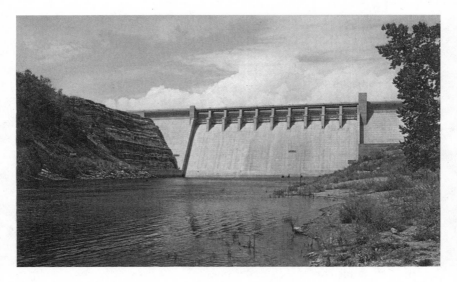

Table Rock Dam, circa 1960. Postcard from the author's collection

activities around Branson. Yet despite these boons, many residents of Stone and Taney counties challenged its construction. Bridges, roads, houses, and even towns had to be relocated. The dam also displaced the local float-fishing industry, which relied on an unhindered White River for its livelihood. Finally, its implementation meant that Ozarkers would have to deal with many land speculators, government agents, and similar outsiders who had always been viewed with suspicion.[28]

In the midst of Table Rock Dam's construction, opposition became so great that rumors of sabotage circulated. Stories of huge rafts laden with dynamite and floated into the structure during cover of night were bantered about. When the lake began to fill, Jim Owen, Branson's most successful float-fishing guide, sent out hundreds of postcards in a funeral-announcement style which lamented the death of the White River. This "Battle of the Dam" presented onlookers with two contrasting views of humanity's relationship with nature. Boosters stressed the harnessing of the landscape for the sake of flood control and electricity, while opponents emphasized environmental and agricultural losses that would be precipitated by such heavy-handed stewardship. Although this debate hinged on competing visions of ideal Ozark topography, it also involved the effect changes had on the emotions of residents and the overarching perception of the region as resistant to modern transformation. Such sentiments were frequently expressed by lifelong Branson attorney, businessman, and author Douglas Mahnkey, who took the Army Corps of Engineers to the Missouri Supreme Court to try to stop the construction of Bull Shoals Dam, the first lake project in southern Missouri. Gazing on the startling land alteration caused by Table Rock Dam, he expressed sadness and longing for an era now passed when he stated, "Times they air a changin'—hit's a pity, pity."[29]

With this famous pronouncement, Mahnkey added philosophical and cultural concerns to an already complex social and environmental dispute. Table Rock Dam and Lake altered the demographic composition of residents and visitors. During 1958, the number of businesses in southwestern Missouri and northwestern Arkansas increased 28 percent over the previous year, and an influx of construction workers created a minor population explosion. From 1950 to 1960, bank deposits in the area leaped from $2.4 million to $9 million, and investments in new homes and businesses more than quadrupled. Since its opening in 1960, Table Rock has always been an attendance leader among Missouri state parks.[30]

Branson quickly became the prime beneficiary of this increased regional visitation. In part this was a passive development because the city's competitor for tourists, Rockaway Beach, was dealt a crushing commercial blow by the Table Rock project. When water was released from the dam and entered Lake Taneycomo (which backed up to its base), it emerged at a chilly sixty degrees Fahrenheit. Prior to 1958, Rockaway Beach drew families that stayed between two weeks and an entire summer on the lake. This change in water temperature made it unsuitable for swimming and inhospitable for warm-water fish. Although cold-tolerant trout were quickly introduced and have since made Lake Taneycomo renowned for that species, Rockaway Beach faded from the Ozark tourism map in the 1960s and has never benefited from Branson's remarkable late-century growth.[31]

Realizing that Branson could rise to the forefront of the southwestern Missouri tourism industry on the completion of the lake, groups such as the Table Rock Boosters Association phrased their support for the venture in terms of morally necessary progress and admonished opponents to rise above "petty selfishness" and to look to the common good that would result from the project. In a 1955 open letter, the association asked its foes to remember that "the world is in flux. We are in 'Changing Times.' The death rattle of a passing age mingles with the birth pangs of a new order." Although admitting that this transition would be somewhat painful, dam backers co-opted the virtue-laden words of their adversaries to envelop modern progress in similar verbiage of principled innovation. As a result, Table Rock Dam became a geographic symbol for both environmental and ideological change, and the controversy over the project demonstrated an often uneasy connection between geography, tourism, and spiritualized ethics which continues to be a factor in the contemporary Ozarks.[32]

OTTO ERNEST RAYBURN AND HIS ARCADIAN OZARKS

Although he had sizable competition during the early years of Ozark tourism, folklorist, educator, and author Otto Ernest Rayburn became the most ardent voice for the unique and consecrated nature of the regional landscape. Born in Iowa in 1891, he first became acquainted with the Ozarks when he read *The Shepherd of the Hills*, felt "kinship with the people," and "walked off the level land never to return." In 1917, he bought a 40-acre plot a short distance from Branson on the White River. Building a cabin, Rayburn there began his sojourn in the "land of God's special favor." Dubbed Hideaway Lodge, this Ozark property served as a summer writing retreat while he spent the school year teaching in Kansas and Arkansas.[33]

Never shying away from utopian sentiments, Rayburn often admitted that his arrival in the Branson area was motivated by a quest for the "poetic symbol" of Arcadia. Hideaway Lodge was to resemble Thoreau's dwelling at Walden Pond, with nature serving as his "companion" and the earth as his "timepiece." Within his capacious body of writings, in fact, he would often ally himself with nineteenth-century transcendentalists and their understanding of the human-environment relationship. Like Thoreau and Emerson, he sought to quietly "preach" the Arcadian way of life and advocate the simple merits of living in a pastoral environment. During the last thirty-five years of his life, Rayburn would undertake myriad publishing ventures, all of which were permeated by these bucolic themes and wrapped Ozark topography in nebulous spiritual rhetoric. Although he loved the entirety of the region, he deemed "Shepherd of the Hills Country" the "jewel in the heart of the lotus" and saw Branson as the "idyllic little city" whose "luster increases with the years."[34]

Beginning with *Ozark Life,* a journal first printed in June 1925, Rayburn was not without a regional magazine until his death. *Ozark Life* was published in Winslow, Arkansas and, like all of Rayburn's ventures, took the greater Ozark region as its subject. The journal served many constituencies, including those interested in regional folklore and folk life, conservationists, tourists, and potential homeowners and investors. Like others of his time, Rayburn's initial writings often derided the onset of modernity in the hills. He had fallen in love with the solace (or idea of solace) that accompanied life in the region. Such "glorious rest" was unavailable amid the "maddening hum of modern machinery" and the "mess of

materialistic pottage" found in urban areas. Throughout his career, Rayburn traf-
ficked in such idealism. Seeking to "write not so much of the Ozarks in reality as
what the region stands for in the imagination," he frequently waxed poetic about
inspirational landscapes, "straight thinking" inhabitants, and the merits of plain
living. Although none of his journals achieved great success, all had circulations
in the tens of thousands. And in yet another paradox of regional boosterism,
many outsiders became exposed to the Ozarks through these writings, chose to
visit, and thereby initiated the problems that he criticized and sought to curtail.
Commenting on modern anxieties and the ways that a later Rayburn publication
inspired visitation to a site deemed immune from such ills, a reader wrote, "I see
sense of values warped. . . . The trouble is, city life has nothing very simple to
offer. One is caught up in a web of circumstances. So as you can see, when the
Ozark Guide comes to us we are transported into another part of the world."[35]

Like all purveyors of heritage and nostalgia, Rayburn wanted outsiders to
experience his adopted land. When he began his publishing career in the 1920s,
regional tourism was still in its infancy. Then, as *Ozark Life* gave way to its succes-
sors, *Arcadian Magazine* (1931–1932), *Arcadian Life* (1933–1942), and *Rayburn's Ozark
Guide* (1943–1960), his "protest against artificiality and plea to return to nature
and obey her laws" were increasingly accompanied by advertisements for area
motels, attractions, and real estate agents. The paradox of the modern Ozarks
had begun.[36]

As vacationers responded to his invitations, Rayburn's editorials grew increasingly wistful. For instance, shortly after the completion of Table Rock Dam, he
wrote:

> Gone are the days, the "good old days," in the Ozarks. The atmosphere of pasto-
> ral enchantment is now a memory. . . . Now the country is threaded with paved
> highways, crowded with tourists and homeseekers, and commercialism is king.
> Our swift streams, symbolizing Arcadian enchantment, are being clogged with
> concrete to meet the demands of the restless age. It is a push-button era with all the
> comforts, conveniences, and luxuries at nod and beck, but we are burdened with a
> troubled, divided world that totters on the brink of destruction. Everything moved
> at a slower pace in the old Ozarks. We knew less about the world then, but we had
> a pretty good knowledge of life's values. We found contentment in simplicity. . .
> . Now, with all our multiplied wants and satisfactions, life is troubled with uncer-
> tainty. We have everything, but don't know what to do with it.[37]

Rather than choosing to ignore the arrival of modernity and its effects on consecrated topography, as did many of his contemporary writers, Rayburn always

saw the Ozarks as remedy for these dilemmas or a site where the modern milieu could be put through a cleansing wringer. Much of this abiding faith during a midcentury torrent of change can be attributed to a unique spiritual vantage. Though frequently claiming to "preach" within the pages of his journals, he also had a brief formal stint as a minister during his younger years. At the age of twenty, he decided that this might be his appropriate calling and was issued a preacher's license by a Methodist church in Woodson County, Kansas. He gave only seven sermons in Kansas but almost two decades later resumed the practice. In 1929, Rayburn briefly assumed pastoral duties at a Presbyterian church in Arkansas, yet by his own admission he was "a complete failure" in this vocation. Instead, by promoting the pursuit of faith outside official sanctuaries, he urged visitors through his writings to realize that spiritual gifts could be gleaned from experiences of immersion in the regional landscape.[38]

Rayburn's religious allusions drew only loosely from biblical narratives and rarely cited specific Christian precepts. For instance, he wrote that, if he were allowed to transfer his mind's eye to "history's pages," "Jacob's well would be in the Shepherd of the Hills country." Within another imaginative rendering, the Ozarks was "an enchanted land of milk and honey where the gates of paradise stand ajar." Alternately, the hazards of modern civilization were described with the aid of *Pilgrim's Progress,* as Rayburn equated Bunyan's Christian with the ailing modern who must "carry through the Slough of Despair, the City of Vanity . . . and the Valley of Death."[39]

Because he sought to station himself among the great nature philosophers, Rayburn's spiritual outlook was one that promoted ongoing revelation of the divine within the realm of human practice. For him, the "church problem" resulted from individuals who simply immersed themselves in social organization and refused to truly "experience Christ." In words that almost directly echoed those of Harold Bell Wright and would resonate with many later commentators, he found the Ozarks to be a place where "the unseen world becomes the real world," where "religious creeds steeped in superstition" had no currency, "and where inhabitants and visitors alike could find "God and the Kingdom of Heaven within themselves."[40]

Despite such debates about the merits of formal Christian practice, Rayburn's message was not limited to a singular mode of religiosity. Throughout thirty-five years of publishing, his syncretic vantage combined ancient mythology, indistinct Native American mysticism, and other vaguely spiritual stances. Annunciating his philosophy of idealism, he merged the seeking of the Golden Fleece, the quest for the Holy Grail, and the parable of the Pearl of Great Price to illustrate a

path to physical, mental, moral, and spiritual "transfiguration." Envisaging himself an American Indian, he imagined the building of a "sacred fire" and the production of a "smoke prayer to the Great Spirit" that would free his soul from the
"hypocrisy" of modernity. And further drawing on such metaphors to augment
his placing of the divine within nature and his rebuke of institutionalized faith,
Rayburn christened forests as "heavenly bliss" and springs as "a place of prayer"
while declaring that "man-built churches fit like store-clothes on an Indian."[41]

Amid frequent criticisms of official religiosity, Rayburn identified the materialism and commercialism of modern civilization (and specifically Ozark tourism) as the most perilous conduit for moral digression. In the early years of his
writing, he took a vehement stance against such depravations. In 1929 he labeled
the increasingly prominent motorist the "prophet of Beddlam" whose "philosophy is saturated with gasoline," and in 1930 he wrote that tourists were trapped
in a "standardized boomerang of experience" that precluded the real spiritual
transformation offered by his Ozark hills. At the root of this madness was a failure to appreciate the thorough permeation of the celestial into daily life. This
lack of acquaintance was said to result from the mechanized and homogeneous
character of modernity. For Rayburn, the ills of the institutional church were
troublesome but merely symptomatic of a larger social and cultural conundrum
of disenchantment. Extolling the virtues of the "Redman" once again, he proclaimed, "He saw no need for only the seventh day of worship, since to him all
days belonged to the Great Spirit of the Universe." Thus, such a bracketing of
worship symbolized a gamut of modern parameters placed on existence. For an
author who took nature as both his testament and his pulpit, these constraints
could only lead to a decline in righteousness and a failure to locate providence
within the bustle of contemporary life.[42]

Post–World War II prosperity and rapid modernization (including the emergence of these accretions in the Ozarks) effectively convinced Rayburn that there
was no returning to his idealized regional Arcadia. In 1945 he had still hoped to
preserve the "spirit and flavor of that halcyon period in the hills," but by 1953 he
was praising "the Ozarks of tomorrow" as a "veritable Garden of Eden" where
new dams would provide low-cost electricity, good roads would offer easier access, and the tourist trade would generate multimillion-dollar revenues.[43]

During the last decade of his life, Rayburn still dreamed of fencing off "a
few townships in the hills" and keeping them "entirely primitive" by prohibiting
automobiles, highways, and electricity. Yet the author had also realized that the
average American of the late 1950s did not share his premodern idealism. Appre-
hending that he could not stop the march of progress, he called for, in the final

years of his publishing, moderate stances toward modernity rather than absti-
nence from it (a view that may have also been prompted by his entrance into the
Ozark real estate trade). As he wrote in 1954:

> Life has become a complicated affair in recent years for a large part of our popula-
> tion. . . . This condition makes a paradox of civilization. We have all the benefits
> of science at nod and beck, but we have been unwise in its application. We have
> become slaves of a system that should be our servant. . . . America is indeed a land
> of opportunity, but we have been sold on material comforts to the extent that we
> make them the end instead of the means of existence. There seems to be a general
> misunderstanding as to what makes for happiness. The spiritual and mental aspects
> of life should come first. The happiest man lives in tune with the infinite. Peace in
> a mountain cabin is better than frustration in a palace. The trouble with our push-
> button civilization is that we put security ahead of opportunity, substituting the
> illusions of material things for the unseen realities that make life worthwhile.[44]

In this way, Rayburn's original Luddite tendencies were tempered by a realiza-
tion that social and cultural development had established more than a toehold
in the Ozarks.

Despite ever increasing concessions to modernity, the aging Rayburn continued to avow that he preferred to write about the Ozarks of his imagination and
that "Ozarkadia is a state of mind as well as a geographical unit." Although confessing in his autobiography that he always looked at the region "through rose
colored glasses," he left a voluminous body of writing that amounted to more
than facile idealism. Within his periodicals, Ozark Country (a 1941 study published
as part of the American Folkways series), a 229-"volume" Ozark Folk Encyclopedia, and numerous other writings, he went beyond mere boosterism to enumerate the many social, cultural, and environmental issues that imperiled his Ozark
Arcadia.[45]

On the death of its publisher in 1960, Rayburn's Ozark Guide was succeeded by
the Ozark Guide Yearbook, a magazine produced in Reeds Springs, Missouri. This
venture continued until 1966 but was almost entirely devoted to advertisements
for local tourist attractions and businesses. As a magazine that highlighted "Vacation & Retirement in the Lakes and Rivers Region," the Yearbook mentioned that
it had been established by Rayburn and sometimes featured reprints of his editorials. However, its unabashed promotion bore little similarity to its founder's
more idealistic and contested vision of the Ozark landscape. By thoroughly embracing the commercialism with which Rayburn grappled, this successor publication abandoned his philosophical hope that the unacquainted would make the

Ozarks their "geographic niche" and "the more abundant life" their "spiritual province."[46]

SANCTIFYING THE SOCIAL LANDSCAPE

As Branson became a tourism mecca in the latter part of the twentieth century, a multiplicity of voices continued to extol the city's ability to unite experiences of the landscape with spiritual sentiments, and this union sometimes emerged from unlikely sources. In 1974, Elmo Ingenthron published a history of Taney County, Missouri. Although the vast majority of the text was devoted to objective accounts, Ingenthron included in his preface words that praised the blessedness of Branson-area topography. Attempting to outline the many reasons why settlers chose the upper White River valley, he cited the opportunity for free land and escape from the travails of city life. However, the author then claimed that spirituality was the true motivating factor for most pioneers. This inspiration was said to arise from a variety of institutional and noninstitutional sources, such as standing on a "lofty hilltop" and beholding humble cabins and contented hill folk; observing a dewdrop that slowly faded away at sunrise and "returned to its maker;" witnessing a rainbow that "revealed the path to eternity"; discovering a "God-made altar" in the hills; or having an awakening at an "unpretentious country church house." Regardless of cause, Ingenthron finally asserted that the Ozark hills possessed "spiritual wealth" and were a consummate place for individuals to "rest and commune" with God.[47]

Ingenthron's status as a Taney County native certainly is a viable explanation for his portrait of the area, but it is nonetheless remarkable that his optimism appeared at a time when Branson was facing its most pressing environmental challenges to date. As he was writing, for example, biologists at the School of the Ozarks had issued a solemn warning concerning the fate of Table Rock Lake and its environs. In a study that examined the dangers of "prolific uncontrolled growth," Kenton C. Olson outlined the mounting pollution of waterways by solid waste treatment plants that deposited phosphorous into the lake and spawned algae growth. Furthermore, despite a popular perception that "ecology is on everyone's mind," tourist garbage continued to litter the terrain. Holding that some call these issues the result of "progress," the author instead marked them as a biological "cancer" that could result in massive destruction. Thus, as had been witnessed throughout the twentieth century, this virtuous landscape continued to breed vice, and its divinely sanctioned beauty remained the chief catalyst for its potential demise.[48]

Expansion and environmental degradation continued relatively unabated throughout the closing decades of the twentieth century. From 1970 to 1980, Taney County's population increased 57 percent, and from 1980 to 1990 it grew 25 percent. Simultaneously, Stone County's population swelled 57 percent during the former period and 22 percent during the latter, thus doubling the 1970 population of each county. Moreover, tourist visitation grew in leaps and bounds throughout this era, and on Branson's early 1990s boom, residents were forced to confront the despoiling of their surroundings. In November 1992, the Branson Area Environmental Task Force issued an executive summary that outlined a series of threats: inadequate sewage treatment and its impact on lake and stream water quality, poor septic tank sewage disposal, untenable storm water management programs, and insufficient groundwater protection strategies. A 1988 survey of Taney County residents demonstrated that 70 percent of those polled felt "the environment needs maximum protection" and 87 percent wanted "gradual development." Solidifying these anxieties was an incident on Memorial Day weekend in 1992 when tourist numbers were so high that the city's sewage system became overburdened and its treatment plant was forced to dump twenty thousand gallons of sludge directly into Lake Taneycomo.[49]

By the mid-1990s, tourist-driven growth was literally trashing Branson's landscape. Yet in 1992, a writer for *Branson Traveler Magazine* still described the region as "an excellent example of nature and man working together" to create a place "close to paradise." The Renfro Landfill, which serves Taney and five other counties, came under state investigation in the early years of that decade for leaching contaminants into nearby waterways. Additionally, the site doubled its volume of trash from 1993 to 1995 and grew 100 feet in height from 1987 to 1995. Improvements were made, of course. Branson's sewage treatment plant was expanded in 1993, and a second facility was slated to be built two years later. That same year, the city banned the use and sale of phosphate detergents in an attempt to slow algae growth in area lakes. However, these measures were not a complete fix. In the summer of 1998, for example, algae exploded on area lakes, jeopardizing the $26 million in revenue and more than 300 jobs generated by anglers at Table Rock and the $8 million and more than 100 jobs spawned from fishing at Taneycomo—earnings and livelihoods dependent on tourism yet endangered by the by-products of tourism's growth.[50]

Just as these issues were being addressed, the environmental priorities of residents switched from water quality to soil erosion and storm water runoff, thereby demonstrating the snowball effects of pollution in a tourism boomtown. In the early 1990s, Branson's Planning Commission was unable to monitor one hundred commercial properties that were regularly under construction simultaneously. By stripping the land of its trees and vegetation, such developments allowed unchecked runoff that both overburdened storm drains and denuded topsoil. Although residential builders like Cooper Communities sought to "change the future without changing the beauty" of their surroundings and area entertainers banded together for benefit concerts to combat growth "without any concern for the environment," construction illegalities persisted. In February 1994, the Branson Building Department discovered seventeen theaters, hotels, and restaurants opened since 1992 which could not pass mandatory inspections. More troubling for area watchdogs was that this finding was the result of a random sample—one that included only seventeen sites.[51]

As concerns mounted over environmental dangers, Branson continued to attract guests with promises of a spiritual experience of landscape. As documented, the Shepherd of the Hills Homestead and Theatre, Silver Dollar City, and myriad variety show venues profited from the region's 1990s explosion by linking visions of pristine nature with sentiments of divine natural creation and protection. Although these attractions did not make conservation a priority, they did make at least some efforts in that direction. One of the most astute individuals in this regard was Springfield architect Alan Bates, who designed Branson theaters, motels, and restaurants in the early 1990s and realized the necessity of making vacationer perceptions of the region conform to reality. As he stated, "Branson still has an image to the public of a place in the Ozark Mountains. . . . If we turn it into an environmental disaster with huge expanses of buildings and parking lots, they will stop coming."[52]

In 1999 three local properties affiliated with Silver Dollar City were recognized by Audubon International for contributions to environmental quality, and co-owner Jack Herschend was acknowledged by the National Arbor Day Foundation for his environmental stewardship. It is certainly undeniable that one can enjoy immaculate surroundings protected by sincere conservationist outlooks on the grounds of Silver Dollar City and the Shepherd of the Hills Homestead. These sites have grasped the import of such efforts for their business since rising to regional prominence during the middle of the twentieth century. However, as Branson's Strip became the city's premier tourist draw, similar sentiments were difficult to locate there. Theater owners such as Andy Williams may have made an attempt to integrate their buildings' design into the surrounding topography, but within a sea of asphalt and neon, such vernacularly inspired architecture-landscape correspondences were growing increasingly tenuous. Additionally, since the mid-1990s local politicians have sought ways to curb pollution caused by tour bus drivers who idle their engines while waiting for riders at area attractions. Thus, although a recent visitor from Kentucky described Branson as "a breath of fresh air," this assertion has spoken more to the city's moral rather than physical atmosphere since its boom.[53]

Many regional commentators apprehended the paradox of "neon and nature" (a slogan adopted by the Branson/Lakes Area Chamber of Commerce and Convention and Visitors Bureau in 1997), yet most of them nonetheless found it difficult to resist furthering bucolic and spiritually laden sentiments. For instance, Leland Payton, in a book of photographs entitled *The Beautiful and Enduring Ozarks* (1999), publicized the fortitude of the area's landscape amid "the crawling chaotic sprawl of our times." Through pictures of pristine rivers, lakes, and hills, Payton continued to advertise the Ozarks as a place capable of positioning one "far from the maddening crowd." Although he did not directly address the material undertakings necessary to maintain these utopian aspects, the author emphasized two familiar "value systems" that would ensure vitality. As long as an "appreciation of natural beauty" upheld its relationship with "rural Christian culture," the region would remain an escape from the problems of contemporary American society and continue to evade the environmental despoiling that seemed an inevitable product of this flight.[54]

In April 1998, *National Geographic* ran another feature on the Ozarks. Unlike previous coverage, this article devoted little time to valorizing premodern cultural remnants and instead focused on ecological hazards resulting from a now booming tourist economy. Page after page was filled with discussion of Branson's rise to national prominence (describing the city as "not much more than a bait stop 25 years ago"), and glossy photos illustrated the polished techniques of local entertainers Tony Orlando and Andy Williams. Detailing the "repercussions of this explosive growth" on residents and the landscape, author Lisa Moore LaRoe saw traffic congestion and waterway pollution as an inevitable aspect of local population increasing at twice the national average. Outside Branson, the expansion of poultry, logging, cattle, and mining industries was producing similarly damaging environmental effects. Although conservation still had much currency in the Ozarks, loggers argued that a "happy medium" must be struck—one that took wilderness values into consideration but also respected the needs of the human component of the landscape. As one sawmill owner argued, "Maybe those plants need to survive, but us folks need to survive too." As the region continued to develop, this almost century-old battle between the furthering of resident livelihoods and the safeguarding of the Arcadian aspects of the terrain sought by vacationers raged on a variety of fronts.

This story's spiritual focus was mainly cast on the popular variant of religiosity offered by Branson's entertainment industry rather than on folksy churches or rural evangelists. The article included a discussion with the Haygoods, eight children who presented their variety act at Silver Dollar City. The Haygoods described their noninstitutional and performative expression of belief as one that touted "faith, family, and freedom"—a triumvirate of virtues said to be invoked at "virtually all Branson shows." Although the author saw this nebulous brand of domestic and civic spirituality as much of the reason for the city's appeal, she found personal succor at more conventional services. After itemizing numerous concerns that were the cause of ever increasing discord in the region, LaRoe discovered "harmony" at a nondenominational church on the outskirts of Branson. As the "sweetest notes" sprang from the preacher's guitar, she stumbled on the bedrock that still underscored the increasingly fragile Ozark landscape. Like many commentators before her, she thus posited simple faith as perhaps the only element capable of fostering tranquility amid the chaos of regional development.[55]

During the late twentieth century, the spiritualizing of the physical and human components of the Ozark landscape was primarily the bastion of tourism boosters.However, Branson's institutional churches also addressed this issue to a degree. In the winter of 1992, dozens of area construction workers, aspiring entertainers, and their families faced homelessness as the city's building and vacation seasons came to a close. Unable to find employment during cold weather, these individuals could not secure affordable housing or money for food or clothing and were subsisting in tents and makeshift pickup truck campers. This deluge of people who had come to Branson with hopes of establishing a toehold within its economy resulted in a January 1993 unemployment rate of 20.6 percent in Taney County and 24.3 percent in Stone County—both figures two times as high as those of the previous January and nearly seven times greater than those in the summer months. As summarized by John Brown, owner of a Branson campground populated by many facing this plight, "You're looking at the new pioneers of the '90s, in trailers and vans instead of covered wagons."[56]

A city of only a few thousand permanent residents, Branson did not have governmental infrastructure to address this crisis. Instead, victims of tourism's growth were aided by the Branson Hills Assembly of God Church and a consortium of local faith communities and entertainers. In December 1992, Branson Hills' pastor, Howard Boyd, turned the lower level of his church into a homeless shelter. During the three-month winter period, it served approximately 6,000 meals and provided nearly 2,400 overnight stays. This effort drew on the resources of many congregations. During the first year of the initiative, five other churches served food and consoled people in need. The shelter continued for three consecutive winters. Each year, participation increased, with eight churches taking part in 1993–1994 and eleven in 1994–1995. Additionally, representatives of the tourism industry joined these religious bodies. Silver Dollar City's Jack Herschend implemented a fund-raising campaign among local businesses, and benefit concerts were organized to generate revenues for the building of affordable housing by interdenominational Christian organizations. Thus, through a church-instituted endeavor that then garnered the support of the entertainment industry—a community-wide undertaking described by Pastor Boyd as bordering on "the miraculous"—the shelter was able to stem the mounting tide of homelessness.[57]

Although housing became less of a concern after the boom years of the early 1990s, other threats to the city's sense of place have necessitated ongoing attention by coalitions of church officials and tourism administrators. Gambling has been one of the more contentious concerns. Under the Indian Gaming Regulatory Act (IGRA), which became law in 1988, Native American tribes were allowed to operate gambling facilities on tribal land after reaching compacts with state governments. In 1994, plans were proposed by New Jersey–based Creative Learning Products for an 800-acre site 10 miles north of Branson. As part of this design, the company entered into a "letter of understanding" with the Eastern Shawnee tribe, a group already operating a bingo facility outside Seneca, Missouri. Although they owned no property near Branson, under provisions of the 1988 law the Eastern Shawnee were vested with the ability to acquire new land with the permission of the Department of the Interior and the state governor. In the fall of 1994, Creative Learning formed a subsidiary company, Creative Gaming International, and announced that it had $25 million to spend on a Branson-area gaming project to be initiated jointly with the Eastern Shawnee.[58]

Word of these plans inspired a range of negative reactions from local residents and vacationers, many of whom phrased their objections in religious language. Although the proposed casino was to be erected north of Branson in Christian County, it would have still been easily accessible by the city's millions of travelers. Many of the responses posited Branson as the antithesis of America's gambling citadel, Las Vegas, and contrasted that city's Sodom with the Ozarks' consecrated terrain. Tommy Thompson summoned this dichotomy when he stated, "Keep it in Las Vegas—we don't want it here. Why do you think they call us *Christian* County?" Even Peter Jegou, the founder and president of Creative Learning Products, realized the impossibility of establishing gaming within Branson's city limits. As he asserted, "I don't think you'll ever see gaming in Branson. We want to become part of the community in Branson, and I know Taney County is a Bible Belt area."[59]

Throughout 1994, casino opponents outweighed supporters by a four-to-one margin in the *Springfield News-Leader's* editorial columns. In that paper, M. A. Jones claimed that gambling was a "sin" and that "God will not bless a nation that sinks deeper and deeper into more sinful things." Linda Blazer asserted, "As a Christian, getting gain from someone else's losses . . . is foreign to the principles given in the Bible." Some residents expounded that this ethical hazard might be the gateway to virtually all other social evils. Vicky Lada wrote, "If you have gambling, then you have bars, and along with all that atmosphere, someone will want to have a nude bar. Then there'll be prostitutes, and alcohol leads to more accidents on the highways." Ann Roberts added, "I pray we never get gambling down here. That'll bring in thieves, professional gamblers. It isn't so much the gambling; it's what follows gambling." Frequent visitor Linda Purvis declared that "gambling would be a disaster in Branson" and that "there is enough distasteful things in life all around us, every day!" Tourist Fred Browning added that the orientation of the area would "totally change" on the implementation of gaming and that the Ozarks may no longer be able to "encourage Christian values."[60]

Branson entertainers also banded together to combat this threat to their virtue-inspired industry. In September 1994, musician and comedian Jim Stafford drafted a letter sent to twenty-four politicians, including Missouri governor Mel Carnahan and Secretary of the Interior Bruce Babbitt, which bluntly pronounced that gambling was "not acceptable for this area." The protest was signed by twenty-five Branson artists, including Mel Tillis, who suggested that the city was one of the final tourist meccas to "hold out" against such corrupting influences. Boxcar Willie furthered this sentiment by adding that Branson was "the last bastion of family entertainment" and that tourists accustomed to good, clean shows would view gambling as a mar on this image. An event at the Glen Campbell Goodtime Theatre brought together local performers and tourism administrators, chamber of commerce members, and city government officials, all of whom agreed that a casino would not enhance the region's "quality of life." At this emotionally charged event, Jim Stafford even broke down in tears as he recounted an experience at a Las Vegas pawn shop. There, the owner showed him a jar of gold fillings sold for gambling money, some of which had been extracted on site by patrons with the use of pliers. Unable to continue his speech beyond this story, Stafford thus demonstrated the physical and spiritual effects of gaming—a combination of dangers feared by all at the meeting.[61]

Although gambling could harm bodies and souls, its Branson opponents also cited economic impacts that would damage the city's reliance on religious sentiment as a salable commodity. People felt that such "unwholesome" tourism alternatives would siphon moneys out of the local community and introduce criminal elements unseen in the city up to that point. As detailed in Chapter 3, Silver Dollar City has indeed led Branson's charge against what co-owner Peter Herschend termed the "cancer of gambling." Vocalizing this concern from a marketing standpoint, he further stated, "It would be disastrous on our established entertainment community." Ultimately, Creative Learning's venture could not move forward without gubernatorial approval. Governor Carnahan, who had been approached by numerous companies with similar aspirations during his term yet assuredly realized the importance of Branson for the state's economic livelihood, forthrightly declared, "I have spurned all of them and indicated I have no interest in that."[62]

The debate over legalized gambling in Missouri has a long and contentious history, one that has often been motivated by religious interests and groups. In Branson, the pastoral assault was spearheaded by Jay Scribner, who served First Baptist Church from 1977 to 2005, founded a local Christian radio station and school, and is a former president of the Missouri Baptist Convention. In an attempt to defeat the state's first bill permitting riverboat casinos in 1992, Scribner brought ten phone lines into his church, and congregants spent several weeks calling voters in Taney County. Under the auspices of "Citizens for Good Government," the church initially devoted its attention to contacting several thousand unregistered voters who expressed opposition to the measure. Subsequently, eighteen thousand registered individuals were called, and those in disagreement with the proposition were offered rides to the polls and reminded of the election date. In November, Taney County led the state in opposition to the referendum, with 76 percent of residents voting against it. Although riverboat casinos on the Missouri and Mississippi rivers were legalized through constitutional alteration in 1998, the vast majority of the county's residents have remained staunchly opposed to gambling. According to Scribner, this steadfastness has occurred because Branson's "Christian people keep a vigil" and in the city there exists "a conscious effort by churches, Christians individually, and business people who either are Christian or have good values, good morals, good ethics . . . to use the Bible as the standard for living."[63]

Throughout the past two decades, Scribner and the First Baptist Church have also led community efforts to combat a variety of other social evils. In March 1990, a group of male exotic dancers began performing in town. Their act lasted only four days, however, before pressure from First Baptist and other local churches compelled an ordinance to regulate adult entertainments. Four months later, the dancers returned to perform at a lounge north of Branson. Once again gratifying the concerns of area Christians, Taney County prosecutor James Justus filed for an injunction forbidding further shows by citing state obscenity laws. According to those statutes, any material or performance could be declared obscene if it breached community standards by having a predominant appeal to prurient interest in sex without artistic, political, or scientific value. On this investigation, the dancers and Jacquelyn M. Smith, owner of the lounge, quickly fled the city before lawsuits could be served. Shortly thereafter, Taney County also passed a ban against such entertaining.[64]

Whether battling gambling, exotic dancers, or a host of other social concerns, Scribner has always invoked Branson's unique "atmosphere" or "environment." Moreover, he has frequently marked it as a moral exemplar for the rest of the nation and noted that its recreationally mediated religious climate possessed myriad evangelical possibilities. Iterating the sentiments of millions of Branson devotees, Scribner asserted that the city is "America the way it ought to be." Through the "mission-minded" attitudes of local churches, theaters, and other attractions, he hopes that the Ozarks will continue to function as a vacation-motivated springboard for a larger revival of moral fortitude. Encapsulating the reach of this unified church-entertainment front and its persistent maintenance of the area's sacred landscape, he proclaimed, "God has commissioned us to take the city—meaning we're trying to do everything we possibly can to make it extremely difficult to go to hell from Branson, Missouri."[65]

Since Branson's rise to national prominence, area Christians inspired by Scribner's edict have sought to further notions of sacred placefulness by means of ministries to tourists, performers, and pastors. Mountain Country Ministries is an arm of the Tri-County Baptist Association, a consortium of fifty-seven Southern Baptist churches in Taney, Stone, and Christian counties. Through a variety of programs, including motor-coach, hotel/motel, and summer resort ministries, the association hopes, in the words of its director, Jim Wells, "to make disciples and see people come to Christ." Its motor-coach initiative (now called Chapel Ministry) began in 1995 to serve the 10,000–12,000 tour buses arriving in Branson each year. It was instigated by a tour-company president who contacted Tri-County because he was concerned with travelers not having an opportunity for Sunday worship. As most such tours had people of different religious preferences, vacationers could not be transported to the church of their choice. Moreover, most trips ended on Sunday, and so there was little opportunity to attend a more formal house of worship. Since 1995, twenty-minute Bible devotions that "transcend denominational boundaries" have been conducted by volunteers for tourists desiring "Chapel on the Coach"—a service described by one vacationer as "the Amen to our Branson trip." As an offshoot, thirty-minute hotel/motel services composed of religious music and devotionals are conducted at a variety of Christian-owned establishments. Although these meetings have drawn as few as two people, as many as eighty have attended at the Honeysuckle Inn—a hotel that frequently hosts religious events and conferences.[66]

Mountain Country Ministries' longest-running endeavor is its summer resort program. Since 1973, teams of youths have come into the Branson area from all over the United States for a summer mission trip. For nine weeks, 900–1,200 volunteers conduct daytime activities at campgrounds and perform a variety act on the porches of entertainment venues or other public sites in the evening. High school and college students must arrange for their own housing while on these trips. Accommodations can usually be found at Christian-owned lodges, local Baptist and non-Baptist church facilities, and in the homes of people sympathetic to their mission. Volunteers are also often provided complimentary tickets to Branson venues and attractions. As a result of all three undertakings, Mountain Country Ministries facilitated 125 professions of faith from tourists in 2001—an accomplishment that Wells claimed was the result of Christian faith permeating Branson's "physical landscape" and "the fabric of the people."[67]

Six miles south of Branson on Table Rock Lake is the Stonecroft Conference Center, another ministry that hopes to capitalize on tourists seeking a "scenic and inspirational setting" by offering "vacations with a purpose." The conference center is part of the larger Kansas City, Missouri–based Stonecroft Ministries, an organization begun in 1938 by Helen Duff Baugh. In addition to its Branson-area center, Stonecroft has for more than sixty years sponsored Christian Women's Clubs (brunch, luncheon, or dinner meetings), Friendship Bible Coffees (small-group, in-home weekly studies), Bible correspondence classes, conferences, and a variety of print resources. It is a nondenominational ministry operating in eighty-four countries, and its "Statement of Faith" allies Stonecroft with an evangelical variant of Christianity through the promotion of the inerrancy of scripture, the inherent sinfulness of humanity, the necessity of new birth, the literal resurrection of Jesus, and worldwide evangelism.[68]

The conference center's facilities include 71 guest rooms, a 450-seat auditorium/sanctuary, and a 240-seat dining area. Approximately half of the staff consists of senior citizen volunteers who provide their services in return for the opportunity to lodge in a Christian setting. Guests can enjoy hiking trails, a large

Good Shepherd Inn, circa 2000. Postcard from the author's collection

indoor swimming pool, exercise room, and easy access to the gamut of Branson attractions. Throughout the year, Stonecroft hosts retreats for women, men, families, and pastors, all of which must be booked at least two years in advance. In addition, the center offers twelve weeks of seminars featuring speakers, musicians, and workshops. Stonecroft attracts visitors from across the Christian spectrum, but all groups must guarantee that they will offer "Christ-centered programming," and an agenda is required four months prior to any event to ensure that this content is present.

Consonant with a time-honored strategy of Branson tourism, Stonecroft offers religiously motivated vacationers an escape from modern tribulations and an experience that tempers Ozark rusticity with contemporary conveniences. According to Brian Smith, director of sales and guest services, his center believes "Christians should not have to settle for second rate" and thus indulges guests with a wide variety of amenities and services. At the same time, domestic comfort is not lost within experiences of luxury. Visitors have constantly iterated in their poststay feedback that they felt "safe" and that visiting the site "was like coming home." Some of this sentiment assuredly derives from Stonecroft's all-Christian staff and emphasis on renowned regional friendliness. However, an ethical climate and a palatable godly presence add to this mood. As stated by Smith, "The reason they come home is that we can't deny the power of the Holy

Spirit either. People come through those doors and say, 'I feel the Holy Spirit in this place.'" By merging this vantage with proximity to wholesome and spiritual Branson attractions, Stonecraft enables its visitors to partake of a multitiered experience of sacred space.[69]

Mountain Country Ministries and Stonecroft are only two of a wide variety of initiatives in the Branson area which employ notions of sacred space to enhance the Christian vacation. As a corollary, a number of ministries have adopted a slightly different focus by concentrating on the thousands of Christians employed by the tourism industry. Jeff and Emma Hurst are the founders of Victory Mountain Ministries, an initiative that caters to the spiritual needs of area performers. Both people have a long history of involvement with Christian entertainment within and outside Branson. On the national level, they worked for the Christian Broadcasting Network in the mid-1980s as production assistants. Emma has done wardrobe for Pat Robertson. Jeff played the role of Jesus at an outdoor theater on the grounds of Praise the Lord Ministries. In Branson, they have also been involved with Passion plays and religious productions. In the early 1980s the Hursts helped to open *Love's Greatest Story*, a short-lived production about the life of Christ staged at a now defunct amphitheater off the Strip. Jeff once again assumed the role of Jesus, and Emma was the set manager. Both have also been involved with Dino Kartsonakis's spiritually guided act.[70]

Although they are still active in the performance aspects of Branson tourism, a decade ago the Hursts turned their attention to the fallout of an industry that was attracting scores of Christian entertainers. As Emma has said, "A lot of people prayed all through the '90s for God to bless this area and really make it a Christian area," and consequently, it became known for its pious product and equally as virtuous players. However, it is sometimes difficult to ally image with reality; commenting on "many of the people who have been elevated in this town as being really strong Christians," Jeff noted, "I've been backstage with them and watched them cussing, swearing, going through temper fits, and not showing any signs that they were a Christian at all." Thus, Victory Mountain Ministries was formed with the intention of helping entertainers grapple with the pressures of being on-stage moral exemplars for millions of vacationers while struggling with ethical shortcomings in their off-stage lives. During their many years in town the Hursts have counseled performers dealing with drug and alcohol addictions, sexual abuse, marital infidelity, and a host of other concerns. By offering worship services and religious gatherings, they have tried to help individuals unite their "stage persona" with who they "really are." According to Emma, "What you say about God on stage doesn't matter. It's what you say about God backstage that matters."[71]

In 1996 former Branson entertainer, revival musician, and ordained Southern Baptist minister Larry Wilhite founded Backstage Ministries—an endeavor that also supplies Branson performers and support people with spiritual succor. As he maintained, "Entertainers are susceptible to the 'God syndrome.' It's easy for a performer to think, 'I'm on stage, thousands of people are there to see me—whew—I'm God.'" In an attempt to assuage such hubris, Wilhite combats pretense by allowing artists to voice their anxieties in a confidential setting. By visiting theaters once a week, conducting Bible studies, and offering moments for prayer within the chaos of the theater trade, he tries to address "financial, emotional, or spiritual" needs. Concurrent with these attempts, Backstage Ministries views Branson as a "missionary field." As Wilhite avowed, "The only difference between me and a missionary in Africa is I'm in my backyard." Evidencing the import of this ministry was a February 2000 reunion concert to benefit it, with performances by popular Branson entertainers from the 1970s and 1980s such as the Foggy River Boys, the Plummer Family, the Baldknobbers, and the Presleys. As individuals who had experienced the travails of an ethically driven tourism industry, all expressed sympathy for contemporary performers who face even greater pressures to model Christian virtue in public while toiling to manifest this same religiosity in their private lives.[72]

Since Branson's boom, the area has also witnessed the emergence of ministries by pastors for pastors. Bill McPhail, an ordained minister in the Missionary Church who has devoted much of his career to counseling people in the Christian entertainment industry, came to the Branson area in 1994. On arrival he established En-Gedi Ministries—a retreat for pastors. Appropriately, the ministry's namesake is the largest oasis along the western shore of the Dead Sea. There, according to 1 Samuel 23:29–24:1, David sought refuge in a cave while being pursued by Saul and his armies. Additionally, En-Gedi is mentioned as a site of beauty, restoration, and spiritual prosperity in the Song of Solomon 1:14 and Ezekiel 47:10. Drawing on these precedents, McPhail hopes his site will become a place for pastors to "sit on the porch, look out over the hills, download frustrations, get a fresh perspective," and see "that they are not alone dealing with the frustrations of modern-day ministry." Among this body of dissatisfactions, he included "theological shifting," lack of denominational loyalty, deficient commitment to "ideals" by the baby boomer generation, changes in worship style and music, and the dawn of the "megachurch"—issues that have resulted in massive departures from pastoral positions and "a major crisis in America across . . . every denomination."[73]

McPhail left his home in Michigan after "the spirit of God" told him to end his pastorate and come to Branson. In 1994 he purchased 21 acres 7 miles north of town replete with caves, springs, and other natural features that reminded him of En-Gedi (which he has visited on numerous occasions). Proximity to Branson was vital for this ministry, for as he stated, this "refuge in the Ozarks . . . is a great entertainment town where God and country are at the forefront." Like Victory Mountain and Backstage Ministries, which endeavor to help specific groups of people, En-Gedi hopes to relieve stress caused by pastors having always to model exemplary thought and behavior for their congregations. Moreover, McPhail trusts that after experiencing his retreat ministers will effect change in both their vocational and personal lives. Echoing the focus on lived religiosity that has permeated Branson since the days of Harold Bell Wright, he declared, "I don't know care how high you jump when you shout. I care about how straight you walk when you come down." McPhail envisions En-Gedi Ministries as an oasis and an immersion in a "rebirth of authentic Christianity" taking place in the area. He thus feels that when his site is completed, it will mimic the aforementioned biblical haven and allow visitors to draw inspiration from its scenic splendor and nearness to the nation's premier Christian vacation mecca.[74]

A wide variety of individualized ministries have sought to actualize a regionally situated vantage that utilizes notions of sacred landscape to further Christian sentiments. However, in the contemporary Ozarks, members of the clergy have also joined together to promote interdenominational efforts focused on that same end. In 1996, a number of local pastors united for a four-day retreat that grew out of the International Renewal Ministries Prayer Summits. Not dealing with theological or social issues, the group focused instead on divine entreaty and cooperation. As a consequence of this ongoing yearly event, Branson-area pastors have also organized a weekly prayer group (now called the Tri-Lakes Pastors Prayer Summit Group) intent on demolishing denominational walls and fostering a united front of religious people to pray for the continuance of Branson's special religious climate. The assembly is currently facilitated by Branson Hills Assembly of God pastor Howard Boyd, who avowed that it takes the ministers "out of roles of competition into collaboration." The gathering convenes on Wednesday mornings at churches, theaters, or business establishments and is composed of members from a variety of churches. According to Bill McPhail, he has never been in a community where there is such "spiritual bonding" or where one finds "a Presbyterian praying for an Assemblies of God praying for a Baptist."[75]

Designed to emulate the Tri-Lakes Pastors Prayer Summit Group, a weekend-long convocation was held in August 2002 which brought together thirty-five Christian entertainers and business professionals. Meant, according to Jay Scribner, "to cross economic lines, cross business lines, and bring people together with the one common denominator that they have a relationship with Jesus Christ," this event also has resulted in weekly meetings (dubbed the Marketplace Prayer Group) to support antigambling initiatives and to foster Branson's spiritual atmosphere. Because this consortium of pastors and businesspeople is locally based, their meetings are integrally linked to the maintenance of sacred space. As phrased by Howard Boyd, "When you pray together God does something with people's hearts that just alters the landscape. What we've discovered is that God calls pastors to a geography. What we're now finding is that it's not just pastors that God calls to a geography. It's like God calls business and professional people, laity, to a geography as well."[76]

Despite overwhelming support for interdenominational collaboration by local pastors, the movement is not totalistic. Father Richard Kellogg became rector of Branson's Shepherd of the Hills Episcopal Church in January 2002. As his church is obviously linked with Harold Bell Wright and even, on dedication in 1960, included an entire wall devoted to the memory of the author, it would seem logical that Shepherd of the Hills Episcopal would be a leading player in local interdenominational efforts. However, according to Kellogg, "[Other area clergy members] tend to look at me as probably more Catholic than I am," an assessment that he claimed placed him outside the "mostly evangelical Protestant persuasion" of the prayer summits. This difference not only is ideological but also has a variety of material manifestations. For instance, he recounted a recent clergy meeting in which there was hardly anyone from a "mainstream church" and surmised from that assembly that he is the only cleric in the city that "wears a collar." Though seemingly insignificant, this costuming comment speaks to both the conservative Protestant emphases of Branson's collective pastorate and their focus on lived religiosity. A newcomer to the area, Kellogg expressed amazement that local ministers do not "dress the part." However, as demonstrated over the past century, a thorough integration of faith into daily existence has often expunged such marks of distinction to suffuse all aspects of society and culture with religious presence.[77]

Considering the preponderance of Southern Baptist and Assemblies of God churches in the area, it is not surprising that representatives from Our Lady of the Lakes Catholic Church are also infrequent participants at ecumenical activities. Monsignor Phil Bucher, pastor from 1993 to 2005, attributed this lack of involvement to both structural and theological reasons. Wednesday morning interdenominational meetings were impossible to attend because of morning mass, and since he was the church's only clergyman, he was also prevented from being present at weekend-long prayer summits. Additionally, as part of a "ritualistic" or "sacramental" church, Bucher claimed that some local pastors feel that the Catholic perspective is not based enough on biblical materials to merit inclusion and that the "fundamentalist approach" of some congregations dissuades him from active membership in those groups. Addressing Branson's vaunted Christian placefulness, Bucher labeled the mind-set "a dream of my fellow ministers" while adding that he questions "the reality of it." In his perspective, this sanctified outlook has elided recognition of many social ills that still imperil the local landscape—an ironic view given that Branson's first contemporary interdenominational efforts centered on alleviating such community quandaries.[78]

PLACE AND PROPHECY

Branson's divinely mandated sense of place has been augmented in recent decades by a vague prophecy offered by Corrie Ten Boom, a Christian who led resistance to the Nazis in Holland, survived the Ravensbruck concentration camp, and became an influential author and lecturer. Her thoughts on the city are difficult, if not impossible, to corroborate, yet they have much currency among numerous local Christians. According to musician Dino Kartsonakis, who once worked with her ministry, Ten Boom traveled to Branson in the late 1970s. After surveying the city from above, she declared that it would become a "beacon of light for the world to see" and that soon "great blessings would come to the area." A similar account has been offered by Mike Radford, one of Branson's chief purveyors of civil religiosity. In his description, Ten Boom was flying over the area in the early 1960s and asked the pilot to tell her the name of the city below. When informed that it was Branson, she replied that "the Lord had just spoken to her heart" and that God "was going to use Branson for his glory." In light of this narrative, Radford has described Branson as "a city of destiny" with the ability to "change our nation for the better, one person, one family at a time." These accounts appear in none of Ten Boom's published materials, but during my fieldwork similar versions were cited on a several occasions by pastors, entertainers, and tourism boosters. One interviewee who recounted the anecdote, director of the Branson Gospel Music Association Phyllis Rotrock, bluntly stated that "there is really no proof" of this prophecy but then nevertheless asserted it as integral for understanding the play of the sacred in the area.[79]

Ten Boom's divination has not only underscored the conceptualization of Branson as sacred space but has also resulted in substantive remembrances. According to Phyllis Rotrock, while meditating in the late 1990s she was divinely instructed to write a book entitled "What God Is Doing in Branson." Skeptical of her literary skills and ability to convey all the wondrous things going on in town, she balked at the idea before receiving another celestial message. In this second disclosure she was told to go with friend Carolyn Daniels to evangelist Billye Brim's Prayer Mountain—a rustic retreat 18 miles outside Branson inspired by Ten Boom's insights. This site regularly hosts workshops focused on study of the "last days" and is driven by Brim's revelation that "angels were holding the land" for her project. There, while praying near a little brook, Daniels conceived of the Hiding Place Café and Ministry, a local restaurant that also provides jobs and lodging to women and children in crisis situations. Daniels derived her organization's name from two sources—Psalm 32:7 ("You are a hiding place for me; you preserve me from trouble; you surround me with glad cries of deliverance" [NRSV]) and Ten Boom's book, *The Hiding Place,* which documented her experiences during World War II. Since 2001, this organization's work, supported by a host of area entertainers, has sought to emulate Ten Boom's sanctuary. According to Daniels, "God brings things for the ministry and meets the needs we have. . . . Every day He does miracles."[80]

In addition to such Ozark-specific prophecy, modern-day Branson has also perpetuated a more standardized expression of premillennial dispensationalism. As the city boomed in the early 1990s, a *U.S. News & World Report* poll indicated that 61 percent of Americans believed Jesus will return; 53 percent held that some world events in the twentieth century fulfill biblical prophecy; and a significant percentage felt that the Bible should be taken literally when it speaks of a final Judgment Day (60 percent) and the Rapture of the church (44 percent). Shortly after the city's rise to national prominence, Tim LaHaye and Jerry B. Jenkins published the first novel in their incredibly popular Left Behind series—a sequence of books built around such end-time themes as the Second Coming, the Antichrist, and a variety of tribulations that will befall the unchurched. This apocalyptic epistemology permeates the worldviews of millions affiliated with the Southern Baptist Convention, various Pentecostal and charismatic denominations (including the Ozarks-based Assemblies of God), and thousands of independent "Bible churches" and is thus integral to Branson's contemporary evangelical Christian tourist base. Daniel Wojcik has described premillennial dispensationalism as a "profound fatalism for a world believed to be irredeemably evil" entwined with faith in a "predestined, perfect age of harmony and human fulfillment." In light of the ways that Branson has historically conjoined a critique of modern depravity with promises of an Ozark utopia, this more theologically oriented merger of faith and fatalism seems an apt fit for the regional ethos.[81]

To codify such sentiments, in recent years Branson has hosted a variety of prophecy conferences. For instance, in August 2001 Sherlock Bally Ministries sponsored the Branson International Prophecy Summit, an event that included a presentation by renowned premillennial author Hal Lindsey and drew three thousand attendees. Speaker Zola Levitt, a Jewish Christian whose ministry focuses on the place of Israel in prophecy, stated that the gathering possessed "a hidden level of joy" and that Branson visitors should feel no apocalyptic trepidation because "prophecy is threatening only to the nonbeliever." Further, in October 2002 the First International Messianic Encounter Conference was held at Branson's Grandvista at the Woods and featured Eddie Chumney, who discussed the Jewishness of the Christian Messiah and the prophetic significance of the Middle East peace process. Finally, in June 2006, the local Thousand Hills Resort hosted "Transmillennial 2006." Although emphasizing aforementioned themes, this four-day event also offered participants the chance to visit Silver Dollar City, variety shows, and other area attractions. In feedback, attendees lauded the area's "beautiful scenery" and, even while at a symposium on end-time tribulations, cited Branson's now familiar merger of "theology, personal experiences, and humor" as a primary draw.[82]

In September 2002, a conference entitled "Roots: The Spiritual History of the Branson Region" was hosted by Steve and Gaye Lisby, the founders of Lion of Judah Ministries. Though much more diminutive than the international conferences discussed above, this event best illustrates the fusion of prophetic aspirations and a sanctified Branson landscape. Thirty people attended this conference, including a variety of local Pentecostal, charismatic, and other conservative Protestant pastors. The meeting's primary intention was to discern ways that the divine destiny and purpose of the region could be achieved. This goal required a three-part process: research into the "sins of our fathers," repentance for these transgressions, and removal of their taint on lives and land. Providing a synopsis of this plan, the symposium's opening prayer declared:

> Oh Lord, our God, by the end of this conference may our hearts have been convicted of our sins and the sins of our forefathers. May we truly feel the sorrow of these sins, and "stand in the gap" for our land, our people and all those who will come after us. May we humble ourselves before you and repent so that you can heal our land and our people that we may become all that you have called us to

become. May this city and this region become the "city of refuge" for all of broken and lost humanity. May we fulfill our destiny according to your divine will and foreknowledge, that you may be glorified and that all may know that you are God and Jesus Christ, your son, is the only "way, the truth and the life."

Although all attendees concurred that significant divinations pronouncing the blessedness of Branson and its import for end-time prophecy had been leveled throughout the 1990s, they also agreed that these transformations had yet to come about. According to conference organizers, historical research offered explanation for this failing. Much of the event consisted of exploring the region's past and marking a range of sins that continue to contaminate the landscape. Through this process of "spiritual mapping," one was thus able to identify "strategies and methods" employed by "spiritual forces of darkness to influence the people and the churches" of southwestern Missouri. The need for such mystical cartography was deemed imperative because it allows "God's people to take back the land, occupy it, and multiply in it," provides "supernatural vision of the enemy," and paves the way for evangelism.

In these discussions, speakers broached a gamut of past and present transgressions that still haunt Branson: witchcraft, lawlessness, murder, drug abuse, racial supremacy, church discord, oppression of the poor, profanation of the Sabbath, homosexuality, adultery, and incest. To demonstrate the ways that these indiscretions have permeated regional history, participants engaged in protracted study of the area's Native American heritage to unearth "racist," polygamous, and pagan practices; discussed issues of murder and lawlessness perpetrated by bushwackers and Baldknobbers during the tumultuous Civil War period; investigated the historical and contemporary presence of "cults" such as Wicca and Mormonism; detailed the work of secret societies like the Freemasons; explored divisiveness among Christian denominations; and looked at data related to contemporary drug abuse, divorce, and domestic violence in Branson. In response to this list of wrongdoings, one participant proclaimed, "It is time for the Lion of Judah to roar and heal our land. It is time for us to repent of indifference, lack of empathy, complacency. God has given us the time, for us to be vessels through whom he can transform our area."[83]

A recent Branson tourist connected herself to the prophetic vantages of many local religious leaders when she wrote, "God is in most of the people I've met and the Spirit is moving, for things will come to those that believe." Although pundits often posit Branson as a site of homogeneous faith, there is certainly not unanimity concerning the role of the city within an intricate web of premillennial prophecy. As might be expected based on the Vatican's relative silence about such issues, Our Lady of the Lakes' Monsignor Phil Bucher questioned the social utility of this conjecture. Instead of meeting to discuss ways that the city can promote its standing as divinely sanctioned, he instead thought pastors should be considering issues of inadequate housing, the dynamics of Mexican immigration to the Ozarks, or the securing of a livable wage. If Bucher were directing these gatherings, he would "temper all of that prophetic stuff" with such public concerns and make "how we treat our neighbor" of primary importance. Moreover, even those of an evangelical persuasion have expressed similar reservations. Bill McPhail, an active participant in interdenominational meetings and a pastor who has invoked the divine sanctioning of Branson, nevertheless stated in relation to Corrie Ten Boom's heralded prediction, "Prophecies will have validity when they are lived out in a practical way in our lives." These dissenting outlooks thus reverberate with time-tested, pragmatic religious approaches in Branson, but as demonstrated by many local Christians, in the modern day they are sometimes trumped by desires to station the city as vital for the fulfillment of eschatological deliberations.[84]

By professing a belief in divine endorsement yet enumerating a wide variety of spiritual and social evils that imperil this sanction, Roots conference participants implicated themselves in a deep-rooted and often paradoxical contest over the dynamics of Branson's sacred space. Early boosters such as Harold Bell Wright and Otto Ernest Rayburn extolled the pristine, premodern, and God-ordained nature of the Ozark landscape while at the same time beckoning tourists with the potential for modernizing the area and despoiling its Arcadian visions. Advocates throughout the first half of the twentieth century continued to assert that the region was a premier example of nature and humanity working in accord despite increasing evidence that residents were ravaging the land and outsider construction was drastically altering topography and demographics.

Vacationers drawn to Branson by promises of immaculate surroundings directly and indirectly created multiple development-oriented environmental damages. Laborers and entertainers summoned by this growth soon realized the pitfalls of boomtown prosperity. Ministries arose in the 1990s to address the problems of spiritual seekers in transit, performers asked to model Christian virtue who struggled to manifest it in their daily lives, and pastors who sought the comforts of a pastoral atmosphere. At that same juncture, ministerial and business alliances focused on the contours of consecrated terrain and invoked a style of religious cooperation first promoted by the region's original booster. Ultimately, these poetic and political incongruities, struggles, and debates reveal that even claiming a nearness to the heavenly is wrought with countless difficulties. Many continue to praise the city's sacred placefulness, but beneath sentiments of sui generis human-divine harmony and intrinsic godly presence exists a century-long process whereby notions of sacred space have been created, deconstructed, maintained, and challenged.

CHAPTER SIX

Hillbilly Heaven

Labor, Leisure, and the Ozark Trickster

Pearl Spurlock, Branson, Missouri's first tour guide, often told her guests, "God has to keep people chained up in heaven for fear they'll come to the Ozarks and become hillbillies." Within a place renowned for religiously oriented tourist offerings and often called "the buckle of the Bible Belt," it might seem surprising that Spurlock would sanctify this icon. The melding of the persona of the hillbilly—best known in popular imagination as shabbily clad, apparently drunken, sexually promiscuous, impoverished, and indolent—with Ozark, particularly Branson, tourism is an ostensibly perplexing alliance. However, thorough examination of the uses of this moniker by local people and boosters reveals a situation far more complex than the stereotypes just mentioned. In fact, the history of the hillbilly figure attests to a time-tested merger of this persona and a wide variety of regional values—a union that has often positioned the hillbilly as a symbol of Ozark morality.[1]

Although Branson's growth is attributable to many factors, a positing of inherently virtuous local residents has been integral for the success of a values-driven market since Harold Bell Wright first celebrated the righteous Ozarker. Hazel Dagley Heavin highlighted this theme through a 1949 poem entitled "Hillbilly." In it the poet bestowed numerous merits on this persona, including honesty, simplicity, neighborliness, industriousness, and other qualities that did not leave "much room for sin." Although a diligent worker, the hillbilly also was said to possess a love of recreation that was often mixed with religious sentiment. He could "Dance all night and sees no wrong, / Conscience clear as he plods along, / Singin' an old camp meetin' song." The poem then concluded with an allusion to paradise that mimicked Spurlock's vision of the other-worldly realm full of souls sympathetic to the Ozark worldview: "Near the throne of God where the angels stay / They'll point with pride at him and say: / 'That's a hillbilly!'"[2]

Heavin's ode is complicit in historical processes that have hallowed the hillbilly, but it also suggests the dual nature and indefinite constitution of that character. The consensus is that the hillbilly is both materially impoverished and morally rich, destined for a life of agricultural toil yet content with whatever bounty nature may offer, and grounded in ethical standards despite outsider perceptions couched in terms of depravity. As will be demonstrated, these ambiguities position the emblematic Ozarker as a classic trickster figure. Because the persona is important in the creation of regional culture, the hillbilly mimics the role of tradition inventor assumed by most tricksters. Simultaneously, however, both archetypal conventions also suggest behaviors and vantages that can sully these foundations. Any investigation of the Ozark hillbilly must therefore wrestle with elements of contradiction to reveal the ways that the character has underscored a cohesive system of religious and philosophical principles while concomitantly illuminating issues that jeopardize the integration of piety and pleasure in Branson.

THE OZARK TRICKSTER

As religion scholar S. G. F. Brandon has noted, the many "guises" of the trickster consist of "deceiver, thief, parricide, cannibal, inventor, benefactor, magician, perpetrator of obscene acts," and a host of other roles that reflect "common occurrence in human experience." This multiplicity of characteristics makes any attempt at an all-encompassing definition a tenuous undertaking. Although indigenous mythologies still constitute the primary focus of work on the trickster, incredibly diverse manifestations beyond these bounds are now becoming obvious. Over the past fifty years, scholars have identified tricksters in such sundry locations as Greek mythology and African American folklore and even within the images of American popular culture icons such as Bugs Bunny and Bart Simpson. In light of this variation, one may safely add ubiquity to a set of defining attributes mired in what William J. Hynes has referred to as "polysemous diversity and endless semiotic activity."[3]

Recent scholars have drawn on the work of Victor Turner to suggest that a liminal nature is possibly the only universally defining feature of the trickster. As Turner wrote, "The attributes of liminality . . . are necessarily ambiguous" because they "elude or slip through the network of classifications that normally locate states and positions in cultural space." While Turner viewed society as a constant interplay of structure and antistructure, Mary Douglas's landmark study of cultural boundary making described the ways that purity and impurity create "unity in human experience." Such seminal scholarship, therefore, has underscored theorizations that refuse to limit tricksters to a singular construction and instead focus on representations immersed in changeable meanings.[4]

The juxtaposed functions embedded in these characterizations and the inability to situate them as wholly benevolent or malevolent prompted folklorist Barbara Babcock-Abrahams to write, "The distinctive feature of trickster tales (like Trickster himself) may well be their ability to confound classification." Through this indefinite relationship with creation, such accounts function as an anamnesis, or recollection of existential complexities. Like tricksters elsewhere, the hillbilly represents cherished regional standards but also embodies a multiplicity of social taboos; offers residents and tourists the opportunity to safely mock established ethical dictates but solidifies them by means of a process of symbolic inversion; and lies at the foundation of Branson-area consumer culture while representing a host of ideologies and behaviors that are contrary to the codified values of local tourism. He is, in other words, "of the margins yet somehow of the center."[5]

A trickster's oppositional nature allows people to celebrate and remember ontological stances ensconced in contradiction. When examining the uses of the hillbilly motif in Branson, it becomes evident that the term and its embodiments have indeed permitted locals to represent their collective values (religious or otherwise) and to demarcate the merits of the Ozarks from those of America at large. By ambivalently modeling the worldview of a culture, the southwestern Missouri hillbilly (in all its forms) has affirmed and negated extant ethical understandings, thereby mimicking ethnologist Klaus-Peter Koepping's description of tricksters as "the chaos on which order depends." In this manner, the archetype differentiates itself from the better-known Appalachian variant, sustains and confutes what is often perceived as a hegemonic body of regional principles, and deserves treatment as a unique but equally multifaceted expression of the trickster.[6]

In 1900, a reporter from the New York Journal coined the term hillbilly and applied it to residents of Appalachia: "A Hill-Billie is a free and untrammeled white citizen who lives in the hills . . . has no means to speak of, dresses as he can, talks as he pleases, drinks whisky when he gets it, and fires off his revolver as the fancy takes him." Many of the initial written impressions concerning this region were the product of the Hatfield-McCoy "feud" of the 1880s, a conflict routinely described by eastern authors as the epitome of a culture of violence. Such accounts created the first iconic images of mountaineers as ominous, savage, and irrational.[7]

During the late nineteenth century, Americans began associating the qualities of laziness, squalor, and an overall propensity for cultural backwardness with the southern mountaineer. As Henry Shapiro wrote, between 1870 and 1900 many felt the "strange land and peculiar people" of Appalachia did not fit with contemporary conceptions of a homogeneous nation. Adding fiscal abnormality to this sense of deviance, New Deal policies portrayed the South as the nation's primary "economic problem," and President Lyndon Johnson concentrated on Appalachia in particular as a central battleground in the "War on Poverty." Furthermore, countless manifestations of these stereotypes have appeared in popular literature, music, film, and television, with the horrific aspect reaching its pinnacle with the portrayal of inbred and brutal sodomites in 1972's *Deliverance*. Historian Allen Batteau described the roots of this characterization as descending from literary and political interpretations that highlighted "the animality and rural cacophony of Appalachia."[8]

Unlike Appalachia, the Ozark region has not historically been subjected to intense scrutiny by national media or politicians. This is not to say that no negative portrayals have been produced by outsider imaginations. For instance, Henry Rowe Schoolcraft, whose 1818–1819 explorations took him throughout southern Missouri, described the society of early white inhabitants as "not essentially different from that which exists among the savages." H. L. Mencken, a later traveler with an equally harsh tone, commented after a trip to the Ozarks in the early 1930s that he saw "dreadful people" who pick lice off their children like "mother monkeys in a zoo." Finally, *New York Times* book reviewer Joe Queenan depicted Branson as a "Mulefuckers Mecca" and "cultural penal colony" in a 1999 book on America's "white trash."[9]

Most Ozark commentaries, however, have been much more complimentary than their Appalachian counterparts. To illustrate, an early 1960s article in *American Mercury* was typically benign when the author wrote that these "hillbillies . . . have no set standard of living, no respect for money, nor fame, nor caste. They know no greed, no envy, no subserviency. These unimpressive men in unimpressive garb, though poor, they seem, are immensely rich." Not chiefly couched in terms of senseless violence, sheer slothfulness, contemptuous family relationships, or deplorable ignorance, the Ozark hillbilly instead presents commentators with a more diverse, complex, and at times problematic set of meanings than the inhabitant of Appalachia.[10]

According to regional journalist Sarah Overstreet, "Ozarkers know that some of the stereotypical 'hillbilly' characteristics are founded in truth." This candor is demonstrated in a jocular but insightful manner by a 1975 article in a Springfield, Missouri, newspaper which posed the question, "What IS a hillbilly?" To answer, the author offered the experience of a family that had come to the area for a vacation. On arrival in Branson, the father asked a well-dressed man standing on a street corner, "Where can I find a real, live hillbilly?" The local responded, "Why, you're looking at one rah cheer." Not matching his preconceived notions, the vacationer responded, "Pshaw and double-pshaw. It's gettin' to whir you can't believe a thing you see or hear. It's also getting to whir you can't tell a hillbilly from people." As attested to by the social and cultural history of Branson, countless instances exist in which the boundary between hillbillies and hill folk has been expunged. Through such erasure, locals and boosters have been able to represent and enact a variety of ultimate concerns.[11]

The line between hillbilly fact and fiction is often revealed within the realm of tourism. At midcentury, newspaper commentator Elsie Upton described the hillbilly in a manner that bears striking similarities to other confounding tricksters. As she wrote, the figure has "two distinct meanings," and these "vary almost as much as high or low, true or false, good or bad." A native will always "assert himself a hillbilly," and when the term is exercised in this "honorable" manner, it becomes "an eminence worthy of owning." Problems arose, however, when this definition was mediated by nonlocal boosters and vacationers in order to match extant negative stereotypes. Thus, an evaluation of this regional identity necessitates discussion of the ways that it has been co-opted by residents, given a sometimes hackneyed and exaggerated usage by interlopers, and reinscribed in local identities to encapsulate numerous virtues that resonate with and have been perpetuated by the area's tourism industry. Such an analysis reveals that Ozark inhabitants have negotiated the ramifications of the idiom within everyday existence and the world of vacationing to craft a predominantly upright, and even sanctified, variant of the hillbilly signifier employed for both pride and profit.[12]

Although it was said in 1911 that "the Hill Billy has a traditional history, reaching into the dim and distant past," this chapter does not intend to fully unearth such precedents.[13] Nor will it suggest that an entirely unified hillbilly paradigm has been proffered by Ozarkers since the beginning of the twentieth century. However, evidence intimates that the characterization of the word has more often been affirmative than negative. Moreover, through scrutinizing its many ambiguous uses, one can identify the signifier's ability to mediate a rather consistent body of ethics. Ozarker Malinda Donaldson demonstrated this play of contradictory meaning in a 1943 essay:

> He [the hillbilly] is equally great and humble; he is equally the master and the servant. He is a world, a law, a king in his own right. He draws no line between the King of England and a ditch digger. . . . NO matter who you are, or how famous you may be, if you felt your importance or fame in the presence of a Hillbilly he'd make you feel like a fool. And he'd do it with poise and dignity for he never loses face. He's a good neighbor, the best there is, but you can't take liberties or he'll put you in your place. . . . One thing more that few people know, there are not many Hillbillies in the Ozarks. There never was at any time. Most of us who live in the Ozarks are just hillfolks, pretending to be Hillbillies.[14]

Donaldson thus highlighted numerous ways that Ozarkers have made a virtue of hillbillyism—a category that represents what is extraordinary about Ozark hill folk and, through this function, enhances relationships to fundamental values and an exalted regional spirit.

Despite the frequent infusion of positive principles into the term, *hillbilly* has also sometimes been a "fightin' word" for Ozarkers. Folklorist Vance Randolph cited a murder that occurred in 1934 as a result of this label. Although he recognized that such violence was an anomaly, natives throughout the twentieth century have adversely reacted to the term. A 1944 article entitled "Don't Call Me a Hillbilly" claimed that, for all mountaineers, the word "smacks of ridicule" and carries a sullying "stigma." In 1955, champion of Ozark folklore and folk life Otto Ernest Rayburn claimed that he preferred "hillfolks" rather than "hillbillies" because "the average Ozarker is neither ignorant nor stupid." In 1995, a Branson resident wrote in *Newsweek* that such stereotypes consistently "oversimplify and misunderstand" rural culture and are "as unmerciful as they are unfounded." Chastisements have even persisted into a new century, when in 2001 a former English professor at Springfield's Drury University stated that "hillbilly" is "the single most derogatory word in the Ozarks." However, most insider criticisms are written in less decisive terms and tend to chastise certain aspects of the representation while valorizing others. Demonstrating this ambiguity, a brochure for Silver Dollar City's Festival of Ozark Craftsmen from the early 1970s stated, "Ozark mountainfolk do not relish being characterized as 'hillbillies.' However, they are proud indeed that their relatively remote way of life helps to preserve the inspiring skills of their doughty forbearers."[15]

Further exhibiting the ubiquitous and sometimes contentious nature of the characterization is a 1960 court case involving the use of hillbilly terminology. In that year, the Springfield (Missouri) Court of Appeals heard the case of *Moore v. Moore,* a divorce request by husband Lowell against his wife, Minnie, on the grounds of indignities. Lowell claimed that, in addition to committing many indiscretions, his spouse had once disparagingly referred to her in-laws as "hillbillies" —the coup de grâce of her many years of insults and abuses. In his decision for the defendant denying the divorce, Judge Justin Ruark addressed the term as follows:

> We suggest that to refer to a person as a "hillbilly" . . . might or might not be an insult depending upon the meaning to be conveyed, the matter of utterance, and the place where the words are spoken. . . . But without the added implication or inflection which indicates an intention to belittle, we would say that, here in Southern Missouri, the term is often given and accepted as a complimentary expression. An Ozark hillbilly is an individual who has learned the real luxury of doing things without the entangling complications of *things* which the dependent and overpressured city dweller is required to consider as necessities. . . . The hillbilly is often not familiar with new models, soirees, and office politics. But he does have the time and surroundings conducive to sober reflection and honest thought, the opportunity to get closer to his God. No, in Southern Missouri, the appellation "hillbilly" is not generally an insult or an indignity; it is an expression of envy.[16]

Here, the judge paid deference to the various usages of the hillbilly moniker while conclusively intoning the many virtues that had been bestowed on it prior to the case and which would continue to be invested in it later in the century. Since the inception of Branson tourism, millions have indeed traveled to southwestern Missouri to covet the lifestyles of simple, honest, natural, and contemplative individuals (actual and contrived) and to grow closer to their own God through these examples.

Ruark's decision is certainly the most famous judicial pronouncement on the nature of hillbillyism. In the legislative realm, Congressman Dewey Short, the "Orator of the Ozarks," most thoroughly expounded on the term. Short was born in Galena, Missouri (just a few miles northwest of Branson), in 1898 and lived in Stone County until going to college in 1915 and subsequently entering the ministry. While pursing religious credentials, he also continued his studies and attended universities in Berlin, Heidelberg, and Oxford. Eventually he worked as a professor of philosophy and psychology at Southwestern College in Winfield, Kansas, from 1923 to 1924 and 1926 to 1928.[17]

Most notable, Short served as a congressional representative from 1929 to 1931 and 1935 to 1957 for the district that included Stone County. Like his independent constituency, he was known for supporting individual initiative and criticizing Franklin Roosevelt's interventionist New Deal programs. His oratorical flair became the talk of Washington, D.C., during the mid-1930s, with national commentators describing his plainspoken yet stinging style as "revivalistic."[18] Even with his vast academic training, worldwide travels, and political fame, Short always emphasized his Ozark upbringing and the values it inculcated in him. For instance, he once stated: "I take pride in the fact that I am a hillbilly from the Ozarks. I like hillbillies. They are frank, candid and honest. Their generosity is unbounded, their hospitality is sincere. They are genuine folks. If they like you, they will die for you; if they dislike you they may let you die. Not all of them are over-industrious for Nature is bountiful, and it is rather easy to live in the Ozarks."[19] This most famous of all self-proclaimed hillbillies again illustrates the many facets of that term. Despite a well-known career as an academic, pastor, and congressman, he insisted on being buried in Galena. He had always felt most comfortable there because locals "do not write their name across the stars" but rather "write it in the hearts" of their fellow human beings. According to Short, such simple "hillbilly" merits "are the things of his greatness."[20]

Amid heated mid-twentieth-century debates over hillbilly terminology, the *Ozarks Mountaineer* came into existence as a periodical meant to rebut negative portrayals of hill folk. Founded in 1952 as a small tabloid featuring stories of political interest for residents of southwestern Missouri, the publication came under new ownership in 1967 and began to attend more thoroughly to Ozarks history, folklore, and pioneer life. In that year, the editor addressed the name of the journal in a brief column that spoke to the relationship between "mountaineer" and "hillbilly." Expressing a desire to dispel stereotypes, "project an image of a proud heritage," and look toward a "progressive future," the piece ultimately concluded that these goals could be accomplished by a local renegotiation of the "hillbilly" idiom. Likening that term to initial derogatory uses of the word *Christian* by nonbelievers, the piece claimed that numerous "valuable traditions" are still encapsulated within the moniker and that, contrary to recurrent outsider characterizations, "what we are speaks loudest of all."[21]

THE PROTESTANT ETHIC AND THE SPIRIT OF OZARK LEISURE

Jim Owen, a Branson float-trip operator, bank president, owner of numerous businesses, and six-term mayor, was dubbed "King of the Hillbillies" in a 1972 obituary. Reflecting on Ozarkers' relationship with work in *Jim Owen's Hillbilly Humor* he wrote, "A genuine hillbilly is a person who is shrewd enough and lazy enough to do it right the first time." In a chapter entitled "Hill-Osophy," he went on to describe the belief system of "a special breed of men and women" which places much value on independent, simple, and honest work but tempers this impulse with an equally hearty appreciation for recreation. By conjoining these inclinations, people claiming hillbilly affiliation have facilitated a century-long process of cultural creation in Branson.[22]

Many first-wave white immigrants arriving in southwestern Missouri in the early nineteenth century were yeoman farmers of Scots-Irish stock. Some scholars deduce that it was this ethnic group that, in fact, created the term "hillbilly." These farmers were descended from Lowland Scots who immigrated to Ulster Plantation in Northern Ireland in the early seventeenth century. Accustomed to the hardships of the Irish wilderness, the Scots-Irish became the frontier vanguard on arrival in North America. First settling in Appalachia, they brought with them many songs and ballads that dealt with William, Prince of Orange, who defeated King James II at the Battle of Boyne, Ireland, in 1690. Supporters of King William were known as "Billy Boys," and some of their North American counterparts were soon referred to as "hill-billies."[23]

Also known as the Presbyterian Irish, these pioneers entered the United States with a particular religious heritage that informed their relationship with work. The Reformed theology practiced by their Calvinist ancestors and the ways that it enlightened perceptions of labor have been much discussed. Max Weber initiated this dialogue in *The Protestant Ethic and the Spirit of Capitalism* when he analyzed Calvinism's affinity with early capitalist enterprise, the roots of Reformation-derived individualism, and the psychic effects of a modern cultural shift toward personal rather than communal notions of success and salvation. Weber's subjects were driven by the opportunity for "forever renewed profit" commandeered by means of "rationalistic capitalist organization"—a piously motivated ontology that eventually informed "all areas of culture." Although his study was not meant to detail religious understandings of leisure, the author did conclude that the *"summum bonum"* of this mind-set was "the earning of more and more money, combined with the strict avoidance of all spontaneous enjoyment of life."[24]

Many of Weber's claims rest on the doctrine of predestination. According to this principle, individuals have fallen from grace and thereby lost their ability to influence salvation. Yet despite this somber condition, people still longed to know their fate and to at least partially validate their claims of election. With a lack of self-confidence being equated with insufficient faith, intense worldly activity became a way to bolster assurance. One's success served as a "divine tool" to express this faithfulness. Ultimately, Weber's Protestants viewed work as a way to assuage religious anxiety, identified wealth as something to be earned not enjoyed, defined leisure as sinful indulgence of the flesh, and marked acquisition as wicked when pursued with the goal of "living merrily and without care."[25]

Iterating Weber's thesis, Ozark scholar Don Holliday claimed that in the early history of the region, the Scots-Irish positioned work as "the social Bible." Similarly, historian and Ozarker Robert Gilmore wrote that generations of residents have grown up with the words of the mid-nineteenth-century hymn "Work for the Night Is Coming" serving "not just as a religious metaphor but as a prescription for everyday living." These sentiments certainly stand in opposition to the patented representations of the languid Ozarker which have permeated the area's popular culture offerings. However, Holliday, who grew up as a third-generation resident of Taney County, refuted this stereotype and complicated *The Protestant Ethic*'s theory when applied to the area's first-wave settlers. Because of their Calvinist vantage and the tumult of their hardscrabble lives, the Scots-Irish Ozarkers possessed a "sense of fatalism." Summarizing this worldview, he stated, "You work as hard as you can but there is a limit beyond which you can't go," and this approach provides "a kind of physical and moral fiber." Thus, the Scots-Irish did view work as a "calling," or moral justification for worldly activity. However, this notion did not disallow leisure spawned from the fruits of one's toil—an accretion that may be the product of adopting Methodist, Baptist, or other non-Calvinist perspectives during the great revivals of the early nineteenth century. In light of this juxtaposition, Holliday's conclusion therefore echoes Jim Owen's maxim concerning the ethical yet tempered nature of hillbilly labor.[26]

From the beginning of white settlement in southwestern Missouri, religiously motivated industriousness has been epitomized by the circuit preacher. American religions scholar David Embree wrote that the Ozarks area "has long been a 'frontier region' for religion." Some local itinerants actually adopted accoutrements of the prototypical frontiersman. For instance, U. G. Johnson, an early twentieth-century Baptist minister out of Taney County, traveled the region with a long duster coat and a pair of pearl-handled Colt .45 pistols accompanying his pulpit and Bible. Since the mid-nineteenth century, Protestant preachers (and eventually the Branson tourism industry at large) have championed an individualistic theology that emphasized the dire necessity of a personal and emotive commitment to Christ; the gratuitous nature of clerical mediation between believers and the divine; simple answers to existential questions rooted in unwavering religious certainty; and the obligation to bring others into the flock by proclaiming the good news of salvation. In turn, this religious perspective helped to create and fortify a sense of radical independence and self-sufficiency made manifest in other sociocultural arenas.[27]

Numerous accounts of Ozark circuit riders attest to their extraordinary commitment to church building and faith promotion throughout that sizable region. For instance, a diary entry from Jacob Lanius—an itinerant pastor for the Methodist Episcopal Church—described a quarterly meeting held in Stone County in June 1839. At this event, he and another local minister platted a circuit of about 200 miles with eighteen different preaching places. Within this immense territory, the men located only twenty-four church members. The life of Sadie McCoy Crank is a further demonstration of solitary religious labor. A Christian Church (Disciples of Christ) minister, she accepted her first pastorate in 1891 and began a fifty-year career as church organizer, minister, traveling revivalist, and temperance speaker. During this period, she planted or revived fifty houses of worship, baptized approximately seven thousand people, and performed more than a thousand funerals and weddings. According to religion scholar Lora Hobbs, "One would be hard-pressed to find a town in southwest Missouri in which Mrs. Crank did *not* preach."[28]

Certain denominations thrived in this isolated Ozark context because of theologies well suited for the individualistic and populist ideology of inhabitants. The Methodist circuit system allowed missionary work among disparate communities. Baptist support for lay clergy prompted an amalgamation of farmer and preacher which rejected notions of ecclesiastical hierarchy. The Christian Church (Disciples of Christ) stressed its call for a return to "primitive" New Testament Christianity that rejected complicated liturgies and church structures. And the egalitarian stance of Cumberland Presbyterians resonated nicely with a regional frontier ethic. According to Brooks Blevins, however, "most Ozark churches were very similar" because each "shared a reliance on evangelical, revivalistic methods and a faith in a righteous, caring, and omnipotent God." Such commonalities often led to the establishment of "union churches," or sites assembled through the combined efforts of a variety of denominations. As demonstrated in previous chapters, nondenominationalism has coursed its way through the history of Branson. From Harold Bell Wright's condemnations of "churchianity" to the popular religion proffered at Silver Dollar City and the area's variety show theaters, and then to numerous social initiatives by consortia of local churches, the city has continued to enact the religious impulses of the Ozark frontier period.[29]

The establishment of permanent houses of worship was a primary goal for peripatetic Ozark preachers, but they also offered more temporary religious ser-

vices in the form of brush arbor or camp meetings replete with emotional messages that aroused penitence, altar calls, and conversion experiences. Revivalists attracted participants from across the denominational spectrum regardless
of their own affiliation. The Reverend Allen Ledbetter, of Ava, Missouri (approximately 50 miles northeast of Branson), was ordained in the General Baptist Church in 1935. By 1981, he claimed to have pastored twenty-seven different
churches and preached nearly four hundred interdenominational revivals in the
Ozarks and beyond. Further attesting to the nonsectarian spirit of these meetings, Joe Cranfield of Taney County stated, "I've seen as many as forty or fifty
preachers at one of them. . . . Every preacher around in the whole country would
come. It didn't make any difference about his denominational standing. . . . They
left off their denominations. They preached the Bible."[30]

Despite the fire-and-brimstone sermons of revival ministers and the grave
pleas for forgiveness from many of the people assembled, camp meetings also
served a vital social and recreational function. Although small revivals were frequently held at schoolhouses or lodge halls, it was the protracted yearly event
that was cause for the most excitement. As communal gatherings for widely dis-
persed frontier populations, camp meetings drew citizens of all faiths who came
from many miles away in late summer for a week-long experience. On a social
level, they facilitated the making of new friends, the rejuvenation of old relationships, opportunities for courtship, and easy channels for the sharing of community-wide news. Although a minister's alliance in Springfield, Missouri, declared
in 1897 that "killing time" was "a grievous sin against God," for Ozarkers with
few opportunities for group amusement these meetings also were a prime occasion for leisure. As local resident Emmett Yoeman stated, "I think 'recreation'
would be a pretty good term to describe them [camp meetings]. . . . I would say
that it was as much a matter of entertainment and was devised for that purpose
more so than any spiritual purpose." Campers were amused by their cohorts and
found pleasure in the affective tone and mannerisms of ministers. Somber ora-
tions were peppered with jokes and anecdotes, and because audience participation was encouraged, the crowd could easily join in "the show." Thus, according
to Ozark historian Robert K. Gilmore, multifaceted revivals offered the opportunity for "communication, self-realization, and enlightenment."[31]

This uniting of theologically driven individualism, creedal independence, and
religious labor (and often leisure as well) has, on occasion, been subsumed under
the hillbilly appellation. In this it adds further nuance to that term. Jim Owen
referred to the exciting nature of "hillbilly revivals" in his description of the local
ideological structure. An advertisement for Gainesville, Missouri's 1966 Hootin'

an' Hollarin' Celebration made mention of a brush arbor revival on the grounds to be "set up just like they had them years ago." In the early 1970s, journalist Donna Scott also encountered a similar meeting at the annual "Hillbilly Days" held at southwestern Missouri's Bennett Springs State Park. Most relevant to the topic, in 1959 I. E. Holden published *The Hillbilly Preacher,* a work that details his career as a minister in the Fire Baptized Holiness Church. Raised in south-central Missouri, Holden was ordained in 1932 and spent the next three decades trekking throughout Kansas, Missouri, and Oklahoma to organize revivals and churches. During his travels he was always quick to herald his Ozark heritage, cite this up-bringing as vital for status as an "old time Christian," and thereby position the hillbilly as one capable of facilitating evangelization and sanctification.[32]

PLAYING HILLBILLY

As discussed in Chapter 1, roving Christian Church (Disciples of Christ) minister Harold Bell Wright's semifictional *The Shepherd of the Hills* essentially created Branson's tourism industry. In this text, Wright only once employed the term "Hill-Billy." On this occasion, however, the word was meant to represent "every native" in the area, even the "wildest" of the lot. Consonant with this rowdy characterization, the author also made use of several negative portrayals of mountaineers that existed in his turn-of-the-century milieu. The malevolence of hill folks was primarily represented through the book's antagonist, Wash Gibbs, and his gang of vigilantes. Echoing carnal stereotypes, Gibbs was depicted as having a "brutal face that had very little of the human in it." He and his men made a livelihood of drinking, fighting, cursing, and essentially refuting the propriety that Wright penned as inherent in this Ozark community. To craft these figures, the author drew on more than hillbilly typecasting. In a melding of fact and fiction which has since infused all periods of Ozark popular culture, he also harked back to some historical precedent. For example, Wright certainly knew about Taney County's infamous late nineteenth-century vigilante group, the Bald Knobbers, when he formulated the Gibbs gang.[33]

Despite the actions of Wash Gibbs, the overarching tone of *The Shepherd of the Hills* celebrates rather than censures the lifestyle of Wright's subjects. For instance, their stance toward work resonates with later understandings that made a virtue of mitigated labor. When facing the possibility of marriage to the economically endowed Ollie Stewart, the young heroine of the novel declared, "It would be nice to have lots of money and pretties, but somehow I feel like there's a heap more than that to think about." Further deliberating on this dilemma, her father advised that she not consider "what he's got 'stead of what he is." If Wright's characters were to embrace urbane ways, such "cheap culture" would signal "death to all true refinement." The heroes in *The Shepherd of the Hills* are industriousness enough to eke out a living from a difficult terrain and possess an inspiring frontier work ethic that embraces the travails of intense physical labor. However, they also demonstrate an appreciation for leisure and a worldview that makes moral lifestyles a higher priority than material gain. These attributes established them as templates for the simple and righteous Ozark hillbilly. Furthermore, as the religio-philosophical impetus behind a nascent tourism industry, they can also be easily positioned as tricksters bequeathed with an ability to create culture.[34]

After the publication of *The Shepherd of the Hills,* thousands of readers arrived in Stone and Taney counties in the early twentieth century to meet Wright's mostly fictional subjects. This quest could have easily resulted in disappointment. But natives, who understood the economic value of perpetuating the book's myths, gladly stepped in to play their hillbilly parts and offer tourists Ozark "reality." Historian Lynn Morrow has recounted an episode that demonstrates the burgeoning work of such "put-on." In 1915, honeymooners made a trip to Shepherd of the Hills Country. On arriving at the Cliff House Club across the river from Forsyth, they were greeted by locals who introduced themselves as "hillbillies." During their stay, which lasted several weeks, they toured sites made famous by Wright's novel, "met" and dined with people who were supposedly fodder for its characters, and visited "actual" caves, cabins, and scenic vistas described in the book. Quickly realizing that sojourners wanted to consume a vision of the essentialized hill person, Ozarkers learned to cash in on this image. As southwestern Missouri native and Springfield newspaper columnist Lucille Morris wrote in 1937, once being a hillbilly became "good box-office," residents were more than willing to "push [their] split-bonnet back . . . smooth out the creases in [their] store boughten calico dress and coyly say 'Jest call me hillbilly.'" Although this willing implication in stereotypes was the fodder for "cheap crudities," Morris invoked the hallowed nature of the archetype by concluding that it had "ancient and significant foundation."[35]

In 1929, *Missouri Magazine* (a publication of the Missouri State Chamber of Commerce) addressed the growing environment of manufactured hillbillies through an appeal to Branson's tourism industry: "Let us not develop into bunk artists for the purpose of filling credulous visitors with half truths or exaggerated ideas about our state." Consonant with this call, scholars of Ozark tourism Lynn Morrow and Linda Myers-Phinney have described these early self-imposed caricatures as "demeaning." Further elaborating on such debasement, regional historian Brooks Blevins used religious imagery to portray the enacting of hill-billyism as identity forfeiture and the willful bearing of others' sins: "The Ozark region has been sacrificed at the altar of American nostalgia. . . . In many ways, the region has scaled the sacrificial heights as a willing if anxious Isaac." How-ever, evidence suggests that local industriousness has crafted a more complex, and often fulsome, notion of the hillbilly than that represented by these com-mentators and that much of the region's vaunted yet ambivalent work ethic has been employed to this end.[36]

Early innovators of Branson-area tourism often extolled the meritorious as-pects of hillbilly labor and its accompanying virtues of simplicity, independence, and authentic living. J. K. Ross, taken to be the model for Wright's "Old Matt," defined the hillbilly in a 1915 (Branson) White River Leader editorial. For him, this term implied living without many material goods but also possessing an intimate knowledge of nature and its bounty. This station, however, did not exclude an ability to engage in professions such as judge, lawyer, teacher, or merchant. Ul-timately, the hillbilly was "a MAN capable of the position he holds," and to join this assembly one must only "go to work and do something." Pearl Spurlock, the most renowned tour guide in the early years of Shepherd of the Hills Country, often reiterated a similar sense of pride in vocation-related identity. Not a na-tive of southwestern Missouri, she claimed that it took her ten years to advance through the rigorous ranks of this fraternity. After a decade, she received her "H. B." degree and became a "full-fledged hillbilly," adding that she was "really proud to be classified as one, among these real mountain people."[37]

Spurlock recounted numerous instances of tourist appreciation for the pious facets of indigenous labor. Most compelling is an account of the erection of a rudimentary tombstone by two siblings who had recently lost their parents. Un-able to purchase a traditional marker, the children constructed a rustic cross on which they hung a crude birdhouse. As the grave was located in the Shepherd of the Hills Cemetery, Spurlock often highlighted it for her guests. Moved by its simple yet meaningful craftsmanship, a tourist wrote to her that this "'Hillbilly' tombstone was as sacred and holy" as the "vast, costly mausoleums" in her city. Here, the writer took the enacting of mountaineer motifs one step further by valorizing work not specifically intended for vacationers' eyes and, in doing so, demonstrated that all facets and rituals of the righteous hillbilly lifestyle were available in some form for tourist consumption.[38]

Over the past one hundred years, thousands of Ozarkers have implicated themselves in a value-laden variant of hillbillyism. However, Jim Owen was the

undisputed "King" of this construct. According to Dan Saults, a former administrator with the Missouri Department of Conservation, "There are those in
America that suspect Jim invented the hillbilly." Owen was born upstate from
Shepherd of the Hills Country in Elkland, Missouri, in 1903. In 1934 he moved to
Branson to operate a drug store owned by his father. An avid outdoorsman, he
began a small float-trip business one year later and promoted it by detailing the
glories of the White River to the fishing editor for *Outdoor Life Magazine*. Beginning with only six boats and one guide, his operation peaked in the late 1940s
with more than one hundred vessels and one hundred employees.[39]

The Owen Boat Line was known for an ability to attract wealthy patrons. According to a 1955 *Saturday Evening Post* feature, this "circle of disciples" included
"princes of industry, prelates of the church, persons prominent in professions,
politics and the theater, and some one-gallussed Ozark hillbillies"—all of whom
possessed a "fierce reverence" for rivers and would "rather go floating than go
to heaven." In accord with the historical melding of rustic experiences and modern comforts, Owen provided guests with portable toilets, bar boats that ferried
between fishing craft, and an extensive commissary list. Such luxuries attracted
Charlton Heston, Gene Autry, Smiley Burnett, and many other lesser stars.[40]

Through a combination of folksy hillbilly vernacular and mystical language,
Owen lured more than ten thousand anglers during the twenty-five years of his
float service. His operation graced the cover of *Life* and was featured in *Look*, the
American, Sports Afield, and dozens of large newspapers. Owen also built Branson's first movie house (once known as the Hillbilly Theater) and the city's original bowling alley. He was a bank president, realtor, and newspaper columnist;
owned an auto dealership, hamburger stand, and dairy; and bred champion fox
hounds and bird dogs (which ate only his self-designed brand of food). Moreover,
he was elected mayor of Branson on six occasions beginning in the mid-1930s and
even made a run for the state legislature in 1954.[41]

Despite this incredible work ethic, Owen immersed himself in a now familiar
Ozark attitude toward industry—one that necessitated a balance between labor
and recreation. He frequently voiced the adage "If you're too busy to fish, you're
too busy," and his business career keenly demonstrated the ways that hillbillyism
reworks Weber's Protestant ethic. According to Paul Henning, creator of *The
Beverly Hillbillies* and longtime friend, Owen was a "hillbilly by choice" and, like
many rural religious folks, was "converted" to that ideology and lifestyle "in the
river." Owen himself claimed that it took him nearly four decades to be accepted
as a "real hillbilly." As with many before him, he adopted that persona originally
for the sake of tourists but then shaped the image into one laden with a variety

of meritorious qualities. Without resorting to extant stereotypes, he employed the hillbilly lingua franca and catered to outsider perceptions of how a hill person ought to talk. It was even rumored that he held language classes for his guides to be sure that they mispronounced correctly. However, this dialect also often expressed a poetic reverence for Ozark natural wonders, with Owen sometimes remarking that flowering dogwoods in the spring were "nature's way of saying grace before breakfast."[42]

Owen's hillbilly philosophy, or "Hill-Osophy," was codified in a 1970 book of anecdotes and aphorisms entitled *Jim Owen's Hillbilly Humor*. Amid the stories and sayings, a reader is offered a distinct view of the appropriate mix between work and leisure. His witticisms were decidedly in favor of independence and self-sufficiency and opposed to outsider aid ("Used to be, my advice to young men deciding on a career was for them to go into a business or a profession. Now I tell them to skip all that and go into poverty—that's where the big money is.") Owen persistently extolled the merits of honest work in a modern culture that was neglecting this sentiment ("Nowadays, there is a lot being said about tranquilizers. But even back in Grandpa's time there was something to make you sleep. They called it work.") But in classic hillbilly trickster style, he also embraced a sense of righteous poverty and soulfully beneficial relaxation. For instance, he quipped, "We don't have psychoanalysis here in the hills. We're considered poor people so we have friends instead." On the subject of recreation he added, "A hillbilly doesn't get excited about things that worry city people. . . . He likes to take life easy." Merging these outlooks with staunch antimodernism, clever anti-intellectualism, a disavowal of government intervention into the lives of Ozarkers, and appreciation for a time-tested regional brand of nondenominational religiosity, Owen thus offered an all-encompassing hillbilly worldview.[43]

The Owen Boat Line met its demise when Table Rock Dam impounded the lower White River in 1957, and the proprietor then moved on to other business endeavors. In recognition of his contributions to the local economy, Branson hosted Jim Owen Day on May 13, 1967. This event served as the climax of the city's Plumb Nellie Days—an annual "Hillbilly Festival and Craft Show" that began in 1960. Described by a Branson entertainment news service as a celebration of the customs and artistic heritage of Ozark "hill folk," it invites guests to don "hillbilly costumes and clothes in 1890's styles." Owen's acknowledgment at the celebration demonstrated the many ways that he facilitated the merger of "authentic" mountaineer culture with hillbilly lore. On his death in 1972, Paul Henning eulogized him as "the best friend the Ozarks ever had."[44]

STAGING THE OZARK TRICKSTER

Although Paul Henning's Uncle Jed, Granny, Elly Mae and Jethro are the most famous pop culture Ozark hillbillies, such characters have been portrayed in film since 1915. In that year, *Billie—the Hill Billy* stereotypically told of a city dweller who travels to the region, encounters a backwoods family headed by a tyrannical father, falls in love with his daughter, and eventually whisks her away for an urban life. Other early offerings set in the area featured more stock characters (both positive and negative), including feuding mountain families in *The Big Killing* (1928); a pedophile in *Child Bride of the Ozarks* (1937); a Nazi-fighting regional heroine in *Joan of Ozark* (1942); and poor, antimodern, yet ethical mountaineers in *The Kettles in the Ozarks* (1956). As this limited sample demonstrates, the cinema (like the rest of America) situated Ozark hillbillies within a dichotomy of meaning. As cultural historian Anthony Harkins has asserted, because the region was not subject to the degree of outsider scrutiny that plagued Appalachia in the early twentieth century, film producers and viewers more easily defined the Ozarks as "mythic space."[45]

In addition to fame from films set in the region, a few residents of Arkansas and Missouri became actors during the 1930s and 1940s. Van Buren, Arkansas's Bob Burns starred in numerous B films that played on hillbilly stereotypes. These included *Comin' round the Mountain* (1940), which featured "the only surviving species of the genus homos hillbillicus Americanious." Frank, Leon, and June Weaver, better known as the Weaver Brothers and Elviry, came from Springfield, Missouri, and had been successful vaudeville comedians in the opening decades of the twentieth century. Between 1930 and 1943 they starred in twelve films that portrayed hillbillies who, aware of the foibles of human nature, used simple astuteness and plain virtue to triumph over city slickers. For instance, the director of *Friendly Neighbors* (1940) described the actors (like their characters) as "grand, simple, honest, sincere, fun to be around." Finally, Chester Lauck and Norris Guff of Mena, Arkansas, created their Lum and Abner personalities in 1931 and captivated radio audiences with life in the fabled Ozark town of Pine Ridge until 1951. During this run, they also made six movies that played on archetypal mountaineer themes. Although some critics said the fictitious Pine Ridge gave the Ozarks a national "black eye," Lauck responded with the upright hillbilly model: "We have endeavored to depict a good, clean, wholesome, down-to-earth way of life. . . . Those who don't know that type of life want to dream of it. Those who do know it want to return to it. We have tried to picture Pine Ridge as a Shangri-La."[46]

Ozark hillbillies made their first television appearance in 1968 when Jack Benny returned to his supposed roots by portraying fiddler "Zeke Benny and his Ozark Hillbillies" on a single show. It was Paul Henning who truly invented this regional television persona, however, by defining it for a national audience and allying it with modern Branson tourism. Henning was born in Independence, Missouri, in 1911. Prior to creating and producing *The Beverly Hillbillies* (whose mountaineer family named the Clampetts supposedly came from the Ozarks), he was instrumental in other television programs such as *Fibber McGee and Molly, Burns and Allen,* and *The Bob Cummings Show.* Recounting boyhood Scout trips to southwestern Missouri, he asserted, "I fell in love with hillbilly characters. I thought they were independent and had always been a fan of hillbilly humor." When *The Beverly Hillbillies* debuted in 1962, an estimated 50 percent of television viewers watched, making the series America's number one rated show by the end of its first month. The most watched program of 1962 and 1963, *The Beverly Hillbillies* still boasts the highest rated half-hour individual episode in television history and counts eight episodes among the fifty most viewed. During the show's run from 1962 to 1970, Henning also served as creator and producer of *Petticoat Junction* (1963–1970) and executive producer of *Green Acres* (1965–1971). These credentials thus make him the undisputed king of rural situation comedy.[47]

Many aspects of *The Beverly Hillbillies* might account for its incredible success. Within a 1960s context of social and cultural upheaval, the show offered simple escapism and a sense of "down-home" security. Moreover, mountaineers had come to national attention during the 1960 West Virginia Democratic primary when John F. Kennedy made the poverty of Appalachia central to his presidential campaign. On an intellectual level, however, the show possessed an ability to cleverly combine banal comedy with social criticism. By illustrating the idiosyncrasies of consumer culture, censuring the pretense of social elites, epitomizing traditional value systems that necessitated support from family and kin, and modeling a democratic egalitarianism that was deemed by some to be rapidly waning in the United States, *The Beverly Hillbillies* had many interesting nuances that often escaped commentators of the time yet mimicked the Branson ideology. Through these reappraisals, Horace Newcomb has claimed that the program promoted "the moral superiority of rural wisdom" and that the Clampetts functioned as a metaphor for a set of "truly American values."[48]

Most vital for this study, *The Beverly Hillbillies* also instituted a national redefinition of "hillbilly." The program did perpetuate a number of patented images, of course, including shotgun wielding, government fearing, and moonshining mountaineers; signature attire of plaid shirts, overalls, and slouched hats; superstitious matriarchs (as epitomized by Granny); innate sexuality that is sultry yet immature (as represented by Elly Mae); and ingrained naïveté-cum-stupidity (as characterized by Jethro). However, a *Saturday Evening Post* writer described Buddy Ebsen (Jed Clampett) as a "hand-me-down philosopher" and repository of folk knowledge. Furthermore, Paul Henning depicted Granny (Irene Ryan), whom he modeled after his mother, as having "the accumulated wisdom of self-sufficient generations." Reflecting on this infusion of integrity into the hillbilly icon, an executive for Filmways (the project's production company) claimed that through "simple, but not stupid" depictions "the word 'hillbilly' will ultimately have a new meaning in the United States as a result of our show." Again demonstrating hillbilly dualism, this program provided viewers with a more virtuous construct of that signifier and embraced its moral fortitude and regard for principled (if not sometimes misguided) labor accented by an appreciation for leisure.[49]

In 1967, four episodes of *The Beverly Hillbillies* were filmed at Silver Dollar City in Branson. Aired as the debut of the 1969 season, they focused on the family's return to its Ozark home in order to find a suitable husband for Elly Mae. Entering the city limits, the characters immediately imbibed the rarified air of the Ozarks. On a breath of it, Jed concluded, "This clean stuff is going to take some getting used to." Many local celebrities and attractions provided cameos, and mention was made of famous sites from *The Shepherd of the Hills*. As a result of the episodes, Silver Dollar City witnessed its greatest one-year increase in visitation to date, and newfound national interest pushed guest totals above one million by the early 1970s. Reflecting on this upsurge and the ways that these TV tricksters facilitated a process of cultural formation, co-owner Pete Herschend stated, "*The Beverly Hillbillies* moved Silver Dollar City, and therefore Branson, out of the regional business and into a national attraction. That was *the* change. That made *the* difference. And this community has never looked back since that time."[50]

As Branson began to establish an identity with variety show entertainment in the late 1960s, the hard work of "playing hillbilly" became the bastion of on-stage, rather than on-screen, performers. When the Presley Family opened the Ozark Mountain Jubilee (the first theater on the now famous Highway 76 Strip) in 1967, it featured not only country and gospel music but also the antics of Gary Presley, a.k.a. Herkimer—a comedian described by his theater as a "savant hillbilly." Travel writer Bruce Cook utilized typically paradoxical language when describing Presley as "swaggering and sort of dim" on stage but "intelligent" and "direct" outside this role. He was further extolled as "a remarkable combination of businessman and performer"—a characterization that again demonstrates the ambiguities of the hillbilly persona and the ever present merger of Ozark labor and leisure.[51]

During a performance I attended in the mid-1990s, Herkimer warmed up the crowd in a manner that exhibited the hillbilly's role as mediator of values. The act began with a joke about a chance meeting between Moses and former president George H. W. Bush and then continued with a succession of religiously motivated yarns that laid bare the production's ideological vantage. Herkimer made clear that the Presleys' Country Jubilee endorsed Christianity and conservative politics—a civil religious merger that finds expression in almost every contemporary production. While serving as a prelude to a medley of gospel numbers, his comedy focused on the evangelistic work of preachers and ministers awaiting entrance into heaven. It also included several jabs at the Clinton administration and "liberal" politics writ large. For instance, Herkimer proposed that he would run for president. After the emcee responded that people would not vote for a hillbilly, he replied that since enduring the Clinton White House Americans may very well want a "real clown" in office.

Comments from guests who attended the Presleys' show during the fall of 2004 and spring of 2005 indicate the ways that an ostensibly facile production can fuse a range of regional values with hillbilly antics. For instance, a Missouri visitor wrote that friends who accompanied her from across the country "really appreciate the values/morals/etc." An Iowa couple who had seen the show during three different decades proclaimed that they "love Herkimer" yet followed up by praising Branson's ever present civil religiosity: "Thanks for honoring the vets." A teenage girl from Oklahoma attested to her love of "the colors of the clothes" and the theater's "comedy" but then added value-laden texture when she wrote, "But most of all the gospel music and the atmosphere." Finally, a Colorado vacationer stated that she had seen the show as a child and most remembered its hillbilly jester. However, she visited again as an adult in 1991 and has returned on three other occasions. Closing her review, she asserted, "What a job to make people laugh. You have truly been blessed!!" This last comment can certainly be read as one that is merely extolling the skills of the theater's comics. However, as evidenced throughout this chapter, Branson boosters and entertainers have worked for many decades to forge a more literal link between hillbilly enactment and blessedness.[52]

Although Branson's hillbilly comics pepper their acts with humorous com-

Presley Family promotional photo, circa 2000. From the author's collection

ments on religious and political subjects, they also include much material that is seemingly objectionable within the local entertainment context. In doing so, they further demonstrate the dichotomous nature of their character. The Bald-knobbers Jamboree (originally the Baldknobbers Hillbilly Jamboree) was the first musical show in Branson and, in 1968, became the second act on the Strip. Throughout the course of almost four decades, its hillbilly component (the Mabe brothers) has mixed droll discussions of Ozark values with what commentator Lori A. Robbins has called "toilet humor." Creating a template still utilized by all regional comics, they have blended outhouse wit with jokes about flatulence, senior citizen sexuality, immoderate alcohol consumption, and other "taboo" Branson subjects. In doing so, the Mabe brothers and other area jesters offer a brand of comedy that mimics the often salacious nature of tricksters worldwide and, like the antics of their folkloric counterparts, permits invited guests to laugh at the hopes, fears, and crudities of their common humanity.[53]

Since the late 1960s, the Presleys and Baldknobbers have inspired countless imitators in the Branson entertainment scene. Nearly every venue offers some variant of the hillbilly guise. However, this characterization is not static. Instead, the nebulous hillbilly trickster has adapted to changing social and cultural climates. For example, in 1987 Herkimer began wearing sequined overalls and inspired a move toward this more brassy attire among all area performers. Similarly, Terri Sanders, a participant in the local industry for more than twenty years who plays a jester named Homer Lee at the Braschler Music Show, attested to the need to "mutate" and "evolve." During a 2002 performance, Sanders lampooned the Latin maids now prominent at local hotels and motels, performed a version of the River Dance, and leveled numerous jokes about Wal-Mart (supposedly the Branson tourist's favorite retail store). Ultimately, Gary Presley astutely addressed the moral vision that underscores such an ever transforming yet "simple and ancient" genre when he posited this type of humor as perfect for the "Bible Belt."[54]

In an atmosphere sated with performances of the Ozark trickster, Bruce Seaton was the consummate example of the integration of hillbilly enactment, lifestyle, and religious promotion. An Ozark native, he spent fifteen years away from the region before returning in the early 1960s to take a job as a Linotype operator for the *Stone County Republican*. Possessing little knowledge of contemporary machinery, Seaton instead began work on an antique hand press at his editor's print shop at Silver Dollar City. There he realized his true career objective—to reenact a prototypical variant of nineteenth-century pioneer life. Soon after, he entered his family in Branson's Plumb Nellie Days parade. Attired in overalls and a fake shabby beard, he was accompanied by his wife in a tattered calico skirt and bonnet and assisted by his eight barefoot children. The Seatons won the event's "Best Hillbilly Family" award on several occasions.[55]

The family's success as hillbilly performers led to a career. Attired in their parade garb and situated around dilapidated cabins or rickety outhouses, the Seatons began selling pictures of themselves to a Springfield photographer. For nearly a decade, they forged a life as "professional hillbillies." Their likenesses appeared on postcards, cookbooks, and calendars. Then in 1963, the family further blurred the line between fact and fiction by purchasing a plot of land and a little shack in rural Stone County. In a setting replete with a tar-paper roof and sagging front porch, they butchered and cured their own meats, chopped wood for heat, and did their own barbering. Further demonstrating hillbilly ambiguity, Seaton asserted that everything in the house was modern "but it don't look it."[56]

Leon Fredrick, Seaton's former print-shop employer, once labeled him "a genuine manufactured hillbilly." Although most of this appearance was forged through pictorial representations, he also constructed his hillbillyism by play-

Camp Meetin' Bound

Seaton Family hillbilly postcard, circa 1970. Postcard from the author's collection

ing Preachin' Bill in the Shepherd of the Hills pageant. Seaton came to the production shortly after it debuted. Preachin' Bill, while not a major character in Wright's work, possesses special significance because he is the first to speak in the book. He declares, "When God looked upon th' work of his hands an' called hit good, he war sure a lookin' at this here Ozark country." Seaton died at a young age in 1976. However, his dual persona as archetypal hillbilly and Ozark-sanctifying vicar united outwardly disparate roles into a career that typified the virtues of mitigated labor and the encouragement of regional sanctity.[57]

J. W. Williamson, a historian of Appalachian popular culture representations, has described the hillbilly as "an outlaw on the fringes of the economy" and "the idiot of capitalism." Dissecting the character's market-based function, he stated:

> If capitalism operates by inducing its workers to believe in the virtues of work and by condemning the evils that interfere with work, such as strong drink, roaming the woods and hunting, and various social indiscretions including murder, mayhem, and bastardy . . . then clearly the hillbilly fool is a warning, a keep-away sign enjoining us to avoid the rocky rural edges outside the grasp of the urban economy.[58]

It is true that the Ozark hillbilly perpetrates acts prohibited by the ethos of the larger Branson entertainment industry and is thus involved in some of the chicanery mentioned by Williamson. It is also accurate that constructions of this vague figure have historically been based in an aversion to capitalist enterprise. However, for nearly a century area natives have made a merit of simple, independent, and honest work; stressed the equally necessary nature of deserved recreation; and folded these qualities into the hillbilly persona. On translation into the tourism industry, this ethic as enacted by a seemingly indolent character has been vital for the region's fertile consumer culture.

Unlike in the Appalachian context, willful participation in a stereotype mostly molded from within has produced what one Springfield journalist called "hillbilly tycoons." The author held that, in contrast to other business magnates, this mogul does not have to work on Wall Street, engage in a lengthy commute, or "risk his life on the subway." Possessing a tricksteresque ability to change and reshape, the Ozark hillbilly can "go to college and travel in Europe undistinguishable from other tycoons," but on return to the hills he "resumes his native character and costume, smokes his corncob pipe, whittles his walnut walking sticks, hitches up his galluses, and watches the dollars roll in." Thus, for this writer and many people throughout Branson's history, the hard work of facilitating the recreation of others through enacting hillbillyism has been valorized as an ethic worth cultivating.[59]

RACIALIZING THE OZARK TRICKSTER

In the United States, hillbilly stereotypes and tensions were heightened by a massive out-migration of Appalachian residents in the three decades following World War II. Spawned by loss of jobs in the area's coal mines and employment opportunities in northern cities, the diaspora reached its height in the 1950s. In total, more than three million southern Appalachian people abandoned the hills during this period. In 1958, an author for *Harper's Magazine* described such a group in Chicago as resistant to change, clannish, disorderly, drunken, content in their dire poverty, and devoid of a moral code. Representing "the American dream gone berserk," these "hillbillies" "confound [ed] all notions of racial, religious, and cultural purity." Thus, for this writer and many others, when Appalachian hill folk invaded urban areas, any vestige of quaintness or down-home virtue was lost. The anomalous makeup of mountaineer culture became anathema to majority understandings of propriety, especially in regard to normative whiteness. As the Appalachian hillbilly often served as an ominous signifier of antimodernism, the trope also became indicative of a perilous racial standing. And, through "othering" Appalachian residents whose authentic whiteness was being called into question, urbanites thereby affirmed historian Matthew Frye Jacobson's contention that "Caucasians are made and not born."[60]

Again demonstrating the sometimes vast divide between Ozark hillbillies and their eastern counterparts, and highlighting the play of contradictory meaning inherent in the signifier, boosters in southwestern Missouri have frequently remade this racial dynamic. For these commentators, the Ozarks served as an ethnic refuge—one that preserved racial purity amid various waves of immigration and demographic diversification. Although most original immigrants to the region were Scots-Irish, their settlement was by no means totalistic. Within the larger Ozark setting, French Creoles were the first to establish communities along the Mississippi River. By 1840, remnants of the Cherokee nation had settled near the Trail of Tears in the western Ozarks, and sizable populations of free blacks existed throughout the area. Yet despite this racial and ethnic variation, voices throughout the twentieth century frequently connected southwestern Missouri culture to a monolithic Anglo-Saxon heritage and, by association, praised the genuine and often sanctified whiteness of the hillbilly icon.[61]

May Kennedy McCord and Otto Ernest Rayburn were two of Branson's primary boosters from roughly 1920 to 1970. Each frequently recruited hillbillies to combat the ills of modernity, including a perceived loss of meritorious whiteness. Dubbed "Queen of Hillbillies" on her death in 1979, McCord grew up just a few miles northwest of Branson and had a forty-year career as author, radio host, musician, and folk festival organizer. She is best known for a column entitled "Hillbilly Heartbeats" published weekly by Springfield, Missouri, newspapers from 1932 to 1943 and a radio program of the same name that ran for twenty years. In print and on air she spoke of the hillbilly with great reverence. For instance, in 1933 she stated, "I'm of his tribe and his clan, and I love every bone in his body. And if I or any contributor of mine ever mis-represents the Hillbilly may the blackness of the desert hide us, the sand fleas devour us and our bones bleach till judgment day."[62]

McCord also invited readers and listeners to offer comments on her work and thus facilitated a communal sense of hillbilly pride. In fact, her column became so popular that it generated more letters than all of the newspaper's other features combined. Reflecting on this community-building project, she declared, "Come on, hillbillies, let's get together. Let's rave about it all. Write some poetry and some essays and some love letters to the hills!" For many, her Sunday morning radio broadcast served as an on-air church of nostalgia through its melding of McCord's folksy religious hymns and discussion of local traditions. According to journalist Lida Wilson Pyles, "There were those who vowed that they got more good from her . . . than from the preacher's sermon at church. Many elderly people who were not physically able to attend church substituted just listening to May Kennedy McCord." Signing off every week with "I'll see you next Sunday, the Lord willin' and the creek don't rise," she catered to listeners who pined for glimpses of Ozark history, with its supposed deep-seated religiosity and dignified hillbilly heritage.[63]

Despite her interest in popularizing Ozark life, McCord claimed that her concern did not spring from the lure of tourist dollars. Her goal instead was to preserve the culture of "honorable and industrious" Ozarkers who "directly descended from the colonizers of America" and were "the only true Anglo-Saxons left." Affirming this sentiment, a 1930 column featured a poem entitled "The Hillbilly":

> Hillbilly, Hillbilly
> Who are you,
> Dreaming and dreaming the
> Whole day through?
> Blood of the Cavalier
> Bold and true
> Blood of the Puritan
> *That* is you!

Aside from this allusion to religious heritage, such environmentally determined racial superiority was also claimed through Ozark folk songs said to descend from ancient English ballads and through "picturesque and lyrical" mountaineer vocabulary said to contain "about 2000 words that can be traced directly to the Elizabethan or Chaucerian periods."[64]

Although McCord was not the first Ozarker to make such declarations, she greatly influenced outsider perceptions of the region because of her role as tour guide for national journalists and scholarly researchers. For instance, in the early 1950s she accompanied a writer and photographer from *Life* into the region and told him specifically that residents shared "the blood of the Seventeenth Century Colonists." That constitution led to characteristics such as pride, individualism, and loyalty to family and community. During her long career, McCord did much to promote and defend what she believed was a virtuous hillbilly legacy. As with most conceptions of the signifier discussed thus far, her vision sought to salvage the Ozark native from occasional claims of backwardness leveled from without. Yet crucial for this notion was an erasure of regional diversity and a glorification of locally cultivated whiteness.[65]

Until his death in 1960, folklorist, educator, and author Otto Ernest Rayburn served as another ardent voice for the unique and consecrated nature of the Ozark landscape and its residents. In the various publications discussed in Chapter 5, Rayburn also frequently intoned a racial makeup that mimicked the region's pristine hills and rivers. As the "'seedbed' of Anglo-Saxonism in the United States and the last surviving Elizabethan culture in the western world," his Ozarks represented a "veritable Garden of Eden" exempt from the unseemly aspects of modern life. In 1924, he moved to northwestern Arkansas to become school superintendent for the Kingston Community Project. Sponsored by the Board of Missions of the Presbyterian Church, this initiative extended the town's educational system from only elementary grades to a high school and a summer-session college, thereby creating the "Little Harvard of the Hills." Kingston was the brainchild of the Reverend Elmer J. Bouher, a missionary and preacher who came to the Ozarks in 1915. Like Rayburn, he considered the region an Anglo-Saxon preserve. As he wrote to a local, "You and your family have maintained the British character exemplified when their ancestors first settled on the Atlantic seaboard. There is no melting pot in these mountains. Your people have maintained your integrity, habits and racial purity."[66]

Drawing inspiration from an American eugenics movement rising in popularity during the early decades of the twentieth century, Bouher crafted a juxtaposition between the "pure clean-bred" and "sturdy" stock of Ozark Anglo-Saxons cut from the same cloth "as Jackson and Lincoln" and the mounting numbers of southern and eastern European immigrants to the United States. As he suggested in the 1920s, "America's greatest problem today is the flood of immigration from the lower levels of European society that is threatening to submerge and destroy our American ideals." Through this statement, he not only allied the Ozark hillbilly with now familiar traits of idealism, purity, industriousness, and democratic standards but also implicitly situated the prototypical mountaineer as a racial redeemer in a country being overrun with unsavory shades of whiteness. Although Rayburn resisted positing this dynamic in such crisis-ridden terms, he too hoped that this seedbed of Anglo-Saxonism would remain unsullied.[67]

Although the discourse focused on slight permutations of whiteness subsided at midcentury, in modern-day Branson one finds the continuation of a nearly homogeneous racial landscape. The city's permanent population has been and continues to be almost exclusively white. In the mid-1990s, out of a combined populace of 44,000 people, only 14 in Taney County and 6 in Stone County were African American. These figures had increased somewhat by the 2000 census, but Taney County was still 96.2 percent white and Stone County 97.6 percent (sta-

tistics that, in light of my time spent in the area, also reflect the racial constitution of Branson's visitors). Such numbers might actually account for the dearth
of nonwhite performers in the entertainment business. Many variety shows are
composed of family members and local musicians, and thus their racial makeup
may result from the character of this labor pool. In addition, Branson's theater
industry was built on country-and-western music, a genre that attracts few nonwhite performers. This dynamic was addressed by Charley Pride, Branson's only
longtime black headliner, when he stated, "People say, 'Why are there no black
musicians in your band?' Well, how many blacks play steel guitar?" Yet despite
these structural explanations for a lack of diversity, numerous black performers have claimed that it is difficult to find work in the city. For instance, Arthur
Duncan, a dancer with the Welk family since the 1960s, asserted that hundreds
of African Americans would like to work in Branson, but "it seems like there is
still a good-old-boy mentality here. It seems people want it to stay the way things
were 50 years ago."[68]

Reflecting on this social constitution, travel writer Arthur Frommer noted the
"undeniable racism" of some contemporary local promoters, and a journalist for
Gentlemen's Quarterly characterized the city as possessing a "foul smell of bigotry."
Despite nearly fifty theaters and more than one hundred acts, Branson's current
offerings include only a handful of black entertainers. The industry's primary
exception, Charley Pride, arrived in town in 1994. He is a member of the Grand
Ole Opry, presents a traditional Nashville sound, and seldom, if ever, includes
themes or styles related to African American music in his act. Such an approach
therefore suggests that nonwhite performers must engage in a tricksterlike erasure of their racial composition and perform a certain variant of whiteness to
profit in the local industry.[69]

In light of the area's history of vaunted Anglo-Saxonism, it is at first confounding that Shoji Tabuchi, a Japanese-born entertainer, is currently one of
Branson's most popular acts. However, he has worked for many years to gain
acceptance through implicating himself in Ozark hillbillyism. Though Tabuchi
was trained as a classical violinist, his musical affinities drastically changed when
he attended a concert by country music star Roy Acuff. In 1967 he moved from
Osaka to San Francisco to pursue a career as a fiddler. A year later, he received his
big break when Acuff invited him to appear at the Grand Ole Opry. In 1981, he
went to Branson and played at the Starlite Theatre. Remaining in town through
the 1980s, he won "Instrumentalist of the Year" at the Ozark Music Awards from
1984 to 1987. In 1990, he opened his own 2,000-seat venue and since that time has
often been dubbed the "King of Branson."[70]

Promotional materials from Tabuchi's theater claim that he "contradicts all ideas about American Country music." Although he does not don the attire of a hillbilly, numerous aspects of his act mirror the incongruous nature of that signifier. Many musical genres permeate the show, including jazz, conga, polka, classical, country, and gospel. In the late 1990s, Tabuchi even added a 2,000-pound Japanese taiko drum to the production—an instrument that, like the more conventional fiddles and banjos of the hillbilly craft, was embraced in rapidly modernizing post-1945 Japan as a way to supposedly preserve endangered cultural traditions. It is the ostentatious style of his theater, however, that is most discussed by tourists—a further example of this venue's paradoxical disposition in a Branson context that persistently makes a virtue of simplicity. In particular, the auditorium's bathrooms, attired with granite and onyx pedestal sinks, gold-leaf mirrors, marble fireplaces, pool tables, and velvet drapes, are cited as a "must see." Finally, in a city that regularly derides Las Vegas–oriented glitz and glamour, Tabuchi is the most sequined of all stars, his site utilizes a host of high-tech theatrics (animated laser art, mirror balls, and neon lights), and he claims that more indoor pyrotechnics are ignited during his show than in any other production in the country.[71]

Despite Tabuchi's eccentricities, his biography and act nevertheless resonate with the hillbilly moral standard, thereby functioning to expunge much of his ethnicity. Like that of the acclaimed mountaineer of actuality and lore, his livelihood had a humble beginning, and he rose to prominence only through a virulent work ethic. When asked what he appreciated most about the United States, he responded, "If you work hard, you can find a job and you can eat," thus intoning what he has labeled a personal "pioneer spirit." As with the semimythical hill people and their on-stage counterparts, he supports a set of core regional values within his performance. Family is marked as vital to this construct. Tabuchi's white wife and daughter frequently appear in the show, and he lauds respect for elders. Christianity is endorsed through numbers such as "The Old Rugged Cross." And every performance is punctuated by a patriotic finale—a component that was recognized in 2004 when he was awarded the "Americanism Medal" by the Daughters of the American Revolution. Finally, Tabuchi has adopted the self-effacing and hackneyed humor of Branson hillbilly comics as a way to both remind people of and make light of his heritage. For instance, he frequently jokes that he and friend Mel Tellis often fish together but Tillis is afraid to turn his back for fear that the Japanese star might "eat the bait." Thus, Tabuchi, like Charley Pride, has infiltrated Branson's predominantly white industry by espousing many elements of the hillbilly motif. Considering the demographic makeup of the

Bathroom, the Shoji Tabuchi Theatre, circa 2000. Postcard from the author's collection

area's residents and guests, this embrace may be the only way that a nonwhite celebrity could be christened an entertainment "king" within a region that has often proclaimed its pure racial legacy.[72]

Shoji Tabuchi may sometimes make light of his ethnic heritage, but Branson's most troubling racial development is the recent presence of Christian Identity groups. Followers of this ideology believe that whites are God's chosen people; mark Jews as descendants of Satan; claim that nonwhites derive from pre-Adamic races and are thus other species; and posit Armageddon as apocalyptic race war. The FBI estimates Identity membership at fifty-thousand nationwide, and the Arkansas-Missouri border is the center of the movement. With more Identity affiliates in Missouri than any other state, many feel that Branson has become the group's main gathering place. Such formal meetings began in the mid-1990s. In 1995, the International Coalition of Covenant Congregations Conference convened at Branson's Lodge of the Ozarks one day after the Oklahoma City bombing. This symposium, which drew six hundred attendees, featured guest speaker Peter J. Peters. Peters heads Scriptures for America (an organization that also believes the Bible authorizes the execution of gays and lesbians), pastors a church in LaPorte, Colorado, and is the country's leading exponent of the Identity belief system. Beyond that date, he engineered similar Branson rallies over the Memorial Day weekends in 2001, 2002, and 2006.[73]

An analogous gathering entitled "Songs for His People" was held in Branson in February 2000 and attracted nearly three hundred individuals. Speaker Charles A. Jennings, an Identity minister and owner of Truth in History Publications in Springdale, Arkansas, expressed pleasure with "the quality of our race in this room," extolled the moral superiority of the antebellum South, and promised listeners that his movement would take the Bible Belt as the new promised land. Other presenters included Thom Robb, who lives 30 miles south of Branson and is the Grand Dragon of the Knights of the Ku Klux Klan. Furthermore, Ted R. Weiland, who leads the Mission to Israel affiliate in Scottsbluff, Nebraska, labeled Jews the "enemies of Christ" and claimed that he preaches in Branson "more than anywhere in the United States."[74]

Although Branson tourism boosters have unremittingly drawn on Christian themes and ideals and sometimes used the area's Anglo-Saxon heritage as a calling card, locals have not embraced the far less benign presentations of these premises by the Christian Identity Movement. Each Identity gathering has met with protest, as residents paraded in front of meeting sites with placards such as "Hate is Not a Neighborhood Value." Moreover, the city's Chateau on the Lake resort canceled a contract for an event to be held in May 2001, with general manager Steven Marshall stating, "We have to take a stand." According to protester Rosemary Stewart-Stafford, when Christian Identity proponents "dare to call themselves Christian," resistance to their message becomes a "duty." The local entertainment industry has certainly been criticized for offering a "fundamentalist" variant of faith, yet the city's construct of wholesome family values has never included the vitriolic rhetoric of this small segment of the overall leisure market. And although the Ozark hillbilly has been put forth in ambivalent terms, that signifier's racial standing has connoted a prideful and principled local heritage rather than overt and contemptible racism.[75]

TRICKING THE TOURISTS

Numerous progenitors exist for the stereotypical hillbilly. Most vital for this study is the image of the Arkansas backwoodsman presented in the "Arkansas Traveler" legend. This account was first published as music in 1847 and since has been conveyed both verbally and pictorially. The story details an encounter between a hill man distrustful of strangers and a visitor who happens upon his ramshackle cabin. The native engages in a verbal game of cat and mouse with the foreigner—conversational deception that apes the purposeful vagueness of tricksters worldwide. For instance, asked by the traveler "Will you tell me where this road goes to?" the native responds, "It's never gone any whar since I've lived here; It's always thar when I git up in the mornin'." Furthermore, the sojourner inquires whether the mountaineer has "any spirits," and he replies, "Lots uv 'em; Sal seen one last night by that ar ol hollar gum, and it nearly skeered her to death." In the end, this contested exchange dies down, and the stranger is given food, drink, and a place to sleep for the night. Full of typecasting that would be thoroughly elaborated on in later decades, the "Arkansas Traveler" describes Ozarkers as lazy, inebriated, content in squalor, and unversed in the ways of coherent discourse. However, it also set the precedent for a communicative device whereby what appears to be hillbilly ignorance alternately becomes cunning intellect and what seems local foolishness instead reveals the traveler's (or tourist's) own credulity.[76]

In the introduction to an anthology of Ozark tall tales entitled *We Always Lie to Strangers,* folklorist Vance Randolph wrote, "There's no harm in 'stretchin' the blanket' or 'lettin' out a whack' or 'sawin' off a whopper' or 'spinnin' a windy' when they involve no attempt to injure anybody. 'A windy ain't a lie, nohow,' said one of my neighbors, 'unless you tell it for the truth.' And even if you do not tell it for the truth nobody is deceived, except maybe a few tourists." Randolph was not a native Ozarker, but no folklorist is more thoroughly associated with the region or has more comprehensively assembled accounts of tourist gullibility at the hands of area natives. His *The Ozarks: An American Survival of Primitive Society* (1931) was the initial book-length study of the region. Although unabashedly neglectful of the more modern elements of the area's society and culture, he forcefully argued that "the Ozark hill-billy is a genuine American—that is why he seems so alien to most tourists." Enamored with notions of isolation and stubborn traditionalism, Randolph commented extensively on virtues long lost within contemporary America. While some saw the nostalgia in *The Ozarks* as folkloric invention, he insisted that "there is not a line of fiction or intentional exaggeration in it."[77]

Throughout his life, Randolph tenuously grappled with the ever increasing stream of vacationers pouring into the hills and their effect on traditional culture. He always said that such things disinterested him but nevertheless realized that tourism was good business and desired to see hill folk profit from outsider dollars. Offering opinion on this subject during a speech at a 1934 Eureka Springs, Arkansas, folk festival, he stated, "The professional Ozark boosters would do well to put more of this primitive stuff into their tourist advertising, and not talk so much about our splendid highways and excellent new hotels. . . . They [city people] come here to see rugged mountain scenery and quaint log cabins

"Hillbillies on Vacation" postcard, circa 1960. Postcard from the author's collection

and picturesque rail fences and romantic-looking mountaineers." Through this premise, his much cherished primitivism could actually be protected rather than threatened by outsider interventions. If natives continued to cultivate the illusion of the past, they would both financially profit and preserve aspects of their heritage made available in consumable form.[78]

Randolph documented many natives who took great pride in their ability to deceive city-dwelling tourists. For instance, in his *Funny Stories about Hillbillies* (1944) he cited an individual who avowed it was "taken as a compliment to be called a liar," and another who professed, "You can hear anything in Stone County except the truth."[79] Such yarns continue to be spun for modern-day Branson vacationers. Commenting on the hillbilly's image within the contemporary tourism industry, Raeanne Presley stated:

> In the mind of the people that live here that would call themselves a hillbilly, that didn't mean stupid. It might have meant that they were uneducated but it never meant that they weren't smart. . . . So, that's what carries over and what Gary [Herkimer in the Presleys' Country Jubilee] tries to do with his comedy. Although you might laugh because he didn't pronounce the word right or he used it incorrectly in a sentence or he looked kind of silly in his clothes, the end of the joke is always that he outsmarted the other guy. That's why I think people are not insulted by that. The play is the smart city guy and the dumb hillbilly but the dumb hillbilly

wins. . . . The people that might consider themselves hillbillies are never insulted by that. Usually the ones that don't want the Ozarks known for hillbillies aren't hillbillies.[80]

One may then securely adjoin deliberate backwardness or an intentional lack of knowledge to the myriad ambivalences that characterize the Ozark trickster. By deceiving visitors in such a manner, the hillbilly fortifies virtues of simplicity, individualism, and relaxed industriousness. Such chicanery furthers a sense of "otherness" in the minds of outsiders and also assists in the cultivation of moun-taineer pride, for behind a veil of ignorance is astuteness, just as underneath a shroud of debauched stereotypes is a multifarious set of regional values.

Tricksters play tricks. Utilizing a strategy of deception, they achieve ends that are self-serving, culturally necessary, or a mixture of the two. The hillbilly trick-ster has effectively enacted this process for nearly one hundred years within the Ozark tourism industry. Words from countless natives throughout this period suggest a complicit involvement in the practice—one that was necessary for the construction of the region's vast consumer culture. Likewise, the moniker has been worn by many as a badge of honor and used to denote a cohesive group of ethical and religious dictates that lie beneath the tourist's misperceptions, foibles, and follies. Reducing the function of the hillbilly trickster to a singularity does a disservice to the richness of the semiotic tradition and pigeonholes a signi-fier with a demonstrable ability to resist coherent description. Positioned on the margins of an Ozark construct of propriety, the figure also resides at the center of the tourism enterprise. Stationed within a mythical lifestyle of indecency and squalor, it also bears connotations of admired simplicity and deep-seated moral-ity. Within a vacation industry intent on offering a strictly delineated portrait of principled thought and action, the ambiguous hillbilly has simultaneously granted reminders of that which imperils its authority and presented an ideo-logical map that charts the path for its continuance.

CHAPTER SEVEN

"The Aroma of God's Spirit"

Branding Branson's Future

After a guest lecture at Missouri State University in 2005, I was approached by Don Gabriel and given a document entitled "The Branson Manifesto." Gabriel heads BransonFunTrip, a travel service company that was recently developed to attract a new cohort of vacationers to the region. He also founded the area's Christian Business Men's Committee, was a member of the Branson/Lakes Area Chamber of Commerce, and is the father of a prominent local entertainer. Targeting baby boomers, his company believes that through fresh marketing approaches this new audience will embrace the region's religiously guided commodities. As he stated, "The Spirit that permeates this community will minister to them. . . . These new visitors will experience what Branson is really like and the tremendous variety that is available. They will leave this town transformed. . . . There are blessings around every corner."[1]

Gabriel's "Manifesto" emerged as an atypical local development project was about to be unveiled in the spring of 2006. Labeled "Branson Landing," this $420 million venture features a scenic boardwalk on the Lake Taneycomo waterfront; a town square large enough to accommodate five thousand guests for special events; a frequent synchronized water, light, sound, and fire display created by producers of shows for Las Vegas's Bellagio Hotel; and a wealth of retail and dining establishments. Prior to this expansion, downtown Branson resembled archetypal small-town America. All variety show theaters are situated to the east of this area, and the downtown section was filled with five-and-tens, diners, and establishments selling "down-home" antiques. However, amid the approximately one hundred new shops planned for inclusion in the Landing are upscale retailers such as Ann Taylor, J. Jill, Children's Place, and even Victoria's Secret.

The development also includes luxury condominiums, two Hilton hotels, and a 220,000-square-foot convention center equipped with technological innovations such as video conferencing and satellite uplink capabilities.

Despite these chic aspects of the Branson Landing project, there will still be businesses that possess a more traditional Ozark feel. For instance, a 40,000-square-foot Bass Pro Shop and a moderately priced and southern-based Belk department store will anchor the area's retail offerings. The Landing will be divided into five themed districts, including one entitled "The Country," described by promoters in standard Branson terms as a celebration of "American life and culture in a Tom Sawyer and apple pie sort of way." However, adjacent to this quarter will be "The Downtown," "rich with the urban flavors of jazz and blues, café and bistro dining, funky shops and galleries." Backers have presented this project as one capable of "breathing new life" into the city's famed Strip and other time-tested local attractions, but the people responsible for Branson Landing have in fact said very little about the venues and accompanying ideologies that brought the region's consumer culture to prominence. Instead, the "Branson Landing lifestyle" has been advertised in a way that seems utterly dissimilar to issues that pervade the body of this study, and this type of promotion thus raises many questions about the fate of the city's religio-tourism enterprise. The director of sales and marketing for the Landing exemplified this incongruent approach as he beckoned individuals to his development:

> Imagine: step outside your condo in the heart of fine, eclectic restaurants, colorful galleries, and trendy boutiques. Take a stroll on the Boardwalk, feel the crisp, fresh breeze from Lake Taneycomo while you sip gourmet coffee and munch a buttery croissant. Pick up a paper at the corner newsstand. Shop in your favorite of nearly 100 retail stores. Meet friends for cocktails in the evening. . . . Now that's living . . . on the Boardwalk at Branson Landing.[2]

In a twenty-four-page promotional magazine about Branson Landing that was published in 2005, no mention was made of the city's thorough linkage to Christian sentiments. Confronting this absence, Don Gabriel's "Manifesto" began by addressing the intended "message" of an expanded tourist market. Wary of this new, ostensibly secular direction, he wrote:

> I believe that Branson is a community founded on Christian principles and unashamedly proclaims these principles. People discover when they visit here that God is honored, Biblical family values are upheld and genuine patriotism (recognizing the Christian foundation of our nation) abounds. . . . Take Christian values

and principles, and the public statement of them, away and Branson fundamentally changes, for the worse.

Later asserting that "some people with an investment in the success of this area will say that we should not emphasize this, for it will keep people from coming," Gabriel instead held that the Christian underpinnings of Branson tourism should be declared rather than elided. When promoting a "blessed" place, such sanctity must be made known, for as he stated, that is the city's "marketing appeal." However, like all boosters throughout the past century, Gabriel avowed that regionally dependent evangelism should not be blatantly preachy. Rather, Branson and its attractions possess an ability to innately communicate such wonders. Demarcating the ways that this spiritual vapor wafts through the Ozark hills and pleading for its continued promotion, he wrote, "The aroma of God's Spirit permeates this area and the theaters, the attractions, the hotels and motels and restaurants, the marinas and lakes, and even the glorious natural beauty itself."[3]

Although Branson Landing signals a bold, and in some people's opinions, misguided new direction for local tourism, even those instrumental in its conception continue to acknowledge the city's primary allure. As stated by Ross Summers, president of the local chamber of commerce, "Branson will always be a slice of America. We never intend to alienate our base." Undeniably, this core constituency has always been the Christian tourist. Even though the nature of religious attractions has mutated over time, thereby drawing individuals with partly different sensibilities, a century of visitors have nevertheless been bound together by a now familiar type of popular faith. As some boosters have recently pushed for more upscale attractions that somewhat rebuff the middle-class-oriented, value-laden approach that has historically guided the industry, others have intensified their efforts to attract this bedrock cohort. Thus, as Branson enters the twenty-first century, it must once again grapple with ambivalences that have permeated its tourism endeavor.[4]

"A MIGHTY CENTER FOR REVIVAL"

The Branson/Lakes Area Chamber of Commerce and Convention and Visitor's Bureau and Silver Dollar City are the area's primary surveyors but collect no demographic information concerning the religious affiliation of tourists. However, *Washington Post* writer Lois Romano, who visited Branson in 2005, found that every visitor she approached "professed to be a practicing Christian," and in asking vacationers about their faith, I reached a similar conclusion. This conjecture is confirmed not only by the unadulterated religious worldviews put forth by area attractions but also by local efforts to entice and maintain visitors with this perspective. In 1999, the city's convention and visitor's bureau for the first time held an event at the annual meeting of the Religious Conference Management Association, a group of travel planners for church groups that represents $50 million in yearly revenues and is one of the fastest-growing meeting sectors nationwide. In addition, seven area businesses signed on as $3,000 apiece Gold Sponsors. City representatives had participated in this convention to a lesser degree in the two previous years and tracked more than 10,000 visitors to Branson who arrived after being contacted on-site. These boosters therefore hoped to increase this number considerably through their 1999 effort.[5]

In the past few years, Branson has also witnessed the emergence of tour operators who cater specifically to a Christian clientele. For instance, Ed Szuszalski owns Trinity Tours of Branson, a company that began in 1997 and books approximately two hundred groups a year. Originally realizing the Christian inclinations of local tourism through working at Silver Dollar City, Szuszalski has found that vacationers enjoy booking their trips with a person of the same faith. Attracting guests from across the Christian spectrum, he does not provide discounts for area attractions or lodgings. Instead, Szuszalski's business is built on religiously motivated hospitality. By meeting his clients on arrival, collecting tickets to shows so they do not have to wait in lines, and ensuring that they will avoid any production that might have "undesirable" content, he functions as "their Christian brother in Branson." His strategy demonstrates that devout tourists are drawn to the Ozarks not only because of the substance of attractions but also because of the seemingly mundane conveniences offered by individuals inspired by piety and profit.[6]

Although Branson tourism has for many decades refashioned the meaning of religious experience and offered innovative modes of recreation-situated worship, the recent emergence of the "show-service" is perhaps the most telling way that some within the local industry hope to maintain a Christian tourist base through more overt (yet still popular in style) modes of proselytism. While in town on a Sunday morning in November 2003, I decided to go to church. Although there were numerous denominational options, I chose a service at the Jim Stafford Theatre. On Monday through Saturday, this venue is filled with patrons who come to see a popular comedian and guitar picker. A few pages of the King James Bible are framed in the building's lobby, and Stafford's wife prays that God will "bless our theater," but amid signature hits such as "Spiders and Snakes" and a barrage of hokey humor, little suggests that on Sundays the site becomes a formal place of worship. However, as I stepped into the "sanctuary" that hosted the Cross Roads International Revival Prayer Gathering, I joined hundreds of others who sought a final dose of faith to cap off their vacation.[7]

This event at Stafford's theater was begun in 1993 by Glenn and Sheila Artt of Branson's Cross Roads International Revival Center. During the week, the Artts pastor a small nondenominational congregation focused on biblical teachings, Spirit-filled fellowship, and evangelism in anticipation of an immanent Second Coming. But on the Sabbath, their ranks swell, as sometimes upwards of six hundred people fill Stafford's locale for an event that offers a decidedly muted presentation of this theology wrapped in the paradigmatic mode of Branson entertainment.

The show-service I attended began like all Branson productions. Audience members–cum–congregants were asked to introduce themselves, and assistant pastors told hackneyed jokes that resembled those tendered by their more obvious hillbilly counterparts. On this particular day, the crowd's constitution was global in scope. Attendees hailed from England, Australia, Kenya, and Canada, as well as from almost every U.S. state. This overture was followed by sacred songs and a few specifically Jewish rituals such as the blowing of a shofar to signal the group's loyalty to Israel. As the service moved from international religio-politics to the realm of civil religiosity, women in sequined costumes mounted the stage / altar waving red and green flags. While not the American banner, this ensign (red representing the blood of Jesus and green the life he gave) was nevertheless offered as a symbol under which the nation could unite.

As witnessed throughout Branson's history, religion has been mediated by myriad cultural forms. At this gathering, it found expression by means of ventriloquism. Calling all children to the fore, the ventriloquist discussed giving thanks to God as the true meaning of Thanksgiving and led the audience in a song entitled "Godo" that was a rough take on "Bingo." This pious frivolity was followed by a twenty-minute sermon that broached the more serious themes of churchly unity and the pending nature of a worldwide anointing. After the passing of collection plates and mention of Branson's blessed status among American communities, the service concluded with an altar call. In the only reference to the noninstitutional nature of his event, Pastor Artt admitted that a public pronouncement of faith in a theater setting might make some people feel odd or uncomfortable. However, numerous individuals did come forth with requests to be spiritually healed. Thus, taken in its entirety, this event included all elements of the city's "secular" productions but went a step further by enacting formal evangelistic techniques only implied by its counterparts. Although I departed wondering whether I had just been to a church or a show, I also knew that such lines of distinction mean little in the Branson context.

In 2001, Sheila Artt claimed that more than 7,000 people had made first-time commitments to Christ during her Prayer Gatherings, and that over 100,000 individuals had attended her services. Because of this popularity, the Cross Roads ministry has commenced plans for a new 61,000-square-foot revival center to occupy the city's vacant 2,500-seat Yellow Ribbon Theatre. Recently, a ministry spearheaded by Tim Hill assumed the Artts' place at the theater and began offering his "Sons of Thunder" morning worship service. Hill believes that God sent him to evangelize in the Ozarks and that this premonition was validated when he was befriended by Christian relationship expert and author Gary Smalley and learned of Corrie Ten Boom's prophecy concerning the region. Reflecting on the city's larger show-service enterprise and its function as "an incredible harvest ministry for souls," he stated, "We are seeing miracles. People are accepting Jesus Christ and people are being healed in the theaters in Branson." The religious gathering at Jim Stafford's venue is one of the most popular, but not the only, show-service in town. In 2003, at least seven other ministries offered Sunday fare at sites such as the Welk Theater and Resort, the IMAX Entertainment Complex, a local horse ranch, and even the Golden Corral restaurant.[8]

Branson's "alternative" worship opportunities have drawn the ire of several area pastors, including Jay Scribner of the First Baptist Church, who called them "just entertainment." However, many other local authorities feel that the city's wealth of Christian tourists cannot be fully accommodated even through the combined efforts of institutional and noninstitutional religious organizations. As Barbara Fairchild, who has conducted such gatherings since 1992, asserted, "If every church and every theater was full, there would still be lots more people who need God than we can reach." In light of this apparent demand, show-services provide a glimpse into an interesting trajectory of future Branson tourism.[9]

Gospel music has been a mainstay in Branson since the 1970s, but formal show-services did not begin until 1990. The first such event, the Sunday Gospel Jubilee with Max Bacon and Family, was held in the afternoon at the Plummer Theater and is still featured at the 76 Music Hall. This performance primarily highlights religious music without the use of sermons or testimonies. It was not until 1992 that Branson offered a production that incorporated these more official liturgical elements. In that year, the Jim Stafford Theatre hosted the Branson Gospel Hour featuring the talents of Dewey Atchison, an Assemblies of God minister with a background in country music. At his first service, thirty people made commit-

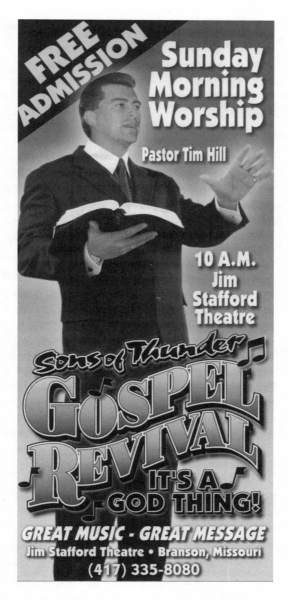

Sons of Thunder Gospel Revival brochure, 2005. From the author's collection

ments to Christ, and soon thereafter he was turning away 300 guests a week who could not fit into the 800-seat locale.[10]

Tourist Seth Golding attended one of the Gospel Hour services, and his encounter serves as an example of the type of religious experience available to visitors. Golding was initially drawn to the event because Glen Campbell, a born-again Christian, was performing. On reflection, however, he was more deeply affected by Atchison's focus on nondenominationalism and the lack of prescribed church establishments or rules. Remaining in contact with the preacher once he departed Branson, Golding returned a few months later to be baptized in Table Rock Lake and married at a country chapel on the edge of the city. Commenting on this and other evangelical successes, Atchison stated, "Branson has got America's attention and what I see is that this is a platform for a tremendous outreach to the world."[11]

Barbara Fairchild, a 1970s country-pop icon turned gospel artist, also commenced a show-service in 1992. When a minister who had been conducting a Sunday gathering at the Willie Nelson Theater could not finish the season, Fairchild filled in. In contrast with Atchison, the singer had a markedly different approach to proselytism but garnered equally as many worshipers. As Fairchild avowed, she tries to "keep 'religion' out of this thing" by avoiding authoritative sermons and altar calls. Her first appearance at Nelson's theater attracted 735 people, and the following Sunday that number doubled. Although she has rotated through a variety of venues, patrons continue to seek her out, and many profess that they attend despite not having gone to an official church in decades.[12]

Because she is also a popular non-Sunday performer, Fairchild's position in the Branson entertainment market raises further questions about what is defined as a house of worship and what amounts to a religious experience. Although claiming that the "show is the show" and the "service is the service," she also has maintained in relation to both productions that "if they come to see [her] they are going to hear about Him." Gospel hymns, patriotic melodies, sanctification of family, and discussion of social concerns such as prayer in public schools and the teaching of evolution pervade each of Fairchild's formats. The "secular" production includes performances of some of her pop hits, and the "sacred" variant offers more frequent references to Christ, but here the contrast ceases. Fairchild has asserted that she does not "preach" during the former happening but also believes that God chose her to evangelize within both approaches because Branson is a "city set on a hill." In manner that further underscores the free play of the divine in all Branson leisure offerings, she claimed that the Holy Spirit is the motivation for all her performances: "Sometimes you'll be sowing, sometimes you'll be watering, sometimes you'll be reaping, and most of the time you won't know the difference. . . . When the presence of the Lord takes over . . . then you just follow that."[13]

In trying to discern what a church is and what it is not, the Grand Old Gospel Hour provides additional complications. Started in 1996 by Sam Stauffer, this show-service now often attracts two thousand visitors to its Sunday event at the Grand Palace (Branson's largest entertainment venue). Stauffer has defined his ministry as a church because it is a legally recognized religious organization and has a local membership of approximately two hundred people. However, he professed that this congregation does not think like more traditional counterparts because it dismisses the notion that a church means "a steeple" or "a stained glass window." Drawing guests from across the Christian spectrum for praise and worship, the pastor offers a presentation that resists denominational affiliation by uniting all within one "body of Christ." It is this sense of accord that distinguishes the Grand Old Gospel Hour from more formal institutions. As he stated, "You have really the same message but you leave off those doctrinal differences. . . . . I see myself as beyond the church. . . . I believe in heaven they are not going to ask you, 'Are you a Baptist? Or a Lutheran? Or a Methodist?' They'll ask, 'Do you know Christ?'"[14]

At the Grand Old Gospel Hour, knowing Christ is a process of the heart rather than the intellect. In the centuries-old Christian debate concerning the proper way to receive and interpret divine mandates, Stauffer opts for an affective approach that can lead to personal transformation and a dynamic relationship with God—a method of "strategic relationalism" that Christian Smith has claimed permeates the history of evangelicalism. Validating the efficacy of this technique, a ministry newsletter described a variety of "healings, financial breakthroughs, spiritual reconnections, and basic 'about faces'" that have resulted from attending the service. As Stauffer asserted in relation to such testimonies, "If you get control of a person's heart then you change their actions. . . . Our faith needs to be living and active." But rather than viewing his mode of religiosity as a lifelong alternative to traditional churches, he sees it as something that can facilitate change on a vacationer's return to home—a desire for ethical makeover in the realm of everyday experience which is at the root of all Branson leisure. Detailing this tactic, he affirmed, "We say, 'Don't leave your church. Go back and pray for your church. Go back and be a spark plug in your church. Go back and do it from within.' . . . We're not there to tear something down. We're there to ignite a fire."[15]

Like others in the show-service genre, Stauffer's presentation had adopted all the trappings of any Branson act and is done "just like a full-scale production." It begins with introductions and banal comedy, progresses through rousing hymns, includes prayers for the nation, and is capped off by moments of reflection on the integration of Christian principles into lived existence. The Grand Old Gospel Hour has become the most popular and financially prosperous of all such productions. Yearly attendance figures exceed 40,000, and the ministry's budget now tops $300,000. Funds generated by the Sunday gathering are funneled into missionary work in India, Mexico, and the United States, and a television ministry is planned. Yet despite its governmental standing as a church, its local congregation, and its evangelical efforts, even Stauffer recognizes the ambiguity inherent in his undertaking. A diminutive permanent assembly combined with an often massive body of transient worshipers has led him to label the Grand Old Gospel Hour a "very small, big church." Moreover, when trying to resolutely categorize his venture, he struggled with classification: "We're not a show but we're not totally a service. So we're kind of like a service. We're kind of the in-between. You have a lot of the elements that are in all churches but then again I don't think we take ourselves as seriously, but we do take ourselves seriously." In the end, the pastor's inability to catalog his presentation matters little and resonates with the many varieties of "betweenness" found throughout the history of the larger entertainment industry. For guests, it ultimately offers a popular respite from adopted creeds and a chance to better appreciate Christ's presence in all facets of social and cultural existence.[16]

Summarizing the reasons why so many are attracted to the Grand Old Gospel Hour, Stauffer claimed that Branson is becoming "a mighty center for revival." His first job on arriving in town reflects this assertion: he worked as the general manager for Cecil Todd's Revival Fires Ministries, an organization that has sponsored two local large-scale camp meetings a year since 1992. Todd started Revival Fires in 1964 in Joplin, Missouri, and then hosted a one-hour program on Trinity Broadcasting Network before moving to Branson in the late 1980s. Like many others, this relocation was partially motivated by *The Shepherd of the Hills*. Racked with stress and illness on arrival in town, Todd identified with the tribulations of novel's protagonist. After only a few months, he recovered his health and initiated his biannual revival, which he has called "a preview of heaven."[17]

Todd's first camp meeting welcomed only 125 individuals, but Revival Fires currently attracts more than 10,000 people to its spring and fall events held at the Grand Palace and other sizable Branson venues. Each camp meeting incorporates a large quotient of star power. In past years, guest speakers have included Pat Robertson, Jim Bakker, John Hagee, and other evangelical and Pentecostal mainstays. Additionally, local performers such as Buck Trent and the Haygoods have lent their talents. The events also incorporate now familiar familial aspects, including preaching by Todd's son, Tim. Civil religiosity pervades the gatherings, as witnessed by 1998's spring theme, "Calling America to Repentance and Revival (from the Church House to the White House)." Moreover, featured ministers invoke area amusements to communicate theological messages. As Dudley Rutherford, utilizing patented Christian fishing imagery, quipped, "God sets the hook in a person's heart. . . . We're thrilled just bringing them in one at a time." Finally, lecturers often prompt visitors to translate their faith into action within morally imperiled American life. As one attendee concluded about the camp meetings, "Christians get encouragement in a world that discourages them all the time."[18]

An appearance by featured speaker Roy Moore at Todd's revival in 2004 exemplified an ability to engage conservative Christian tourists discouraged with the contemporary political milieu. Moore, former chief justice of the Alabama Supreme Court, emblematizes national debates over the place of Christianity within the public square. Beginning in 1995, he faced challenges from the American Civil Liberties Union (ACLU) over the display of the Ten Commandments in his courtroom and his use of prayers during sessions. When elected chief justice in 2001, he unveiled a 5,280-pound granite monument featuring the directives in the court building rotunda, and three months later the ACLU filed suit. In 2003, a U.S. District Court judge ordered Moore to remove the monument or face contempt charges and heavy fines. He subsequently refused, was suspended, and had his appeal denied by the Supreme Court. During his Revival Fires speech, he discussed the undue separation of church and state, America's Christian underpinnings, and the personal trials he has faced while promoting this agenda. As his spokeswoman attested, "He really connects the dots for us about how the Ten Commandments are the basis of our moral law." Sensing that tourists were amenable to his message, Moore returned later in 2004 to speak alongside Gregory Thompson, the former superintendent of schools in Humansville, Missouri (80 miles north of Branson). Thompson was then being sued over the presence of the Ten Commandments in a cafeteria and his push to include Christian principles in public school curricula. Despite an almost certain legal defeat, Thompson and Moore professed that they would inevitably emerge victorious within the broader battle for the soul of America: "If you obey the Ten Commandments and the book they're written in, we win."[19]

Like the Grand Old Gospel Hour, Revival Fires engages in evangelism outside the parameters of its two yearly gatherings. The organization has a mailing list of 35,000 people and a yearly budget of $3.5 million that is spent primarily on foreign missionary work. This proselytism is focused on Russia, where, as of 2002, the ministry had sent 10,000 followers on more than a hundred occasions. As with Stauffer's initiative, missionaries say that their intention is not to lead people away from their home churches but to reinvigorate participation in these institutions. This strategy was attested to by Gary and Janice Voegtle, who first took Bibles to Russia in 1993 after attending one of Todd's revivals. Instead of trying to convert citizens to a particular Christian vantage, they claimed that their efforts brought countless individuals back to their traditional Russian Orthodox communities. Many of those who work abroad for Revival Fires joined its ranks after attending the ministry's Branson events. Drawn by an experience that has maintained the recreational tones of historical camp meetings, these individuals merged this brand of pious leisure into a more formal religious affiliation. Situating his events within the larger context of the area's faith-based tourism and furthering notions of an increasingly collapsed distinction between religion and recreation in the region, Todd stated, "What is happening here in Branson is that where you have the church here and the entertainment up here, you're seeing these two come to closer balance."[20]

If Branson theaters can easily be transformed into houses of worship, some of the city's institutional churches have also donned the characteristics of entertainment venues or relied on tourist patronage. For instance, when Branson Methodist Church first opened, its services were conducted in a downtown dance hall. Prior to the development of the city's Highway 76 Strip, the congregation relocated to a lonely hillside along that route. Building on this site, what is now Branson United Methodist Church became the first auditorium on a stretch of road currently lined with brassy theaters and neon signs. This locale has been both a blessing and a curse for pastor Don Keithly. By being nestled amid the city's musical attractions and even bearing architectural similarities to these venues, the church has great visibility and sometimes counts half of the people in attendance as vacationers. However, Keithly also has claimed that these "endless tourists" cause "many distractions" for local adherents and that it is hard for him to "compete with the professional show environment and mentality." This latter remark speaks to the types of traditional religiosity that fit easily with area entertainment as opposed to those variants that struggle to realize this correspondence. The emotive and often raucous approach of Pentecostal churches and nondenominational fellowships easily resonates with Branson's variety show entertainment, for example, whereas the more subdued liturgy of United Methodism was situated by Keithly as in competition with rather than a corollary to such "secular" rites.[21]

The history of Branson's only Catholic church is also ensconced in a tourism narrative. When Our Lady of the Lakes' former pastor, Monsignor Phil Bucher, arrived in 1993, masses were being held at the Christy Lane Theater to accommodate overflow from the church's undersized sanctuary. Shortly thereafter, a different structure was erected close to downtown, but by 2002, even this 600-seat building was too small. To fund a new house of worship, Bucher called on vacationers, who often constitute 90 percent of his 3,000-person congregation. Able to accommodate 1,300 attendees, the recently completed 40,000-square-foot church cost $4 million and is the largest sanctuary in the Springfield–Cape Girardeau diocese—a huge expanse of religious geography that covers most of southern Missouri. Because visitors made this transformation viable, Bucher felt the need to incorporate tourists into the church by embracing them as "parishioners in their home away from home," a viewpoint that requires getting out of "the mentality that it is 'our' church." This new religiosity not only mandates a redefinition of religion, religious experience, and church but, in this case, also requires a reclassification of what constitutes a community of worship. According to Bucher, "every weekend it's a new parish."[22]

In modern-day Branson, theaters temporarily become formal worship sites on Sundays, and worship sites rely on theater patrons for their livelihood and growth. However, the most extraordinary examples of the merger of religion and recreation are two local entertainment venues that have actually been transformed into full-time churches. In July 2002, Mel Tillis announced that he was selling his 2,700-seat auditorium to a partnership created by David Green, the owner of Hobby Lobby. In turn, Green planned to lease the location to Tri-Lakes Cathedral, an Assemblies of God church. Tillis, a devout Christian, embraced this transfer because the property was going to be "in the hands of God and it can't get no better than that." When I visited in late 2003, ticket booths, concession stands, and other reminders of the property's former purpose still remained, but officials hoped that these would soon be transformed into places for welcoming guests and distributing literature. Pastor David Plank asserted that remodeling was in store but also hoped a sanctuary that at least alludes to a Branson theater would allow Tri-Lakes "to touch as many people [tourists] as possible."[23]

Despite hoping to evangelize to a larger constituency in his theater-turned-church, Plank expressed many reservations about branding Branson as a sanctified town and positing its entertainment as a snug fit with Christian principles. Instead, he equated the city's "spiritual quality" with "a denial of what a true Christian is" because area religious leaders and adherents have failed to address mounting divorce rates, poverty, drug abuse, and homosexuality. Moreover, performers who did not incorporate biblical doctrine into their own lives were augmenting this general climate of pious malaise. To allay this pervasive "false impression of true Christianity," Plank urged both residents and vacationers to "take ownership" of Branson—a message he believed that not many religious leaders were willing to present because of tourists' "fickleness" and desire to embrace only the "fun" elements of faith. Thus, while one may think that Tri-Lakes would fuse entertainment with religiosity more than any other Branson church, its pastor instead saw the popularity of pleasurable piety as eliding an essential focus on pressing sociocultural issues and the cultivation of what he considered authentic Christianity.[24]

David Green has stated that "Hobby Lobby is basically a ministry." In accordance with this injunction, Mardel (a company subsidiary) sells Christian materials and educational products, Hobby Lobby does not do business on Sundays, and its Web site offers many prayers and scriptural quotations. This Web site also describes a variety of ministry projects supported by the corporation and lauds the faith-oriented, full-page ads it takes out every Christmas Day and Easter in more than 250 newspapers nationwide. Like Branson entertainment at large, Hobby Lobby firmly allies Christianity with patriotism, as witnessed by Max Lucado's "A Prayer for America," a piece prominently displayed on the company's home page. It also has a vested interest in infusing religion into lived existence—an approach made manifest by involvement with Bearing Fruit Communications (a marketer of Christian messages through radio and television programs) and Book of Hope (an organization that evangelizes to children). Hobby Lobby also hopes to "share the Lord's blessing" with employees and conduct business "in a manner consistent with Biblical principles." The company currently generates more than $1 billion in sales a year and has more than 300 locations. However, its owner is always quick to emphasize that increased profits are less important than Christian-based commerce. This understanding is codified in Hobby Lobby's "Statement of Purpose," which claims the enterprise has endured "by God's grace."[25]

In 2002, David Green facilitated another theater-to-church conversion in Branson, one that was described in miraculous language by representatives from Skyline Southern Baptist Church. For many years Skyline had tried to relocate to the city's vacant Gold Rush Theater, but the price for the site was too high for the small congregation. After Skyline gave up these plans, the experience of a sixteen-year-old member employed at a local restaurant altered the church's fate. Striking up a conversation with a patron in early 2002, the waitress told him that she attended Skyline, that it was a growing congregation, and that it could not afford to buy the aforementioned theater property. This guest happened to be one of Green's best friends and offered to help. He subsequently contacted the church and declared that Hobby Lobby was willing purchase the Gold Rush for them and then broker a lease. Skyline Southern Baptist took possession of its new home on January 1, 2003, and since then Sunday morning attendance has increased by approximately 650 people. Expressing his awe in relation to this series of events, Pastor Larry Craig asserted, "It was like God said, 'You tried and couldn't do it. Now let me show you what I can do.'"[26]

In light of these various amalgamations of church and entertainment venue, one might expect that a Passion play would meet with great success in Branson. Catering to this perceived demand, *The Promise,* a musical based on the life of Jesus, debuted in 1995 and ran continuously through 2001, but it has been featured only sporadically since that year. Replete with flying angels, an array of live animals, and a raging storm on the Sea of Galilee, this production blends religion and pageantry in a more dramatic fashion than any other local performance while claiming religious authenticity by having a script drawn verbatim from biblical texts. *The Promise*'s Jesus, like the Christ of nineteenth-century American revivalism, is portrayed as kind, gentle, and vulnerable—a characterization meant to make the Christian savior easily available to believers and nonbelievers alike.[27]

Although the show's marketing and public relations director, Geoff Steel, claimed that his production's representation of Jesus is not meant to be "holier than thou" and that believer status is not "a criteria [sic]" for attendance because "there is no altar call after the show," some associated with *The Promise* have maintained otherwise. Randy Brooks, who has portrayed Jesus throughout the musical's stay in town, definitely views his acting as ministry. As he stated, "I feel I am called to do this, just as a minister might be called to preach. . . . *The Promise* is like nothing you've seen before, just simply because of the anointing that the Lord has on it. . . . We need churches to bring their lost and the unsaved to see *The Promise*." Thus, the show is intended for proverbial sheep and goats. The cast members—all Christian actors and actresses—often express their work in terms of a divine vocation, thereby iterating an impulse toward proselytism that seems unavoidable in such an act and further substantiating Branson as a locus for traditional conversion experiences. Attesting to the effectiveness of this approach, tourists Rocco and Evelyn Youmans of Summerville, South Carolina, wrote, "For those who have not accepted Christ as their personal savior—seeing this show should help convince them!"[28]

During its years in the Ozarks, *The Promise* has not only effected conversions but also facilitated miraculous healings. As detailed by Randy Brooks:

The Promise advertisement, 1999. From the author's collection

We have gotten many letters. One letter was about a little girl. Her parents wrote and said she had been having seizures all of her life. During the show's healing scene (when Jesus is healing people as the chorus is singing "there is power in the name of the Lord"), something happened to their seven-year-old daughter. The girl said she felt "something really warm" come over her body. They had noticed she hadn't experienced a seizure since she had seen *The Promise* and the healing scene. Seeing that scene on stage, she had enough faith to believe in healing for herself.

At this production guests can have their own belief systems reaffirmed, challenge nonbelievers to adopt a Christian outlook, and conceivably even achieve physical or psychological restoration—all within the confines of dramatic theater. More-over, the musical has been a favorite among the thousands of church tour groups that come to Branson and is often promoted by leaders as superior entertain-ment and stirring testimony (a combination of merriment and solemnity which has been historically necessary within the realm of religiously motivated leisure). It once was also much acclaimed by local tourism authorities and received nu-merous citywide awards. Considering this ostensibly direct fit with regional ide-ology and niche markets, the show should still be enjoying great material suc-cess. In reality, however, *The Promise* has struggled to stay solvent.[29]

For a number of years the production did indeed play to sellout crowds. Be-ginning in the late 1990s, however, it filled its host theater only to 25 percent ca-pacity. Some people attribute the problem to structural elements such as mount-ing overhead costs (utility bills, actors' salaries, and so on) that precipitated an increase in ticket price. Others say the decline was the product of competition with the even more famous Great Passion Play in Eureka Springs, Arkansas—a production only a short drive from Branson which has for many years been America's number one outdoor drama with regard to attendance. Perhaps, too, the problems were hastened by a recent push by local boosters to attract younger visitors and tout outdoor recreation in the Ozarks.[30]

Although all these factors undoubtedly play a role in the musical's struggles, another and probably critical element is that *The Promise* does not offer the va-riety show ingredients that have spelled success elsewhere in Branson. Its overt Christian themes definitely are not a detriment, but its presentation is univo-cal. Vacationers with religious inclinations are familiar with its patented (though dramatically spectacular) presentation and the biblical literalism it promotes. Though familiarity is never to one's disadvantage in the local vacation market, this study has demonstrated that tourists want their religion infused with secular amusement. Affirming this thesis, Phyllis Rotrock, director of the Branson Gos-pel Music Association, stated in a 2002 interview that "gospel is hard to sell in Branson. People in this area do not expect to pay to go see a gospel show." This claim demonstrates that success in the industry is predicated on offering more than what is available for free in the institutional church setting or narratives that are frequently recounted within houses of worship. Acts must tender lively and multifaceted entertainment skillfully cloaked in a metanarrative of Christianity if they are to prosper.[31]

The success of embedded rather than unequivocal approaches to evangelism was evident when I attended a show by Kirby Van Burch in 1997. Van Burch is one of a number of Branson magicians and has been featured in town since the mid-1990s. It may seem as though the Christian tourist would opt for a plethora of other acts that more explicitly showcase faith, but Van Burch has always been a favorite with visiting church groups—an appeal that makes sense after the production's surprise ending. The show began like most others by featuring jokes from a hillbilly comic. The main attraction greatly resembled similar acts found in Las Vegas or elsewhere, with the magician integrating a variety of lavish sets, exotic animals, a dance troupe, and a heavily sequined wife/assistant who was the object of much trickery. As a penultimate deception, Van Burch made a 35-foot helicopter disappear in four seconds. However, he had promised throughout that the real astonishment was reserved for the end.

The true crescendo began with Van Burch revealing the secrets behind a few facile tricks. Revelations then became more forthright as he boldly pronounced that his act was merely *illusion,* for God was the sole entity bestowed with magical capabilities. Instead of then offering one final spectacle, he closed by talking about reading Bible stories with his grandmother and trying to "walk in God's light" through his vocation. Van Burch's show has been described as one that leaves patrons "not only truly astounded, but powerfully affected," and his unconventional mode of testimony has been heralded by tourists. As a pastor who visited with his congregation affirmed, "When you came out near the close, sat down and said there was no magic, only illusions, and that God can do miracles, we were moved. Such an effective sharing of your faith probably does more than many of my sermons."[32]

The Sunday show-service has been described in the *Branson Church Getaway Planner* as an event that offers "a front row seat to the marvelous thing God is doing here, a chance to see the real reason why people from all over the country one day find themselves suddenly attracted to Branson, Missouri!" Stepping into theaters where the previous night they might have been enjoying country music, patriotic displays, and family-values rhetoric subtly enveloped in religiosity, show-service attendees are offered a more firm testament concerning the spiritual intentions of the tourism industry at large. Like Kirby Van Burch's show, these events are marked by a variety of surprise integrations of faith and frivolity. Because productions such as *The Promise* have failed to evangelize by means of a mode that delicately straddles lines between sacred and secular, the show-service must remain cognizant of its beneficially liminal status—a "betweenness" that signals success in the local market. A recent visitor to Silver Dollar City, the Ozark attraction that has most nimbly negotiated this divide over the past fifty years, commented that his visit was "just like going to church," but he invoked that site's desire to make faith pleasurable by adding, "Except my kids sure enjoyed it more than church." Later defining all of Branson as a "religious com-munity," this vacationer identified the chief way, in the minds of many, that the area's tourism enterprise will remain vital—an understated, popularly mediated, and deep-rooted integration of Christianity and culture.[33]

As ground was being broken for the Branson Landing project, Peter Her-schend, co-owner of Silver Dollar City, delivered a speech at a 2004 Billy Graham Crusade in Kansas City. Speaking to a crowd of 51,000 during an event that in-spired more than 10,000 commitments to Christ, Herschend discussed his own religious conversion in 1969 and the ways that experience has affected his busi-ness endeavors. Suddenly and without planning, he asked listeners how many had visited Silver Dollar City since it opened in 1960. By show of hands, roughly two-thirds of the audience responded affirmatively. In an interview that detailed this occurrence, Herschend was asked to identify "the great leaders of today." The response of the undisputed overseer of Branson's religio-tourism endeavor interestingly speaks to the ideological vantage and value structure that most tourists arrive to consume: "I only have one name: Billy Graham."[34]

Graham rose to stardom by preaching a message of Christian inclusiveness often reviled by more fundamentalist factions and a willingness to evangelize in nontraditional ways and locales. Despite anticommunist rhetoric in the 1950s and entanglements with Richard Nixon, he has for many decades emphasized the cultivation of personal relationships with Jesus Christ rather than the place of Christianity within politics. Such nondenominational approaches, creative pros-elytism, and lack of an overt political agenda course their way through Silver Dollar City. Herschend's theme park has been the leading Branson attraction for more than forty years and a model of success emulated by most subsequent tourist sites. It is hence safe to assume that the overwhelming show of hands at the 2004 revival demonstrates that the nebulous style of evangelicalism offered by Graham is also a chief impetus for modern-day visitation to Branson.

Branson's rise to national prominence in the 1990s coincided with the emer-gence of American evangelicalism as a potent social, cultural, and political force. As evangelicals fully surfaced from the subcultural insularity that had character-ized the movement since the 1930s, the Ozarks became a potent site for facilitat-ing this transition. Not alone in presenting a popularly styled brand of evangeli-calism, Branson was one facet of a larger trend that included coincidently huge growth within Christian music, film, and fiction. Moreover, as increased political awareness and activity among evangelicals abetted the "Republican Revolution" of the mid-1990s, the city also did its part by offering a platform to prominent Christian Right leaders who found Branson's longtime promotion of family values and civil religiosity a snug fit for their sensibilities. By linking such vantages to other elements that have always had traction in the region—antimodernism, nostalgia, affability, and affordability—the city solidified what Peter Herschend has labeled the Branson "brand." As efforts to modify this trademark continue to unfurl, the imbroglio surrounding them speaks not only to the city's future but also to the future of evangelicalism, sociopolitical conservatism, and the overall place of faith within American life.

A "NEW ERA" IN BRANSON?

At a ribbon-cutting for Branson Landing on May 27, 2006, host and local magician Darren Romeo proclaimed, "Today, we gather to open a new era." Many have indeed talked about the citywide growth facilitated by this development as the beginning of a twenty-first-century boom. In 2005, construction skyrocketed to $121.5 million, thereby breaking a record set in 1993. In addition to the Landing, this value reflected a profusion of home building. As finishing touches were being put on downtown improvements, more than 8,000 houses and condominiums throughout the city were planned or being built. By October 2005, 106 residential condominiums had been sold at an average price of $425,000. Buyers hailed from thirty-eight states, but the majority were from the east and west coasts. Moreover, a bond issue of $80 million to finance the Branson Convention Center sold out in two days. And golf course communities such as the Tribute Golf Club, slated to open in 2007, have sprung up hoping to capitalize on the region's push to attract baby boomers and upwardly mobile professionals seeking to relocate or purchase a second home.[35]

A chief impetus for all recent development in Branson has been a mounting concern over a stagnant market that cannot attract new guests. For most of the latter part of the 1990s, only 20 percent of all vacationers were first-time visitors. In 2004, a task force (the "Branson Branding" initiative) instigated by the local chamber of commerce hired Sterling Marketing Group to develop a framework and direction for 2005 in the hope of increasing this number. After experiencing Branson as customers, reviewing previous research, conducting focus group discussions, and completing "man on the street" interviews, the company discerned two target audiences: repeat visitors, primarily senior travelers and parents with children who love Branson the way it is ("Loyals"); and people who do not vacation in the Ozarks because they have a one-dimensional view of its product, primarily empty nesters and recent retirees over the age of forty-five or parents who are skeptical that Branson can entertain their children ("Resistors").

Many of Sterling's findings are not surprising in light of Branson history. "Values" was placed atop a list of industry features and benefits. This inventory also included "family entertainment productions," a "world-class theme park," a "beautiful, natural setting," "personal attention to each guest," a "safe" atmosphere, "affordability," and "clean, modern accommodations." Three platforms were then created to organize these attributes. Denoting links to the very roots of the area's tourism enterprise, Sterling first enumerated "Authentic Connections" as a chief enticement by stating that "in a mass produced world, a real atmosphere and products are rare." A second platform was titled "Live Entertainment Bonanza" and highlighted long-standing issues such as quality productions suitable for every member of the family, shows prefaced on "style and respect," and the fostering of an "up-close and personal connection with performers." Finally, "Active Relaxation" emphasized the striking of a delicate balance that has always characterized the local industry. Playing on this dynamic, the report called for "plenty of things to get your heart going, but nothing too frightening."

All conclusions were encapsulated in a statement entitled "The Branson Promise." This list of seven regional convictions included time-tested Ozark themes: association with the genuine aspects of existence ("We believe that a vacation is not an escape from reality but a connection to what is real"); promotion of the city as an idealized domestic sphere ("We believe you deserve a break from your regular life while preserving the security and comfort that comes from feeling 'right at home'"); endorsement of emotive and heartfelt recreation ("We believe the best experiences are live and personal. They affect you—and you affect them"); sanctification of "American values" ("We believe in . . . respect for the individual, patriotism, faith, hope, optimism, family, courage, generosity, and opportunity for all"); and reasonable expense ("We believe that world-class entertainment doesn't have to cost a world-class fortune"). Yet although the Sterling Group felt that these familiar premises and precepts provided foundation for a "great product," they alone could not inspire first-time vacationers. Therefore the chamber of commerce was encouraged to craft a strategy that would "appeal to the Resistor without alienating the Loyal guest." To negotiate this divide, the firm suggested making "Branson will surprise you" the "guiding principle" for local marketers. Misguided perceptions and skepticism would then be allayed through a demonstrative approach that mimicked the area's long-standing promotion of lived principles and aversion to dogmatism in a variety of forms (labeled a "show, don't tell" technique). These unexpected elements would then be conveyed through a central "brand position": "Entertainment you can touch. Entertainment that touches you."[36]

Most of the Sterling Group's suggestions are far from surprising when one considers the past century of regional tourism. However, the ways that the company's directives have been made manifest within the Branson Landing project are certainly astonishing, especially in light of the demographic composition of local visitors since its early 1990s boom. At the onset of this expansion, a 1991 study concluded that its largest cohort was couples with children (40 percent of all visitors), 29 percent of guests were couples without children, 20 percent were couples over age fifty, and 11 percent were singles. In addition, this report discerned that visitors predominantly hailed from midwestern states. Moreover, a 1994 survey revealed that the city inspired much "brand loyalty," as 75.8 percent of all tourists stated they were likely to return the following year. Finally, most early 1990s vacationers were categorically middle class, with 85 percent having a combined yearly family income between $35,000 and $49,000 and spending only $60 per day.[37]

Current tourist dynamics are still much the same. Branson has seen its vacationer population slightly age over the past decade. Only 35 percent of guests now are families with children, and the average age of a vacationer has increased to fifty-seven years. More people travel from greater distances to reach the town, with 62 percent coming from farther than 300 miles away. But despite these changes, Branson remained a middle-class destination in 2004, with vacationers having an average yearly income of roughly $52,000 per family per year and still spending about $60 per person per day. Furthermore, its 4.75/5.0 visitor satisfaction rating has ensured that repeat customers will continue to frequent the city.[38]

Feedback at the Branson Landing ribbon cutting seemed to signal a move away from the devout, middle-class, senior and family cohort that has been the basis for tourism industry success since the early twentieth century. These responses also suggested that visitors were ready to embrace attractions beyond the long-standing local entertainment paradigm. Tourist Jerry Holloway commented, "It kind of looks like Country Club Plaza" (a very upscale shopping and dining area in Kansas City, Missouri, that is adjacent to one of the wealthiest suburbs in America). Another visitor added, "Now there's something to do besides see the shows." Area resident Jerry Wicklein furthered this sentiment when he suggested, "I think this is going to be the biggest thing in Branson." Finally, local entertainer Ron Retherford highlighted the disjunction between the Landing and the rest of Branson when he asserted, "It almost feels like a town itself. Like a town within a town." In a place that has always promoted its social cohesion and accompanying consistency of values, this last contention is the most startling. Although this study has highlighted a variety of ambivalences that have permeated the history of regional consumer culture, it has also showcased an ability by boosters and visitors alike to maintain an integral vision of sanctified consumption. If Branson Landing indeed becomes "a town within a town," it might jeopardize what Peter Herschend has labeled a "culture of values." As he averred, the city possesses "a culture you don't find in any other rural vacation destination in America. It's a culture of entertainment that has values to it as opposed to entertainment that only has spectacle."[39]

Branson Landing will bring heretofore unseen and spectacular housing, retail, and entertainment opportunities to the city, but close investigation does reveal that it is implicated in a "culture of values" in a variety of small ways. Rick Huffman, president of the development company spearheading the project, moved to Branson in the early 1990s. Although labor could fill all his time, he has integrated himself into local Christian culture and will "never work on Sundays." Mike Rankin, Branson's economic development director, explained worldwide interest in this new boom by stating, "It's a safe haven in the central U.S. with a perception of family values." Layne Morrill, a native Ozarker who recently sold 50 acres of his land to a planned community centered around a golf course, suggested that newcomers are arriving to partake of rather than alter the region and its ideals: "I believe the majority look at this area more like we do. They kind of like the world they see, and they want to be part of it, not change it." Tim Benolken, area vice president for the Hilton Hotel Corporation, rationalized the presence of his upscale lodgings in a city renowned for its modest prices by harking back to familiar area criticisms of modernity and promotions of authentic communal experiences within this milieu: "We enjoy long-standing reputations of valuing our customers, and in an increasingly chaotic world, Branson and Hilton stand firm as brands that represent civility and genuine family fun." Finally, Dennis Evans, director of sales and marketing for Branson Landing, linked his project to bucolic Ozark visions that have saturated regional boosterism: "People across the country are embracing the quality of life they see here in the Ozarks and they consider their purchase an investment in not just their own futures, but the future of one of the most unspoiled places in the country."[40]

Even as show-services and other religiously oriented attractions prosper, glaringly absent from this catalog of familiar Branson rhetoric is any specific mention of God or Christianity. Although tourists have expressed incredible interest in Branson Landing (the volume of phone inquiries to the chamber of commerce increased by nearly 50 percent in 2006), not even the most renegade marketer is calling for a strategy that ostracizes the Christian—or specifically, the evangelical—vacationer. Rather, the Landing and associated upscale developments may, in fact, reflect the changing economic status of American evangelicalism. In 1929, H. Richard Niebuhr described born-again Christianity as the "religion of the disinherited." However, over the past forty years, evangelicals have pulled steadily closer to and even surpassed the income and educational levels of the average American. A subscriber report produced in 1999 by *Christianity Today,* a popular evangelical publication, described its typical patron as a "54 year old married man with a post graduate degree. He works full-time in a professional occupation. His total household income is over $63,000." Compared with an average household income of $49,692 in the U.S. population that year, the financial status of the typical evangelical household meant that the family was thus well into and even above the middle-class income bracket. Furthermore, as late as 1965, a white mainline Protestant was two and a half times as likely to have a college degree as a white evangelical. But by 2000, the former group was only 65 percent more likely to have the same degree. And since 1985, the percentage of incoming freshman at highly selective private universities who said they were born again rose by 50 percent. Some of the most remarkable evidence for the growth of evangelical affluence comes from the Assemblies of God, a Pentecostal denomination headquartered about thirty minutes north of Branson. Founded by rural and working-class individuals and for many decades reviling the secular world, this group has partially retailored its message to make it compatible with an upwardly mobile middle class through emphasizing material blessings God might provide in this world. By the 1970s, Assemblies churches were sprouting up in wealthy suburbs across the country, and recent surveys have revealed that the denomination's members are more educated and better off than the general public.[41]

This growth in evangelical economic prosperity has precipitated a marked expansion of political power and a gradual shift from the Democratic Party to the Republican. In turn, according to Thomas Frank, this increased wealth has produced a split within the Right between moderate and conservative factions. "Moderate Republicanism," with its "distinctively upper-class flavor," has placed its focus on fiscal policies while condemning "blue-collar people, with their funny religions and [socially] conservative politics." Alternately, "conservative Republicanism" has continued to emphasize hot-button issues such as a ban on abortion, the prohibition of gay marriage, and the merger of church and state. It is this latter group of aspiring middle-class individuals focused on a full integration of Christianity into the public sphere and averse to the ongoing "degeneration" of society and culture which has invigorated Branson's market since the early 1990s.

Highlighting this constituency, Don Gabriel wrote in his "Manifesto," "We are the most politically incorrect community in the world. God likes this, and so do millions of tourists."[42]

Such sentiments, which denote Branson as a bastion of tradition, or according to Thomas Frank, a locus of "backlash" against progressive culture, have had credence for decades in the area. Vital for this construct has been a regional accentuation of populism framed by antimodern notions, anti-intellectual championing, the valorization of idyllic rurality, and a lived religiosity that censures nonpragmatic theologies, elite control over ultimate truth, and the limitation of religious experience to formal sanctuaries. A 1-cent sales tax approved in 2005 is expected to boost the Branson/Lakes Area Chamber of Commerce's marketing budget by $2.5 million annually and allow promoters to reach out beyond a prototypically midwestern base and its accompanying ideology. As stated by Ed Michel, who owns a local travel agency, "We've not had any money to tap into the East and West Coast with advertising. When we hit 10 or 12 million [visitors] those East and West Coast people will know who we are. This money will let us play with the big boys." Such an increase in visitation seems feasible in light of recent development, but the question remains whether the more affluent tourist will desire and help to maintain Branson's established pious product. Commenting on the now tenuous position of such value-laden commodities, Peter Herschend stated that Branson's tourism industry is "like a fine piece of china that you have to work constantly to protect because if allowed to drop, it will crack."[43]

Herschend's statement was put forth almost one hundred years after Harold Bell Wright published *The Shepherd of the Hills,* but the men's attitudes concerning regional development are nearly identical. Wright's trepidation was caused by the arrival of a rail line that runs through a parcel of land now occupied by Branson Landing. As current local alderman Ron Huff arrived for that project's ribbon cutting, he stated, "I looked down there and saw that skyline. This is definitely a landmark in our history." Although a seemingly insignificant quotation, Huff's words are packed with symbolic import. *The Shepherd of the Hills* described the Ozarks as the antithesis of corrupt urban life and free of the many vices associated with cityscapes. Contemporarily, tourists continue to mark Branson as such a retreat. As stated by Melissa Egli of Fort Dodge, Iowa, "Here, we found a lot of people like us. We found a place where we connected. It's a draw for us . . . very important. Any more you're made to feel uncomfortable being a Christian." Yet just as Wright feared that the region would become "the haunt of careless idlers" if loosed from its ethical underpinnings, Egli and others may, in light of the city's new brand of leisure, increasingly find it difficult to position Branson as an asylum for the devout.[44]

Branson's tourism industry has certainly prospered through offering vacationers a sense of bucolic sanctuary. However, such solace has always resisted the uncompromising tones of Don Gabriel's "Manifesto" and instead keenly negotiated a variety of seemingly insurmountable dichotomies. The most important of these conciliations has been the assuaging of friction between "premodern" and "modern." The city has unremittingly marketed itself as one of the few surviving bastions of American "tradition." This term has been replete with connotations of unswerving patriotism, firmly entrenched family values, and meritorious country life. Concomitantly, it has also ever infused visions of modern prosperity into its rustic offerings and thereby satisfied visitors who want an experience of a fabled past, the comforts of home, and images of opulence. Through implication in regional consumer culture, tourists have thus sought to employ ideological vantages derived from the realm of leisure in their everyday lives. In this way, the Branson experience has functioned as tool for remaking modernity through its time-tested chastisements of intellectual pretense, conspicuous consumption, and relativistic values. Boosters have always worried that this purpose would be lost as the Ozarks drew more influence from the outside world. And as a new century unfolds, Branson must again grapple with this dynamic and forge ways to reconcile its strains.

The city may now face its most difficult dualism as the wares of Branson Landing seem to oppose rather than complement show-services and other spiritually infused commodities. Popular religious stances have always guided local recreation, and promoters have ardently tried to position Branson as a place where faith flows out of church walls and into the very fabric of society and culture. A divine "aroma" has thus been able to permeate discourses concerning gender, sexuality, race, class, and nation; inform the telling of Ozark and American history; enlighten responses to the natural environment; provide guidance for individuals seeking to assuage dilemmas such as gambling or poverty; and impact views of appropriate leisure itself. Although the people responsible for the area's new development have in slight ways deferred to regional religiosity, it is hard to see how their attractions infuse this variant of faith into other value-creating arenas. Branson consumer culture has not only modeled the many facets of religious tourism in the United States but has also represented and helped to craft the contours of a loosely defined and ever mutating mode of American popular Christianity. In doing so, the city has been a national locus for broadcasting nostalgic visions of an idealized yet waning past, the necessary merger of

God and country, normative nuclear family relations, and middle-class propriety. Many still feel that Branson can continue to be such a multifaceted "mighty center for revival." However, if the city alters its approach and thereby caters to a more affluent tourist cohort (evangelical or otherwise) through wholly secular attractions and commodities disassociated from a distinct moral paradigm, it thereby loses much of its restorative capacity. It could thus squander its time-tested ability to arbitrate social, cultural, and political affairs and exhaust its role as an ideological architect for millions who venture into these holy hills.

Notes

INTRODUCTION. "THE MORAL VINEYARDS"

1. Robert Fyan to his sister, 17 Apr. 1862, Western Historical Manuscript Collection, University of Missouri–Rolla, Rolla. The Ozarks is an approximately 40,000-square-mile area that encompasses southern Missouri, northern Arkansas, and parts of Oklahoma and Kansas. Its boundaries are roughly delineated by a series of waterways that outline the region: the Missouri River in the north; the Arkansas River in the south; the Mississippi River in the east; the Black River in the southeast; and the Spring River in the southwest.

2. Ostling, "Of God and Greed," 70; Ostling, "TV's Unholy Row," 60; Hanna Rosin, "Jim Bakker's Revival," *Washington Post*, 11 Aug. 1999, C1.

3. Kathryn Buckstaff, "Bilked Believers Forgiving of Jim Bakker," *Springfield News-Leader*, 15 Sept. 2002, 8A; Todd, interview; Bill Smith, "Bakker Returns to TV Pulpit in Branson, Mo.," *St. Louis Post-Dispatch*, 19 Nov. 2003, A13; "Flock Forgives Televangelist of His Trespasses," *Houston Chronicle*, 26 Apr. 2003, 1.

4. David Usborne, "Bakker's Back," *Independent on Sunday (UK)*, 15 June 2003, 1–2.

5. "Branson, Mo., Developer Proposes Christian-Themed Community," *St. Louis Post-Dispatch*, 30 Jan. 2005, D8; Smith, "Bakker Returns to TV Pulpit in Branson, Mo.," A13.

6. Frommer, *Arthur Frommer's Branson*, 31; Merle Haggard quoted in "Arts and Leisure," *New York Times*, 21 Aug. 1994, 28; Rafferty, *Ozarks*, 248; Charles Gusewelle quoted in *Water & Fire: A Story of the Ozarks*, prod. Michael Murphy, Kansas City Public Television (KCPT), 2000, videocassette.

7. Smith, "Melodrama, Popular Religion, and Literary Value," 237; Millard, "Personality of Harold Bell Wright," 464; Ferre, *Social Gospel for Millions*, 6–7.

8. Herberg, *Protestant, Catholic, Jew*, 77; Ammerman, "Golden Rule Christianity," 201, 203, 211.

9. Bebbington, *Evangelicalism in Britain*, 2–17.

10. Millard, "Personality of Harold Bell Wright," 464.

11. Williams, *Popular Religion in America*, 7; Lippy, *Being Religious American Style*, 18; Orsi, "Everyday Miracles"; McDannell, *Material Christianity*.

12. Hulsether, "Interpreting the 'Popular' in Popular Religion," 128–129.

13. Allcock, "Tourism as a Sacred Journey."

14. Karlis, Grafanaki, and Abbas, "Leisure and Spirituality."

15. Morgan, *Puritan Family*, 16; Daniels, *Puritans at Play*, 7, 17; Hall, *Worlds of Wonder, Days of Judgment*.

16. Moore, *Selling God*, 93. In the late 1960s, sociologist Peter Berger was the foremost critic of religious commodification. In *The Sacred Canopy* (1967), he claimed that this orientation damaged both the uniqueness of American denominational polities and the distinctiveness of their doctrines by forcing homogenization for the sake of mass appeal. Because of this focus on marketability, faith communities were losing their capacity to "legitimate" the world. See Berger, *Sacred Canopy*. For arguments that counter Berger and other secularization theorists while addressing issues of American religious consumption and the use of economic language to describe religious growth/decline in the United States, see Kelley, *Why Conservative Churches Are Growing*; Iannaccone, "Religious Markets and the Economics of Religion"; Iannaccone, "Why Strict Churches Are Strong"; and Finke and Stark, *Churching of America*.

17. Orr, *Pictorial Guide to the Falls of Niagara*, 155. On the religious nature of nineteenth-century tourism, see Sears, *Sacred Places*.

18. Moore, *Selling God*, 149; Walt Whitman quoted in Reynolds, *Beneath the American Renaissance*, 25.

19. Brown, *Inventing New England*, 77–78, 99.

20. Messenger, *Holy Leisure*, 5, 26.

21. Gilmore, *Ozark Baptizings, Hangings, and Other Diversions*, 33–35.

22. The best source for information on outdoor religious dramas is the Institute of Outdoor Drama at the University of North Carolina–Chapel Hill. Founded in 1963, this organization documents the histories of such productions while providing leadership in fostering artistic and managerial excellence and expansion of the outdoor drama movement. See its Web site at www.unc.edu/depts/outdoor. On the history of American Passion plays, including the Great Passion Play in Eureka Springs, see Monk, "Passion Plays in the United States."

23. On the Sacred Arts Complex, see the Great Passion Play's Web site at www.greatpassionplay.com. Information on its history and development can also be gleaned from a biography of its controversial founder, Gerald L. K. Smith. See Jeansonne, *Gerald L. K. Smith*. On the Holy Land Experience, see the "What Is the Holy Land Experience." Branson entertainment has also included a variant of the Bible museum genre. The traveling Fires of Devotion exhibit has stopped in town on a number of occasions since 1998. This display includes a tour of ancient artifacts, a multimedia presentation that tells the history of biblical versions and translations, and a full-size facsimile of the Dead Sea Scrolls. See Kathryn Buckstaff, "Exhibit Teaches Visitors the Story of the Bible," *Springfield News-Leader*, 28–30 Aug. 1998, 15E.

24. Moore, *Selling God*, 251. For the most thorough description of Heritage USA, see FitzGerald, "Reflections."

25. Moore, "Walt Disney World," 216; The Project on Disney, *Inside the Mouse*, 7.

26. On Marian apparition sites in the United States, see Garvey, *Searching for Mary*. On pilgrimage as the central framework for all religious tourism, see Vukonic, *Tourism and Religion*.

27. Doug Johnson, "Leap of Faith Succeeds in Branson Attraction," *Washington Times*, 29 Apr. 2000, E2.

28. On Walt Disney's boyhood in Missouri, see Viets, "Walt Disney," 50–55.

29. Freihofer, "Can You Solve the Mystery," 3; Freihofer, "Heart of the Matter," 4; Freihofer, "Planning an Effective Church Getaway," 6.

30. LaRoe, "Ozarks Harmony," 76.

31. Hulsether, "Interpreting the 'Popular' in Popular Religion," 127.

32. Urry, "Social Relations, Space and Time," 30; Desmond, *Staging Tourism,* xviii.

33. Branson/Lakes Area Chamber of Commerce and Convention and Visitors Bureau, Branson/Lakes Area 2005 Fact Sheet.

34. MacCannell, *Tourist,* 131, 160.

35. Tuan, "Space and Place," 236; "Perfect American Town," 25.

36. Strenski, *Four Theories of Myth in Twentieth-Century History,* 2; tourist response, "Branson Is Fun for Everyone!" marketing campaign, fall 2004, in the author's collection.

37. Branson/Lakes Area Chamber of Commerce and Convention and Visitors Bureau, Branson/Lakes Area 2005 Fact Sheet.

38. Cohen, "Tourism as Play," 291–304; Entrikin, *Betweenness of Place,* 134.

39. Randolph, *Stiff as a Poker and Other Ozark Folk Tales,* 5.

CHAPTER I. "TEMPLES OF GOD'S OWN BUILDING"

1. Wright, *To My Sons,* 196.

2. Jones, "Brother Hal," 395.

3. Dickinson, *Best Books of Our Time,* 201; Mott, *Golden Multitudes.* On the novels of Harold Bell Wright written after his departure from the ministry, see Ferre, *Social Gospel for Millions,* 90–97. Quantifying book sales continues to be a precarious undertaking and was even more problematic in the early twentieth century. Thus, numerical support for Wright's popularity is partially suspect. For instance, newspaper accounts claim that for a period of twenty years his books outsold all others except the Bible. Furthermore, biographer Elsbery W. Reynolds wrote in 1916 that *The Shepherd of the Hills* was the "fourth most widely read book in the English language." Perhaps offering a more accurate assessment, Harper and Brothers audited the records of his books' sales prior to his death and found that an average of 737,443 copies were sold of each of his first twelve novels—a total of 10 million copies. *The Shepherd of the Hills* alone accounted for more than 2 million of these sales. See Deffenbaugh, "Ministry of Harold Bell Wright," 29; Reynolds, *Harold Bell Wright,* 3; "Harold Bell Wright, Novelist, 72, Dead," *New York Times,* 14 May 1944.

4. Hart, "One Hundred Leading Authors," 287; Mencken, *Prejudices,* 32; Hawethorne, *Harold Bell Wright,* 104; Tagg, *Harold Bell Wright,* 42.

5. Milstead, "Harold Bell Wright," 501; Wright, *Shepherd of the Hills,* 284.

6. Reynolds, *Harold Bell Wright,* 4 (first published for free distribution by the Chicago Book Supply Co.); Jones, "Brother Hal," 391–393; Wright, *To My Sons,* 200.

7. Wright, *To My Sons,* 141–142. On the history of the Christian Church (Disciples of Christ), see McAllister and Tucker, *Journey in Faith,* and Garrett, *Stone-Campbell Movement.*

8. Jones, "Brother Hal," 395–396.

9. Wright, *To My Sons,* 201.

10. "Harold Bell Wright Memorial Library," 1; Wright, *To My Sons,* 203, 204; "Harold Bell Wright" (in *Lawrence County Historical Society Bulletin*), 26; "Harold Bell Wright Found His Calling in a Little Church in Pierce City, Mo.," *Daily Reporter (Independence, KS),* 30 Jan. 2000, 5.

11. Wright, *To My Sons,* 208, 216–217. On the history of Pittsburg, Kansas, see the special

centennial issue of the *Pittsburg (KS) Morning Sun*, 20 May 1976. Although beginning with an initial press run of 50,000 copies in 1895, the *Appeal* boasted a circulation of more than 750,000 by 1913. On Wayland and the *Appeal to Reason*, see Green, *Grass-Roots Socialism;* Quint, "Julius A. Wayland"; and Nord, *"Appeal to Reason* and American Socialism."

12. Gladden, *Applied Christianity.* On the Social Gospel movement, see Handy, *Social Gospel in America,* and Hutchinson, *Modernist Impulse in American Protestantism.*

13. Wright, *To My Sons,* 106; Ferre, *Social Gospel for Millions,* 8. On the anti-intellectual and populist tendencies of early American evangelicalism, see Hofstadter, *Anti- Intellectualism in American Life,* and Hatch, *Democratization of American Christianity.*

14. Wright, *That Printer of Udell's,* 74–75. In his autobiography, Wright noted the influence of Charles Sheldon (pastor of Central Congregational Church in Topeka, Kansas, from 1889 to 1924) on the socially oriented Christianity espoused within *That Printer of Udell's.* See Wright, *To My Sons,* 211.

15. Van Doren, *American Novel,* 269; Ferre, *Social Gospel for Millions,* 67–68.

16. *Pastoral Call,* 6 Dec. 1904; Wright, *To My Sons,* 207.

17. Madsen, *History,* 6–7; Ross, *Old Matt's View of It,* 15; Van Buskirk, "Shepherd of the Hills Country," 23–25. The year in which Wright first encountered the Rosses is a cause for contention. Some claim that he was introduced to the family by a mutual friend in 1903 while spending a year recuperating from poor health in Aurora, Missouri. The Shepherd of the Hills Historical Society, an organization that produces the only authorized theatrical production of the novel, claims that he visited in 1896 while taking a break from his pastorate in Pittsburg and boarded at the homestead when his horse was unable to cross the flooded White River. While these events accord with those described above, this dating seems erroneous. In his autobiography and in other historical sources cited throughout this chapter, Wright's ministry in Pittsburg is said to have begun in the fall of 1898. Thus, perhaps this is yet another case of the fusing of fact and fiction that epitomizes much of the history of the Branson tourism industry. For a synopsis of these various dates and accounts, see Frizell, "History of 'The Shepherd of the Hills' Dramatizations," 11–13.

18. On Wright's time in Lebanon, Missouri, see Don O. Vernon, "Harold Bell Wright Reminiscences Recalled by Don O. Vernon," *Lebanon (MO) Rustic Republican,* 31 May 1944; Tudor, "Famed Author Harold Bell Wright"; Eric D. Tudor, "'Shepherd of the Hills' Author Drew Inspiration from Lebanon," *Lebanon (MO) Daily Record,* 1 Feb. 1999, 2B; and Jones, "Brother Hal," 408–409.

19. Ferre, *Social Gospel for Millions,* 2–3.

20. The multifaceted function of the rural church proposed by Country Life advocates is succinctly stated in the 1910 minutes of the United Presbyterian Church in the USA's Department of Church and Country Life. The board stated that the department will "endeavor to restore the country church to the place it once had in the religious activities of the country—to make it the potent factor in every community of social and moral regeneration, of intellectual and spiritual life." This sentiment was not only embraced by individual denominations but also found currency among mainline Protestant federations such as the Federal Council of Churches of Christ in America, which created an office in 1912 to serve as a clearinghouse for information from the formal and informal denominational Country Life efforts. On Christian church involvement in the Country Life Movement, see Swanson,

"'Country Life Movement' and the American Churches," and Gall, "Presbyterians, Warren Wilson, and the Country Life Movement."

21. Wright, *Shepherd of the Hills*, 13; Wilson, *Church of the Open Country,* 74–75. Also see Bowers, *Country Life Movement in America.*

22. Wright, *Shepherd of the Hills*, 170–174; Mills, *White Collar,* 9.

23. Smith, "Melodrama, Popular Religion, and Literary Value," 218; Wright, *Shepherd of the Hills*, 170–174. On the Men and Religion Forward Movement, see Bederman, "'Women Have Had Charge of the Church Work Long Enough.'" On the masculinity of Christ as portrayed in popular religious art, see Morgan, *Visual Piety,* 97–123. On the history of the YMCA, see Mjagkij and Spratt, *Men and Women Adrift.*

24. Wright, *Shepherd of the Hills*, 180–181.

25. Ibid., 57, 287.

26. Ibid., 265; Munday, "Wright Trail," 118.

27. Patten, *New Basis of Civilization,* 61; Ferre, *Social Gospel for Millions,* 77. In Lears, *Fables of Abundance,* the author insists that the dominance of corporate advertising in the early twentieth century promoted both a physical and psychological perfectionism within consumers and that this strategy was meant to erode essential ties between humans and nature by prompting an embrace of capitalist technology. Like Wright, Lears expressed disgust over the orchestration of selves undertaken by people who stand to profit from unlimited consumption, and he seemed to hope for a reactualization of rustic insularity as well as that social order's accompanying morality of personal sacrifice and selflessness. Both Wright's early twentieth-century and Lears's late twentieth-century apprehensions rested on a fear that commodity-made selves would triumph or have been victorious over selves grounded in deep-seated ethics and strong, individualized emotion. Thus, although many of Wright's critics opined that his texts were nothing but sentimental schmaltz, one of his central concerns has been at the forefront of social criticism and the analysis of American capitalism for nearly a century.

28. Wright, "What about God," 90, 102.

29. Wright, *Calling of Dan Matthews,* 105–106. Wright's disdain for sectarian machinations was further articulated in *The Uncrowned King.* Here the author offers an allegory that provides yet another argument for the unification of all Christian churches. Similar to Bunyan's *Pilgrim's Progress,* Wright's story tells of his hero's journey to the "Outer-Edge-of-Things" and the "Beautiful Sea." After many trials and travails, he is allowed to enter the "Temple of Truth" only after affirming that he has denied the "Wealth of Traditions," "Holy Prejudices," "Sacred Opinion," and the "Honors of the World." Ultimately, a singular mode of simple and forthright worship is deemed all that is necessary for salvation, with the antidenominationalism of *The Calling of Dan Matthews* permeating the work's pages.

30. 1 Cor. 12:20, 12:26, 3:18 (NRSV).

31. Wright, *Calling of Dan Matthews,* 172, 183, 187.

32. Ibid., 346. In *God and the Groceryman,* a sequel to *The Calling of Dan Matthews* written to boost the sale of Wright's literature by means of a return to Ozark-based novels, this theme of applied Christianity outside the confines of the institutional church continues to be invoked. In the novel, Dan Matthews has become an immensely prosperous businessman but believes he has failed to make a true ministry of his work. The text addresses Dan's at-

tempts to correct this failure by incorporating all the churches of Westover into a unified whole. In conjunction with his on-site agent, John Saxton, Matthews plans a church with no denominational tie which follows a simple rendering of Christ's teachings. Furthermore, through the analogy of the groceryman, Wright emphasizes that Christian ethics must be integrated into all that one does, even if engaged in the seemingly secular and mundane undertaking of a shopkeeper. See Wright, *God and the Groceryman*.

33. Wright, *To My Sons*, 252.

34. Howard, *Walkin' Preacher of the Ozarks*, 36. In *The Re-Creation of Brian Kent*, the protagonist is, at the story's commencement, an unethical bank clerk who steals money from his employers to fund his wife's extravagant lifestyle and the couple's frivolous and profligate "jazz age" routine. Discovering his spouse's infidelity, Brian attempts suicide by drowning but is saved by his elderly Ozark relative, Aunt Sue. Through the good works and righteous attitudes of Aunt Sue and her companion, Judy Taylor, the protagonist regains his ethical standards. Brian is thus "re-created" physically, mentally, morally, and spiritually by a now familiar pairing of upright Ozarkers and resplendent Ozark geography.

35. "'Walkin' Preacher' Dies," *Springfield Leader & Press*, 13 May 1966, 13; "Ozarks Have Had Two Walking Preachers," 51. Though perhaps the most famous, Guy Howard was not the first person to be dubbed the Ozarks "Walkin' Preacher." John Crockett, D.D. (also referred to as the "Bishop of the Ozarks"), often preached at the Stone Chapel in Forsyth, Missouri, and was for a short time president of the School of the Ozarks. Beginning in the late nineteenth century and continuing into the 1930s, he ministered throughout the hills and founded myriad remote congregations. On Crockett, see "Ozarks Have Had Two Walking Preachers," and Baker, "Bishop of the Ozarks."

36. Howard, *Walkin' Preacher of the Ozarks*, 182, 177, 52.

37. Ronald Reagan to Mrs. Jean B. Wright, 13 Mar. 1984. This letter is on display at the Harold Bell Wright Museum, Shepherd of the Hills Homestead and Outdoor Drama, Branson, Missouri. Numerous other examples of *The Shepherd of the Hills* influence could also be noted. For instance, prominent Ozark folklorist and tourism booster Otto Rayburn wrote, "I am deeply indebted to Harold Bell Wright. He opened my eyes. Without him I might have missed the Ozarks entirely." See Rayburn, *Forty Years in the Ozarks*, 18, 54.

38. Millard, "Personality of Harold Bell Wright," 464; Smith, "Melodrama, Popular Religion, and Literary Value," 225; Overton, *American Nights Entertainment*, 120. Furthermore, in *New York Times* book reviews from 1919 and 1921, critics noted that Wright had a "predestined audience . . . in little towns all over the country," and they furthered attacks on his popularly consumable romanticism by claiming that he continued to make appeals to the "obviousness of American yokels." See *New York Times Book Review*, 31 Aug. 1919 and 28 Aug. 1921.

39. Morrow, "Wright Connection (Part I)," 19. The original correspondences between Marian Wright Powers and Harold Bell Wright are housed at the Powers Museum in Carthage, Missouri.

40. Morrow and Myers-Phinney, *Shepherd of the Hills Country*, 62–68, 10; Myers-Phinney, "Arcadia in the Ozarks," 7.

41. Myers-Phinney, "Arcadia in the Ozarks," 10; "Galena, Missouri," 50. Lynn Morrow and Linda Myers-Phinney write that "the float trip provided an exotic adventure to relax impatient capitalists and calm the anxieties, real or perceived, of urban living." Thus, a theme

of Ozark antimodernism still perpetuated in the modern day finds its roots in this early tourist draw. See Morrow and Myers-Phinney, *Shepherd of the Hills Country*, 115.

42. Wright, *Shepherd of the Hills*, 292, 259, 288; Morrow Postcard Collection.

43. "Presbyterian Hill Purchased Long Ago by Springfield Men," *Springfield Press*, ca.1929,
Shepard Room Collection; "Presbyterian Mecca Overlooks Hollister," *Springfield Leader*, 25
Sept. 1925, 2–4; Morrow and Myers-Phinney, *Shepherd of the Hills Country*, 155–156, 161. The
earliest institutionalized church in Branson was affiliated with the Presbyterian faith. Dedicated in April 1911, the Branson Presbyterian Church was erected at the corner of Fourth
and Pacific streets, a short distance up the hill from the White River. See Godsey, "Branson
Presbyterian Church," and Kathryn Buckstaff, "Restoring Branson's First Church," *Springfield News-Leader*, 9 June 1998, 3B. There had been a Presbyterian presence in southwestern
Missouri since the 1820s, when missionaries arrived to evangelize the Osage Indians. The first
formal churches were built in the early 1840s. Even prior to the construction of the Branson
church, Stone County hosted the Crane Presbyterian Church (organized in 1905), and E. E.
Stringfield mentions Stone County's Pierson Cumberland Presbyterian Church and Taney
County's Forsyth Southern Presbyterian Church in *Presbyterianism in the Ozarks*.

44. "Program, Mid-Summer Meeting of The Ozarkians," 1928, Wiley Collection; Shep-
herd of the Hills Estates brochure, ca. 1927, Western Historical Manuscript Collection,
University of Missouri–Rolla, Rolla; Smith, "Melodrama, Popular Religion, and Literary
Value," 239.

45. Presbyterian Hill brochure, "Where Will You Spend Your Vacation?" ca. 1920, Shepard
Room Collection; Morrow and Myers-Phinney, *Shepherd of the Hills Country*, 157–158; "To the
Honorable County Court and All Other Good Citizens of Taney County, Missouri," *White
River Leader*, 5 Feb. 1915.

46. "Presbyterian Mecca Overlooks Hollister," 4; Presbyterian Hill brochure, "Where
Will You Spend Your Vacation?"

47. Vincent, *Chautauqua Movement*, 4; Tapia, *Circuit Chautauqua*.

48. Hively, "When the Chautauqua Came to Town," 41; "Missouri Committee Recom-
mends Offer Hollister Properties to Southern Baptists," *Word & Way*, 19 Sept. 1946; Vincent,
Chautauqua Movement, 13.

49. Morrow and Myers-Phinney, *Shepherd of the Hills Country*, 162–163.

50. Ibid., 162–164; White River Booster League, "Come to Lake Taneycomo and the
White River Country: The Vacation Paradise of the Ozarks," 1940, Western Historical Manuscript Collection, University of Missouri–Rolla; Milstead, "Harold Bell Wright," 502; Morrow Postcard Collection.

51. Van Buskirk, "Kanakuk Kamps," 187–188; "History of Kanakuk"; Wright, *To My Sons*,
43, 120, 104.

52. Van Buskirk, "Kanakuk Kamps"; "History of Kanakuk"; Wright, *To My Sons*, 43,
120, 104.

53. Ifkovic, "Harold Bell Wright and the Minister of Man," 24.

54. Wright, *Ma Cinderella*; Wright, *Shepherd of the Hills*, 302.

55. Milstead, "Harold Bell Wright," 501; Meadows, *Short Stories and Poems of the Ozark
Hills*, 63. Commenting on the effects of Wright's literature on the Ross family, local historian
Phyllis Rossiter wrote that "it has been said that they never forgave" Wright for "betraying

their friendship" and forcing them to deal with scandalous and untrue allegations about a ruined daughter. See Rossiter, *Living History of the Ozarks,* 203.

56. Wright, *To My Sons,* 242.

CHAPTER 2. "HILLS OF TRUTH AND LOVE"

1. Nahum Tate (son of Dow Tate), phone interview; Morrow Postcard Collection.

2. Dow Tate to Sammy Emmie Tate, 29 July 1913 (in the author's collection and used with the permission of Nahum Tate).

3. Ibid.

4. MacCannell, *Tourist,* 131, 160; Boorstin, *Image,* 77–117; Taylor, "Authenticity and Sincerity in Tourism," 8.

5. Trilling, *Sincerity and Authenticity,* 93; Cohen, "Tourism as Play," 294.

6. Eco, *Travels in Hyperreality;* Baudrillard, *Simulations;* MacCannell, *Tourist,* 6–7.

7. Urry, "Sociology of Tourism," 51; Hobsbawm and Ranger, *Invention of Tradition;* Culler, "Semiotics of Tourism"; Duncan, "Social Construction of Unreality." On authenticity theories and their relationship to tourism studies, see Wang, "Rethinking Authenticity in Tourism Experience"; Hughes, "Authenticity in Tourism"; and Taylor, "Authenticity and Sincerity in Tourism."

8. "There's Gold in Those Ozark Hills," *St. Louis Post-Dispatch,* 29 Aug. 1965, quoted in Morrow and Myers-Phinney, *Shepherd of the Hills Country,* 32; Morrow, "Old Matt's Cabin," 29; Hendrickson, "Book People Come True," 193; Shepherd of the Hills Historical Society, Inc., *Shepherd of the Hills Souvenir Program 1976,* 8.

9. Van Buskirk, "Shepherd of the Hills Country," 28.

10. Harold Bell Wright to W. Gibbons Lacy, 1 Sept. 1932, Godsey Papers.

11. Morrow, "Wright Connection (Part II)," 18; "Sammy Lane Boat Line" brochure; Terry, "Shepherd of the Hills," 4.

12. "Storied Locality Is Objective of Local Travelers," *Decatur (GA) Review,* 17 Aug. 1930.

13. Kathryn Buckstaff, "David and Karen Cushman Plan Few Changes to Branson's Oldest Resort," *Springfield News-Leader,* 2 Mar. 2001, 8A; Tinsley, "Old Branson"; DuBois, "Early Days on Taneycomo," 22.

14. Hendrickson, "Book People Come True," 193; Ross, *Old Matt's View of It,* 9, 18, 17.

15. Morrill, *Story of Uncle Ike.* In the nearly one hundred years since the publication of *The Shepherd of the Hills,* there have been a multitude of publications that seek to verify or falsify the actual identities of the novel's characters. Other works include Grizzard, *Characters and Community of the Shepherd of the Hills;* Stout, "Memories of Sammie Lane" (here the author claims to be the daughter of Jim Lane and sister of Sammy Lane); and Madsen, *History.* This last publication continues to be sold at the Shepherd of the Hills Homestead and Outdoor Drama and speaks to the historical authenticity of all the novel's sites and characters.

16. Madsen, *History,* 43; Kirshenblatt-Gimblett, "Objects of Ethnography," 414; Munday, "Wright Trail," 121–122.

17. Madsen, *History,* 45; Spurlock, *Over the Old Ozark Trails,* 26. Spurlock, more than any local booster, was responsible for preserving the legacy of Wright's "authentic" characters. In 1924, she initiated a monument fund to erect a grave marker for John and Anna Ross in

the Shepherd of the Hills Cemetery which identified them as "Old Matt" and "Aunt Molly." Additionally, her tourist lectures constantly witnessed to truthful links between regional personalities and Wright's characters. As poet and Branson resident John G. Neihardt wrote in the foreword to *Over the Old Ozark Trails in the Shepherd of the Hills Country,* "Her talks to tourists have served to give a 'local habitation and a name' to this or that fictitious character in the famous tale."

18. Spurlock, *Over the Old Ozark Trails,* 28–29, 15.

19. Terry, "Shepherd of the Hills," 4; Laugeson, "Old Matt's Cabin," 8; "Shepherd Legend Still Growing," *Springfield News & Leader,* 4 Aug. 1957, C1.

20. Rossiter, *Living History of the Ozarks,* 203; Robbins, "A' Lyin' to Them Tourists," 19.

21. Herbert, "Literary Places, Tourism and the Heritage Experience," 312; Schouten, "Heritage as Historical Reality," 21; Madsen, *History,* 35; Morrow Postcard Collection.

22. *Ozark Guide Yearbook* (1962): 8; "Jim Lane's Cabin," 7; Madsen, *History,* 35; Pipes, *Fabulous Barefoot Horizons,* 82; *Ozark Guide Yearbook* (1964): 32, 38–39.

23. *Springfield Leader & Press,* 25 Feb. 1946, 10.

24. Van Buskirk, "Shepherd of the Hills Country," 30.

25. Powell, "Red Letter Books Relating to Missouri," 353; Hartman, "Shepherd of the Hills Drama," 6; Flannagan, *Arena,* 150.

26. Frizell, "History of 'The Shepherd of the Hills' Dramatizations," 29–31; *Shepherd of the Hills* movie brochure (1919).

27. Review of *The Shepherd of the Hills, New York Times,* 31 July 1941, 13.

28. Review of *The Shepherd of the Hills, Variety,* 18 June 1941, 16.

29. Madsen, *Branson,* 24.

30. Waldo Powell, whose father was believed by many local residents to be the model for the Shepherd in Wright's novel, is said by *Newsweek* to have "groaned throughout the performance." Additionally, in a manner complicit with the stereotypes presented in Paramount's film, the magazine closed its article by noting that, despite the chagrin of Branson residents, "no studio official has been reported missing in the hills." See *Newsweek,* 21 July 1941, 52.

31. Townsend Godsey, "The Shepherd" (essay), 1957, 60, Godsey Papers.

32. Thompson, "Saga of the Shepherd of the Hills, Part II," 27; Pipes, "Meet the People in the Shepherd of the Hills Country," 55; Eddie Bass, "A Place to Show Ozarks Culture," *Springfield News & Leader,* 13 Aug. 1950, D3.

33. Angus, "Rose O'Neill," 122; Gilmore, "Rose O'Neill's Bonniebrook," 19. Also see O'Neill, *Story of Rose O'Neill.*

34. Cochran, *Vance Randolph,* 170; Angus, "Rose O'Neill," 122–123; Abernathy and Trimble, *Rose O'Neill.* Rose O'Neill died in 1944, but Bonniebrook continues as a tourist attraction. The mansion was destroyed by fire in 1947, but a replica was completed in 1993 with funds raised by the Bonniebrook Historical Society and is open to tourists from April through November. In addition, the International Rose O'Neill Club was formed in Branson in 1967. Hundreds of club members and collectors meet in Branson each year to celebrate the four-day convention known as Kewpiesta.

35. Alma Jones Laugeson, *A Day at the Shepherd of the Hills Farm,* 1964, 8, Shepard Room Collection. Artistic representations of angelic children in heavenly scenes continue to draw tourists to the Ozarks. On average, 500,000–750,000 people per year visit the Precious Mo-

ments Chapel in Carthage, Missouri. Precious Moments, the world's most popular collectible items, are porcelain figurines inscribed with sayings that promote family, religion, or basic moral tropes. Sam Butcher, the creator of these figurines, has described his journey to Carthage as divinely inspired and has decorated his chapel with murals of his collectibles situated in biblical scenes. Some pilgrims claim to have received divine aid during their visits, and for many more, the site functions as a shrine for ritual purification by dispelling anxieties about both this life and the promised hereafter. The chapel's feature mural, "Hallelujah Square," depicts the entrance into heaven and saintly children who have already gained admittance. The majority of these figures represent people who have died over the past fifteen years, and guides narrate the horrible deaths suffered by these individuals and the joy loved ones have experienced by seeing the afterlife portrayed in such a benign fashion. In a 1984 interview, Butcher stated, "Precious Moments is the pulpit that I preach behind. People who won't go to church to hear the same message will go to the store and buy it." This quotation strikes at the heart of popular religion in the Ozarks by reflecting its extraecclesiastical nature, its alliance with lived experience, and its partnership with consumer culture. See Ketchell, "Precious Moments Chapel," 27–33.

36. Frizell, "History of 'The Shepherd of the Hills' Dramatizations," 44; Albers, interview; Kathryn Buckstaff, "Branson Rings in Season with Record Parade," *Springfield News-Leader*, 4 Dec. 1995, 1A. Although the contemporary Adoration Parade is a boon for newly burgeoned Christmas-season tourism in Branson, organizers have fought to keep corporations from advertising as part of the celebration. Claiming to represent the true spirit of the holiday, parade planners implicate the event in a "Jesus is the Reason for the Season" ideology by symbolically and materially banishing evidence of rampant Christmastime consumption. Though the late 1990s witnessed numerous local entertainment venues that decided to stay open through the winter as part of an "Ozark Mountain Christmas" campaign, and though thousands of tourists consume these offerings in conjunction with their attendance of the parade, the pageant's explicitly Christian nature is said to be preserved through its "noncommercial" approach. See Kathryn Buckstaff, "Penguins, Camels and Dogs, Oh My," *Springfield News-Leader*, 2 Dec. 1996, 1B, and "Parade Banishes Ads," *Springfield News-Leader*, 5 Dec. 1997, 10A.

37. Frizell, "History of 'The Shepherd of the Hills' Dramatizations," 37–42; Hartman, "Shepherd of the Hills Drama," 7–8.

38. Frizell, "History of 'The Shepherd of the Hills' Dramatizations," 44–50.

39. Van Buskirk, "Shepherd of the Hills Country," 31; Trimble, *Story of Old Matt of the Shepherd of the Hills*, 13. In 1968, Grossett and Dunlap estimated that it had sold one million copies per year of its edition of *The Shepherd of the Hills* during a seventeen-year period. See Gideon, "Shepherd's Show," 9. Since 1957, four additional statues have been added to the display atop Inspiration Point, all crafted by Ozark native Michael Lee. See Van Buskirk, "Shepherd of the Hills Country," 35.

40. Thompson, "Saga of the Shepherd of the Hills, Part II," 27–28; Van Buskirk, "Shepherd of the Hills Country," 32; Frizell, "History of 'The Shepherd of the Hills' Dramatizations," 59. Roughly in conjunction with the first performance by the Old Mill Players, television station KYTV in Springfield aired a narrated musical production of Wright's novel. Actors were cast from the drama department at Central Missouri State College at Warrensburg, and a four-

teen-verse "Ballad of the Shepherd of the Hills," composed by Will Mercer, accompanied much of the play's action. Sponsorship for this production came from local businesses and civic groups, including the Shepherd of the Hills Farm, Marvel Cave, the Retail Merchants Committee of Branson, and the chamber of commerce. See *TV Radio Mirror,* Apr. 1960.

41. Thompson, "Saga of the Shepherd of the Hills, Part II," 28; Thompson, "Saga of the Shepherd of the Hills, Part III," 56.

42. Laugeson, *Day at the Shepherd of the Hills Farm.*

43. Ibid., 21.

44. Lake Area Parish of the United Presbyterian Church, "Worship in the Outdoors" brochure, 1965, Shepard Room Collection. Though there is no evidence to suggest that Sunday morning services continued to be conducted at the Shepherd of the Hills Farm into the 1970s, a 1971 souvenir program does advertise "Sunday Night Gospel Sings." This program is supplemented by ever present praise of the area's inhabitants and geography, including a testimony from the U.S. representative from Missouri, Durward G. Hall, who proclaimed that the attraction "has nurtured and preserved our most valuable principles and traditions" by recognizing the merit of "simple truths." See the Shepherd of the Hills Historical Society, Inc., Shepherd of the Hills Souvenir Program, 1971.

45. Gene Gideon, "'The Shepherd of the Hills' Enters 14th Season," Shepherd of the Hills Farm press release, Jan. 1973, Shepard Room Collection; Frizell, "History of 'The Shepherd of the Hills' Dramatizations," 61–66; Gideon, "Shepherd's Show," 9; Thompson, "Saga of the Shepherd of the Hills, Part III," 58. Although very popular, the production at the Shepherd of the Hills Farm outshined national rivals primarily because it had a longer season than any other outdoor drama. Running six months, it thus easily surpassed attendance at other well-liked productions such as *Unto These Hills* (a Cherokee, North Carolina, performance about the Eastern Band of Cherokee), Spearfish, South Dakota's *Black Hills Passion Play,* or the Shepherd of the Hills Farm's only local competitor, *The Great Passion Play* in Eureka Springs, Arkansas.

46. Mike Penprase, "Branson Man Buys Shepherd of the Hills," *Springfield Daily News,* 5 Nov. 1985, 2A; Rossiter, *Living History of the Ozarks,* 205.

47. Van Buskirk, "Shepherd of the Hills Country," 35; Rossiter, *Living History of the Ozarks,* 205.

48. Don Mahnken, "Extended Tourist Season Works," *St. Louis Post-Dispatch,* 27 Dec. 1988, 3B, 4B; Van Buskirk, "Shepherd of the Hills Country," 35.

49. Steve Koehler, "'Shepherd' Novel Kept Current," *Kansas City (MO) Star,* 6 June 2004, B5; Thurman, interview; Frizell, "History of 'The Shepherd of the Hills' Dramatizations," 72.

50. Frizell, "History of 'The Shepherd of the Hills' Dramatizations," 79; post to the *St. Louis Post-Dispatch* online forum, 4 June 2003, http://forums.stltoday.com/viewtopic.php?t=63742&postdays=0&postorder=asc&highlight=branson&start=20. (In an attempt to solicit opinions from Branson tourists concerning their experiences in the Ozarks, in June 2003 I began posting online queries to newspaper forums in St. Louis, Tulsa, Dallas, Wichita, Des Moines, Memphis, Shreveport, and Topeka. The comment quoted in the text was in response to my queries.) A possible explanation for a conflating of the Shepherd of the Hills pageant with a Passion play is the nearness of the Great Passion Play in Eureka Springs, Arkansas—roughly an hour south of Branson.

244 NOTES TO PAGES 53–61

51. "Christian Family Weekend." This more explicit contemporary fusion of religion and popular culture was also evident during my recent visit to a gift shop at the Shepherd of the Hills Homestead. There I purchased a T-shirt that bore the Oscar Meyer hotdog logo with the company's name replaced by "Jesus Christ." Underneath, a caption reads, "My Savior Has a First Name, It's J-E-S-U-S . . . " (an obvious play on the company's well-known jingle). Perhaps to indicate that such a juxtaposition is not welcomed or well received in all of Oscar Meyer's markets, the shirt also includes the words "Branson, MO," thus suggesting that at least in this town faith trumps consumption, or alternately, that faith is readily available for consumption.

52. "Shepherd of the Hills Outdoor Theater."

53. Bourdieu, *Outline of a Theory of Practice*, 164, 82–83, 28–44.

CHAPTER 3. "I WOULD MUCH RATHER SEE A SERMON THAN HEAR ONE"

1. Goforth, "Not Your Parent's Branson" (*Kansas City*) *Metro Voice* 14, no. 6 (2003): 24.

2. Stacey Hamby, "Silver Dollar City: Owners Build Empire on Christian Principles," *Word & Way*, 10 June 1999, 9; S. T. Lambert's comments were posted as a review of Silver Dollar City on the Epinions.com Web site, 31 Dec. 2000, www.epinions.com/kifm-review -2307-2039366B-3A4F0229-prod4 (accessed 15 July 2005).

3. Thompson, "Herschends," 37–38; Gubernick, "Curb on the Ego," 418–420.

4. Crystal Cody, "Silver Dollar City Hits Slump," *Arkansas Democrat-Gazette*, 8 Aug. 2003, 3.

5. Rafferty, *Ozarks*, 8; Sears, *Sacred Places*, 38; *The Visionaries: The Herschends of Branson, MO*, dir. Dave Hargis and prod. Roy Speckman, Universal Midwest Media, 1992, videocassette. Missouri boasts more caves than any other state. See Weaver, *Wilderness Underground*, for a further examination.

6. McCall, "'Down Under' at Silver Dollar City," 42; Martin, *Official Guide to Marvel Cave*, 14. Despite Martin's assertion, Marble (later "Marvel") Cave has primarily been described in a language of religiously inspired awe. However, other Ozark caves have been bestowed with a more demonic character. For instance, regional promoter Otto Ernest Rayburn detailed a 1949 trip by students from the University of Tulsa who came to the area looking for a fissure labeled the "Opening into Hell." The group was motivated by Native American lore that depicted a "hole that spits fire," but the students failed to locate such a devilish cavern. See Rayburn, "Opening into Hell," 35.

7. Madsen, *History*, 30; Morrow and Myers-Phinney, *Shepherd of the Hills Country*, 38–40.

8. Emery, "Description of Marble Cave, Missouri," 614–615. The notion of Ozark healing waters apparently still held currency as late as 1929. In an article from that year, travel writer J. Fred Long wrote that "a myriad of underground streams and rivers" possesses "purifying lime rocks, curative magnesium deposits and invigorating mineral elements that beset every molecule of water coursing through to implant in it the purity and health-giving qualities that are evident at once in the water visitors see gushing out of hill sides and chasm bottoms." See J. Fred Long, "Oldest Land on the Western Hemisphere Rediscovered by Vacationists," *Ozarks*, 1929, Wiley Collection.

9. Rafferty, *Ozarks*, 200–204; Westfall and Osterhage, *Fame Not Easily Forgotten*, 2, 7. On late nineteenth-century accounts of Eureka Springs' spa tourism, see Cutter, *Cutter's Guide to Eureka Springs, Arkansas*, and Kalklasch, *Healing Fountain*. After the turn of the twentieth

century, many Americans began to view modern medicine with less skepticism, and fewer people sought healing spas. Claiming to be the fourth largest city in the state in 1900, Eureka Springs saw its population drop to roughly 1,400 by 1960.

10. Morrow and Myers-Phinney, *Shepherd of the Hills Country*, 40–42; Martin, *Official Guide to Marvel Cave*, 16. In a semantic move that seems to indicate that investors changed their focus from health spa development to mineral extraction, the mining town's name was changed to Marmaros (Greek for "marble") in 1886. See Madsen, *History*, 30.

11. "Pioneer of Ozark Awakening," 9; Miles H. Scott, "The Marvelous Cave," *White River Valley Historical Quarterly* 8, no. 10 (1985): 4–5; Thompson, "Herschends," 38.

12. Payton, *Story of Silver Dollar City*, 24–25; Bohner, "It All Started with a Hole in the Ground," 32.

13. "Mystery of Marble Cave," *White River Leader*, 13 Dec. 1913; Tidgwell, "Marvel of a Cave," 27; *Scientific American* 68 (1893): 65; Noble, "Creatures of Perpetual Night," 432, 430.

14. Martin, *Official Guide to Marvel Cave*, 21; Chandler, "Tale of Two Men Leads to One City," 26. By the time that Miriam and Genevieve assumed ownership of Marvel Cave, a number of similar attractions could be found in Stone and Taney counties. A tourism map produced about 1930 by the Missouri State Department of Resource Development details four other caverns within a short distance from Marvel Cave (Indian Creek Caverns, Keithley Cave, Wonder Cave, and Fairy Cave.) The most popular of these, Fairy Cave (now Talking Rocks Cavern), was opened by Waldo Powell, son of Truman Powell and the supposed model for Harold Bell Wright's Ollie Stewart character. See Missouri State Department of Resource Development, "The White River Country of Missouri," ca. 1930, Wiley Collection.

15. Marge of Sunrise Farm, "Fresh from the Hills . . . Ozark Cave Women," ca. 1944, Shepard Room Collection; Milstead, "Harold Bell Wright," 502.

16. Martin, *Official Guide to Marvel Cave*, 24; Madsen, *History*, 30; McCall, "'Down Under' at Silver Dollar City," 43.

17. Payton, *Story of Silver Dollar City*, 23; McCall, "'Down Under' at Silver Dollar City," 43; Martin, *Official Guide to Marvel Cave*, 54.

18. Thompson, "Herschends," 37–38; Doug Johnson, "Leap of Faith Succeeds in Branson Attraction," *Washington Times*, 29 Apr. 2000, E2; William Childress, "A City as Popular as Pretzels," *St. Louis Post-Dispatch*, 5 Apr. 1997, 7T.

19. Payton, *Story of Silver Dollar City*, 39–44; "Branson Mainstays Continue to Thrive," *Springfield News-Leader*, 26 Aug. 1996, 68.

20. Payton, *Story of Silver Dollar City*, 40; Thompson, "Herschends," 39; William Childress, "Silver Dollar City Gets Worldly," *St. Louis Post-Dispatch*, 27 Apr. 1997, 8T.

21. Payton, *Story of Silver Dollar City*, 51; "Mary Herschend Dies at 83," *Branson Beacon & Leader*, 21 Mar. 1983, 1.

22. Silver Dollar City Chamber of Commerce, "Silver Dollar City in Marvel Cave Park" brochure, Shepard Room Collection; Hartman, "Alf Bolin's Reign of Terror," 127–130; Payton, *Story of Silver Dollar City*, 58.

23. Schickel, *Disney Version*, 267; Doctorow, *Book of Daniel*, 289.

24. On the use of religious and spiritual language to describe Disneyland and Disney World, see King, "Disneyland and Walt Disney World," and Salamone and Salamone, "Images of Main Street."

25. Payton, *Story of Silver Dollar City*, 126, 58–59.

26. Peggy Soric, "A Temple of Wood, a Message of Truth," *Springfield News-Leader*, 26 July 1986, 4B.

27. Ibid.

28. Ibid.; Roebuck, "Coaster Thrills and Mountain Skills," 48; Kathryn Buckstaff, "They're Getting Married in a Theme Park," *Springfield-News Leader*, 9 June 1997, 3B.

29. Soric, "Temple of Wood," 4B; Deeds, interview.

30. Ron Sylvester, "There's Silver in These Hills," *Springfield News-Leader*, 13 Feb. 2000, 3B; "Mary Herschend Dies at 83," 1.

31. Chandler, "Silver Dollar City's Future Is Its Past," 23, 27–29; Brunson, "Behind the Boom in Branson, Mo.," 49; Roebuck, "Coaster Thrills and Mountain Skills," 48; Thompson, "Herschends," 69; Freihofer, "From 'Sorta' . . . to Saved," 37.

32. Daly, "Church at Risk," 1–6.

33. Kellogg, interview; Johnson, "Leap of Faith," E2.

34. Moore, *Selling God*, 244–248; *Encyclopedia of Fundamentalism*, 402–403, 470–473; Wacker, "Searching for Eden with a Satellite Dish," 441.

35. Corliss, "If Heaven Ain't a Lot Like Disney," 80; Ostling, "Of God and Greed," 70; Ostling, "TV's Unholy Row," 60; Johnson, "Leap of Faith," E2; "New Jim Bakker TV Show Acquires Camelot," 10.

36. Johnson, "Leap of Faith," E2; Herschend, interview; Hamby, "Silver Dollar City," 9.

37. Jack Herschend quoted in Roebuck, "Coaster Thrills and Mountain Skills," 48.

38. Kathryn Buckstaff, "Ozarker Spearheads Nazareth Village," *Springfield News-Leader*, 9 May 2002, 2B.

39. Payton, *Story of Silver Dollar City*, 126; Doug Johnson, "Branson's Silver Dollar City Theme Park Takes a Christian Slant," *Minneapolis Star Tribune*, 21 May 2000, 10G; Roebuck, "Coaster Thrills and Mountain Skills," 48; Bates, "Herschends Turn SDC into Multi-Million Dollar Empire," 3–4. The Herschend Family Entertainment Corporation's explicitly Christian mission statement has not been without controversy. Its southern-themed attraction located within Stone Mountain State Park in Georgia was leased from the state for thirty years. Originally the mission statement was posted on Web sites for the park. However, after the American Civil Liberties Union raised questions about advertising a public park as a Christian space, its religious references were removed in December 2000. Additionally, in November 2000, Stone Mountain management withdrew a question from its telephone surveys which asks visitors to rate the park's "Christian atmosphere." See "Silver Dollar City Alters Mission Statement," *Springfield News-Leader*, 15 Dec. 2000, 1A.

40. Orville Conrad and Alicia Bolin's comments were posted to the Silver Dollar City Fan Club Web site, 12 July 2005, http://groups.yahoo.com/group/SDCFans/message/866 and http://groups.yahoo.com/group/SDCFans/message/865.

41. Roebuck, "Coaster Thrills and Mountain Skills," 48.

42. Thompson, "Herschends," 39; Sarah B. Hansen, "Silver Dollar City Turns to Gold," *Springfield News-Leader*, 17 Dec. 1990, 2D; Gubernick, "Curb on the Ego," 418–420; "For New Operations Chief, First Priority Is to 'Glorify God'," *USA Today*, 30 Apr. 1987, 7A; "Higher Calling," *Springfield Business Journal*, 3–9 Aug. 1998, 2.

43. Elliot, "Ozark Mountain Magic," 58; Carolyn Olson, "Theme Park Offers Award-

Winning Entertainment, Christian Values," *St. Louis Post-Dispatch,* 14 May 2000, T3; "Silver Dollar City."

44. "Group to Be at Silver Dollar City," *Baxter Bulletin (Mountain Home, AR),* 4 Sept. 2004, 1B.

45. Kathryn Buckstaff, "Veggie Tales Takes Branson," *Springfield News-Leader,* 2 June 2002, 10B; "Veggie Tales Phenomenon Hits Branson," *PR Newswire,* 3 June 2002; John Wooley, "Silver Dollar City Launches Kids' Fest Celebration," *Tulsa World,* 9 June 2002, 7.

46. Arline Chandler, "Village Celebrates a Story More Precious Than a Silver Dollar," *Arkansas Democrat Gazette,* 24 Oct. 1999, 1H.

47. Johnson, "Branson's Silver Dollar City Theme Park," 10G; Juliana Goodwin, "Christian Soldier Mounts K.C. Crusade," *Springfield News-Leader,* 7 Oct. 2004, 1A; Noll, *American Evangelical Christianity,* 50–51.

48. Brunson, "Behind the Boom in Branson, Mo.," 49; Hamby, "Silver Dollar City," 9; Roebuck, "Coaster Thrills and Mountain Skills," 48.

49. Silver Dollar City promotional booklet, "Sharing and Caring in the Spirit of Community," 2002, in the author's collection.

50. Tom Uhlenbrock, "Branson Cheers President's Tune," *St. Louis Post-Dipatch,* 22 Aug. 1992, 1A; Scott Charton, "Republican President of Education Board Praises Democrat Carnahan," Associated Press Political Service, 18 Jan. 1996; Randy Buseman, George Klenovich, and Rusty Goode, "Honoring Achievement: The Ernst & Young Entrepreneur of the Year Awards," *Business Record (Des Moines, IA),* 27 June 2005, 14.

51. Corn and Moldea, "Did Ashcroft Take the Low Road on the Highroad?"

52. David Johnston and Neil A. Lewis, "Religious Right Made Big Push to Put Ashcroft in Justice Dept.," *New York Times,* 7 Jan. 2001, 16.

53. Kathy O. Buckstaff, "Branson Residents Oppose Gambling," *Springfield News-Leader* 10 Sept. 1994, 4A; Pete Herschend quoted in Robert Siegel, Noah Adams, and Dan Collison, "Boats in Moats," *All Things Considered* (radio program), 8 Oct. 1998; Oscar Avila, "Vote for Amendment Raises Gambling Fears in Branson," *Kansas City Star,* 12 Nov. 1998, B1; Boyd, interview.

54. "Records Indicate Family Bankrolling Casino Opposition," *Columbia (MO) Daily Tribune,* 15 July 2004; Allen Palmeri, "Defeat of Branson Casino Proposal Shows 'Prayer over Money,'" *Baptist Press News,* 4 Aug. 2004, 30.

55. Goforth, "New 'Celebration City' Adds to Family Fun in Branson."

56. Henry, "Silver Dollar City Exit Summary"; AOL CityGuide Web site, http://cityguide.aol.com/stlouis/entertainment/search.adp?cat=vt%5f%5fst%5f&page=detailReviews&id=111907188&rskip=20&layer=venues, 5 Aug. 2001 (accessed on 18 July 2005). Silver Dollar City conducts many exit polls to gauge customer satisfaction. In 2002, roughly 30 percent of the people surveyed (92 of 307) mentioned the park's "safety," "friendliness," "cleanliness," "order," and "Christian values" as the things they most enjoyed about their experience. (After 2002, the Herschend Family Entertainment Corporation came under new management, and the sharing of different types of customer information with the press, competition, or people engaged in educational pursuits was disallowed.)

57. Payton, *Story of Silver Dollar City,* 126; TripAdvisor.com Web site, www.tripadvisor.com/ShowUserReviews-g44160-d103201-r2519146-Silver_Dollar_City-Branson_Missouri.html, 8 Sept. 2004 (accessed on 27 July 2005).

58. "Family Fun Feeds Silver Dollar City,"(Oklahoma City) Journal Record, 27 Apr. 2000.

59. TripAdvisor.com Web site, www.tripadvisor.com/ShowUserReviews-g44160-d106415 -r644301-Marvel_Cave-Branson_Missouri.html, 23 July 2001 (accessed on 29 July 2005).

CHAPTER 4. JESUS IS "THE GREATEST STAR"

1. Wes Neal, Branson Stars Booklet (Branson, MO: Champions of Excellence Ministries, 1999), n.p. The Branson Stars Booklet can also be located online at www.fountaingateway .com/coe/ministrynews.htm.

2. Branson/Lakes Area Chamber of Commerce and Convention and Visitors Bureau, Branson/Lakes Area 2005 Fact Sheet.

3. McKinney, "Like Family," 28–29, 36.

4. Malone, Country Music, U.S.A., 131; McKinney, "Like Family," 32. On the life and work of Albert Brumley, see Hively, I'll Fly Away (The Story of Albert E. Brumley), and Cusic, Sound of Light.

5. Robbins, "A' Lyin' to Them Tourists," 61, 70; Terry, "Show That Put a Town on the Map," 11. The Assemblies of God established its headquarters in Springfield, Missouri, in 1918 when it purchased a former grocery and meat market at Pacific and Lyon streets. Today, the denomination has become the largest Pentecostal group in the world. As of 1999, the Assemblies of God claimed 2.5 million members in the United States and 32 million adherents worldwide. On the history of Pentecostalism in the Ozarks, see Gohr, "Snapshots of the Pentecostal Movement."

6. Mark Marymount, "Still Fresh at 40," Springfield News-Leader, 25 June 1995, 6B; Pryor, "Then Came Branson," 28; Lancaster and McGill, "Branson," 37–38. The history of the Presley Family, like much of the telling of Branson's past, is wrapped in folksy, familial narratives that appeal to the city's nuclear-family tourist cohort. According to Lloyd Presley's daughter-in-law, the family patriarch traded his loyal hound dog to his brother for a well-worn guitar and, through this sacrifice, set out on a musical course that would become his "life long passion." Presley, interview.

7. Baldknobbers Jamboree Show press packet, 2002, in the author's collection; Klise and Payton, Insiders' Guide, 113–114; Klopfer, How Branson Got Started, 34.

8. Lancaster and McGill, "Branson," 38; Presley, interview; Vorhaben, interview; Linebaugh, interview; Howard, "America's Hometown," 84.

9. Baldknobbers Hillbilly Jamboree promotional brochure, ca. 1969, in the author's collection.

10. "Over 25 Years of Music History," Southwest Missourian (Kimberling City, MO), 20 Feb. 1986, 18, 24; Lancaster and McGill, "Branson," 39; "Biography," Randy Plummer Web site; Green, "Proud as Plumb Pudding," 10; Randy Plummer, "An Ozark Prayer," Plum Puddin' Productions, 2000; Klopfer, How Branson Got Started, 35. Randy Plummer's Web site includes many items and elements that demonstrate a link between Branson-area musical entertainment and conservative, evangelical Christianity. For instance, it provides links to the Web site of the Jerusalem Prayer Team, an organization that regards peace in Israel as a precursor to the fulfillment of Christian apocalyptic thinking, and that of the Presidential Prayer Team, a group with civil religious intentions which encourages nationwide prayer for the president.

These links are accompanied by a daily Bible verse, advertisements for various Branson ministries, and other "inspirational" materials.

11. Fredrick, "Little Helping Hand"; Trent, interview. *Urban Cowboy*'s effect on Branson is still evidenced by the presence of Mickey Gilley, a cousin of Jimmy Swaggart's, in Branson. Gilley's Texas honky-tonk inspired the film. His mother wanted him to become a gospel performer and a minister, but Gilley instead found success with popular country music. In 1990 he opened a 996-seat theater in Branson which still continues to draw sizable crowds. See Klise and Payton, *Insiders' Guide*, 131–132.

12. Tourist response, "Branson Is Fun for Everyone!" marketing campaign, fall 2004, in the author's collection; Karla Price, "Branson Fashion Mixes Glitz, Understatement," *Springfield News-Leader*, 23 May 1993, 1F. According to journalist Karla Price, essential elements of the "Branson style" include the color mauve or any shade of purple in a theater's decor, rhinestones, custom-made cowboy boots, shoulder-length drop earrings, and big hair. It is interesting how this style mimics what may be termed "televangelical chic"—the fashion adopted by wives of prominent televangelists such as Tammy Faye Bakker or Jan Crouch which also has its roots in the 1980s. This comparison seems more cogent when one considers the large number of contemporary Branson performers who have fused Ozark entertainment with the promotion of evangelical or charismatic Protestantism. See Ron Sylvester and Karla Price, "What's Branson Style? Country Music, City Chic and Lots of Sequins," *Springfield News-Leader*, 23 May 1993, 5F.

13. Wolff, *Country Music*, 301; Klise and Payton, *Insiders' Guide*, 139; Roy Clark quoted in Ellison, *Country Music Culture*, 114; Cook, *Welcome to Branson*, 162; Lancaster and McGill, "Branson," 41. Clark's presence in the Ozarks further illustrates an intriguing yet contested connection between Branson and Las Vegas, as he was the first country music artist inducted into the Las Vegas Entertainers Hall of Fame (as a charter member). See Cook, *Welcome to Branson*, 164. Furthermore, as recounted by Leena Hughes—who now owns the building that housed Roy Clark's Celebrity Theater—during the mid-1980s the site included a bar in its mezzanine which functioned as an after-hours dance hall. Testifying to a move within the city's entertainment industry toward a more socially conservative, temperance-oriented vantage, a de facto ban on alcohol is now in place at all Branson shows. See Hughes, interview.

14. Ron Sylvester, "Room for Everyone," *Springfield News-Leader*, 8 Oct. 1989; "The Tourism Boom," *Springfield-News Leader*, 4 Apr. 1992, 6F; Ron Sylvester and Sara B. Hansen, "Field of Dreams: Branson Built It and They Came," *Springfield News-Leader*, 8 Apr. 1990, 1A. A count of citywide yearly visitors has been kept only since 1986. That year, the Ozark Marketing Council reported 3.1 million tourists. See Carney, "Branson," 26.

15. Lancaster and McGill, "Branson," 45–46; Bland, "Country Music's New Mecca," 64; Karla Price, "Branson Applauds '60 Minutes' Coverage," *Springfield News-Leader*, 9 Dec. 1991, 1A; Martha Hoy, "'60 Minutes' Gives Tourism Boost," *Branson Beacon*, 11 Dec. 1991, 3; Traci Bauer, "Media Helps Branson," *Springfield News-Leader*, 21 May 1992, 6B.

16. Don Zimmerman, "Country's Mecca in Missouri," *USA Today*, 24 June 1994, 1D; Kathy Buckstaff, "Despite Pains, Growth Moves Ahead," *Springfield News-Leader*, 26 Feb. 1995, 8A; "First There Was Nashville . . . Then Came Branson," *Atlanta Journal-Constitution*, 4 July 1993, N4.

17. Kathryn Buckstaff, "Branson Sees Decline in Tourism," *Springfield News-Leader*, 21 Feb. 2001, 6A; "Magazine Says City No. 1 for Families," *Springfield News-Leader*, 30 July 1999, 3B; Kathryn Buckstaff, "Poll Ranks Branson Top Holiday Destination," *Springfield News-Leader*, 9 Dec. 1997, 3B; Klise and Payton, *Insiders' Guide*, 24; Branson/Lakes Area Chamber of Commerce and Convention and Visitors Bureau, Branson/Lakes Area 2004 Fact Sheet.

18. Michael Ediger, e-mail correspondence with the author, 8 June 2003.

19. Malone, *Country Music, U.S.A.*, 11; Bruce, *And They All Sang Hallelujah*, 123, 136.

20. Williams, *America's Religions*, 233.

21. Malone, *Country Music, U.S.A.*, 12–13; Smith and Rogers, "Political Culture and the Rhetoric of Country Music," 185–198; Don Williams, "I Believe In You," MCA, 41303, 1980; Tom T. Hall, "Me and Jesus," Mercury, 73278, 1972. On the history of southern gospel music, see Goff, *Close Harmony*. The vitality of gospel music in Branson is safeguarded by the Branson Gospel Music Association (BGMA). Founded in 1998, the association sponsors a monthly "Jammin' for Jesus" concert series and an annual all-night session that, on average, attracts 2,000–3,000 people. Although these are primarily southern gospel events, they also feature artists who perform Christian bluegrass, country, and even hip-hop. Intimating the intricate fusion of sacred and secular within Branson musical entertainment, Phyllis Rotrock, director of the BGMA, stated that even though individuals provide "testimony" at her events, they are not a "worship service." However, whereas the jams used to be free, $5 per head is now charged because the BGMA "is a ministry." See Rotrock, interview.

22. Braschler, interview; Walters, interview.

23. Mark Marymount, "Braschlers Put Traditional First," *Springfield News-Leader*, 8–10 Sept. 2000, 18E; Worden, "Get Ready for a Great Feeling at the Braschler Music Show"; "Church Group Feedback," 12. Like the Braschler Quartet, Carol Wimmer advocates ministry through the arts. She is the author of Christian-themed musicals, plays, and scripture memory songs for children published by Sheep School Press.

24. Howard, "America's Hometown," 95; Lancaster and McGill, "Branson," 45. On the career of Bill Gaither, see Gaither and Jenkins, *Homecoming*.

25. Carlin, *Big Book of Country Music*, 153–154; Fairchild, interview; Mark Marymount, "Fairchild Happy in New Place," *Springfield News-Leader*, 16–18 July 1999, 17E. Numerous other performers who have fused country and gospel have achieved a degree of success in Branson. For instance, Cristy Lane, best known for her hit "One Day at a Time, Sweet Jesus," came to town in 1989 and operated her own theater until the mid-1990s. Her show consisted of country standards such as "I Fall to Pieces" and contemporary gospel melodies.

26. "Branson Singing Star Guided by Psalm 37:4," 16.

27. Tipton, "Cancer Doesn't Impair Don Gabriel's Vision," 14.

28. "Church Getaway Feedback," 8.

29. Sara B. Hansen, "Theater Is Gatlin 'Miracle,'" *Springfield News-Leader*, 5 Oct. 1991, 6B.

30. Francaviglia, "Branson, Missouri," 65–66; Carlin, *Big Book of Country Music*, 195–196; "Arts and Leisure," *New York Times*, 21 Aug. 1994, 28.

31. Ron Sylvester, "Willie Soon to Shine with Branson Stars," *Springfield News-Leader*, 16 Sept. 1991, 1A; Sara B. Hansen, "Nelson Anticipates Branson," *Springfield News-Leader*, 9 Oct. 1991, 1A; Ron Sylvester, "Nelson on the Road Too Much for Ticket Holders," *Springfield News-Leader*, 1 Dec. 1992, 1A. Commenting on both Haggard's and Nelson's unwillingness

to "Bransonize" their shows, Cindy Merry, a consultant for ten local productions, stated, "Their opinions of why they couldn't make it are a lot different than someone like me. They couldn't make it because they thought that if they put their name on a marquee that's all it would take to sell tickets. The truth of it is that the visitor to Branson is very sophisticated when it comes to the type of entertainment they want. They won't take somebody on stage not working for them." See Merry, interview.

32. Ellison, *Country Music Culture*, 112; Patty Cantrell and Kathy Oechsle, "Cash Country Creditors Reap Rewards," *Springfield News-Leader*, 6 May 1994, 6B, 8B; Ron Sylvester, "'Man in Black' Cashes Out of Branson Shows," *Springfield News-Leader*, 22 Nov. 1994, 1A. Cash is not the only renowned country artist to abandon Branson because of its older, evangelical, and conservative patrons. In 1992, Kenny Rogers partnered with Silver Dollar City to develop the White Water Landing theme park (featuring a thousand-seat showboat) and a massive shopping center on Branson's Strip. Rogers also performed occasionally beginning in 1992. In 1995, however, he ended his partnership with Silver Dollar City and left the Ozarks to, in his words, pursue a "younger and hipper" audience in Myrtle Beach, South Carolina. On the other hand, born-again country musician Glen Campbell has had long-lived success in Branson. See Kathy Oechsle, "Rogers to be Partner," *Springfield News-Leader*, 1 May 1992, 1A; Mark Marymount, "Rogers Folds Branson Hand, Ends Partnership," *Springfield News-Leader*, 21 Dec. 1995, 1A, 13A.

33. Pryor, "Then Came Branson," 28. The Tillis quotation concerning his decision to move to Branson appeared in the *Topeka Capital-Journal*, 24 July 1992, D1. In the fall of 2002, the Mel Tillis Theater in Branson was purchased by David Green, owner of the Hobby Lobby stores. Tri-Lakes Cathedral, an Assemblies of God church, now leases the building. Commenting on this transition, Tillis stated, "I've been thinking about it and praying about it for about the last year or so. . . . When I leave here in January [2003], I will know my theater is in good hands. It's going to be in the hands of God, and it can't get no better than that." See "Mel Tillis Theater Becomes Church," 8.

34. Cusic, *Sound of Light*, 181–182.

35. Gary Indiana, "Town of the Living Dead," *Village Voice*, 21 Sept. 1993, 35; Bill Duryea, "Come to the Boom Town," *St. Petersburg Times*, 31 July 1994, 2F; Laskas, "Branson in My Rearview Mirror," 170; Frommer, *Arthur Frommer's Branson*, 188; Cal Thomas, "Branson Remains the Town That Slime Forgot," *Springfield News-Leader*, 22 June 1995, 6A.

36. Queenan, *Red Lobster*, 166–167, 173; Scribner, interview.

37. Walker, "Down toward Arkansas," 111; Cook, *Welcome to Branson*, 170.

38. Tourist response, "Branson Is Fun for Everyone!" marketing campaign, fall 2004, in the author's collection; Cook, *Welcome to Branson*, 170.

39. "Perfect American Town," 26; Tourist response, "Branson Is Fun for Everyone!" marketing campaign, fall 2004, in the author's collection. On some occasions, a performer's urban inclinations have led to his or her own discomfort in Branson as well as that of audiences. For instance, in 1994 the edgy New York comedian David Brenner abruptly canceled a three-month run at Branson's Ozark Theatre after only a dozen performances. During this period, the largest crowd Brenner had drawn was 404 people in a venue that seated 1,300. Although theater owner Kent Emmons attributed this failure to "stretching the parameters of Branson entertainment," he also cited Brenner's uneasiness with the Ozarks: "He's more

city. He's a city guy. He got to the point where he thought this wasn't the place for him. . . .
I think the people were too slow for him." A central point of contention for the comedian
was the refusal of a Branson supermarket to extend him a credit account—a typically easy
process in a small town (especially for a multimillionaire) but one not afforded this New York
native in the symbolic hub of America's heartland. See Karla Price, "Brenner Views Branson
from Rearview Mirror," *Springfield News-Leader*, 10 June 1994, 1A, 4A.

40. Greaux, "Architecture," 28; Cook, *Welcome to Branson*, 215. Other local purveyors of pop-
oriented nostalgia not discussed in this chapter include Bobby Vinton, who opened his Blue
Velvet Theater in 1993, and John Davidson, who debuted at the Jim Stafford Theatre in 1991.

41. Ron Sylvester, "Williams Slams Branson," *Springfield News-Leader*, 9 Jan. 1992, 1A, 8A;
Cook, *Welcome to Branson*, 216. During a 1992 performance that included a guest appearance
by composer Henry Mancini, Williams demonstrated his ongoing "Bransonization." At one
moment in the act, Mancini praised Williams for "working his ass off" to get the theater
ready. Williams quickly responded, "We don't use words like that in Branson," and the crowd
responded with a rousing ovation. See Pryor, "Then Came Branson," 28.

42. Cook, *Welcome to Branson*, 220; Klise and Payton, *Insiders' Guide*, 110; "Forum Index";
Wolfe, interview. Another anecdote related by Wolfe further illustrates the continued tenuous relationship that Williams has with Branson's entertainment ideology. In preparation
for one show, Andy was supposed to come out in a cowboy hat, although as a flamboyant
urbanite in his mid-seventies he does not look much like a cowboy. Glen Campbell, who has
performed with Williams in recent years, was to say to him, "Who are you supposed to be?"
Andy was to reply, "I'm a cowboy." Glen was then to declare, "You look more like the gay
caballero." It was jokingly suggested in this practice that Andy should subsequently respond,
"Fuck you." Mistakenly, this retort was typed into the teleprompter by the stage manager.
When this moment in the act arose at that evening's show, Campbell read the teleprompter
and began to laugh. Andy described to the crowd what had occurred by stating that "F You"
was typed on the screen. Although he avoided actually speaking a vulgar word, the theater
received a number of letters of complaint saying that Andy had said "fuck" in the performance, thus demonstrating that even alluding to profanity is beyond the realm of accept-
ability for many Branson tourists.

43. Klise and Payton, *Insiders' Guide*, 146–147; Robert Keyes, "Newton Sues Theater Owners," *Springfield News-Leader*, 17 Feb. 1994, 2A, 5A; Kathy Oechsle, "Newton Fired by Theater
Owners," *Springfield News-Leader*, 12 Apr. 1994, 1A; Dean Curtis, "Creditors Nipping at Newton's Heels," *Springfield News-Leader*, 23 June 1994, 1A, 5A.

44. Ron Sylvester, "Newton's Show Does a U-Turn Back to Branson," *Springfield-News
Leader*, 23 Nov. 1994, 1A; Traci Shurley, "Orlando Sues Newton over Split," *Springfield News-
Leader*, 29 Apr. 1999, 1A; "Newton Files Suit against Orlando," *Springfield News-Leader*, 22
June 1999, 1A; Ron Davis, "Seat 210, Front Row, Center," *Springfield News-Leader*, 18 July 1993,
10G; Duryea, "Come to the Boom Town," 3F. A seemingly benign yet, in the Ozark context,
controversial example of Newton's "too Vegas for Branson" style can be seen in one of his
patented jokes. An assistant asks, "How long have you been wearing that girdle?" and gets
the reply, "Ever since my wife found it in the glove compartment." Though on the surface
innocent, even this allusion to bodies and light-hearted take on adultery proved too contentious for many of Branson's faithful.

45. Sylvester and Hampton, *Branson,* 61, 63; Laskas, "Branson in My Rearview Mirror," 171–172.

46. Klise and Payton, *Insiders' Guide,* 134; Esther 2:10.

47. Don Mahnken, "Extended Tourist Season Works," *St. Louis Post-Dispatch,* 27 Dec. 1988, 4B; Kathryn Buckstaff, "Branson's Traditional Celebration of Christmas Stays True to Holiday's Spiritual Beginnings," *Springfield News-Leader,* 8 Dec. 2003, 1A; Schmidt, *Consumer Rites,* 190.

48. Vecchio, interview.

49. "Tony's Testimony," 22.

50. Ron Sylvester, "'Liberace of Gospel Set' to Ply Trade in Branson at Legends," *Springfield News-Leader,* 5 Mar. 1992, 1B; Kathryn Buckstaff, "Long Years of Effort Put Dino at Palace," *Springfield News-Leader,* 5 Nov. 1996, 7A.

51. Freihofer, "Dino," 10.

52. Ibid., 11; "Testimonies"; Freihofer and Tipton, "Our Talks with Dino, Cheryl, and Gary," 10.

53. Freihofer, "Review," 20.

54. Layher, interview.

55. Lennon, interview.

56. Rodnitzky, "Back to Branson," 98; Drew Jubera, "The Year That Changed America," *Atlanta Journal-Constitution,* 27 Dec. 2001, A1; Dan Lennon, e-mail correspondence with the author, 20 July 1999.

57. Bellah, *Beyond Belief,* 175; Bellah, *Broken Covenant,* 84.

58. Freihofer, interview.

59. Presley, interview.

60. Vecchio, interview; Jubera, "Year That Changed America," A1. Iterating the sense of American exceptionalism promoted in Branson and melding it with an endorsement of antimodern nostalgia, Branson historian Jessica Howard stated, "People who think the U.S. is going down the toilet go to Branson. Branson represents the kind of America everyone fought the wars for." See "In the World of Newt and Rush, Branson Is Hip," *Springfield News-Leader,* 26 Feb. 1995, 8A.

61. "Branson Honors Those Who Served," *Springfield News-Leader,* 27 May 2001, 7B; Kathryn Buckstaff, "Branson Rolling Out Red Carpet for All Veterans," *Springfield News-Leader,* 4 Nov. 2001, 1A. Tony Orlando's multidecade popularity in Branson is a product of his esteem among veterans—a relationship that dates from his 1973 hit "Tie a Yellow Ribbon round the Ole Oak Tree." This success might also be contingent on his often religiously phrased Branson boosterism. As he has stated about the city, "It's a miracle. . . . If the United States had a heart and it were a living, breathing animal, Branson would be right where the heart is." See Laskas, "Branson in My Rearview Mirror," 171.

62. Branson Veterans Task Force (Web site); Buckstaff, "Branson Rolling Out Red Carpet for All Veterans," 4A.

63. Duede, "Vietnam Veteran Visits Branson," 48. Nationalism is further institutionalized and sanctified in Branson at the National Center for Patriotic Studies (an arm of the Branson Veterans Task Force), located in the Mansion America theater. The mission of the center is to "promote an understanding of and a commitment to our American patriotic

value system." This is accomplished through endeavors such as the creation of a variety of "experiential programs" that combine "our country's heritage with the entertainment industry in Branson" and the development of Branson as an "educational tourism market" by bringing models of patriotic monuments from across the country to town. In doing so, the center hopes to "stimulate the study and practice of patriotism as a function of citizenship." Harking back to a notion of education that elides dialogue about the justifiable nature of war while consecrating the acts of the American military, Debbie Ikerd (executive director of the Branson Veterans Task Force) stated: "Our goal is not only to honor those who have served, but also to educate our youth regarding the sacrifices veterans have made to preserve our freedom." See Debbie Ikerd, "Branson Salutes Our Veterans," *Kansas City Star,* 10 Feb. 1999, F4.

64. Neal, *Branson Stars Booklet,* n.p.

65. Jubera, "Year That Changed America," A1.

66. Pfister, *Insiders' Guide to Branson and the Ozark Mountains,* 128–129; Mark Marymont, "Smirnoff Uses Culture Shock for Patriotic Fun," *Springfield News-Leader,* 17–19 Sept. 1999, 22E; Ron Sylvester, "Comedic Smirnoff Coming to Town," *Springfield News-Leader,* 14 May 1993, 1B; Freihofer, "Comedy on a Mission," 37. "Yakov Smirnoff Show: Traveler Reviews."

67. Freihofer, "Celebrate America"; tourist response, "Branson Is Fun for Everyone!" marketing campaign, fall 2004, in the author's collection.

68. American Highrise (Web site); John Rogers, "Entertainer's 'Doodle' Catches Postal Service's Eye," *Springfield News-Leader,* 25 Oct. 1997, 1B.

69. Jorstad, *Holding Fast/Pressing On,* 113.

70. Tom Uhlenbrock, "Branson Cheers President's Tune," *St. Louis Post-Dipatch,* 22 Aug. 1992, 1A; Kathryn Buckstaff, "Reed Exhorts Crowd to Vote," *Springfield News-Leader,* 31 Aug. 1996, 1A; Dawn Peterson, "U.S. Needs God, Speaker Says," *Springfield News-Leader,* 2 Apr. 1998, 1A; Traci Shurley, "Pat Robertson Fans Turn Out for Taping," *Springfield News- Leader,* 13 June 1998, 10A; Jennifer Barnett, "Singing Senators Cut Loose," *Springfield News-Leader,* 22 Sept. 1997, 1B.

71. Robert Schmuhl quoted in Lois Romano, "Branson, Mo., Looks beyond RVs and Buffets," *Washington Post,* 8 Aug. 2005, A3.

72. Laskas, "Branson in My Rearview Mirror," 175; tourist response, "Branson Is Fun for Everyone!" marketing campaign, fall 2004, in the author's collection.

73. Diane Majeske, "Mister Marriage," *Springfield News-Leader,* 20 Feb. 2002, 4G.

74. Ibid., 1G; Smalley and Smalley, "Eight Great Reasons to Date"; Smalley, "Women Are from the Classroom."

75. Griffith, *God's Daughters,* 22, 204; Smalley, "Persistence."

76. "Our Guiding Principles"; Freihofer, "Youth Getaways," 18.

77. Wiebe, interview. "Raising America," a song-and-dance revue performed by the American Kids at Branson's Majestic Theater, is an example of a local entertainment act that reflects the concerns of Kanakuk Kamps. The American Kids was founded by a former Oklahoma high school principal, Dr. Dale Smith, in the late 1970s. It is now a national organization that helps young people develop character in a Christian context by using the performing arts as a vehicle. Values stressed include courage, commitment, dedication to family

and country, loyalty, and the fullest use of one's God-given talents. Currently, more than a thousand children participate in the program and stage their acts in New York, Las Vegas, Nashville, Hollywood, Orlando, and Branson. See Tipton, "American Kids Are Coming."

78. Wiebe, interview.

79. Ibid.

80. Parker, "Engendering Identity(s) in a Rural Arkansas Ozark Community," 148, 153, 148. In Parker's research, it was older women (Laverne was at the time sixty-six, and Rhonda was fifty-two) who cited biblical injunctions for female deference to male authority. However, as seniors are one of Branson's primary tourist cohorts, it might stand to reason that the propagation of such sentiments and their representation in local entertainment would function to attract this niche market.

81. Kathryn Buckstaff, "A Real Christmas Story," *All Roads Lead to Branson: Branson's Entertainment Quarterly,* Holiday 2001 edition; Freihofer, "Hughes Brothers," 51.

82. E-mail correspondence with the author, 25 July 2000. On a similar note, when Pat Boone's "Will Rogers Follies" came to Branson in the mid-1990s, citizens and tourists took umbrage at its scantily clad young women. The tourism industry's uncodified "ethical policing" quickly took charge, and soon thereafter leotards and body stockings were featured under the revealing costumes. See Rosenberg and Silverman, *Ozarks Traveler,* 168. Even with these changes in attire, some visitors still felt that the Follies were outside the Ozark fold. As tourist Peg Adams claimed, because the show is too much like Broadway, "they're not Branson." See Duryea, "Come to the Boom Town," 3F.

83. Mark Marymount, "Jennifer Charms Audiences," *Springfield News-Leader* 25–27 June 1999, 19E; Murray, "Jennifer Says Goodbye," 14, 32; Cox, "Branson's Very Own Yankee Doodle Dandy." Dolly Parton, a better-known, busty starlet, also contributes to Branson entertainment as the co-owner of the Dixie Stampede (a dinner theater that light-heartedly reenacts the Civil War). However, no tourist objections to this buxom singer's presence in town have been noted. One might surmise that this lack of protest is because Parton hails from rural Tennessee, and her breasts can therefore be viewed as the vehicles whereby a country girl made good in show business.

84. Ron Sylvester, "Not Just Dolls," *Springfield News-Leader,* 12 Nov. 1995, 1G; Arline Chandler, "Star Light, Star Bright," *Arkansas Democrat Gazette,* 24 Oct. 1999, 4H.

85. Sara H. Bennett, "Pageant Fever," *Springfield News-Leader,* 31 Jan. 1999, 1G, 7G; Lauren Squires, "Pageant Emcee Marred Branson Image," *Springfield News-Leader,* 31 Jan. 1999, 8A; Kathryn Buckstaff, "Branson Wants Toned Down Pageant," *Springfield News-Leader,* 4 Nov. 1999, 3B. Despite the numerous debacles surrounding Branson's Miss USA Pageant, Dia Webb (Miss Oklahoma), who finished in the top ten, was able to find some Christian-based redemption. The night before the event commenced, Webb presented herself to the producers of Branson's *The Promise,* a musical based on the life of Jesus. After an audition, she was given a part in the show. See "Role in the Promise No Accident for Reigning Miss Oklahoma," 25–26.

86. Bland, "Country Music's New Mecca," 64; tourist response, "Branson Is Fun for Everyone!" marketing campaign, fall 2004, in the author's collection.

CHAPTER 5. "NEAR HEAVEN"

1. Wright, *Shepherd of the Hills*, 30, 101, 144, 158.

2. Ibid., 103, 145, 156, 302.

3. *Water & Fire: A Story of the Ozarks*, prod. Michael Murphy, Kansas City Public Television (KCPT), 2000, videocassette.

4. Wright, *Shepherd of the Hills*, 302.

5. Chidester, "Poetics and Politics of Sacred Space"; David Chidester and Edward T. Linenthal, intro. to Chidester and Linenthal, *American Sacred Space*, 18. As early as the late 1970s, human geographers interested in social and cultural contexts began critiquing the lack of contextual focus on the part of humanistic geography. On initial considerations of this issue, see Cosgrove, "Place, Landscape and the Dialectics of Cultural Geography," and Ley, "Social Geography and Social Action."

6. Smith, *Map Is Not the Territory*, 88–103. The myth-and-symbol approach to sacred space is primarily the legacy of Mircea Eliade. In his *The Sacred and the Profane* (1959) and elsewhere, faith was marked as an independent variable, and the realms of the psychological, social, and economic were to be understood as dependent on it. As a corollary, sacred places were grounded in a unique character and possessed a special nature that could not be conferred on them by mere human action. In such locales, the major vertical divisions of the world intersected via a "symbol of ascent," thereby making them worldly centers filled with the possibility of divine encounters. See Eliade, *Sacred and the Profane*.

7. Birdsong, "Near Heaven," 48.

8. Sauer, *Geography of the Ozark Highland of Missouri*, viii–ix. Interestingly and inaccurately in light of Branson's tourism history, Sauer predicted that the Ozarks would never develop into a banner vacation area. Although admitting that Branson was one of a number of "much visited summer resorts" near Lake Taneycomo, he wrote that such places were unknown to people "outside of the cities lying adjacent to the Ozarks" and that tourist development was untenable because "a vacation in the Ozarks is attended by few of the ordinary amenities of city life and by none of the social allurements with which the established resorts are provided abundantly." As previous chapters have demonstrated, many people came to Branson precisely because it lacked such modern devices, and many more arrived owing to the efforts of Lizzie McDaniel, the Lynch sisters, the Trimbles, and others who effectively merged visions of rustic vacationing with modern conveniences. See ibid., 231–232.

9. Sauer, "Economic Problem of the Ozark Highland."

10. Ferrell, "Ozarks," 27.

11. "Sammy Lane Boat Line" brochure, 13–14; *White River Leader*, 28 Aug. 1914; Lake Taneycomo Chamber of Commerce brochure, 1926, quoted in Myers-Phinney, "Arcadia in the Ozarks," 6. "Land of a Million Smiles" was an early slogan utilized by the Ozarks Playground Association (OPA). Headquartered in Joplin, Missouri, the OPA began in 1919 as a cooperative effort of businesses to promote tourism in the region.

12. Kansas City Southern Railway, *Kansas City Southern Ozarks*, quoted in Sellars, "Early Promotion and Development of Missouri's Natural Resources," 134.

13. Miller, "Ozarks, Synonym for Surprises," 12; "Mecca of All Tourists and Summer Visitors," 11.

14. E. A. Strout Realty Agency Inc. brochure, ca. 1949, Western Historical Manuscript Collection, University of Missouri–Rolla.

15. McNeil, "'By the Ozark Trail,'" 25.

16. Rafferty, "Ozarks Forest"; Morrow, "St. Louis Game Park," 11.

17. Rafferty, "Ozarks Forest," 117; Rossiter, "Burning the Ozarks," 33–34; Gusewelle, "'Continuity of Place and Blood,'" 101. Reports concerning the abundance of wildlife in southwestern Missouri during the early nineteenth century often seem of mythical proportion. For instance, during his three-month tour of the area in 1818–1819, geologist and explorer Henry Rowe Schoolcraft reported a voluminous number of deer, turkeys, wolves, bears, and fowl. On Christmas Day, 1818, on Beaver Creek, near modern-day Branson, his group of hunters killed fourteen turkeys in a matter of two hours. Rafferty, *Rude Pursuits and Rugged Peaks*, 73.

18. Rossiter, "Burning the Ozarks," 33–34; Morrow, "St. Louis Game Park."

19. Rafferty, *Ozarks*, 209–210; Van Buskirk, "Wild White River," 58.

20. Rafferty, *Ozarks*, 210–211; Burton, "Rockaway Beach"; Love, "Making Niagras in the Ozarks," 140. The White River Boosters' League was incorporated in 1919 primarily as a promotional organization for tourism in Branson, Hollister, Rockaway Beach, and Forsythe, Missouri.

21. Saults, "Fifty Years of Missouri Conservation," 24; Keefe, *First 50 Years*, 6–8.

22. Keefe, *First 50 Years*, 21, 334, 337.

23. Love, "World of Townsend Godsey"; Godsey, *Ozarks Mountain Folk*, 128.

24. Keefe, *First 50 Years*, 19; Morrow, "St. Louis Game Park," 15.

25. Simpich, "Land of a Million Smiles."

26. Comstock, "Ozark Pageant," 3.

27. Ozark Mountain Lakes and Rivers, Inc., "White River Lakes of the Ozarks" brochure, Western Historical Manuscript Collection, University of Missouri–Rolla.

28. Fred DeArmont, "Progress at Table Rock"; Hensley, "In the Shadow of Table Rock Dam." Prior to the construction of Table Rock Dam, the U.S. Army Corps of Engineers had supervised the building of Norfork and Clearwater lakes on White River tributaries and Bull Shoals Dam on the White River itself.

29. James F. Barrett, "Times They Air a Changin'—Hit's a Pity, Pity," *Stone County (MO) Gazette*, 17 Apr. 2000; Rayburn, "Dam Talk," 56. Despite his frequently nostalgic writings, Douglas Mahnkey, like many other Ozarkers, sought to strike a balance between progress and preservation of the past. At a twenty-fifth anniversary dinner commemorating the building of Table Rock Dam, he told representatives from the U.S. Army Corps of Engineers, "I hope you don't build any more dams. You've covered up too many good pawpaw patches and fishing holes already." However, Mahnkey also owned a hotel in Forsyth and therefore profited from the large increase in regional tourism which resulted from the construction of Table Rock. Like most with his vantage, he pictured the Ozarks as a woodsy haven for nature lovers rather than a site for hoards of speedboats and music fans. His experience demonstrates that even the most ardent opponents of modern technological accretions have not necessarily been antimodern. Instead they have promoted a tempered form of progress often incompatible with the boomtown history of Branson. See Chris Bentley, "At Least Progress Hasn't Completely Covered Everything," *Springfield News-Leader*, 26 Feb. 1995, 5A.

30. Rayburn, "Big Year," 5; Asbell, "Vanishing Hillbilly," 95; Brown, "Ozark Playgrounds Add New Tourist Attraction," 63.

31. Rafferty, *Ozarks,* 211.

32. Hensley, "In the Shadow of Table Rock Dam," 269–271.

33. Simpson, "Otto Ernest Rayburn," 161; Rayburn, "Rayburn's Roadside Chat" (July 1930), 1; Rayburn, *Forty Years in the Ozarks,* 6, 13. Further describing how *The Shepherd of the Hills* made him feel a part of the regional landscape, Rayburn wrote, "It turned the trick. From that day forward I was a hillbilly of the first water. I couldn't imagine how I had managed to grow to manhood without knowing about the Ozarks." See Rayburn, "Hideway Lodge," 7.

34. Rayburn, "Quest for Arcadia," 5; Rayburn, *Forty Years in the Ozarks,* 32; Rayburn, "Arcadian Echoes" (1950), 61; Rayburn, "Shepherd of the Hills Country," 11; Kimball, "White River Lure," 21. Defining the concept of "Arcadia," Rayburn stated, "The word, Arcadian, means ideally rural. Historically, Arcadia was the province of ancient Greece. It was a land of great scenic beauty where men found contentment in rural simplicity. Today, any contented rural folk may be called Arcadians." See Otto Ernest Rayburn, *Arcadian Magazine,* Mar. 1931, 4.

35. Rayburn, "Rayburn's Roadside Chat" (Sept. 1929), 3; Rayburn, "Rural Musings" (1949), 3; Miller, "What Rayburn's Ozark Guide Means to Me," 47.

36. Rayburn, "Sight Unseen," 5.

37. Rayburn, "Gone Are the Days," 6.

38. Rayburn, *Forty Years in the Ozarks,* 47–48.

39. Rayburn, "Ozarkograms," 12; Rayburn, "Rural Musings" (1949), 3; Rayburn, "Lay My Burden Down," 5; Rayburn, "Arcadian Echoes" (1949), 53.

40. "Rayburn's Roadside Chat" (Mar.–Apr. 1930), 3.

41. Rayburn, "Arcadian Echoes" (vol. 19, 1948), 38; Rayburn, "Pastoral Living," 55; Rayburn, "Rayburn's Roadside Chat" (Sept. 1929), 3.

42. Rayburn, "Rayburn's Roadside Chat" (Sept. 1929), 3; Rayburn, "Rayburn's Roadside Chat" (Sept. 1930), 1; Rayburn, "Harmony of Nature," 18.

43. Rayburn, "Rural Musings" (1945), 115; Rayburn, "Progress in the Ozarks," 3.

44. Rayburn, "Gone Are the Days," 6–7; Rayburn, "Try the Ozarks," 5–6.

45. Rayburn, "Lay of the Legend," E; Rayburn, *Forty Years in the Ozarks,* 8; Rayburn's Ozark Folk Encyclopedia was not intended for print but rather consists of 229 "volumes" or loose-leaf binders preserved as part of the Otto Ernest Rayburn Collection at the University of Arkansas. Each contains pamphlets, clippings, photos, maps, and other materials arranged first in relation to 125 counties in Oklahoma, Missouri, and Arkansas and then rearranged thematically under headings such as "Chickens, "Shooting," and "Zither."

46. Rayburn, "Arcadian Echoes" (vol. 18, 1948), 97.

47. Ingenthron, *Land of Taney,* 18–19.

48. "'Progress' or 'Cancer,'" *Springfield Leader & Press,* 13 Feb. 1973, 7.

49. Branson Area Environmental Task Force, "Executive Summary"; Deborah Barnes and Kathy Oechsle, "Branson and the Environment," *Springfield News-Leader,* 5 Sept. 1993, 1A.

50. Fredrick, "Ozark Mountain Country," 4. Deborah Barnes, "Defending the Land,"

Springfield News-Leader, 7 Sept. 1993, 1A, 5A; Jennifer McDonald, "Keeping Lakes Clean a Challenge," *Springfield News-Leader,* 22 May 1999, 9A.

51. Chris Bentley, "Branson Discovers 17 'Illegal' Buildings," *Springfield News-Leader,* 10 Feb. 1994, 1A. In May 1994, the Ozark Mountain Daredevils, Brewer and Shipley, and other area entertainers performed a concert in Branson which was produced by the Ozark Environmental Awareness Fund. Revenues from the event were donated to area groups that monitor lakes, woods, and wildlife. Kathy Oechsle, "Concert Singers' Refrain to Be Saving Environment," *Springfield News-Leader,* 27 Apr. 1994, 1B.

52. Barnes and Oechsle, "Branson and the Environment," 9A.

53. Silver Dollar City, Inc., "A Company Committed to Protecting and Nurturing the Environment" press release, 2000, in author's collection; Kathryn Buckstaff, "Branson Residents Urge Board to Curb Tour Bus Pollution," *Springfield News-Leader,* 10 Oct. 1995, 5B; Tourist response, "Branson Is Fun for Everyone!" marketing campaign, fall 2004, in author's collection.

54. Payton, *Beautiful and Enduring Ozarks,* 9, 72. According to Claudia Vecchio, former vice president of communications for the Branson/Lakes Area Chamber of Commerce and Convention and Visitor's Bureau, "Neon and Nature" was adopted as a promotional slogan to cater to the desires of baby boomer vacationers. Claiming that this demographic tires of Branson's musical entertainment more easily than does the World War II generation, which spawned the city's early 1990s boom, she stated they must be provided a "total experience"—one that unites variety shows with hiking, biking, and other forms of "adventure travel." As part of this dual-edged approach, Vecchio's organization partnered with the city of Branson in 1998 to create the Environmental Excellence Challenge. This initiative focuses on recycling, water preservation, and the beautification of area properties by means of environmental and legislative committees. See Vecchio, interview.

55. LaRoe, "Ozarks Harmony."

56. Lane Beauchamp, "Branson's Success Scars Land and Lives," *Kansas City Star,* 7 Mar. 1993; A1, A14; Tony Horwitz, "Getting Nowhere: Boomtowns Lure Poor with Plenty of Work—but Not Much Else," *Wall Street Journal,* 16 June 1994, A1.

57. Boyd, interview; Beauchamp, "Branson's Success Scars Land and Lives," A1, A14; Lane Beauchamp, "Tourist Season Begins with Help for the Homeless," *Kansas City Star,* 7 Mar. 1993, A14.

58. Chris Bentley, "Proposed Site North of Branson," *Springfield News-Leader,* 10 Sept. 1994, 1A; Kathy O. Buckstaff, "'The Right Price Always Buys the Property,' Five-Star's Owner Says," *Springfield News-Leader,* 10 Sept. 1994, 1A. Creative Learning Products was founded in 1994 and for a decade focused its production on crayons, children's placemats, videos, and other early-learning materials. However, in June 1994, the company restructured its operations to focus on entertainment and gambling—a move that, according to founder Peter Jegou, was meant to "take its successes in entertaining children to the next level." Creative Learning first invested in Branson when it bought the Five-Star Theatre in the spring of 1994 to house an original musical play based on the life of Roy Rogers. See "Company Cruises from Crayons to Casinos," *Springfield News-Leader,* 10 Sept. 1994, 4A.

59. Bentley, "Proposed Site North of Branson"; Traci Bauer, "Controversy Coming

Neighbors Agree," *Springfield-News Leader,* 10 Sept. 1994, 1A. Contrary to Tommy Thompson's assessment, the naming of Christian County had nothing to do with a particular religious vantage. In March 1859, this political unit was carved from portions of Greene, Taney, and Webster counties. Mrs. Neaves, a landowner hesitant to lose her citizenship in Greene County, agreed to do so if the new area was named for her former residence, Christian County, Kentucky. See Christian County Centennial, Inc., *Christian County.*

60. "Strong Views for, against Gambling," *Springfield News-Leader* 13 Sept. 1994, 4A; "Ozarkers Make Voices Heard on Casino Issue," *Springfield News-Leader* 27 Oct. 1994, 5A; Linda Purvis, e-mail correspondence with the author, 17 Apr. 1997; Fred Browning, e-mail correspondence with the author, 7 Mar. 1997. Although the vast majority of those who wrote to the *Springfield News-Leader* opposed gambling on moral and religious grounds (sixty-two of seventy-nine through late October 1994), a few dissenting voices appeared. For instance, Peggy Pollard saw Native American casinos as a way to atone for past indiscretions throughout American history when she wrote, "I believe that if the Indians want to open a bingo parlor or gambling casino, they should be allowed to do so. We've done a lot of things to them—we've taken their land and we didn't just take the bad land, we took the good land, and I think they should be allowed to do their gambling or play their bingo." Interestingly, even without the influence of gambling some people suggested that crime was becoming a serious problem in Branson during the mid-1990s. In 1996, a commentator on CBS's *Face the Nation* stated that the city's overall crime rate had risen 800 percent from the previous year. See "Mayor Blasts CBS Report on Branson Crime Statistics," *Springfield News-Leader,* 8 Dec. 1996, 1B.

61. Ron Sylvester, "Performers Voice Their Opposition to Gambling," *Springfield News-Leader* 10 Sept. 1994, 4A; Kathy O. Buckstaff, "Branson Groups Unite against Gambling," *Springfield News-Leader,* 24 Sept. 1994, 1A.

62. Kathy O. Buckstaff, "Branson Residents Oppose Gambling," *Springfield News-Leader* 10 Sept. 1994, 4A; Pete Herschend quoted in Robert Siegel, Noah Adams, and Dan Collison, "Boats in Moats," *All Things Considered* (radio program), 8 Oct. 1998; Chris Bentley, "Gambling, Carnahan Don't Mix," *Springfield News-Leader,* 11 Sept. 1994, 1A. Refuting contentions offered by Herschend and other businesspeople, former Chrysler Corporation chairman Lee Iacocca stated in 1994 that Branson-area residents would ultimately be pleased if gambling was allowed. In town for a ribbon-cutting ceremony at the entrance to the Branson Hills housing development (in which he had an ownership stake), Iacocca maintained, "The day when the overbuilt theaters in this town start to close, gambling will become an attractive option here. If done right and controlled and the bad elements kept out, gambling will bring families." See Kathy O. Buckstaff, "Iacocca: Gambling Might Save You," *Springfield News-Leader,* 15 Nov. 1994, 6B, 8B.

63. Scribner, interview.

64. Sara B. Hansen, "Proprietor Flees; Exotic Dance Suit Still Not Served," *Springfield News-Leader,* 24 July 1990, 1B. In 1994, a Scribner-led coalition also combated local licentious sexuality by preventing the establishment of a Hooters restaurant in Branson. Although he had never been to Hooters, Scribner professed the incompatibility of the establishment with the Branson image when he stated, "You don't have to get down to wallow with the pigs to know they stink." See Kathy Oechsle, "Branson Ponders 'Adult Entertainment Zone,' Just in Case," *Springfield News-Leader* 4 Feb. 1994, 1A; Scribner, interview.

65. Scribner, interview; Stacey Hamby, "Christians Make Difference in Missouri's Tourist Mecca," *Word & Way*, 30 Apr. 1998, 5. As an example of other social ills contested by Branson's First Baptist Church, Scribner spoke out against a proposition for more lenient liquor laws because it would degrade "the value system that has in fact made Branson what it is." Alcohol joined the list of regional pariahs during the early 1990s. In March 1995, the chamber of commerce and the board of alderman prevented the sale of alcohol at Branson Jam, the tourism industry's yearly kickoff. In that same month, city leaders unanimously denied plans to bring a microbrewery to town. See Lane Beauchamp, "Beer or Bingo?" *Kansas City Star*, 15 Mar. 1995, A1; Kathryn Buckstaff, "More Lenient Liquor Law Proposed," *Springfield News-Leader*, 29 May 2001, 1B. Substances of a different kind have also been positioned by local boosters as outside Branson's virtuous fold. A 2003 television commercial advertised the city as "a place where getting high means a roller coaster ride."

66. Wells, interview; Gold, interview; "History of Chapel (Formerly Motor Coach) Ministry."

67. Wells, interview; Gold, interview; Hamby, "Christians Make Difference in Missouri's Tourist Mecca," 6.

68. "Stonecroft Ministry," 14; "Statement of Faith" (Stonecroft Ministries). On the history of Stonecroft Ministries, see Baugh, *Story Goes On*.

69. Smith, interview.

70. Jeff Hurst, interview; Emma Hurst, interview. Another example of an organization specifically designed to provide religious outreach to tourists in Branson is Warren Hunter's Sword Ministries. Hunter came to Branson from South Africa because he felt that God was revealing a variety of "signs and wonders" in the Ozarks. See "He Came from South Africa to Impart to You in Branson," 52.

71. Jeff Hurst, interview; Emma Hurst, interview.

72. Stacey Hamby, "Behind the Curtain," *Word & Way*, 30 Apr. 1998, 6; Mark Marymount, "Reunion Brings Familiar Faces to Branson," *Springfield News-Leader*, 25–27 Feb. 2000, 9E.

73. McPhail, interview.

74. Ibid.

75. Boyd, interview; Scribner, interview; McPhail, interview; Linda Leicht, "Churches in Branson Lose Leaders," *Springfield News-Leader*, 6 Oct. 2005, 1A.

76. Scribner, interview; Boyd, interview.

77. Kellogg, interview; Millsap, "Branson Church Will Memorialize Harold Bell Wright," 6.

78. Bucher, interview.

79. Freihofer, "Dino," 10; "Few Words from Mike Radford," 55; Rotrock, interview.

80. Rotrock, interview; Tipton, "Stars Come out for the Hiding Place Ministries," 16–18. Billye Brim was called to the ministry through a baptism in the Holy Spirit in 1967. From 1971 through 1980 she worked for Kenneth Hagin Ministries in Tulsa, Oklahoma. After retiring from that post, she established her own organization and, in the mid-1990s, began plans for Prayer Mountain. As she recounts on her ministry's Web site, "For years I have sensed a call for a special place to pray about God's plans and purposes in these days of the 'former and latter rain together' outpouring. . . . Then about eleven years ago I began to sense a yearning toward Branson. I heard of the prophecy Corrie Ten Boom gave concerning what God

would do there in the last days. At Brother Kenneth Hagin's Winter Bible Seminar in Tulsa, during a powerful Holy Ghost controlled meeting, I was out under the power on the floor for a long time. God spoke to me plainly about this call. The place was to be near Branson. He said angels were holding the land. . . . He said there was to be a Prayer Mountain. A place where people could come for individual prayer. . . . But primarily a place where seasoned prayers would lead to Holy Spirit guided prayers concerning the work of God in the last days. . . . And so this is a God touched project. Prayer Mountain in the Ozarks is now a reality." See Brim, "Vision of Prayer Mountain."

81. *U.S. News & World Report,* 19 Dec. 1994, 64; Wojcik, *End of the World As We Know It,* 4.

82. Levitt, "October 2001 Personal Letter"; "Transmillennial 2006" brochure, in the author's collection.

83. Although not in attendance at the Roots Conference, I was provided with detailed notes and all handouts from the proceedings by Howard Boyd, pastor of Branson Hills Assembly of God Church.

84. Tourist response, "Branson Is Fun for Everyone!" marketing campaign, fall 2004, in the author's collection; Bucher, interview; McPhail, interview.

CHAPTER 6. HILLBILLY HEAVEN

1. While conducting fieldwork in Branson, I heard numerous versions of Spurlock's quotation. The one used here can be found in Pfister, *Insiders' Guide to Branson and the Ozark Mountains,* 25.

2. Heavin, "Hillbilly," 76.

3. Brandon, "Trickster," 623; Hynes, "Inconclusive Conclusions," 215.

4. Turner, *Ritual Process,* 95; Douglas, *Purity and Danger,* 13.

5. Babcock-Abrahams, "'Tolerated Margin of Mess,'" 165; Pelton, *Trickster in West Africa,* 3.

6. Koepping, "Absurdity and the Hidden Truth," 193.

7. Green, "Hillbilly Music," 204.

8. Shapiro, *Appalachia on Our Mind,* x; Batteau, *Invention of Appalachia,* 132. On representations of Appalachia by outsiders from the 1860s through the 1980s, see McNeil, *Appalachian Images in Folk and Popular Culture.*

9. Rafferty, *Rude Pursuits and Rugged Peaks,* 63; H. L. Mencken, "Famine," *Baltimore Evening Sun,* 19 Jan. 1931; Queenan, *Red Lobster,* 166.

10. McAdoo, "Where the *Poor* Are Rich," 13, 83. Early residents of southwestern Missouri did live apart from mainstream society because of the region's relative inaccessibility and maintained traditional folkways. Taney County was perhaps the most isolated place in the region during the early settlement period and as late as 1920 had the lowest population density of any Ozark county (12.5 people per square mile). In 1920, Stone County was only slightly more populated, with a density of 14.4 people per square mile. However, even at the turn of the twentieth century, this remoteness was not complete. Ridge trails and rudimentary roads existed, as did magazine and newspaper subscriptions that offered contact with life beyond the hills. Inhabitants also kept abreast of national and international developments through communication with crossroads merchants. These information channels were supplemented by neighborhood dances and musical parties that brought people to-

gether to share community information and knowledge of world affairs. As historian Edgar D. McKinney once surmised, the level of isolation depended to a great extent "upon the personality and preferences exhibited by individuals" and cannot be reduced to utter geographic seclusion. See Estabrook, "Population of the Ozarks," 25, and McKinney, "Images, Realities, and Cultural Transformation in the Missouri Ozarks," 76.

11. Sarah Overstreet, "Some of the Stereotypes May Be Founded in Truth, but Mostly It's Pure Hollywood Fiction," *Springfield News-Leader*, 10 Mar. 1985, 1L; Dale Freeman, "What IS a Hillbilly?" *Springfield News & Leader*, 2 Feb. 1975, 1. Another piece of Ozark wit further illustrates the difficulties of a tourist's ability to identify "authentic" hillbillies. According to this account, "an old native of the White River Valley, after being queried from time to time by tourists looking for a hillbilly, was once more asked by a New Englander where he might find one. After he was informed that he was talking to a hillbilly and finding that the native looked no different than any one else, he commented: 'These natives aren't like they used to be, are they?' To which the old native replied, 'No, nor they never were.'" See "Ozark Wit and Humor," 6.

12. Upton, "Hillbilly," 23.

13. Quotation from Hibler, *Down in Arkansas*, 33.

14. Donaldson, "Hillbilly," 16–17.

15. Randolph and Wilson, *Down in the Holler*, 252; Roberts, "Don't Call Me a Hillbilly," 4; Rayburn, "Hillbillies," 27; Kirkendall, "Who's a Hillbilly," 22; Doug Johnson, "Hillbilly Jokes Start Opinion War in Ozarks," *Springfield News-Leader*, 14 Jan. 2001, 6B; "Picture Guidebook: Missouri's Annual Festival of Ozark Craftsmen," Silver Dollar City, ca. 1970, Shepard Room Collection.

16. *Moore v. Moore*, 337SW 2d 781 (1960).

17. Stone County Historical Society, *History of Stone County, Missouri*, 236; "Political Shepherd of the Hills," 26; Treese, *Biographical Directory of the American Congress*, 1819.

18. Stone County Historical Society, *History of Stone County, Missouri*, 236–237.

19. "Genuine Folks," 20.

20. "Hillbilly" (*Rayburn's Ozark Guide*), 4.

21. "Hillbillies—To Be or Not to Be," 12. In one of the first issues of the *Ozarks Mountaineer*, a native Ozarker added further nuance to the magazine's negation of the hillbilly idiom. Cora Pinkley Call asserted that despite outsider characterizations, there exists a great diversity of people and lifestyles in the region, and thus the mountaineer is "not a curiosity." Although the author sought to debunk a variety of stereotypes, she did conclude that two overarching regional attributes could be identified—a "strength of character" and a "oneness of purpose to serve the Almighty." See Call, "We Are Mountaineers, Not Hill-Billies," 10.

22. "Jim M. Owen Dies; King of the Hillbillies," *Springfield Leader & Press*, 12 July 1972, 4B; Owen, *Jim Owen's Hillbilly Humor*, 18, 17. Iterating Owen's belief in a hillbilly ideology that embraces both hard work and robust play, southwestern Missouri native Karen Mahan wrote in 1990, "I am proud to bear the title of an 'Ozark Hillbilly.' . . . Hillbillies have been portrayed as lazy, dirty, and ignorant; nothing could be further from the truth. The hillbilly has to work twice as hard as his city cousin just to get by. . . . The city cousin believes himself to be smart, but he's the one who works for 40 years in the city so he can retire next door to the hillbilly. The hillbilly spends his whole life working and playing in the hills he loves." See Mahan, "Hillbilly Heart," 47.

23. Rafferty, *Ozarks,* 55–57.

24. Weber, *The Protestant Ethic and the Spirit of Capitalism,* 21–26, 61.

25. Ibid., 163. Numerous scholars have attempted to rework Weber's thesis to account for religious impulses that sanctioned consumption in addition to labor. This realignment has been most thoroughly effected by sociologist Colin Campbell in *The Romantic Ethic and the Spirit of Modern Consumerism.* Campbell identified a "Purito-Romantic" personality that possessed the religious and emotional wherewithal to produce modern consumption. The author located this sentiment within early eighteenth-century Arminian stances spawned from Calvinism which stressed the benevolence instead of arbitrariness of God. This shift then allowed for the development of divinely sanctioned passion and, as a corollary, God-ordained consumption. Campbell claimed that, with the development of romanticism, God was divested from such emotionally driven morality and a worldview arose that assumed individuals could be morally improved by consuming and enacting a generalized humanitarianism.

26. Holiday quoted in *The Ozarks: Just That Much Hillbilly in Me,* dir. and prod. Mark Biggs, Southwest Missouri State Board of Directors, 1999, videocassette. The first verse of "Work for the Night Is Coming" declares, "Work for the night is coming / Work through the morning hours / Work while the dew is sparkling / Work mid springing flowers / Work when the day grows brighter / Work in the glowing sun / Work for the night is coming / When man's work is done." See Gilmore, "Environment of Work," 8. The sentiment of this hymn is derived from a passage in John 9:4 (NRSV) when the gospel writer declared, "We must work the works of him who sent me while it is day; night is coming when no one can work." *In The Ozarks: Just That Much Hillbilly in Me,* critique of the hillbilly image is offered by southwestern Missouri natives and scholars to provide a rounded portrait of the term. However, the back cover of the video's case ultimately delineates the hillbilly as a virtuous construct accessible to Ozarkers and non-Ozarkers alike: "Through the interplay of archival images, music and commentary by historians, folklorists, artists and ordinary people, it becomes clear that traditional Ozarkers care deeply about what one participant in the film calls 'those old American values' of family, church, community and land. To the extent that we each share those values there's just that much hillbilly in all of us."

27. Embree, "Ozarks," 1; Braden, "Remembering Minister U. G. Johnson," 53. In the realm of Ozark education, no institution better illustrates the merger of religious sentiment and industriousness than the College of the Ozarks. Located just a few miles south of Branson, it was opened in 1907 as the School of the Ozarks. Initially, this Presbyterian-run facility was meant as a high school where youths could meet most of their educational expenses by working. Thus, academic learning and spiritual enhancement were supplemented by cooking, cleaning, plowing, harvesting, or a variety of other tasks. In 1958, a transition began to an institute of secondary education, and by the late 1960s, the School of the Ozarks was populated only by college-age students. In 1991, it changed its name to the College of the Ozarks, but it continued to combine religiously guided education with mandatory on-campus labor—an amalgamation that has provided the college with the nickname "Hard Work U." On the history of the College of the Ozarks, see Godsey and Godsey, *Flight of the Phoenix.*

28. "Ozarks Diaries of a Methodist Circuit Rider," 14; Hobbs, "Sadie McCoy Crank," 6.

29. Blevins, *Hill Folks,* 58.

30. Ledbetter, "Experiences of a Country Preacher," 12; Uncle Joe Cranfield quoted in Gilmore, *Ozark Baptizings, Hangings, and Other Diversions*, 81–82. For detailed accounts of brush arbor meetings in southwestern Missouri, see Robertson, "Campmeeting in the Ozarks," and Bilyeu, "Hundred Nights Revival of 1933."

31. *West Plains (MO) Journal*, 11 Feb. 1897; Emmett Yoeman quoted in Gilmore, *Ozark Baptizings, Hangings, and Other Diversions*, 78; Gilmore, *Ozark Baptizings, Hangings, and Other Diversions*, xxv. On the entertainment functions of revival preachers, see Weisberger, *They Gathered at the River*, and Moore, *Selling God*.

32. Owen, *Jim Owen's Hillbilly Humor*, 99; "It's Time for Our Annual Hootin' an' Hollarin' Celebration"; Scott, "It's a Brush Arbor Meeting," 19; Holden, *Hillbilly Preacher*, 30, 57, 88.

33. Wright, *Shepherd of the Hills*, 163, 68. In post–Civil War southwestern Missouri, numerous vigilance committees formed to combat lawlessness. However, these groups sometimes became unruly in turn—a scenario best illustrated by Taney County's Bald Knobbers in the 1880s. Originally assisting law-enforcement officials with the capture of criminals, they soon began to take justice into their own hands. In 1889, the Bald Knobbers killed two innocent men in Christian County and, because of these misdeeds, lost local and national support for their endeavors. On the Bald Knobbers, see Upton, *Bald Knobbers*.

34. Wright, *Shepherd of the Hills*, 36, 72, 173.

35. Morrow, "For Fun and Profit," 15; Morris, "Good Ol' Hillbilly . . . ," 188–189.

36. "Filling the Tourist with Bunk Stories"; Morrow and Myers-Phinney, *Shepherd of the Hills Country*, 200. Blevins, *Hill Folks*, 221.

37. J. K. Ross, "The Hill Billy," *White River Leader*, 10 Sept. 1915; Spurlock, *Over the Old Ozark Trails*, 10.

38. Spurlock, *Over the Old Ozark Trails*, 59–60.

39. Saults, "Gently down the Stream," 79; "Jim M. Owen Dies: King of the Hillbillies," *Springfield Leader & Press*, 12 July 1972, 43. For a detailed description of an Owen Boat Line float trip written by a former guide, see Sare, *Some Recollections of an Ozarks Float Trip Guide*.

40. Jarman, "Idyll in the Ozarks," 37, 94; Stallcup, "Famous Age of the Owen Boat Line," 29–30. Owen's trips were often described with the use of religious imagery, but on some occasions they exhibited explicit religious practice. For instance, he once entertained a party headed by a Roman Catholic bishop who filled his boat with candles, vestments, and sacred vessels. Each morning the cleric said morning mass on the gravel bars. See Jarman, "Idyll in the Ozarks," 88.

41. Godsey, "King of the Floaters"; Madsen, *Branson*, 23–24. Attesting to the work-related ambiguities that pervade the hillbilly persona, the *Life* cover story on the Owen Boat Line described diligent guides who "did everything" for their guests while at the same time labeling the float trip as the "laziest kind of sport." See "Life Goes Fishing."

42. Owen, *Jim Owen's Hillbilly Humor*, 8–9, 118; Saults, "Gently down the Stream," 79. Paul Henning, the creator and producer of *The Beverly Hillbillies*, wrote a brief introduction to *Jim Owen's Hillbilly Humor*.

43. Owen, *Jim Owen's Hillbilly Humor*, 23, 19, 22, 118. An anecdote from this book best illustrates the author's support for nondenominational religiosity. In this account, several farmers were discussing the merits of their town's various churches and denominations.

Many opinions were expressed, and then the elder of the group was asked his thoughts. He replied, "I'm thinking that there are three ways from here to the cotton gin. But when you get there, the ginner ain't going to ask which way you took. He's going to ask, 'How good is your cotton?'" See ibid., 50.

44. Frank Farmer, "Day as No Other for Jim Owen," *Springfield News & Leader*, 14 May 1967, A1; Brim, "Plumb Nellie Days"; "Jim M. Owen Dies," 47.

45. Williamson, *Hillbillyland*, 37–38, 39–40, 62, 55; Harkins, *Hillbilly*, 160.

46. Harkins, *Hillbilly*, 161; Austin, "Real Beverly Hillbillies"; Parker, "Shangri-La," 23.

47. Harkins, "Hillbilly in the Living Room," 99–109; "Come 'n Listen to My Story 'bout a Man Named . . . Paul."

48. Harkins, "Hillbilly in the Living Room," 114; Newcomb, "Appalachia on Television," 322–323. Although Newcomb posits a rural wisdom tradition in *The Beverly Hillbillies* ethos, he also points to numerous negative stereotypes that permeate the show. Ultimately, he concludes that its "real viciousness" is not the making fun of mountaineers. Instead, because the characters' morality is like the "simple virtue of children," the harm comes in infantilizing adult populations of southerners and thereby projecting viewers' desires for lost innocence (323–324). Other scholars of Appalachia have presented a much less nuanced take on the program. Commenting on *The Beverly Hillbillies* and a host of other media representations of the region, David Whisnant stated, "In their gross insensitivity to the feelings of Appalachian people, to their spiritual and material needs, and to the richness and variety of their culture, the media have been agents of a broader pattern of cultural imperialism." See Whisnant, "Ethnicity and the Recovery of Regional Identity in Appalachia," 129.

49. Lewis, "Golden Hillbillies," 31; "Corn Is Green," 70. Reflecting on the dialectic of meaning found within *The Beverly Hillbillies'* characterizations, eastern Tennessee correspondent and radio commentator Mack Morris wrote, "We alternately seem to swing, as a regional group, from one image to another in the eyes of much of the rest of the nation. . . . This swing from one extreme to the other occurs with remarkable regularity . . . and is enough to set up a sort of schizophrenia—as a matter of fact, I think it has, in us and in the rest of the country regarding us—which may explain the popularity of 'The Beverly Hillbillies.'" Quoted in Day, "Pride and Poverty," 376.

50. "Back to the Hills" (episode of *The Beverly Hillbillies*); Herschend, interview.

51. Cook, *Welcome to Branson*, 156–157.

52. Guest comments, Presleys' Country Jubilee, Oct. 2004–May 2005, in the author's collection.

53. Robbins, "A Lyin' to Them Tourists," 82.

54. Ron Sylvester, "Branson's Style Definition Changes with Musical Scene," *Springfield News-Leader*, 23 May 1993, 1F; Sanders, interview; Cook, *Welcome to Branson*, 157.

55. Jane Bennett, "How to Be a Professional Hillbilly," *Springfield Leader & Press*, 6 Sept. 1970, 1C, 4C; Fredrick, *Ozarks Hillbilly Editor*, 176–179.

56. Bennett, "How to Be a Professional Hillbilly," 1C, 4C.

57. Fredrick, *Ozarks Hillbilly Editor*, 179; Bennett, "How to Be a Professional Hillbilly," 1C, 4C; Wright, *Shepherd of the Hills*, 13–14.

58. Williamson, *Hillbillyland*, 27.

59. Dorothy Roe, "Ozark Hillbilly: Tycoon with 'Fringe Benefits,'" *Springfield Daily News*,

9 Aug. 1965. This notion of hillbilly industriousness has also been invoked outside the param-eters of the tourism industry. For instance, in 1995 Joe McNabb published *Ozark Hillbilly CEO: An Autobiography*. McNabb was born in 1913 in Cotter, Arkansas, and spent his early boyhood on the White River. When he was a teenager, his family moved to Stone County. After a stint in the navy, he began a career as an engineer and accepted a job with the Guy F. Atkinson Company in 1943. While with this firm, he served as construction manager for the Mangla Dam project in West Pakistan (the largest earth-filled dam in the world at the time), became company president in 1975, and was elected CEO in 1979. Echoing sentiments of vigorous work and hearty play offered by many Ozarkers, McNabb wrote, "Hillbillies are incredibly industrious. They are the type of people who would clear the trees from a little patch of ground and use the trees to build a house (usually a log home). Then they would plow the soil around the house and sow corn to make their favorite drink. . . . Hillbillies work hard and play hard. When they wanted to have some fun they cleared a spot in the woods, sawed up some logs, and built themselves a platform for dancing." See McNabb, *Ozark Hillbilly CEO*, 12.

60. Harkins, "Hillbilly in the Living Room," 100; Jones, *Dispossessed*, 209, 212; Votaw, "Hillbillies Invade Chicago," 64–66; Jacobson, *Whiteness of a Different Color*, 4.

61. Rafferty, *Ozarks*, 41–66.

62. "'Queen of the Hillbillies' Reigns No More," *Springfield Leader & Press*, 22 Feb. 1979, 1B; May Kennedy McCord, "Hillbilly Heartbeats," *Springfield Leader & Press*, 6 Aug. 1933.

63. McCord, "Hillbilly Heartbeats" (in *Rayburn's Ozark Guide*), 33; Godsey and Godsey, "Queen of the Hillbillies," 15, 26; Pyles, "Remembering May Kennedy McCord," 68.

64. Stone County Historical Society, *History of Stone County, Missouri*, 238; McCord, "Hillbilly Heartbeats," *Ozark Life*, Jan. 1930, 16.

65. McCord, "Vanishing Ozarker," 55.

66. Rayburn, *Ozark Country*, 36; Rayburn, "Progress in the Ozarks," 3; Simpson, "Otto Ernest Rayburn," 164; Burnett, *When the Presbyterians Came to Kingston*, 38–39.

67. Simpson, "Otto Ernest Rayburn," 162–163; Burnett, *When the Presbyterians Came to Kingston*, 186–187.

68. Ron Sylvester, "Setting the Stage," *Springfield News-Leader*, 9 July 1994, 1G, 10G; U.S. Census Bureau, *Taney County, Missouri, Profile of General Demographic Characteristics, 2000* (Washington, DC: GPO, 2000); U.S. Census Bureau, *Stone County, Missouri, Profile of General Demographic Characteristics, 2000* (Washington, DC: GPO, 2000); Smith, 1A. On occasion, con-temporary commentators still connect southwestern Missouri culture to an Anglo-Saxon heritage. For instance, travel writer Fred Pfister wrote in 2002 that "like their Celtic ances-tors," these modern-day Ozarkers are "passionate about love, politics, and religion" and can be "deeply stirred by the natural beauty of the hills or be emotionally responsive to music and the spoken word." See Pfister, *Insiders' Guide to Branson and the Ozark Mountains*, 25.

69. Frommer, *Arthur Frommer's Branson*, 34; Laskas, "Branson in My Rearview Mirror," 174; Bill Smith, "Branson Attracts Few Blacks," *St. Louis Post-Dispatch*, 23 July 1995, 1A. Other black entertainers in Branson include doo-wop group The Platters and Nedra Culp, a soul singer who has won the city's "Vocalist of the Year" award on several occasions.

70. Tom Uhlenbrock, "From Japan with Love . . . for Country Music," *St. Louis Post-Dis-patch*, 21 Apr. 2002, T1; Morrissey, "King of Branson," 72; Booe, "A Fiddlin'," 21.

71. Shoji Tabuchi Theatre press packet, 1998, in the author's collection; Felton, "Shoji Tabuchi Features Awesome Japanese Drumming," L10; Toni Stroud, "Branson, Mo.: Many Attractions but Music Is King," *Minneapolis Star Tribune,* 14 July 1996, 4G.

72. Freihofer, "Shoji Tabuchi."

73. Carolyn Tuft and Joe Holleman, "Inside the Christian Identity Movement," *St. Louis Post-Dispatch,* 5 Mar. 2000, A8.

74. Ibid.

75. Linda Leicht, "Branson Venues Should Spurn White Supremacists," *Springfield News-Leader,* 2 Apr. 2001, 1B.

76. Masterson, *Arkansas Folklore,* 187–189. According to folklorist William K. McNeil, authorship of the "Arkansas Traveler" is uncertain. He has argued that large portions of the dialogue predate the 1850s, with two of the exchanges going back to at least the early sixteenth century. See McNeil, "By the Ozark Trail," 21.

77. Randolph, *We Always Lie to Strangers,* 3; Randolph, *Ozarks,* 22, v. Randolph's penchant for premodern Ozark society and culture was blatantly exhibited on page 4 of *The Ozarks* when he stated that the region is "the most backward and deliberately unprogressive" in the United States.

78. Rayburn, *Forty Years in the Ozarks,* 89–90.

79. Randolph, *Funny Stories about Hillbillies,* 5–6.

80. Presley, interview.

CHAPTER 7. "THE AROMA OF GOD'S SPIRIT"

1. "BransonFunTrip's Roots Are Secure in the Blessings of Branson," media release, 23 Feb. 2006, in the author's collection.

2. "Branson Landing Is Taking Off," 15; Evans, "Welcome to Branson," 13.

3. H. Donald Gabriel, "The Branson Manifesto," 6 Mar. 2006, n.p., in the author's collection.

4. Lois Romano, "Branson, Mo., Looks beyond RVs and Buffets," *Washington Post,* 8 Aug. 2005, A3.

5. Ibid.; Kathryn Buckstaff, "Branson Courts Religious Groups," *Springfield News-Leader,* 8 Aug. 1999, 1A, 7A.

6. Szuszalski, interview. Although Trinity Tours caters to the Christian tourist more thoroughly than any other area business, many businesses include church group tours and conferences as an area of specialization. For instance, in 1998 Ozark Mountain Tour and Travel brought in five conventions of religious organizations—a Christian constituency that amounted to more than 10,000 individuals. See Buckstaff, "Branson Courts Religious Groups," 1A.

7. Worden, "Stafford Family Values," 58. The term "show-service," which obviously implies the mixture of traditional institutional church ceremonies and procedures with patented elements of Branson's variety show entertainment, is borrowed from Jessica H. Howard. See Howard, "America's Hometown," 95.

8. Kathryn Buckstaff, "Sunday Morning Shows Ruffle Feathers," *Springfield News-Leader,* 11 Aug. 2001, 7B, 8B; Linda Leicht, "Branson Taking the Spiritual Lead," *Springfield News-*

Leader, 4 Mar. 2006, 1C. Other show-services not discussed in this chapter include "Celebrate Sunday," a worship service held at the Remember When Theatre (located in the IMAX Entertainment Complex) and hosted by Sue O'Neal (the wife of Richard Daniel Clark, who created the "American Highrise" mural described in Chapter 4); a gathering conducted by New Horizons Ministry at the Welk Theater and Resort; "The Sunday Happening," led by Allen Edwards and offered at the Golden Corral restaurant; a service at the Majestic Theater led by pastor Dave Hamner; and entertainer Travis Loewen's Cowboy Chapel, a site located at the Canyon Creek Ranch which uses horses and steer to impart a religious message.

9. Buckstaff, "Sunday Morning Shows Ruffle Feathers," 8B.

10. Brunson, "Behind the Boom in Branson, Mo.," 47–48.

11. Ibid.

12. Ibid., 48; Fairchild, interview.

13. Fairchild, interview; Buckstaff, "Sunday Morning Shows Ruffle Feathers," 8B.

14. Stauffer, interview.

15. Ibid.; Smith, *Christian America,* 45; "Prayer of Agreement"; Stauffer, interview.

16. Stauffer, interview.

17. Ibid.; Todd, interview; Dawn Peterson, "Revival Fires Develops Faithful Following," *Springfield News-Leader,* 10 Mar. 1998, 10A.

18. Peterson, "Revival Fires Develops Faithful Following," 1A, 10A; Dawn Peterson, "Revival Expects Record Crowd," *Springfield News-Leader,* 31 Mar. 1998, 1A; Dawn Peterson, "Revival's Energy Renews Faith of Thousands," *Springfield News-Leader,* 2 Apr. 1998, 1A, 6A. Todd's camp meetings bear striking similarities to area show-services, and he actually considered entering that market. He has claimed that the Herschend family of Silver Dollar City, who once owned the Grand Palace, wanted "that [venue] to be used for God." In response, he had "an offer on the table" to purchase the theater and use it for weekly prayer gatherings but subsequently backed off the idea because of his advanced age. See Todd, interview.

19. Linda Leicht, "Ten Commandments Judge to Speak in Branson," *Springfield News-Leader,* 14 Mar. 2004, 1B; Jeff Arnold, "Humansville Stands United on Ten Commandments," *Springfield News-Leader,* 2 Apr. 2004, 1B.

20. Peterson, "Revival Expects Record Crowd," 7A; Robert Kelly, "Couple Delivering Bibles to Russian People," *St. Louis Post-Dispatch,* 13 Mar. 1995, 1; Todd, interview. Sunday show-services and Todd's revivals are only two of the many mergers of theater entertainment and more formal expressions of Christianity in Branson. For instance, in 1998, JoDee Herschend, wife of the Herschend Family Entertainment Corporation's executive vice president, started a venture similar to the Revival Fires camp meetings which was also held at the Grand Palace. Titled "1st Sunday," this event featured Branson-style family entertainment offered by local musicians, highlighted messages of salvation preached by speakers from the Billy Graham Evangelistic Association, and ended with an altar call. Held on the first Sunday of the month from March through October, the gathering was meant to convey the spiritual nature of Branson to tourists and to facilitate experiences of faith in a "nonthreatening environment." Although these services often attracted as many as two thousand people, they are no longer held. However, JoDee Herschend continues to engage in Christian outreach in the region through her Jesus Saves Inc. ministry. Additionally, since 1996 a National Day of Prayer celebration has been conducted at an area theater. The 1998 event drew fifteen

hundred people and included praise and songs by Wayne Newton and Tony Orlando. It also featured sermons by local clergy which asked God's blessing for the nation's military, government officials, educators, families, and media representatives. See Dawn Peterson, "1st Sunday Wins Praise," *Springfield News-Leader,* 8 June 1998, 1B, and Dawn Peterson, "Prayer Show Draws Believers," *Springfield News-Leader,* 8 May 1998, 1B.

21. Glazier, "Methodists Moved Out of a Dance Hall," 3; Keithly, e-mail interview. Glazier's brief article drew further correlations between Branson United Methodist Church and entertainment venues on the Strip by featuring a photo of its similarly styled facade alongside images of the Mel Tillis Theater, the Andy Williams Moon River Theatre, the Johnny Cash Theatre, and the Grand Palace.

22. Kathryn Buckstaff, "Churches Being Fruitful, Multiplying," *Springfield News-Leader,* 23 Feb. 2002, 1A; Bucher, interview. Our Lady of the Lakes is not the only area church to have recently rebuilt with the aid of tourist dollars. The Hollister Church of Christ moved into a new sanctuary in the spring of 2002 with the partial assistance of vacationer monies. Moreover, the First Baptist Church of Forsyth doubled the size of its building and moved it closer to Branson in the summer of 2002 with the use of similar funds. See Buckstaff, "Churches Being Fruitful, Multiplying," 1A, 14A.

23. "Mel Tillis Theater Becomes Church," 8; Plank, e-mail interview.

24. Plank, e-mail interview.

25. Howell, "Hobby Lobby's Heavenly Ascension"; "Statement of Purpose" (Hobby Lobby, Inc.).

26. Bob Baysinger, "Hobby Lobby Chain Stores Purchase Vacant Theater for Growing Church," *BP (Baptist Press) News,* 25 July 2003, www.bpnews.net/bpnews.asp?ID=16369 (accessed on 29 June 2004).

27. Kathryn Buckstaff, "'The Promise' Passes 1,000th Show," *Springfield News-Leader,* 21–23 Aug. 1998, 19E; Mark Marymount, "Show Mixes Religion, Pageantry," *Springfield-News Leader,* 2–4 Oct. 1998, 18E; Freihofer, "Church Leaders," 8.

28. Buckstaff, "'The Promise' Passes 1,000th Show," 19E; Tipton, "The Promise Returns," 24–25; "'The Promise' Customer Comments." Beginning in 2000, *The Promise* briefly shared its stage with *Two from Galilee,* a musical from the same production company which tells the story of Mary and Joseph prior to the birth of their son.

29. Tipton, "The Promise Returns," 25. In 1998, *The Promise* was named Branson's "Production of the Year," and Randy Brooks was honored as the "Male Entertainer of the Year" and the "Male Vocalist of the Year." In addition, that same year the show's cast received the "Gospel Artists of the Year" award at the All-America Music Awards, and it was chosen as one of the top three destination attractions in the United States by the American Bus Association.

30. The ambiguities of *The Promise*'s religious pageant/ministry and its tenuous existence as a profit-seeking and soul-saving venture were further accentuated by Jeff Hurst, cofounder of Branson's Victory Mountain Ministries: "The key is, *The Promise* is a for-profit entertainment production. They're not a ministry. It ministers and fits in the town well, but it's an expensive production and it's for-profit." See Jeff Hurst, interview.

31. Rotrock, interview.

32. "Church Leaders Praise Van Burch," 26.

33. "Branson Theaters Go Gospel," 52. In 2003, I posted a query to an online Branson tourism forum which asked, "I am interested in the religious content of Branson shows and attractions. I wondered if anyone had thoughts on this aspect of the tourism industry?" The tourist quotation offered in this paragraph was taken from a body of thirty-three responses to this inquiry. Other comments included: "You can just sense a Christian atmosphere in Branson"; the city's theaters possess "a very Christian attitude"; "Anyone believing in God would feel comfortable in Branson and in the shows"; people love Branson's religiously oriented attractions because they remind them of "everyday pleasures"; and "With so many non-Christian people/places/things out in the world, it [Branson] really makes for a nice change." All replies can be found on the GetAwaySaver Forums at www.getawaysaver.com/forum/showthread.php?threadid=5670.

34. Freihofer, "From 'Sorta' . . . to Saved," 37.

35. See the following articles by Kathryn Buckstaff in the *Springfield News-Leader:* "'I Am Just Amazed,'" 27 May 2006, 1A; "Sprawling New Subdivision Throttles Up Branson Boom," 10 Jan. 2006, 1A; "Branson Braces for Next Boom," 16 Oct. 2005, 1A; "Convention Center Bonds Sell Quickly," 25 Aug. 2005, 1B.

36. Sterling Marketing Group, Inc., "Branson: A Place, a Destination, a Brand," 26 Oct. 2004, marketing report, in the author's collection.

37. See the following articles in the *Springfield News-Leader:* "Who Visits Branson," 8 Sept. 1992, 6B; "The Tourism Boom," 4 Apr. 1992, 6F; "Branson Visitor Breakdown for 1994," 2 Feb. 1995, 1A; "Survey: Branson is THE Place to Be," 24 July 1992, 1A.

38. Branson/Lakes Area Chamber of Commerce and Convention and Visitors Bureau, Branson/Lakes Area 2005 Fact Sheet.

39. Buckstaff, "'I Am Just Amazed,'" 1A; Kathryn Buckstaff, "Culture of Values Key to Branson's Success," *Springfield News-Leader,* 27 Feb. 2005, 46L.

40. Buckstaff, "Culture of Values Key to Branson's Success," 46L; Buckstaff, "Branson Braces for Next Boom," 1A; Kathryn Buckstaff, "Star-Studded Beginning," *Springfield News-Leader,* 26 Oct. 2005, 1B; "Luxury Condo Demand Drives Record Sales," 5.

41. Kathryn Buckstaff, "Additional Ads May Draw More Visitors," *Springfield News-Leader,* 31 Mar. 2006, 5B; Niebuhr, *Social Sources of Denominationalism;* Laurie Goodstein and David D. Kirkpatrick, "On a Christian Mission to the Top," *New York Times* (online edition only), 22 May 2005, www.nytimes.com/2005/05/22/national/class/EVANGELICALS-FINAL.html?ex=1274414400&en=a745e9fcce50f35b&ei=5088&partner=rssnyt&emc=rss> (accessed on 10 July 2006); Corbin, "Impact of the American Dream on Evangelical Ethics," 340.

42. Frank, *What's the Matter with Kansas,* 89–109; Gabriel, "Branson Manifesto."

43. Kathryn Buckstaff, "Branson's Construction Building Future Prosperity," *Springfield News-Leader,* 26 Feb. 2006, 10J; Buckstaff, "Culture of Values Key to Branson's Success," 46L.

44. Kathryn Buckstaff, "Forty-Eight Stores Ready for Ribbon Cutting," *Springfield News-Leader,* 25 May 2006, 1A; Romano, "Branson, Mo., Looks beyond RVs and Buffets," A3.

Bibliography

MANUSCRIPT COLLECTIONS

Elgin, Robert L., Collection. Western Historical Manuscript Collection. University of Missouri–Rolla.

Godsey, Townsend, Papers. Ozarkiana Collection. College of the Ozarks, Point Lookout, Missouri.

Gunter, Rick J., Postcard Collection. Stevensville, Maryland.

Morrow, Lynn, Postcard Collection. Jefferson City, Missouri.

Rayburn, Otto Ernest, Collection. Special Collections. University of Arkansas, Fayetteville.

Shepard Room Collection. Library Center. Springfield-Greene County Public Library, Springfield, Missouri.

Short, Dewey, Papers. Western Historical Manuscript Collection. University of Missouri–Columbia.

Upton, Lucille Morris, Papers. Western Historical Manuscript Collection. University of Missouri–Columbia.

Wiley, Robert S., Collection. Western Historical Manuscript Collection. University of Missouri–Rolla.

Wright, Harold Bell, Collection. Special Collections. Pittsburg State University, Pittsburg, Kansas.

MOTION PICTURES AND TELEVISION PROGRAMS

The Big Killing. Paramount Pictures, 1928.

Comin' round the Mountain. Universal Pictures, 1951.

Deliverance. Warner Brothers, 1972.

Friendly Neighbors. Republic Pictures, 1940.

Joan of Ozark. Republic Pictures, 1942.

The Kettles in the Ozarks. Universal Pictures, 1956.

The Shepherd of the Hills. Story-Picture Corporation, 1919.

The Shepherd of the Hills. First National Pictures, 1927.

The Shepherd of the Hills. Paramount Pictures, 1941.

"Back to the Hills." *The Beverly Hillbillies.* 24 Sept. 1969, CBS.

"The Hillbilly Show." *The Jack Benny Program.* 20 Mar. 1958, CBS.

"The Hills of Home." *The Beverly Hillbillies.* 1 Oct. 1969, CBS.

"Jane Finds Elly a Man." *The Beverly Hillbillies.* 15 Oct. 1969, CBS.

"Silver Dollar City Fair." *The Beverly Hillbillies.* 8 Oct. 1969, CBS.

INTERVIEWS (ALL TRANSCRIPTS IN AUTHOR'S POSSESSION)

Albers, Jo Stacey. Branson historian. Interview by the author. Branson, Missouri, 23 Sept. 2002.

Boyd, Howard. Pastor, Branson Hills Assembly of God Church. Interview by the author. Branson, Missouri, 29 Sept. 2002.

Braschler, Cliff. Braschler Family Music Show. Interview by the author. Branson, Missouri, 16 Sept. 2002.

Bucher, Msgr. Phil. Our Lady of the Lakes Catholic Church. Interview by the author. Branson, Missouri, 23 Nov. 2002.

Buckstaff, Kathryn. Journalist, *Springfield News-Leader.* Interview by the author. Branson, Missouri, 10 Sept. 2002.

Deeds, Bob. Pastor, Silver Dollar City Wilderness Church. Interview by the author. Branson, Missouri, 20 July 2003.

Fairchild, Barbara. Interview by the author. Branson, Missouri, 12 Sept. 2002.

Freihofer, Richard. Publisher, *Branson Church Getaway Planner.* Interview by the author. Ozark, Missouri, 20 Sept. 2002.

Gold, Nadeine. Resort ministry coordinator, Mountain Country Ministries. Interview by the author. Highlandville, Missouri, 11 Sept. 2002.

Herschend, Pete. Executive vice president, Herschend Family Entertainment Corporation. Interview by the author. Branson, Missouri, 24 Sept. 2002.

Hughes, Leena. Owner, Hughes Brothers Theater. Interview by the author. Branson, Missouri, 19 Sept. 2002.

Hurst, Emma. Cofounder, Victory Mountain Ministries. Interview by the author. Branson, Missouri, 24 Sept. 2002.

Hurst, Jeff. Cofounder, Victory Mountain Ministries. Interview by the author. Branson, Missouri, 24 Sept. 2002.

Keithly, Don. Pastor, Branson United Methodist Church. E-mail interview by the author. 5 Dec. 2002.

Kellogg, Fr. Richard. Rector, Shepherd of the Hills Episcopal Church. Interview by the author. Branson, Missouri, 13 Sept. 2002.

Layher, Ron. Owner, Starlite Theatre. Interview by the author. Branson, Missouri, 12 Sept. 2002.

Lennon, Dan. Director of marketing and performer, Welk Theater and Resort. Interview by the author. Branson, Missouri, 25 Sept. 2002.

Linebaugh, Richard. General manager, Baldknobbers Jamboree. Interview by the author. 19 Sept. 2002.

McPhail, Bill. Founder, En-Gedi Ministries. Interview by the author. Near Reeds Springs, Missouri, 27 Sept. 2002.

Merry, Cindy. Branson entertainment consultant. Interview by the author. Branson, Missouri, 20 Sept. 2002.

Plank, David. Pastor, Tri-Lakes Cathedral. E-mail interview by the author. 10 Jan. 2003.

Presley, Raeanne. Sales and accounting manager, Presleys' Country Jubilee. Interview by the author. Branson, Missouri, 27 Sept. 2002.

Rotrock, Phyllis. Director, Branson Gospel Music Association. Interview by the author. Branson, Missouri, 18 Sept. 2002.

Sanders, Terri. Braschler Music Show. Interview by the author. Branson, Missouri, 16 Sept. 2002.

Scribner, Jay. Pastor, First Baptist Church. Interview by the author. Branson, Missouri, 18 Sept. 2002.

Smith, Brian. Sales/guest services director, Stonecroft Conference Center. Interview by the author. Hollister, Missouri, 17 Sept. 2002.

Stauffer, Sam. Pastor, Grand Old Gospel Hour. Interview by the author. Branson, Missouri, 23 Nov. 2002.

Szuszalski, Ed. Owner, Trinity Tours of Branson. Interview by the author. Branson, Missouri, 19 Sept. 2002.

Tate, Nahum. Telephone interview by the author. 12 June 2006.

Thurman, Keith. Director, Shepherd of the Hills Outdoor Theatre. Interview by the author. Branson, Missouri, 24 Sept. 2002.

Todd, Cecil. Founder, Revival Fires Ministries. Interview by the author. Branson, Missouri, 18 Sept. 2002.

Trent, Jean. Manager, Buck Trent Theater. Interview by the author. Branson, Missouri, 26 Sept., 2002.

Vecchio, Claudia. Former vice president of communications, Branson/Lakes Area Chamber of Commerce and Convention and Visitor's Bureau. Interview by the author. Branson, Missouri, 12 Sept. 2002.

Vorhaben, Shelly. Director of sales/marketing, Baldknobbers Jamboree. Interview by the author. 19 Sept. 2002.

Walters, Johnny. Braschler Family Music Show. Interview by the author. Branson, Missouri, 16 Sept. 2002.

Wells, Jim. Director of missions, Mountain Country Ministries. Interview by the author. Highlandville, Missouri, 11 Sept. 2002.

Wiebe, Ward. Director, Kanakuk Kamps. Interview by the author. Branson, Missouri, 11 Sept. 2002.

Wolfe, Tom. General manager, Andy Williams Moon River Theatre. Interview by the author. Branson, Missouri, 18 Sept. 2002.

BOOKS, ARTICLES, AND WEB-BASED SOURCES

Note: The *Branson Church Getaway Planner*, the source of several articles cited below, is a magazine distributed to approximately twenty thousand Christian congregations and church groups on a quarterly basis. It includes information about lodging, attractions, and performers deemed appropriate for the Christian tourist. The magazine is not held at any library.

However, copies can be requested by contacting Richard Freihofer, Editor and Publisher, *Branson Church Getaway Planner,* 1100 W. Oak St., Ozark, MO 65721. More information is available at www.bransonchurchgroups.com.

Abernathy, Barbara, and Mary H. Trimble. *Rose O'Neill.* Branson, MO, 1968.

Allcock, John B. "Tourism as a Sacred Journey." *Loisir et Societe* 11, no. 1 (1988): 33–48.

American Highrise. www.americanhighrise.com. 5 May 2003 (accessed on 9 Dec. 2003).

Ammerman, Nancy T. "Golden Rule Christianity: Lived Religion in the American Mainstream." In *Lived Religion in America: Toward a History of Practice,* edited by David D. Hall, 196–216. Princeton, NJ: Princeton University Press, 1997.

Angus, Fern. "Rose O'Neill." In *In the Heart of Ozark Mountain Country: A Popular History of Stone and Taney Counties, including Branson, Missouri,* edited by Frank Reuter, 122–124. Reeds Spring, MO: White Oak Press, 1992.

Arnold, Mark J. "Uncertainty in the Gaming Industry: Lessons from Missouri." *Review of Business,* 22 Mar. 1997, 14–19.

Asbell, Bernard. "The Vanishing Hillbilly." *Saturday Evening Post,* 23 Sept. 1961, 92–95.

Austin, Wade. "The Real Beverly Hillbillies." *Southern Quarterly* 19, nos. 3–4 (1981): 83–94.

Babcock-Abrahams, Barbara. "'A Tolerated Margin of Mess': The Trickster and His Tales Reconsidered." *Journal of the Folklore Institute* 11 (1975): 147–186.

Baker, Jesse E. "The Bishop of the Ozarks." *Missouri Magazine,* June 1933, 7–8.

Bates, Patricia. "Herschends Turn SDC into Multi-Million Dollar Empire." *Amusement Business* 103, no. 50 (1991).

Batteau, Allen W. *The Invention of Appalachia.* Tucson: University of Arizona Press, 1990.

Baudrillard, Jean. *Simulations.* New York: Semiotext(e), 1983.

Baugh, Helen Duff. *The Story Goes On.* Kansas City, MO: Stonecroft Publications, 1984.

Bebbington, David. *Evangelicalism in Britain: A History from the 1730s to the 1980s.* London: Unwin Hyman, 1989.

Bederman, Gail. "'The Women Have Had Charge of the Church Work Long Enough': The Men and Religion Forward Movement of 1911–1912 and the Masculinization of Middle-Class Protestantism." *American Quarterly* 41 (1989): 432–465.

Bellah, Robert. *Beyond Belief: Essays on Religion in a Post-Traditionalist World.* 1970. Berkeley: University of California Press, 1991.

———. *The Broken Covenant.* 1975. New York: Seabury, 1992.

Berger, Peter. *The Sacred Canopy: Elements of a Sociological Theory of Religion.* Garden City, NY: Doubleday, 1967.

Bilyeu, Thelma. "The Hundred Nights Revival of 1933." *OzarksWatch* 10, nos. 1–4 (1997): 105.

"Biography." Gary McSpadden Ministries. www.garymcspadden.com. 19 Mar. 2003 (accessed on 11 Sept. 2003).

"Biography." Randy Plummer. www.randyplummer.com. 1 May 2000 (accessed on 21 Oct. 2003).

Birdsong, R. A. "Near Heaven." *Rayburn's Ozark Guide* 26 (1950): 48.

Bland, Elizabeth L. "Country Music's New Mecca." *Time,* 26 Aug. 1991, 64.

Blevins, Brooks. *Hill Folks: A History of Arkansas Ozarkers and Their Image.* Chapel Hill: University of North Carolina Press, 2002.

Bohner, Martha Hoy. "It All Started with a Hole in the Ground." *Ozarks Mountaineer* 48, no. 2 (2000): 32–34.

Booe, Martin. "A Fiddlin'." *USA Weekend*, 2–4 Apr. 1993, 20–21.

Boorstin, Daniel J. *The Image: A Guide to Pseudo-Events in America*. New York: Harper and Row, 1964.

Bourdieu, Pierre. *Outline of a Theory of Practice*. Translated by Richard Nice. Cambridge: Cambridge University Press, 1977.

Bowers, William. *The Country Life Movement in America: 1900–1920*. Port Washington, NY: Kennikat Press, 1974.

Braden, Charles S. *Spirits in Rebellion: The Rise and Development of New Thought*. Dallas: Southern Methodist University Press, 1963.

Braden, Jerry. "Remembering Minister U. G. Johnson." *Ozarks Mountaineer* 45, no. 1 (1997): 53.

Brandon, S. G. F. "Trickster." In *A Dictionary of Comparative Religion*, edited by S. G. F. Brandon, 623. New York: Charles Scribner's Sons, 1970.

Branson Area Environmental Task Force. "Executive Summary." 16 Nov. 1992, 1–16.

"Branson Landing Is Taking Off!" *Branson Landing* 2, no. 2 (2005): 15.

"Branson Singing Star Guided by Psalm 37:4." *Branson Church Getaway Planner* 3, no. 1 (2000): 16.

"Branson Theaters Go Gospel!" *Branson Church Getaway Planner* 4, no. 2 (2001): 52.

Branson Veterans Task Force. www.bransonveterans.com. 6 May 2003 (accessed on 8 Dec. 2003).

Branson/Lakes Area Chamber of Commerce and Convention and Visitors Bureau. Branson/Lakes Area 2004 Fact Sheet.

———. Branson/Lakes Area 2005 Fact Sheet.

Brim, Billye. "The Vision of Prayer Mountain." Billye Brim Ministries. www.billyebrim.com/PrayerMountain.htm. 13 Apr. 2003 (accessed on 11 Mar. 2004).

Brim, Robert. "Plumb Nellie Days." Branson Webzine. www.bransonwebzine.com/content/plumb-nellie_99.htm. 13 May 2004 (accessed on 13 May 2004).

Brown, Dona. *Inventing New England: Regional Tourism in the Nineteenth Century*. Washington, DC: Smithsonian Institution Press, 1995.

Brown, Irene. "Ozark Playgrounds Add New Tourist Attraction." *Ozark Guide Yearbook* (1963): 63.

Brown, Norman O. *Hermes the Thief: The Evolution of a Myth*. New York: Random House, 1969.

Bruce, Dickson, Jr. *And They All Sang Hallelujah: Plain-Folk Camp-Meeting Religion, 1800–1845*. Knoxville: University of Tennessee Press, 1974.

Brunson, Rick. "Behind the Boom in Branson, Mo." *Charisma*, July 1993, 47–50.

Buckstaff, Kathryn. "A Real Christmas Story." *All Roads Lead to Branson: Branson's Entertainment Quarterly*, Holiday 2001 edition, 26–27.

Burgess, Stanley. "Perspectives on the Sacred: Religion in the Ozarks." *OzarksWatch* 2, no. 2 (1988): 4–7.

Burnett, Abby. *When the Presbyterians Came to Kingston, Kingston Community Church, 1917–1951*. Kingston, AR: Bradshaw Mountain Publishers, 2000.

Burton, Stephen. "Rockaway Beach." *Branson Traveler Magazine*, Mar. 1992, 9–11.

Bush, George. "Remarks at a Bush-Quayle Rally in Branson, Missouri, on August 21, 1992."

The Museum at the George Bush Presidential Library. http://bushlibrary.tamu.edu/research/papers/1992/92082102.html. 14 May 2004 (accessed on 17 May 2004).

Call, Cora Pinkley. "We Are Mountaineers, Not Hill-Billies." *Ozarks Mountaineer* 2, no. 4 (1953): 10.

Campbell, Colin. *The Romantic Ethic and the Spirit of Modern Consumerism*. Oxford: Blackwell, 1987.

Campbell, LeAnn. "Forty Years of Life on the Road." *Ozarks Mountaineer* 46, no. 2 (1998): 30–31.

Carlin, Richard. *The Big Book of Country Music: A Biographical Encyclopedia*. New York: Penguin Books, 1995.

Carney, George O. "Branson: The New Mecca of Country Music." *Journal of Cultural Geography* 14 (Spring–Summer 1994): 17–32.

Cartwright, Colbert S. *Candles of Grace: Disciples Worship in Perspective*. St. Louis: Chalice Press, 1992.

Chandler, Arline. "Silver Dollar City's Future Is its Past." *Branson Review* 8, no. 3 (2000).

———. "A Tale of Two Men Leads to One City." *Branson's Review* 8, no. 3 (2000): 26–29.

Chidester, David. "The Poetics and Politics of Sacred Space: Towards a Critical Phenomenology of Religion." In *From the Sacred to the Divine: A New Phenomenological Approach*, edited by Anna-Teresa Tymieniecka, 211–231. Dordrecht, the Netherlands: Kluwer Academic Publishers, 1994.

Chidester, David, and Edward T. Linenthal, eds. *American Sacred Space*. Bloomington: Indiana University Press, 1995.

Christian County Centennial, Inc. *Christian County: Its First 100 Years*. Nixa, MO: A & J Printing, 1959.

"Christian Family Weekend." The Shepherd of the Hills Homestead and Outdoor Theater. www.theshepherdofthehills.com/events/christ_family.htm. 13 Aug. 2003 (accessed on 3 June 2003).

"Church Getaway Feedback." *Branson Church Getaway Planner*, 7, no. 3 (2004).

"Church Group Feedback." *Branson Church Getaway Planner* 6, no. 2 (2003): 12.

"Church Leaders Praise Van Burch and His Award-Winning Illusions." *Branson Church Getaway Planner* 3, no. 3 (2000): 26.

Cochran, Robert. "People of His Own Kind: Vance Randolph's Kansas Years." *Little Balkans Review* 1, no. 2 (1980–1981): 1–18.

———. *Vance Randolph: An Ozark Life*. Urbana: University of Illinois Press, 1985.

Cohen, Erik. "Tourism as Play." *Religion* 15 (1985): 291–304.

"Come 'n Listen to My Story 'bout a Man Named . . . Paul." *Examiner*, 3 Feb. 2001. http://examiner.net/stories/020301/fea_020301001.shtml (accessed on 22 May 2004).

Comstock, G. M. "An Ozark Pageant." *Bull Shoals Gazette*, Oct. 1952, 3.

Cook, Bruce. *Welcome to Branson, Missouri: The Town That Country Built*. New York: Avon Books, 1993.

Corbin, Wyndy. "The Impact of the American Dream on Evangelical Ethics." *CrossCurrents* 55 (2005): 340–350.

Corliss, Richard. "If Heaven Ain't a Lot Like Disney: Theme Parks Created in Uncle Walt's Image Offer a Sanitized Suburban Utopia." *Time*, 16 June 1986, 80.

Corn, David, and Dan Moldea. "Did Ashcroft Take the Low Road on the Highroad?" *Nation* (online edition only), 15 Jan. 2001. http://ssl.thenation.com/doc.mhtml?i=20010129&s=corn20010115 (accessed on 7 Aug. 2005).

"The Corn Is Green." *Newsweek,* 3 Dec. 1962, 70.

Cosgrove, Dennis. "Place, Landscape and the Dialectics of Cultural Geography." *Canadian Geographer* 22 (1978): 66–72.

Cox, Vicki. "Branson's Very Own Yankee Doodle Dandy." *Branson Living* 2, no. 2 (1996): 20–24.

Culler, J. "Semiotics of Tourism." *American Journal of Semiotics* 1, nos. 1–2 (1981): 127–140.

Cusic, Don. *The Sound of Light: A History of Gospel Music.* Bowling Green, OH: Bowling Green University Popular Press, 1990.

Cutter, Charles. *Cutter's Guide to Eureka Springs, Arkansas.* St. Louis: Cutter and Trump, 1884.

Daly, Lewis C. "A Church at Risk: The Episcopal 'Renewal Movement.'" *Institute for Democracy Studies Insights* 2, no. 2 (2001): 1–9.

Daniels, Bruce C. *Puritans at Play: Leisure and Recreation in Colonial New England.* New York: St. Martin's Press, 1995.

Day, Ronnie. "Pride and Poverty: An Impressionistic View of the Family in the Cumberlands of Appalachia." In *Appalachia Inside Out—Culture and Customs,* ed. Robert J. Higgs, Ambrose N. Manning, and Jim Wayne Miller. Knoxville: University of Tennessee Press, 1995.

DeArmont, Fred. "Progress at Table Rock." *Missouri News Magazine,* 19 Sept. 1959, 22–23.

Deffenbaugh, Nola. "The Ministry of Harold Bell Wright." *Ozarks Mountaineer,* 47, no. 1 (1999): 38–39.

Desmond, Jane C. *Staging Tourism: Bodies on Display from Waikiki to Sea World.* Chicago: University of Chicago Press, 1999.

Dickinson, Asa. *The Best Books of Our Time.* New York: H. W. Wilson Co., 1934.

Doctorow, E. L. *The Book of Daniel.* New York: Random House, 1971.

Donaldson, Malinda. "The Hillbilly." *Arcadian Life Magazine,* Spring–Summer 1943, 16–17.

Douglas, Mary. *Purity and Danger.* London: Penguin Books, 1970.

DuBois, Alice Darby. "Early Days on Taneycomo." *Ozarks Mountaineer* 21, no. 2 (1973): 22.

Duede, Angie. "Vietnam Veteran Visits Branson." *All Roads Lead to Branson: Branson's Entertainment Quarterly,* Holiday 2001 edition, 48–49.

Duncan, James S. "The Social Construction of Unreality: An Interactionist Approach to the Tourist's Cognition of Environment." In *Humanistic Geography,* edited by David Ley and Marwyn S. Samuels, 269–282. Chicago: Maaroufa Press, 1978.

Eco, Umberto. *Travels in Hyperreality.* London: Picador, 1986.

Eliade, Mircea. *The Sacred and the Profane: The Nature of Religion.* New York: Harcourt Brace, 1959.

Elliot, Frank. "Ozark Mountain Magic." *Fun World* (official magazine of the International Association of Amusement Parks and Attractions), Nov. 2000, 56–63.

Ellis, Michael. "Just How 'Old' Is Ozarks English?" *OzarksWatch* 8, no. 3 (1995): 26–29.

Ellison, Curtis W. *Country Music Culture: From Hard Times to Heaven.* Jackson: University Press of Mississippi, 1995.

———. "Keeping Faith: Evangelical Performance in Country Music." In *Reading Country Music: Steel Guitars, Opry Stars, and Honky-Tonk Bars,* edited by Cecelia Tichi, 121–152. Durham, NC: Duke University Press, 1998.

Embree, David. "The Ozarks: Buckle of the Bible Belt or Haven for Religious Diversity?" *OzarksWatch* 12, nos. 3–4 (1999): 1–5.

Emery, Capt. J. B. "Description of Marble Cave, Missouri." *Kansas City Review of Science* 8 (1885): 614–622.

Encyclopedia of Fundamentalism, ed. Brenda E. Brasher. New York: Routledge, 2001.

Entrikin, Nicholas. *The Betweenness of Place: Toward a Geography of Modernity.* Baltimore: Johns Hopkins University Press, 1991.

Estabrook, Arthur H. "The Population of the Ozarks." *Mountain Life and Work* 5 (1929): 2–3, 25–28.

Evans, Dennis. "Welcome to Branson!" *Branson Landing* 2, no. 2 (2005): 13.

Felton, Tammy. "Shoji Tabuchi Features Awesome Japanese Drumming." *Travelhost,* June/July 1997, L10.

Ferre, John P. *A Social Gospel for Millions: The Religious Bestsellers of Charles Sheldon, Charles Gordon, and Harold Bell Wright.* Bowling Green, OH: Bowling Green State University Popular Press, 1988.

Ferrell, Will. "The Ozarks." *Ozarks Mountaineer* 14, no. 1 (1966): 27.

"A Few Words from Mike Radford." *Branson Church Getaway Planner* 6, no. 2 (2003).

"Filling the Tourist with Bunk Stories." *Missouri Magazine,* May 1929, 14.

Finke, Roger, and Rodney Stark. *The Churching of America, 1776–1990: Winners and Losers in Our Religious Economy.* New Brunswick, NJ: Rutgers University Press, 1992.

"'First Lady' of the Ozarks." *Rayburn's Ozark Guide* 18 (1948): 27.

FitzGerald, Frances. "Reflections: Jim and Tammy." *New Yorker,* 23 Apr. 1990, 45–87.

Flannagan, Hallie. *Arena: The History of the Federal Theatre.* New York: Benjamin Bloom, 1940.

"Forum Index." Andy Williams: The Official Website. http://andywilliams.com/bb/viewtopic.php?t=96, 22 Mar. 2006 (accessed on 20 June 2006).

Francaviglia, Damien. "Branson, Missouri: Regional Identity and the Emergence of a Popular Culture Community." *Journal of American Culture* 18, no. 2 (1995): 57–73.

Frank, Thomas. *What's the Matter with Kansas?* New York: Henry Holt and Co., 2004.

Fredrick, Leon. "A Little Helping Hand." *Branson's Review,* Oct.–Nov. 1999, n.p.

———. "Ozark Mountain Country." *Branson Traveler Magazine,* Feb. 1992, 4.

———. *Ozarks Hillbilly Editor.* Branson, MO: Leon Fredrick, 1995.

Freihofer, Richard. "Can You Solve the Mystery?" *Branson Church Getaway Planner* 2, no. 2 (1999): 3.

———. "Celebrate America: A Wild Ride beyond the 'Rah-Rah.'" *Branson Church Getaway Planner* 7, no. 3 (2004): 14–16.

———. "Church Leaders: These Hit Shows Can Help Your Church." *Branson Church Getaway Planner* 3, no. 1 (2000): 6.

———. "Comedy on a Mission." *Branson Church Getaway Planner* 5, no. 4 (2002–2003): 34–38.

———. "Dino." *Branson Church Getaway Planner* 4, no. 4 (2001–2002): 10–12.

———. "From 'Sorta' . . . to Saved!" *Branson Church Getaway Planner* 7, no. 4 (2004): 36–37.

———. "The Heart of the Matter." *Branson Church Getaway Planner* 3, no. 2 (2000): 4.

———. "The Hughes Brothers: The Show, the Family, & That Feeling!" *Branson Church Getaway Planner* 7, no. 1 (2004): 50–51, 58.

————. "Planning an Effective Church Getaway." *Branson Church Getaway Planner* 4, no. 2 (2001): 6.

————. "Review: Lost in the Fifties." *Branson Church Getaway Planner* 3, no. 3 (2000): 20.

————. "Shoji Tabuchi: 'Family Is Everything.'" *Branson Church Getaway Planner* 5, no. 4 (2002–2003): 10–14.

————. "Youth Getaways." *Branson Church Getaway Planner* 4, no. 1 (2001): 18.

Freihofer, Richard, and Becky Tipton. "Our Talks with Dino, Cheryl, and Gary, All about Their EasterSpring Spectacular March 24–April 7." *Branson Church Getaway Planner* 5, no. 1 (2002): 9–11.

Frizell, Michael Lewis. "A History of 'The Shepherd of the Hills' Dramatizations: The Branson Productions." Master's thesis, Southwest Missouri State University, 1996.

Frommer, Arthur. *Arthur Frommer's Branson!* New York: Macmillan Travel, 1995.

Gaither, Bill, and Jerry Jenkins. *Homecoming: The Story of Gospel Music through the Eyes of Its Best-Loved Performers.* Grand Rapids, MI: Zondervan Press, 1997.

"Galena, Missouri." *Ozark Magazine,* Jan.–Feb. 1915, 50.

Gall, Jeffrey L. "Presbyterians, Warren Wilson, and the Country Life Movement." *Journal of Presbyterian History* 76 (1998): 215–231.

Garrett, Leroy. *The Stone-Campbell Movement: The Story of the American Restoration Movement.* Abilene, TX: College Press, 1994.

Garrett, Willa. "'Hillbilly Heartbeats'—The 98 Years of May Kennedy McCord." *Ozarks Watch* 11, no. 2 (1998): 40–42.

Garvey, Mark. *Searching for Mary: An Exploration of Marian Apparitions across the U.S.* New York: Plume, 1998.

"Genuine Folks." *Rayburn's Ozark Guide* 18 (1948): 20.

Gideon, Gene. "Shepherd's Show." *Travel,* Aug. 1968, 9.

Gilmore, Robert K. "The Environment of Work." *OzarksWatch* 4, no. 1 (1990): 8–10.

————. *Ozark Baptizings, Hangings, and Other Diversions: Theatrical Folkways of Rural Missouri, 1885–1910.* Norman: University of Oklahoma Press, 1984.

————. "Rose O'Neill's Bonniebrook: An Emerging Tourist Attraction." *OzarksWatch* 3, no. 4 (1990): 19.

Gladden, Washington. *Applied Christianity.* Boston: Houghton, Mifflin and Co., 1886.

Glazier, Bob. "Methodists Moved out of a Dance Hall into the First Auditorium to Be Constructed on Branson's Famous 76 Country Boulevard." *Springfield!* 8, no. 11 (1992): 3.

Godsey, Helen, and Townsend Godsey. *Flight of the Phoenix: The Biography of the School of the Ozarks.* Point Lookout, MO: S of O Press, 1984.

————. "Queen of the Hillbillies." *Ozarks Mountaineer* 25, no. 11 (1977): 14–15, 26–27.

Godsey, Townsend. "Branson Presbyterian Church." *White River Valley Historical Quarterly* 9, no. 6 (1987): 12–13.

————. "The King of the Floaters." *Missouri Life* 5, no. 1 (1977): 67–74.

————. *Ozarks Mountain Folk: These Were the Last.* Branson, MO: Land Press, 1977.

Goff, James R. *Close Harmony: A History of Southern Gospel.* Chapel Hill: University of North Carolina Press, 2002.

Goforth, Alan. "New 'Celebration City' Adds to Family Fun in Branson." American Family

Association Online. http://headlines.agapepress.org/archive/5/afa/272003b.asp. 27 May 2003 (accessed on 15 June 2006).

————. "Not Your Parent's Branson." *Metro Voice* (Kansas City, MO) 14, no. 6 (2003): 8.

Gohr, Glenn. "Snapshots of the Pentecostal Movement." *OzarksWatch* 12, nos. 3–4 (1999): 17–23.

Greaux, E. L. "Architecture: Branson, Missouri." *Theater Crafts International,* May 1993, 27–35.

Green, Archie. "Hillbilly Music: Source and Symbol." *Journal of American Folklore* 78, no. 309 (1965): 204–228.

Green, Cheri. "Proud as Plumb Pudding." *Shepherd of the Hills Gazette,* Spring 2001, 10.

Green, James R. *Grass-Roots Socialism: Radical Movements in the Southwest, 1895–1943.* Baton Rouge: Louisiana State University Press, 1978.

Griffith, R. Marie. *God's Daughters: Evangelical Women and the Power of Submission.* Berkeley: University of California Press, 1997.

Grizzard, Eva Eakin. *Characters and Community of the Shepherd of the Hills.* Point Lookout, MO: Textor Printery, 1934.

Gubernick, Lisa. "A Curb on the Ego." *Forbes* 150, no. 6 (1992).

Gusewelle, C. W. "'A Continuity of Place and Blood': The Seasons of Man in the Ozarks." *American Heritage* 29, no. 1 (1978): 96–108.

Hall, David D. *Worlds of Wonder, Days of Judgment: Popular Religious Beliefs in Early New England.* Cambridge, MA: Harvard University Press, 1989.

Handy, Robert T. *The Social Gospel in America, 1870–1920.* New York: Oxford University Press, 1966.

Harkins, Anthony A. *Hillbilly: A Cultural History of an American Icon.* Oxford: Oxford University Press, 2004.

————. "The Hillbilly in the Living Room: Television Representations of Southern Mountaineers in Situation Comedies, 1952–1971." *Appalachian Journal* 29, nos. 1–2 (2002): 98–126.

"Harold Bell Wright." *Lawrence County Historical Society Bulletin,* Apr. 1988, 25–26.

"Harold Bell Wright Memorial Library." *Lawrence County Historical Society Bulletin,* July 1988, 1.

Hart, Irving Harlow. "The One Hundred Leading Authors of Best Sellers in Fiction from 1895 to 1944." *Publishers Weekly,* 19 Jan. 1946, 285–290.

Hartman, Mary. "Alf Bolin's Reign of Terror." In *In the Heart of Ozark Mountain Country: A Popular History of Stone and Taney Counties, including Branson, Missouri,* edited by Frank Reuter, 127–130. Reeds Springs, MO: White Oak Press, 1992.

Hartman, Viola. "The Shepherd of the Hills Drama." *White River Valley Historical Quarterly* 40, no. 1 (2000): 6–9.

Hatch, Nathan O. *The Democratization of American Christianity.* New Haven, CT: Yale University Press, 1989.

Hawethorne, Hildegarde. *Harold Bell Wright: The Man behind the Novels.* New York: D. Appleton, 1923.

Heavin, Hazel Dagley. "Hillbilly." *Rayburn's Ozark Guide* 21 (1949): 76.

"He Came from South Africa to Impart to You in Branson!" *Branson Church Getaway Planner* 4, no. 3 (2001)

Hendrickson, James. "Book People Come True." *Bookman,* Oct. 1925, 192–193.

Henry, Jerry. Corporate Director of Research, Herschend Family Entertainment Corporation. "Silver Dollar City Exit Summary, Summary of Positive Comments, Year to Date 2002."

Hensley, John R. "In the Shadow of Table Rock Dam: The Army Corps of Engineers, Civil Engineering and Local Communities." *Missouri Historical Review* 53 (1986): 255–272.

Herberg, Will. *Protestant, Catholic, Jew.* New York: Anchor Books, 1960.

Herbert, David. "Literary Places, Tourism and the Heritage Experience." *Annals of Tourism Research* 28 (2001): 312–333.

Hibler, Charles H. *Down in Arkansas.* Kansas City, MO: J. W. Smith, 1911.

Higgs, Robert J., Ambrose N. Manning, and Jim Wayne Miller, eds. *Appalachia Inside Out—Culture and Customs.* Knoxville: University of Tennessee Press, 1995.

"Hillbillies—To Be or Not to Be." *Ozarks Mountaineer* 15, no. 5 (1967): 12.

"The Hillbilly." *Rayburn's Ozark Guide* 48 (1956): 4.

"History of Chapel (Formerly Motor Coach) Ministry." Mountain Country Ministries. www.mtncountryministries.org/Motorcoach/mcmhist.htm. 7 July 2003 (accessed on 11 Mar. 2004).

"The History of Kanakuk." Kanakuk Kamps. www.kanakuk.com/about/history.aspx. 14 Dec. 2006 (accessed on 14 Dec. 2006).

Hively, Kay. *I'll Fly Away (The Story of Albert E. Brumley).* Branson, MO: Mountaineer Books, 1990.

———. "When the Chautauqua Came to Town." *Ozarks Mountaineer* 35, no. 2–3 (1987): 41.

Hobbs, Lora. "Sadie McCoy Crank: Pioneer Woman Preacher." *OzarksWatch* 12, nos. 3–4 (1999): 6–12.

Hobsbawm, Eric, and Terence Ranger. *The Invention of Tradition.* Cambridge: Cambridge University Press, 1983.

Hofstadter, Richard. *Anti-Intellectualism in American Life.* New York: Alfred A. Knopf, 1963.

Holden, I. E. *The Hillbilly Preacher.* 1959. Independence, KS: Religious Press, 1970.

Howard, Guy. *Walkin' Preacher of the Ozarks.* New York: Harper and Brothers, 1944.

Howard, Jessica H. "America's Hometown: Performance and Entertainment in Branson." Ph.D. diss., New York University, 1997.

Howell, Debbie. "Hobby Lobby's Heavenly Ascension." *Discount Store News,* 24 Jan. 2000. http://articles.findarticles.com/p/articles/mi_m3092/is_2_39/ai59177047 (accessed on 29 June 2004).

Hughes, George. "Authenticity in Tourism," *Annals of Tourism Research* 22 (1995): 781–803.

Hulsether, Mark. "Interpreting the 'Popular' in Popular Religion." *American Studies* 36, no. 2 (1995): 127–137.

Hutchinson, William R. *The Modernist Impulse in American Protestantism.* Cambridge, MA: Harvard University Press, 1966.

Hynes, William J. "Inconclusive Conclusions: Tricksters—Metaplayers and Revealers." In *Mythical Trickster Figures: Contours, Contexts, and Criticisms,* edited by William J. Hynes and William G. Doty, 202–217. Tuscaloosa: University of Alabama Press, 1993.

Iannaccone, Laurence. "Religious Markets and the Economics of Religion." *Social Compass* 39, no. 1 (1992): 123–131.

———. "Why Strict Churches Are Strong." *American Journal of Sociology* 99, no. 5 (1994): 1180–1211.

Ifkovic, Edward. "Harold Bell Wright and the Minister of Man: The Domestic Romancer at the End of the Genteel Age." *Markham Review* 4, no. 2 (1974): 22–25.

Ingenthron, Elmo. *The Land of Taney: A History of an Ozark Commonwealth.* Point Lookout, MO: School of the Ozarks Press, 1974.

"It's Time for Our Annual Hootin' an' Hollarin' Celebration." *Ozarks Mountaineer* 14, no. 8 (1966): 2.

Jacobson, Matthew Frye. *Whiteness of a Different Color: European Immigrants and the Alchemy of Race.* Cambridge:, MA Harvard University Press, 1998.

Jarman, Rufus. "Idyll in the Ozarks." *Saturday Evening Post,* 25 June 1955, 36–37, 88.

Jeansonne, Glen. *Gerald L. K. Smith: Minister of Hate.* New Haven, CT: Yale University Press, 1988.

"Jim Lane's Cabin." *Ozarks Mountaineer* 14, no. 1 (1966).

Jones, Charles T. "Brother Hal: The Preaching Career of Harold Bell Wright." *Missouri Historical Review* 1 (1984): 387–413.

Jones, Jacqueline. *The Dispossessed—America's Underclasses from the Civil War to the Present.* New York: Basic Books, 1992.

Jorstad, Erling. *Holding Fast/Pressing On: Religion in America in the 1980s.* New York: Greenwood Press, 1990.

Kalklasch, L. J. *The Healing Fountain: Complete History of Eureka Springs.* St. Louis: Chambers' Print, 1881.

Kansas City Southern Railway. *Kansas City Southern Ozarks.* Kansas City: Schooley Printers, 1924.

Karlis, George, Sotiria Grafanaki, and Jihan Abbas. "Leisure and Spirituality: A Theoretical Model." *Loisir et Societe* 25, no. 1 (2002): 205–214.

Keefe, John F. *The First 50 Years.* Jefferson City, MO: Missouri Department of Conservation, 1987.

Kelley, Dean. *Why Conservative Churches Are Growing: A Study in the Sociology of Religion.* 1972. Macon, GA: Mercer University Press, 1986.

Kelly, Susan Croce. "The First Lady of the Ozarks." *Midwest Motorist,* Aug. 1973, 8–9.

Ketchell, Aaron K. "The Precious Moments Chapel: Suffering, Salvation and the World's Most Popular Collectible." *Journal of American Culture* 22, no. 3 (1999): 27–33.

Kimball, Alice Mary. "White River Lure." *Rayburn's Ozark Guide* 18 (1948): 21.

King, Margaret J. "Disneyland and Walt Disney World: Traditional Values in Futuristic Form." *Journal of Popular Culture* 15, no. 1 (1981): 116–140.

King, Martin. "Another New Day Dawns for Oklahoma's Anita Bryant." *Baptist Messenger,* 12 Mar. 2003. www.baptistmessenger.com/issue/010816/7.html (accessed on 15 Dec. 2003).

Kirkendall, Rebecca Thomas. "Who's a Hillbilly?" *Newsweek,* 27 Nov. 1995, 22.

Kirshenblatt-Gimblett, Barbara. "Objects of Ethnography." In *Exhibiting Cultures: The Poetics and Politics of Museum Display,* edited by Ivan Karp and Steven D. Lavine, 386–443. Washington, DC: Smithsonian Institution Press, 1991.

Klise, Kay, and Crystal Payton. *The Insiders' Guide to Branson and the Ozark Mountains.* Springfield, MO: Gannett River States Publishing Corp., 1995.

Klopfer, Susan. *How Branson Got Started.* Branson, MO: Vanatech Press, 1997.

Koepping, Klaus-Peter. "Absurdity and the Hidden Truth: Cunning Intelligence and Grotesque Bodily Images as Manifestations of the Trickster." *History of Religions* 24, no. 3 (1985): 191–214.

Kropotkin, Peter. "What Geography Ought to Be." *Nineteenth Century* 18 (1885): 940–956.

Lancaster, James D., Jr., and Robert McGill. "Branson: A Country Music Phenomenon." In *In the Heart of Ozark Mountain Country: A Popular History of Stone and Taney Counties including Branson, Missouri,* edited by Frank Reuter, 37–46. Reeds Springs, MO: White Oak Press, 1992.

LaRoe, Lisa Moore. "Ozarks Harmony." *National Geographic* 193, no. 4 (1988): 76–99.

Laskas, Jeanne Marie. "Branson in My Rearview Mirror." *Gentlemen's Quarterly,* May 1994, 169–173, 201.

Laugeson, Alma Jones. "Old Matt's Cabin—A Woman and a Club Saved It for Posterity." *Ozarks Mountaineer* 10, no. 6 (1962): 8.

Lears, T. Jackson. *Fables of Abundance: A Cultural History of Advertising in America.* New York: Basic Books, 1995.

Ledbetter, Reverend Allen. "Experiences of a Country Preacher." *White River Valley Historical Quarterly* 7, no. 9 (1981): 12–13.

Levitt, Zola. "October 2001 Personal Letter." Zola Levitt Ministries. www.levitt.com/letters/2001-10.html. 26 June 2006 (accessed on 26 June 2006).

Lewis, Richard Warren. "The Golden Hillbillies." *Saturday Evening Post,* 2 Feb. 1963, 30–35.

Ley, David. "Social Geography and Social Action." In *Humanistic Geography: Prospects and Problems,* edited by David Ley and Marwyn Samuels, 41–57. Chicago: Maaroufa Press, 1978.

"Life Goes Fishing." *Life,* 23 June 1941, 86–89.

Lippy, Charles. *Being Religious American Style: A History of Popular Religiosity in the United States.* Westport, CT: Greenwood Press, 1994.

Love, Kathy. "The World of Townsend Godsey. " *Missouri Folklore Society Journal* 11–12 (1989–1990): 117–122.

Love, Robertus. "Making Niagras in the Ozarks." *Technical World Magazine* 20 (1913): 140.

"Luxury Condo Demand Drives Record Sales." *Branson Landing* 2, no. 2 (2005): 5.

MacCannell, Dean. *The Tourist: A New Theory of the Leisure Class.* New York: Shocken, 1976.

Madsen, Jerry S. *Branson: A Historical Time Line from 1680.* Galena, MO: Ozark Trails Magazine, 1997.

———. *The History: Those Who Walked with Wright.* Galena, MO: Ozark Trails Magazine, 1985.

Mahan, Karen. "Hillbilly Heart." *Ozarks Mountaineer* 38, nos. 10–11 (1990): 47.

Malone, Bill C. *Country Music, U.S.A.* Austin: University of Texas Press, 2002.

Martin, Ronald L. *Official Guide to Marvel Cave.* Springfield, MO: Ozark Mountain Publishers, 1974.

Masterson, James R. *Arkansas Folklore.* Little Rock, AR: Rose Publishing Co., 1974.

McAdoo, Julia. "Where the *Poor* Are *Rich.*" Reprinted in *Ozark Guide Yearbook* (1962): 13, 83–84.

McAllister, Lester G., and William E. Tucker. *Journey in Faith: A History of the Christian Church (Disciples of Christ).* St. Louis: Bethany Press, 1975.

McCall, Edith. "'Down Under' at Silver Dollar City." *Ozarks Mountaineer* 45, no. 6 (1997): 42–44.

McCord, May Kennedy. "Hillbilly Heartbeats." *Ozark Life,* Sept. 1929, 20.

————. "Hillbilly Heartbeats." *Ozark Life,* Jan. 1930, 16.

————. "Hillbilly Heartbeats." *Rayburn's Ozark Guide* 37 (1953): 33.

————. "The Vanishing Ozarker." *Rayburn's Ozark Guide* 36 (1953): 55–56.

McDannell, Colleen. *Material Christianity: Religion and Popular Culture in America.* New Haven, CT: Yale University Press, 1995.

McKinney, Edgar D. "Images, Realities, and Cultural Transformation in the Missouri Ozarks, 1920–1960." Ph.D. diss., University of Missouri–Columbia, 1990.

————. "Like Family: Kinship Perceptions of Ozarks Radio Entertainers and the Spread of Consumer Culture, 1934–1959." *Gateway Heritage* 11, no. 4 (1991): 26–39.

McNabb, Joe B. *Ozark Hillbilly CEO: An Autobiography.* Santa Rosa, CA: Wordsworth, 1995.

McNeil, W. K., ed. *Appalachian Images in Folk and Popular Culture.* 2d ed. Knoxville: University of Tennessee Press, 1995.

————. "'By the Ozark Trail': The Image of the Ozarks in Popular and Folk Songs." *JEMF Quarterly* 21, no. 75–76 (1985): 20–30.

Meadows, Chris. *Short Stories and Poems of the Ozark Hills.* Point Lookout, MO: School of the Ozarks Press, 1971.

"Mecca of All Tourists and Summer Visitors Centers around Lake Taneycomo District." *Missouri Magazine,* Apr.–May 1930, 11.

"Mel Tillis Theater Becomes Church." *Branson Church Getaway Planner* 5, no. 3 (2002): 8.

Mencken, Henry L. *Prejudices: Second Stories.* 1919. New York: Alfred A. Knopf, 1977.

Messenger, Troy. *Holy Leisure: Recreation and Religion in God's Square Mile.* Philadelphia: Temple University Press, 1999.

Millard, Bailey. "The Personality of Harold Bell Wright." *Bookman,* Jan. 1917, 463–469.

Miller, Harry A. "The Ozarks, Synonym for Surprises." *Missouri Magazine.* Nov. 1928, 12.

Miller, Marge. "What Rayburn's Ozark Guide Means to Me." *Rayburn's Ozark Guide* 35 (1953): 47.

Mills, C. Wright. *White Collar: The American Middle Classes.* New York: Oxford University Press, 1953.

Millsap, Marvin. "Branson Church Will Memorialize Harold Bell Wright." *Ozarks Mountaineer* 8, no. 9 (1960): 6.

Milstead, L. C. "Harold Bell Wright: Press Agent." *Bookman,* Jan. 1931, 501–502.

Mjagkij, Nina, and Margaret Spratt. *Men and Women Adrift: The YMCA and the YWCA in the City.* New York: New York University Press, 1997.

Monk, Charlene Faye. "Passion Plays in the United States: The Contemporary Outdoor Tradition." Ph.D. diss., Louisiana State University and Agricultural and Mechanical College, 1998.

Moore, Alexander. "Walt Disney World: Bounded Ritual Space and the Playful Pilgrimage Center." *Anthropological Quarterly* 53 (1980): 207–218.

Moore, R. Laurence. *Selling God: American Religion in the Marketplace of Culture.* New York: Oxford University Press, 1994.

Morgan, David. *Visual Piety: A History and Theory of Popular Religious Images.* Berkeley: University of California Press, 1998.

Morgan, Edmund. *The Puritan Family: Religion and Domestic Relations in Seventeenth-Century New England.* New York: Harper and Row, 1966.

Morrill, O. R. *The Story of Uncle Ike and the Shepherd of the Hills Characters.* Branson, MO: S. and S. Press, 1948.

Morris, Lucille. "Good Ol' Hillbilly. . . ." *University Review—A Journal of the University of Kansas City* 4, no. 2 (1937): 188–190.

Morrissey, Suzanne. "King of Branson." *Country America,* Nov. 1997, 70–73.

Morrow, Lynn. "For Fun and Profit: Hillbillies in Ozarks Popular Culture." *White River Valley Historical Quarterly* 38, no. 4 (1999): 15–24.

———. "Old Matt's Cabin." *OzarksWatch* 3, no. 4 (1990): 28–30.

———. "The St. Louis Game Park: Experiments in Conservation and Recreation." *White River Valley Historical Quarterly* 36, no. 4 (1997): 7–19.

———, ed. "The Wright Connection (Part I)." *White River Valley Historical Quarterly* 10, no. 1 (1988): 18–19.

———, ed. "The Wright Connection (Part II)." *White River Valley Historical Quarterly* 10, no. 2 (1989): 18–19.

Morrow, Lynn, and Linda Myers-Phinney. *Shepherd of the Hills Country: Tourism Transforms the Ozarks, 1880s–1930s.* Fayetteville: University of Arkansas Press, 1999.

Mott, Frank Luther. *Golden Multitudes: The Story of Best Sellers in the United States.* New York: Macmillan, 1947.

Munday, Dixon Wayne. "The Wright Trail: A Ministry in Print." Master's thesis, Northeast Missouri State University, 1991.

Murray, Barbara. "Jennifer Says Goodbye." *Branson Church Getaway Planner* 5, no. 1 (2002): 14.

Myers-Phinney, Linda. "Arcadia in the Ozarks: The Beginnings of Tourism in Missouri's White River Country." *OzarksWatch* 3, no. 4 (1990): 6–11.

Neal, Wes. *Branson Stars Booklet.* Branson, MO: Champions of Excellence Ministries, 1999.

Newcomb, Horace. "Appalachia on Television: Region as Symbol in American Popular Culture." In *Appalachian Images in Folk and Popular Culture,* edited by W. K. McNeil, 314–329. Knoxville: University of Tennessee Press, 1995.

"The New Jim Bakker TV Show Acquires Camelot!" *Branson Church Getaway Planner* 8, no. 1 (2005).

Niebuhr, H. Richard. *The Social Sources of Denominationalism.* Gloucester, MA: Henry Holt and Co., 1929.

Noble, Kingsley. "Creatures of Perpetual Night." *Scientific American* 139 (1928): 430–432.

Noll, Mark A. *American Evangelical Christianity: An Introduction.* Oxford: Blackwell Publishers, 2001.

Nord, David Paul. "The *Appeal to Reason* and American Socialism, 1901–1920." *Kansas History* 1 (Spring 1978): 75–89.

O'Neill, Rose. *The Story of Rose O'Neill: An Autobiography.* Edited by Miriam Farmanek-Brunell. Columbia: University of Missouri Press, 1997.

Orr, J. W. *Pictorial Guide to the Falls of Niagara: A Manual for Visitors.* Buffalo, NY: Salisbury and Clapp, 1842.

Orsi, Robert. "Everyday Miracles: The Study of Lived Religion." In *Lived Religion in America: Toward a History of Practice,* edited by David D. Hall, 3–21. Princeton, NJ: Princeton University Press, 1997.

Ostling, Richard N. "Of God and Greed: Bakker and Falwell Trade Charges in Televangelism's Unholy Row." *Time,* 8 June 1987, 70.

———. "TV's Unholy Row: A Sex-and-Money Scandal Tarnishes Electronic Evangelism." *Time,* 6 Apr. 1987, 60.

"Our Guiding Principles." Focus on the Family. www.family.org/welcome/aboutof/a000 0075.cfm. 11 Dec. 2003 (accessed on 11 Dec. 2003).

Overton, Grant M. *American Nights Entertainment.* New York: D. Appleton, 1923.

Owen, Jim M. *Jim Owen's Hillbilly Humor,* New York: Pocket Books, 1970.

"The Ozarks Diaries of a Methodist Circuit Rider, 1836–1839." *OzarksWatch* 2, no. 2 (1988): 14.

"The Ozarks Have Had Two Walking Preachers." In *Twice Told Tales and an Ozark Photo Album,* edited by Cliff Edom and Vi Edom, 51. Columbia, MO: Kelly Press, 1987.

"Ozark Wit and Humor." *White River Valley Historical Quarterly* 1, no. 3 (1962): 6.

Parker, H. Jane. "Engendering Identity(s) in a Rural Arkansas Ozark Community." *Anthropological Quarterly* 65 (1992): 148–155.

Parker, Ken. "Shangri-La." *Rayburn's Ozark Guide* 28 (1951): 23.

Patten, Simon. *The New Basis of Civilization.* London: Macmillan, 1907.

Payton, Crystal. *The Story of Silver Dollar City: A Pictorial History of Branson's Famous Ozark Mountain Theme Park.* Springfield, MO: Lens and Pen Books, 1997.

Payton, Leland. *The Beautiful and Enduring Ozarks.* Springfield, MO: Lens and Pen Press, 1999.

Pelton, Robert D. *The Trickster in West Africa: A Study of Mythic Irony and Sacred Delight.* Berkeley: University of California Press, 1980.

"A Perfect American Town: Utopia, Missouri." *Economist,* 24 Dec. 1994, 25–27.

Pfister, Fred. *Insiders' Guide to Branson and the Ozark Mountains.* Guilford, CT: Globe Pequot Press, 2002.

"A Pioneer of Ozark Awakening." *Arcadian Magazine,* July 1931, 9.

Pipes, Gerald Harrison. *Fabulous Barefoot Horizons.* Galena, MO: Ozark Books, 1957.

———. "Meet the People in the Shepherd of the Hills Country." *Rayburn's Ozark Guide* 25 (1950): 55.

"Political Shepherd of the Hills." *Rayburn's Ozark Guide* 18 (1948): 26.

Powell, Benjamin Edward. "Red Letter Books Relating to Missouri." *Missouri Historical Review* 36 (1942): 349–355.

"A Prayer of Agreement." *Grand & Glorious Times* (Grand Old Gospel Hour Newsletter), Fall 2001, n.p.

The Project on Disney. *Inside the Mouse: Work and Play at Disney World.* Durham, NC: Duke University Press, 1995.

"'The Promise' Customer Comments." BransonShows.com. www.bransonshows.com/activity/ThePromise.cfm, 5 July 2005 (accessed on 5 July 2006).

Pryor, Kelli. "Then Came Branson: The Hottest Spot in Country Music Can Be Found Deep in the Heart of the Ozarks." *Entertainment Weekly,* 29 May 1992, 28.

Pyles, Lida Wilson. "Remembering May Kennedy McCord." *Springfield!* 6, no. 6 (1984): 39.

Queenan, Joe. *Red Lobster, White Trash, and the Blue Lagoon.* New York: Hyperion, 1999.

Quint, Howard H. "Julius A. Wayland, Pioneer Socialist Propagandist." *Mississippi Valley Historical Review* 35 (1949): 585–606.

Rafferty, Milton D. *The Ozarks: Land and Life*. 1980. Fayetteville: University of Arkansas Press, 2001.

———. "The Ozarks Forest: Its Exploitation and Restoration." *OzarksWatch* 10, nos. 1–4 (1997): 114–118.

———, ed. *Rude Pursuits and Rugged Peaks: Schoolcraft's 1818–1819 Ozark Journal*. Fayetteville: University of Arkansas Press, 1996.

Randolph, Vance. *Funny Stories about Hillbillies*. Girard, KS: Haldeman-Julius, 1944.

———.*The Ozarks: An American Survival of Primitive Society*. New York: Vanguard Press, 1931.

———. *Stiff as a Poker and Other Ozark Folk Tales*. New York: Columbia University Press, 1955.

———. *We Always Lie to Strangers: Tall Tales from the Ozarks*. New York: Columbia University Press, 1952.

———. *Wild Stories from the Ozarks*. Girard, KS: Haldeman-Julius, 1943.

Randolph, Vance, and George Wilson. *Down in the Holler—A Gallery of Ozark Folk Speech*. Norman: University of Oklahoma Press, 1953.

Rauschenbusch, Walter. *Christianity and the Social Crisis*. 1907. New York: Harper and Row, 1964.

Rayburn, Otto Ernest. "Arcadian Echoes." *Rayburn's Ozark Guide* 18 (1948): 97–98.

———. "Arcadian Echoes." *Rayburn's Ozark Guide* 19 (1948): 38.

———. "Arcadian Echoes." *Rayburn's Ozark Guide* 20 (1949): 53–54.

———. "Arcadian Echoes." *Rayburn's Ozark Guide* 25 (1950): 61

———. "A Big Year." *Rayburn's Ozark Guide* 59 (1959): 5.

———. "Dam Talk." *Rayburn's Ozark Guide* 32 (1952): 56.

———. *Forty Years in the Ozarks*. Eureka Springs, AR: Ozark Guide Press, 1957.

———. "Gone Are the Days." *Rayburn's Ozark Guide* 58 (1958): 6–7.

———. "The Harmony of Nature." *Ozark Life*, Sept. 1929, 18.

———. "Hideway Lodge." *Rayburn's Ozark Guide* 37 (1953): 7.

———. "Hillbillies." *Rayburn's Ozark Guide* 44 (1955): 27.

———. "Kingston-in-the-Ozarks." *Ozark Life*, July 1928, 34–37.

———. "Lay My Burden Down." *Rayburn's Ozark Guide* 38 (1953): 5.

———. "Lay of the Legend." *Rayburn's Ozark Guide* 36 (1953): E.

———. "A Miniature Autobiography." *Rayburn's Ozark Guide* 21 (1949): 83–84.

———. "Opening into Hell." *Rayburn's Ozark Guide* 22 (1949): 35–36.

———. *Ozark Country*. New York: Duell, Sloan, and Pearce, 1941.

———. "Ozarkograms." *Ozark Life*, Sept. 1929, 12.

———. "Pastoral Living." *Rayburn's Ozark Guide* 19 (1948): 55.

———. "Progress in the Ozarks." *Rayburn's Ozark Guide* 35 (1953): 3.

———. "The Quest for Arcadia." *Rayburn's Ozark Guide* 64 (1960): 5.

———. "Rayburn's Roadside Chat." *Ozark Life*, Sept. 1929, 3.

———. "Rayburn's Roadside Chat." *Ozark Life*, Mar.–Apr. 1930, 3.

———. "Rayburn's Roadside Chat." *Ozark Life*, July 1930, 1.

———. "Rayburn's Roadside Chat." *Ozark Life*, Sept. 1930, 1.

———. "Rural Musings." *Rayburn's Ozark Guide* 9 (1945): 115.

———. "Rural Musings." *Rayburn's Ozark Guide* 20 (1949): 3–5.

———. "Shepherd of the Hills Country." *Rayburn's Ozark Guide* 29 (1951): 11.

———. "Sight Unseen." *Rayburn's Ozark Guide* 44 (1955): 5–7.

———. "Try the Ozarks." *Rayburn's Ozark Guide* 39 (1954): 5–6.

Reynolds, David. *Beneath the American Renaissance: The Subversive Imagination in the Age of Emerson and Melville.* New York: Alfred A. Knopf, 1988.

Reynolds, Elsbery W. *Harold Bell Wright: A Biography.* 1916. Lone Creek, MO: Westphalia Press, 1983.

Robbins, Lori A. "'A' Lyin' to Them Tourists: Tourism in Branson, Missouri." Master's thesis, University of Mississippi, 1999.

Roberts, A. W. "Don't Call Me a Hillbilly." *Christian Science Monitor Weekly,* 18 Mar. 1944, 4.

Robertson, Vesta Nadine. "Campmeeting in the Ozarks." *Ozarks Mountaineer* 21, no. 4 (1973): 26.

Rodnitzky, Jerry. "Back to Branson: Normalcy and Nostalgia in the Ozarks." *Southern Cultures,* Summer 2002, 97–105.

Roebuck, Lucas S. "Coaster Thrills and Mountain Skills." *Today's Christian,* July/Aug. 2001.

Rogers, Jimmie N., and Stephen A. Smith. "Country Music and Organized Religion." In *All That Glitters: Country Music in America,* edited by George H. Lewis, 270–284. Bowling Green, OH: Bowling Green University Popular Press, 1993.

"Role in the Promise No Accident for Reigning Miss Oklahoma." *Branson Church Getaway Planner* 2, no. 2 (1999): 25–26.

Roof, Wade Clark. *A Generation of Seekers: The Spiritual Journeys of the Baby Boom Generation.* San Francisco: Harper, 1993.

Rosenberg, Sondra, and Stuart Jay Silverman. *The Ozarks Traveler: An Insider's Guide.* Santa Fe, NM: Red Crane Books, 1996.

Ross, J. K. *Old Matt's View of It.* 1912. Reprinted in *White River Valley Historical Quarterly* 5, no. 7 (1975): 9–18.

Rossiter, Phyllis. "Burning the Ozarks." *Ozarks Mountaineer* 40, nos. 2–3 (1992): 33–34.

———. *A Living History of the Ozarks.* Gretna, LA: Pelican Publishing Co., 1992.

Salamone, Virginia A., and Frank A. Salamone. "Images of Main Street: Disney World and the American Adventure." *Journal of American Culture* 22, no. 1 (1999): 85–92.

"Sammy Lane Boat Line" brochure. 1922. Reprinted in *White River Valley Historical Quarterly* 6, no. 6 (1978): 13–15.

Sare, Ted. *Some Recollections of an Ozarks Float Trip Guide.* Marshfield, MO: Webster County Printing, 1998.

Sauer, Carl O. "The Economic Problem of the Ozark Highland." *Scientific Monthly* 11 (1922): 215–227.

———. *The Geography of the Ozark Highland of Missouri.* 1920. New York: Greenwood Press, 1968.

Saults, Dan. "Fifty Years of Missouri Conservation." *Ozarks Mountaineer* 33, nos. 6–7 (1983): 24.

———. "Gently down the Stream." *Sports Afield,* May 1974, 78–79, 184.

Schickel, Richard. *The Disney Version.* New York: Simon and Schuster, 1968.

Schmidt, Leigh Eric. *Consumer Rites: The Buying and Selling of American Holidays.* Princeton, NJ: Princeton University Press, 1995.

Schouten, F. F. J. "Heritage as Historical Reality." In *Heritage, Tourism and Society,* edited by D. T. Herbert, 21–31. London: Mansell, 1995.

Scott, Donna. "It's a Brush Arbor Meeting." *Bittersweet* 3, no. 1 (1975): 18–24.

Scott, Miles H. "The Marvelous Cave." *White River Valley Historical Quarterly* 8, no. 10 (1988): 4–5.

Sears, John F. *Sacred Places: American Tourist Attractions in the Nineteenth Century*. New York: Oxford University Press, 1989.

Sellars, Richard West. "Early Promotion and Development of Missouri's Natural Resources." Ph.D. diss., University of Missouri–Columbia, 1972.

Shapiro, Henry. *Appalachia on Our Mind: The Southern Mountaineers in the American Consciousness, 1870–1920*. Chapel Hill: University of North Carolina Press, 1978.

The Shepherd of the Hills Historical Society, Inc. Shepherd of the Hills Souvenir Program. 1971.

———. Shepherd of the Hills Souvenir Program. 1976.

The Shepherd of the Hills movie brochure (1919). Harold Bell Wright: The Best Selling American Author of the 20th Century. http://bbw.addr.com/shepmv1919.htm#_postcards2. 6 Aug. 2003 (accessed on 16 July 2003).

"Shepherd of the Hills Outdoor Theater: Traveler Reviews." 12 June 2006. www.tripadvisor .com/Attraction_Review-g44160-d106483-Reviews-Shepherd_of_the_Hills_Outdoor _Theater-Branson_Missouri.html (accessed on 12 June 2006).

"Silver Dollar City: Missouri." *MotorHome Magazine*, 7 July 2005. www.motorhomemagazine .com/shortstops/0009silver.cfm (accessed on 2 Aug. 2005).

Simpich, Frederick. "Land of a Million Smiles." *National Geographic* 83, no. 5 (1943): 589–623.

Simpson, Ethel C. "Otto Ernest Rayburn, an Early Promoter of the Ozarks." *Arkansas Historical Quarterly* 58 (1999): 160–177.

Smalley, Dr. Greg, and Michael Smalley, M.A. "Eight Great Reasons to Date." Smalley Relationship Center. www.smalley.gospelcom.net/artman/publish/article_95.shtml. 11 Dec. 2003 (accessed on 11 Dec. 2003).

Smalley, Gary. "Persistence." Smalley Relationship Center. www.smalley.gospelcom.net/ artman/publish/article_302.shtml. 11 Dec. 2003 (accessed on 11 Dec. 2003).

———. "Women Are from the Classroom; Men Are from the Playground." Smalley Relationship Center. www.smalley.gospelcom.net/artman/publish/article_288.shtml. 11 Dec. 2003 (accessed on 11 Dec. 2003).

Smith, Christian. *Christian America? What Evangelicals Really Want*. Berkeley: University of California Press, 2000.

Smith, Erin A. "Melodrama, Popular Religion, and Literary Value: The Case of Harold Bell Wright." *American Literary History* 17, no. 2 (2005): 217–243.

Smith, Jonathan Z. *Map Is Not the Territory: Studies in the History of Religions*. Leiden, the Netherlands: E. J. Brill, 1978.

Smith, Stephen A., and Jimmie N. Rogers. "Political Culture and the Rhetoric of Country Music: A Revisionist Interpretation." In *Politics in Familiar Contexts: Projecting Politics through Popular Media*, edited by Robert L. Savage and Dan Nimmo, 185–198. Norwood, NJ: Ablex Publishing, 1990.

Spurlock, Pearl. *Over the Old Ozark Trails in the Shepherd of the Hills Country*. 1936. Branson, MO: White River Leader, 1939.

Stallcup, Helene. "The Famous Age of the Owen Boat Line." *Ozarks Mountaineer* 40, nos. 4–5 (1992): 29–31.

"Statement of Faith." Stonecroft Ministries. www.gospelcom.net/stonecroft/html/state ment_of_faith.html. 4 Feb. 2004 (accessed on 11 Mar. 2004).

"Statement of Purpose." Hobby Lobby, Inc. www.hobbylobby.com/site3/company/state ment.htm. 9 Dec. 2003 (accessed on 29 June 2004).

Stone County Historical Society. *History of Stone County, Missouri.* Marionville, MO: Stone County Historical Society, 1989.

"Stonecroft Ministry." *Branson Church Getaway Planner* 3, no. 3 (2000): 14.

Stout, Goldie Shearer. "Memories of Sammie Lane." *Ozarks Mountaineer* 14, no. 1 (1966): 16–17.

Strenski, Ivan. *Four Theories of Myth in Twentieth-Century History.* Iowa City: University of Iowa Press, 1987.

Stringfield, E. E. *Presbyterianism in the Ozarks: A History of the Work of the Various Branches of the Presbyterian Church in Southwest Missouri, 1834–1907.* N.p.: Presbytery of the Ozark, U.S.A, 1909.

Swanson, Merwin. "The 'Country Life Movement' and the American Churches." *Church History* 46 (1977): 358–373.

Sylvester, Ron, and Jeff Hampton. *Branson: Onstage in the Ozarks.* Forth Worth, TX: Summit Group, 1994.

Tagg, Lawrence V. *Harold Bell Wright: Storyteller to America.* Tucson, AZ: Westerlore Press, 1986.

Tapia, John E. *Circuit Chautauqua: From Rural Education to Popular Entertainment in Early Twentieth Century America.* Jefferson, NC: McFarland and Co., 1997.

Taylor, John P. "Authenticity and Sincerity in Tourism." *Annals of Tourism Research* 28 (2001): 7–26.

Terry, Dickinson. "The Shepherd of the Hills: Still Tending His Flock of Thousands of Tourists." *Midwest Motorist,* Aug. 1969, 4–5.

———. "The Show That Put a Town on the Map." *TV Guide Magazine,* 5–11 Aug. 1961, 11.

"Testimonies." Dino: America's Piano Showman, www.dinoplayspiano.com/testimonies .html, 20 June 2006 (accessed on 26 May 2006).

Thompson, Jim. "The Herschends: Catalysts for Ozark Mountain Country's Unprecedented Growth in Tourist Trade." *Springfield!* 13, no. 4 (1992): 34–39, 68.

———. "Saga of the Shepherd of the Hills, Part II." *Springfield!* 15, no. 4 (1993): 26–28.

———. "Saga of the Shepherd of the Hills, Part III." *Springfield!* 15, no. 5 (1993): 56–59.

Tidgwell, Flo Montgomery. "A Marvel of a Cave." *Ozarks Mountaineer* 35, nos. 2–3 (1987): 26–27.

Tinsley, Sandra Holmes. "Old Branson." *Springfield!* 8, no. 11 (1987): 25–26.

Tipton, Becky. "The American Kids Are Coming." *Branson Church Getaway Planner* 5, no. 3 (2002): 22–23.

———. "Cancer Doesn't Impair Don Gabriel's Vision." *Branson Church Getaway Planner* 5, no. 2 (2002): 14.

———. "The Promise Returns." *Branson Church Getaway Planner* 5, no. 2 (2002): 24–25.

———. "The Stars Come Out for the Hiding Place Ministries." *Branson Church Getaway Planner* 5, no. 3 (2002): 16–18.

"Tony's Testimony." *Branson Church Getaway Planner* 7, no. 2 (2004): 22.

Travers, Jerome A., ed. "History of Clowning." *Journal of Pastoral Counseling* 24 (1989): 1–119.

Treese, Joel D., ed. *Biographical Directory of the American Congress, 1774–1996; the Continental Congress, September 5, 1774, to October 21, 1778, and the Congress of the United States, from the First through the 104th Congress, March 4, 1789, to January 3, 1997.* Alexandria, VA: CQ Staff Directories, 1997.

Trilling, Lionel. *Sincerity and Authenticity.* London: Oxford University Press, 1972.

Trimble, Bruce. *The Story of Old Matt of the Shepherd of the Hills.* Hollister, MO: Steve Miller Press, 195–.

Tuan, Yi-Fu. "Space and Place: Humanistic Perspectives." *Progress in Geography* 6 (1974): 211–252.

Tudor, Eric D. "Famed Author Harold Bell Wright Got His Early Roots from the Missouri Ozarks." *KJPW Old Settler's Gazette,* 17 Nov.–31 July 1999, 11–16.

Turner, Victor. *From Ritual to Theater: The Human Seriousness of Play.* New York: PAJ Publications, 1982.

———. *The Ritual Process: Structure and Anti-Structure.* Chicago: Aldine Publishing Co., 1969.

Upton, Elsie. "Hillbilly." *Rayburn's Ozark Guide* 19 (1948): 22–23.

Upton, Lucille M. *Bald Knobbers.* Caldwell, ID: Caxton Printers, 1939.

Urry, John. "Social Relations, Space and Time." In *Social Relations and Spatial Structures,* edited by Derek Gregory and John Urry, 20–48. New York: St. Martin's Press, 1985.

———. "The Sociology of Tourism." In *Progress in Tourism, Recreation, and Hospitality Management,* edited by C. P. Cooper, 48–57. London: Bellhaven, 1991.

———. *The Tourist Gaze: Leisure and Travel in Contemporary Societies.* London: Sage Publications, 1990.

Van Buskirk, Kathleen. "The Kanakuk Kamps." In *In the Heart of Ozarks Mountain Country: A Popular History of Stone and Taney Counties, including Branson, Missouri,* edited by Frank Reuter, 187–188. Reeds Spring, MO: White Oak Press, 1992, 187–188.

———. "Shepherd of the Hills Country." In *In the Heart of Ozark Mountain Country: A Popular History of Stone and Taney Counties, including Branson, Missouri,* edited by Frank Reuter, 23–35. Reeds Spring, MO: White Oak Press, 1992.

———. "The Wild White River." In *In the Heart of Ozark Mountain Country: A Popular History of Stone and Taney Counties, including Branson, Missouri,* edited by Frank Reuter, 56–62. Reeds Springs, MO: White Oak Press, 1992.

Van Doren, Carl. *The American Novel, 1789–1939.* New York: Macmillan, 1940.

Viets, Dan. "Walt Disney: Memories of a Small Town Influence Millions." *Ozarks Mountaineer* 49, no. 5 (2001): 50–55.

Vincent, John H. *The Chautauqua Movement.* Boston: Chautauqua Press, 1886.

Votaw, Albert N. "The Hillbillies Invade Chicago." *Harper's,* Feb. 1958, 64–67.

Vukonic, Boris. *Tourism and Religion.* New York: Pergamon, 1996.

Wacker, Grant. "Searching for Eden with a Satellite Dish." In *Religion and American Culture,* ed. David G. Hackett, 439–458. New York: Routledge, 1995.

Walker, Lisa. "Down toward Arkansas." *New Yorker,* 18 Sept. 1989, 105–124.

Wang, Ning. "Rethinking Authenticity in Tourism Experience." *Annals of Tourism Research* 26 (1999): 349–370.

———. *Tourism and Modernity: A Sociological Analysis.* New York: Pergamon, 2000.

Watts, Patsy. "Is Branson Holding a 'Dead Man's Hand'?" *Branson Living* 1, no. 2 (Dec. 1994–Jan. 1995): 8–11, 30–31.

Weaver, Dwight. *The Wilderness Underground: Caves of the Ozark Plateau.* Columbia: University of Missouri Press, 1992.

Weber, Max. *The Protestant Ethic and the Spirit of Capitalism.* 1904–1905. Upper Saddle River, NJ: Prentice Hall, 1958.

Weisberger, Bernard A. *They Gathered at the River: The Story of the Great Revivalists and Their Impact upon Religion in America.* Boston: Little, Brown, 1958.

Westfall, Jane, and Catherine Osterhage. *A Fame Not Easily Forgotten.* Conway, AR: River Road Press, 1970.

"What Is the Holy Land Experience." The Holy Land Experience. www.holylandexperience.com/about/index.html. 18 May 2004 (accessed on18 May 2004).

Whisnant, David. "Ethnicity and the Recovery of Regional Identity in Appalachia: Thoughts upon Entering the Zone of Occult Instability." *Soundings* 56, no. 1 (1973): 124–138.

Wiley, Robert S. *Dewey Short: Orator of the Ozarks.* Crane, MO: R. S. Wiley, 1985.

Williams, Peter W. *America's Religions: Traditions and Cultures.* New York: Macmillan, 1990.

———. *Popular Religion in America: Symbolic Change and the Modernization Process in Historical Perspective.* Englewood Cliffs, NJ: Prentice Hall, 1980.

Williamson, J. W. *Hillbillyland.* Chapel Hill: University of North Carolina Press, 1995.

Wilson, Warren. *The Church of the Open Country: A Study of the Church for the Working Farmer.* New York: Missionary Movement of the United States and Canada, 1911.

Wojcik, Daniel. *The End of the World As We Know It: Faith, Fatalism, and Apocalypse in America.* New York: New York University Press, 1997.

Wolff, Kurt. *Country Music: The Rough Guide.* London: Rough Guides, 2000.

Worden, Kim. "Get Ready for a Great Feeling at the Braschler Music Show." *Branson Church Getaway Planner* 6, no. 2 (2003): 44–45.

———. "Stafford Family Values." *Branson Church Getaway Planner* 6, no. 3 (2003).

Wright, Harold Bell. *The Calling of Dan Matthews.* 1909. Gretna, LA: Pelican Publishing, 1995.

———. *God and the Groceryman.* New York: D. Appleton, 1927.

———. *Ma Cinderella.* New York: Harper and Brothers, 1932.

———. *The Re-creation of Brian Kent.* Chicago: Book Supply, 1919.

———. *The Shepherd of the Hills.* 1907. Gretna, LA: Pelican Publishing Co., 1994.

———. *That Printer of Udell's.* Chicago: Book Supply, 1903.

———. *To My Sons.* New York: Harper and Brothers, 1934.

———. *The Uncrowned King.* Chicago: Book Supply, 1910.

———. "What about God." *Physical Culture,* Apr. 1931, 90.

"Yakov Smirnoff Show: Traveler Reviews." Tripadvisor.com. www.tripadvisor.com/ShowUserReviews-g44160-d107350-r2379929-Yakov_Smirnoff_Show-Branson_Missouri.html, 20 June 2006 (accessed on 20 June 2006).

Index